ALAN TITCHMARSH

THE COMPLETE COUNTRYMAN

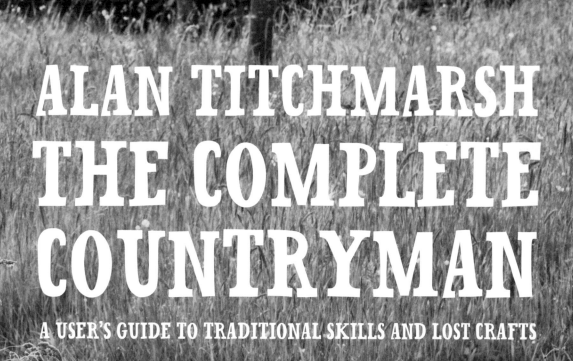

ALAN TITCHMARSH
THE COMPLETE
COUNTRYMAN

A USER'S GUIDE TO TRADITIONAL SKILLS AND LOST CRAFTS

Special photography by
Jonathan Buckley

BBC
BOOKS

10 9 8 7 6 5 4 3 2 1

Published in 2011 by BBC Books, an imprint of Ebury Publishing.
A Random House Group Company

The Random House Group Limited Reg. No. 954009

Addresses for companies within the Random House Group can be found at
www.randomhouse.co.uk

A CIP catalogue record for this book is available from the British Library.

ISBN 978 18 4 607393 9

The Random House Group Limited supports the Forest Stewardship
Council®(FSC®), the leading international forest certification organisation.
All our titles that are printed on Greenpeace approved FSC® certified paper
carry the FSC® logo. Our paper procurement policy can be found at
www.randomhouse.co.uk/environment

Commissioning editor: Lorna Russell
Project editor: Helena Caldon
In-house editor: Caroline McArthur
Design and art direction: Smith & Gilmour
Picture researcher: Sarah Hopper
Photographer: Jonathan Buckley

Colour origination by: AltaImage
Printed and bound by Firmengruppe APPL, Wemding, Germany

To buy books by your favourite authors and register for offers,
visit www.randomhouse.co.uk

Picture credits:
All special photography by Jonathan Buckley. Alamy: 17 bl, 22, 23 r, 27, 32, 37, 39 tl, 46 l, 48 l, 55 l, 57 l, 58, 60 (1), 61, 63, 46 (1), 65 r, 66, 67, 72 t, 73 (3), 79 (1), 79 (3), 79 (4), 83 (5), 90 (1), 90 (3), 90 (4), 94, 101, 104, 115, 124, 129, 143, 145, 149 t, 149 b, 150, 156, 160, 161, 164 tl, 164 tr, 164 bl, 164 br, 179 (6), 179 (8), 179 (9), 180, 185 (7), 193 (7), 193 (8), 193 (10), 197 (6), 197 (7), 201 (2), 201 (3), 203 (16), 208 r, 211 (4), 217 l, 217 r, 218 (2), 218 (4), 218 (5), 218 (6), 218 (7), 218 (8), 219, 221 (1), 221 (2), 221 (3), 221 (4), 221 (5), 221 (6), 221 (7), 221 (8), 221 (9), 221 (10), 226, 228 r, 230, 234 l, 234 r, 235, 236, 251 l, 258, 259 l, 259 tr, 262, 267 (1), 267 (2), 267 (7), 267 (11), 267 (12), 267 (17), 268 (30), 268 (34), 273 (3), 275 (9), 275 (11), 275 (14), 275 (18), 275 (19), 275 (23), 275 (25), 275 (26), 275 (30), 276, 280, 281 (1), 281 (4), 284 (5), 284 (6), 283 (7), 284 (12), 284 (16), 284 (17), 284 (18), 284 (19), 284 (20), 286 (1), 286 (2), 286 (4), 289 (1), 289 (2), 291 (/Beepstock), 292 (3), 292 (4), 295. Bridgeman Art Library 23 l, 33, 36. Burazin: 39 br. Jonathan Buckley: 29, 46 tr, 47, 48 r, 49, 51, 52, 56, 57 r, 59, 70, 72 b, 74, 76 l, 76 r, 80, 82, 85, 86, 87, 90 (2), 97, 112, 113, 117, 119, 120, 144, 157 l, 163, 174, 193 (1-6), 205, 209, 212 r, 241, 265, 282, 284 (10), 293, 294, 297, 298, 303. Jonathan Buckley 2–3 (/Camilla Swift, The Pant, Monmouthshire); 95 (/Design Kate Frey, RHS, Chelsea Flower Show 2003);122, 123, 125 l, 125, 127, 128, 131, 157 r, 248 r (/Sarah Raven, Perch Hill East Sussex); 126 (/ Danae Duthy, country Roses, Essex); 151 (/West Green House, Hampshire); 167 (/ West Dean Gardens, Hampshire); 169 (/Great Dixter, East Sussex); 170 (/Diana Guy, Welcome Thatch, Dorset); 177 (/Alison Houghton, Berkshire); 195 (/Whatley Manor, Gloucestershire); 246 (/Christopher Lloyd, Great Dixter, East Sussex). Corbis: 15, 17 br, 20 r, 25 b, 26 r, 252, 254. FLPA: 45, 46 br, 50, 53 (1), 53 (2), 53 (3), 53 (4), 53 (5), 53 (6), 53 (8), 54, 59, 60 (2), 60 (3), 60 (4), 63 l, 62 r, 64 (2), 64 (3), 64 r, 65 l, 73 (1), 73 (2), 73 (4), 79 (2), 83 (1), 83 (2), 83 (3), 83 (4), 88, 89, 92 t, 92 b, 98, 99, 103 r, 179 (1), 179 (2), 179 (3), 179 (4), 179 (5), 179 (7), 185 (1), 185 (2), 185 (3), 185 (4), 185 (5), 185 (6), 185 (8), 185 (9), 197 (1), 197 (2), 197 (3), 197 (4), 197 (5), 197 (8), 197 (9), 197 (10), 197 (11), 197 (12), 197 (13), 197 (14), 197 (15), 201 (1), 201 (4), 201 (5), 201 (6), 201 (7), 201 (8), 201 (9), 203 (10), 203 (11), 203 (12), 203 (13), 203 (14), 203 (15), 203 (17), 203 (18), 211 (1), 211 (2), 211 (3), 211 (5), 211 (6), 211 (7), 211 (8), 212 l, 215 (1), 215 (2), 215 (3), 215 (4), 215 (5), 215 (6), 215 (7), 215 (8), 216 l, 216 r, 218 (2), 227 tl/bl/r, 228 l, 237, 237 r, 267 (3), 267 (4), 267 (5), 267 (6), 267 (8), 267 (9), 267 (10), 267 (13), 267 (14), 267 (15), 267 (16), 267 (18), 267 (19), 267 (20), 268 (21), 268 (23), 268 (24), 268 (25), 268 (26), 268 (27), 268 (28), 268 (29), 268 (31), 268 (32), 268 (33), 268 (35), 268 (36), 270 (1), 270 (2), 270 (3), 270 (4), 270 (5), 270 (6), 270 (7), 270 (8), 271 (9), 271 (10), 271 (11), 271 (12), 271 (13), 271 (14), 271 (15), 271 (16), 273 (2), 273 (5), 273 (6), 273 (7), 273 (8), 275 (10), 275 (12), 275 (13), 275 (15), 275 (16), 275 (20), 275 (21), 275 (24), 275 (27), 275 (28), 275 (29), 275 (31), 275 (32), 279 (1), 279 (2), 279 (3), 279 (4), 279 (5), 279 (6), 279 (7), 279 (8), 279 (9), 279 (10), 281 (3), 283 (1), 283 (2), 283 (3), 283 (8), 284 (9), 284 (11), 284 (14), 286 (3), 286 (5), 287 (1, 2), 287 (3), 287 (4, 5), 287 (6), 287 (7), 289 (3), 289 (4), 292 (1), 292 (2), 292 (5), 292 (6), 292 (7), 292 (8), 301 (1), 301 (2), 301 (3), 301 (4), 301 (5), 301 (6). Fox Photos: 41. GAP: 18, 20 l, 138, 182, 183, 185, 187 (/Lynn Keddie), 198, 208 l, 218 (3), 231, 249, 250, 251 r. Garden Picture Library: 273 (1), 273 (4), 275 (17), 275 (22), 283 (4), 283 (5), 283 (6), 284 (13), 284 (15). Getty images: 13, 17, 25, 26, 40, 108, 109, 133 tl, 133 tr, 133 b, 147, 244, 248 l, 255. Mary Evans Picture Library: 21, 39 tr, 39 bl, 39 bm, 224, 256. Photolibrary: 179 (10), 204. The National Archives/Heritage Images: 34. Ronald Startup: 26 r. Ken Welsh: 33. Museum of English Rural Life, University of Reading: 44, 102. Stockfood.com: 134, 136, 137. Thorne's Poultry Centre: 53 (7).

The author and publisher gratefully acknowledge the permission granted to reproduce the copyright material in this book. Every effort has been made to trace copyright holders and to obtain their permission for the use of copyright material. The publisher apologizes for any errors or omissions in the above list and would be grateful if notified of any corrections that should be incorporated in future reprints or editions of this book.

CONTENTS

Introduction

CHAPTER 1
Country Ways 10

CHAPTER 2
Working the Land 42

CHAPTER 3
The Country Home and Garden 106

CHAPTER 4
The Wild Garden 173

CHAPTER 5
Country Arts and Crafts 222

CHAPTER 6
Go Wild in the Country 260

Further Information 306
Index 308
Acknowledgements 312

INTRODUCTION 🌿

Now the last thing I want to do is to sound like some old fogey, droning on about 'the good old days'. They weren't entirely. Yes, we had all kinds of things then that we don't have now – school milk, cod liver oil capsules and a whack on the bum with the back of a hairbrush when we misbehaved. But there are some things from those days that I still cherish and that I wish were more widely appreciated.

I was born and brought up surrounded by countryside and all that went on in it. As small children – wait for it – we made our own amusement (that means we were bored but were inventive enough to do something about it). We were allowed out to explore the moors, lanes, riverside, woods and farmland; we'd go fishing (stupidly, with a bent pin that never caught anything), climb trees or track animals. Almost everyone I knew walked to and from school, and there were plenty of diversions en route; we knew the moment the conker season started, and when hollow plant stems were ripe for making peashooters. We recognised when the burdock burrs were ready to throw at girls so they'd stick to their clothes, and when frog spawn was likely to appear and be dolloped into a jam jar. We absorbed natural history on the hoof; it was part of everyday life. And for we lucky few, that state of affairs has coloured and informed our lives.

What saddens me now (and I regret beginning on a negative note) is that children in particular, and therefore a whole new generation of adults, are starting out in life so distanced from the countryside and country ways that they are fearful of it. It usually happens with things we don't fully understand. When you consider that the most important day-to-day issues for most folk today are sell-by dates on food, their ability to kill 99 per cent of household germs, whether or not their mobile phone is charged, which is the best network to use, and how frequently they update their Facebook page, you will see where I am coming from.

If I tell you that I have an iPhone, an iPad and a laptop; that I write on a computer and send emails, you will believe me, I hope, when I claim that I do not stand in the way of progress. What I bemoan is not the acquisition of new skills and new ways of communicating, but the loss of some of the old ones – a lack of communication and loss of affinity with the natural world. At school, 50 years ago, besides regular lessons, we learnt our wildflowers, a little elementary gardening and a few country crafts. At weekends, families 'took the car out for a spin' to enjoy the scenery and visit quaint villages, pubs and beauty spots. We didn't need to spend a fortune; everything we enjoyed was – almost – on the doorstep. The countryside was where we always wanted to go. Parents did not force their children to go there – quite the reverse.

In the fifties, there were still lots of country-people who kept smallholdings, or ran their homes and gardens in much the same thrifty ways our ancestors did centuries ago, even though they were rapidly being considered old-fashioned and out of date. And all those traditional activities helped to shape the countryside and create its unique character and stunning views.

Now that we've become a highly urbanised society where stuff' comes in glitzy packaging, every town and city has the same set of shops, and people get their entertainment and social life via airwaves instead of face to face, it's interesting to see that a lot of crafts and outdoor activities are experiencing a comeback as creative hobbies and that the countryside is becoming an increasingly popular getaway place. Whether it's the call of the wild or an instinctive return to our roots, I couldn't say.

What I can say is that it pleases me no end and gives me hope.

Today families are going out spotting birds, butterflies or bats, discovering traditional rare breeds of livestock at country fairs and agricultural shows, and learning ancient woodland crafts –

maybe even putting them to good use by growing their own hazel hurdles or making their own walking stick, or even a coracle. Oh yes you can!

Nearly four thousand private gardens open to the public each year under a thriving National Gardens Scheme, and the National Trust and English Heritage continue to open houses and gardens for our delectation and delight. There are enthusiasts growing and preserving their own food, keeping hens or bees, and making anything from icecream to herbal remedies, elderflower fizz and sloe gin.

You can have lessons on hedge-laying and dry stone walling, take courses on animal husbandry or gardening – in short, you can connect with the countryside whoever you are and wherever you live if you have the inclination and the energy.

After decades of rampant consumerism, it's heartening to see families today creating their own lifestyle and getting outside and enjoying all that's

best about the British countryside. All I can hope for is that this book will help to foster a fondness and a respect for the natural world, and a feeling that we are its stewards and custodians for those who come after.

I use the word 'countryman' because it encapsulates both a love of, and an involvement with, the countryside. It is not in any way gender-specific, it is just a delightfully wholesome word and a darned sight more rooted in the great outdoors than the more politically correct 'countryperson'. Those of a sensitive disposition will, I hope, forgive me. But then, if they are so easily offended, I suggest that the countryside is not for them. But it really should be. There's such a lot to discover and enjoy out there, and I hope this book will help you to do just that.

Alan Titchmarsh

COUNTRY WAYS
CHAPTER 1

COUNTRY TRADITIONS

Most of today's country traditions grew up in a bygone Britain, when the ebb and flow of country life was driven by what was going on out in the fields and countryside, with jobs like hedging and ditching, sowing or harvesting determined by the seasons. Apart from the slowly changing sequence of farm work, and the length of time that could be spent working being affected by daylight hours, every day must have been pretty much the same – except for Sundays, which were dominated by church and family life spent frugally at home.

There was virtually no entertainment except for story-telling, and with little or no formal education, country folk were naturally superstitious. As a result all sorts of beliefs grew up, and these were elaborated on and passed on to the next generation as myths, legends and old wives' tales. Holidays as we know them today didn't exist, so special occasions such as saints' days, May Day, Easter, Whitsuntide and Christmas stood out as a welcome break from everyday routine, when people would dress up, socialise, feast and maybe indulge in a spot of drunken revelry.

Even when the economy boomed and facilities for town and city dwellers improved in Elizabethan and Victorian times, country people still had to make their own amusement and old traditions thrived. Until the time of the Second World War, village life still centred around local activities such as church fêtes, the flower and produce show, and the activities of groups such as the Women's Institute, cricket team or gardening club, with the church still playing a big part in social life. As a lad in the 1950s, I sang in the church choir and rang the bells. I still ring, but back then both activities were a good way to earn a bit of pocket money and – most important of all – take part in the annual perk: the choir trip to Morecambe or the Lakes each summer.

In the first half of the twentieth century, church festivals and events such as Empire Day, on which people across the world celebrated being a part of the British Empire, were still reflected in school activities. The village hall was the natural centre for meetings, from the model railway society to the amateur dramatic group. And even today, a good few local societies and community activities still survive, despite other attractions.

TRADITIONAL FESTIVALS AND SPECIAL DAYS

A good many British traditions had their roots way back in pagan Britain, and since they were already deeply embedded in the yearly calendar of events, they were 'cleaned up' after Britain became Christian and incorporated into approved religious festivities. Other celebrations, such as Guy Fawkes Night, were added as historical events unravelled.

Right up until the middle of the twentieth century, the local church was a focus for the entire community, and its festivals were markers in the countryman's year.

SHROVE TUESDAY

During the run-up to Easter, the Church called for 40 days of abstinence during Lent:

'Forty days and forty nights
Thou wast fasting in the wild;
Forty days and forty nights
Tempted, and yet undefiled.'

Mere mortals might not have been quite so 'undefiled' as their Saviour in the wilderness, but most of them at least made an effort. Since Shrove Tuesday is the day before Lent begins, it became 'Pancake Day', when housewives had their last chance to use up any rich foods in the house – eggs, cream, butter, honey – in one final delicious treat before enduring 40 days of plain food. Shrove Tuesday was also originally the time when people had fun and indulged in riotous pastimes to 'get it out of their system' in anticipation of 40 days of modest living and good behaviour. Since the fifteenth century, some villages have held pancake races, with pinnie-clad mums racing up the high street (which is often closed off especially for the event), tossing pancakes in a frying pan as they run.

ASH WEDNESDAY

This is the first day of Lent and is so-called because it was originally the day on which penitents had their foreheads marked with ashes as a sign of mourning and repentance.

In 1445, a housewife, late for church, ran down the street with a pancake in her frying pan. This began the popular tradition of pancake races that continues today.

LENT

Lent runs from Ash Wednesday to Easter Sunday. If you have a diary handy, you'll see that the time between Ash Wednesday and Easter Sunday is actually a little bit longer than 40 days, but that's because traditionally only the weekdays were counted. When I was at primary school, we were expected to give up sweets or chocolate for Lent, but in days of yore it was observed far more seriously; it was a time for fasting, penitence and abstinence, so people ate plainly – they had no meat at all, though fish could be eaten – and folk lived quietly.

MOTHERING SUNDAY

The fourth Sunday in Lent was when people gave small gifts to their mothers. In my childhood it was almost always a small bunch of anemones, dripping with water and handed out by the vicar at matins. Creative children would make small items in a craft class at school (raffia mats or a wicker basket were regular favourites), but these days Mother's Day – as it's now usually called thanks to American influence – has 'grown' into a good excuse for a big family get-together with cards, gifts, flowers and often an outing or lunch.

PALM SUNDAY

This is the last Sunday before Easter, which commemorates Christ's entry to Jerusalem on a donkey, with palm fronds being used to strew the way before Him as a symbol of His majesty. It was once celebrated by church processions with clergy and congregation carrying palm fronds; some churches still continue the tradition in a small way and most hand out little crosses made from palm leaves. As children we brought these home from Sunday School and used them as bookmarks in our bibles, though they invariably found their way into stories about Biggles and the Famous Five as well.

GOOD FRIDAY

This usually falls on the last Friday before Easter. As it was a holy day (later corrupted to 'holiday'), folk had a day off work, but they were meant to use it to go to church, not to do domestic chores. It was once considered unlucky to do laundry on Good Friday, for this reason, but gardening was a different matter. In medieval times, Good Friday gave country folk much-needed time to spend in their veg gardens and smallholdings at just the right time of year for sowing and planting most of the rather limited range of crops available to them at the time. (Today, although Easter is still an extremely popular time to catch up on gardening jobs in general, it's not such a reliable indicator of when to plant and sow. A lot of the veg we grow here today originate from warmer countries and so they aren't hardy, which means it's not safe to plant them outside until well after Easter, when the last frost is safely past – usually mid- to late May.)

Crops sown on Good Friday were believed to produce especially high yields; it was also traditional to sow parsley on Good Friday since that was the only day in the year that it did not go 'nine times to the Devil' before germinating. On Good Friday the Devil's influence over the earth was removed. (For non-gardeners, I should perhaps explain that parsley is notoriously slow to germinate, but nowadays we suspect that this is nothing to do with the Devil but that it just needs higher temperatures than you usually find in a spring garden. Fresh parsley seed comes up quite quickly in a pot on the kitchen windowsill or a propagator kept at 70°F.)

EASTER

Easter is quite literally a moveable feast – a church festival whose date changes from year to year. It is always held on the first Sunday after the full moon following the Spring Equinox, so the actual date can vary from anywhere between 21 March and 25 April. It celebrates the resurrection of Christ.

Traditionally people wore new clothes (or at least one item of new clothing) at Easter, since it was a time of renewal and regeneration after 40 days of 'doing without' during Lent. Housewives would make or buy a new set of clothes for their family which would then last all year. (In the past a lot of ordinary working people only owned two sets of clothes, one for everyday and one kept for 'best'.) The Easter bonnet was often the one item of new clothing that young (especially unmarried) women went in for, and they'd save up for ribbons and other trimmings to make it something special.

Churches were traditionally decorated for Easter with white lilies, thought to be due to the old belief that the flowers grew from the drops of perspiration that fell from Christ before the crucifixion, thus making them symbols of resurrection. Confirmed members of the Church of England were expected to take communion at least three times a year, 'one of which shall be Easter'.

The tradition of dancing around the maypole is not a simple case of moving around it, but is actually a complex series of steps which pairs of dancers perform in order to weave the ribbons into an attractive pattern.

MAY DAY

May Day has its roots in the ancient Roman festival of Floralia, which was brought to Britain at the time of the invasion, roughly two thousand years ago. The original festival was held in honour of the goddess Flora and originally ran for three days from 28 April to 1 May, to celebrate the reappearance of spring flowers and the fruit-tree blossom that was necessary for a good crop of fruit later in the season.

After the Romans left our shores, the original pagan festival became a one-day celebration which we still know as May Day. People got up before sunrise and went into the fields and woods to gather spring flowers to decorate their homes. Young unmarried women also washed in dew which they gathered early on May Day morning; this they believed would maintain their clean, pale, youthful complexion and deter freckles, thus improving their chances of making a good marriage. The maypole was then set up on the village green and decorated with flowers and ribbons, ready for a day of traditional dancing, merry-making and sports, which finished at dusk when the May Queen, or Queen of the May, was crowned. She'd usually be the best dancer or the prettiest girl present and, according to tradition, she had to be kissed by every youth she met on her way home. Poor girl.

MAY GOSLINGS

As a Yorkshire lad, born on 2 May, my Yorkshire grandmother would ask me 'Have you been christened a May Gosling?' I wondered for years what she meant, then I discovered there had been a Northern custom, akin to April Fooling, which took place on 1 May. Tricks were played and the successful perpetrators would cry 'May Gosling!', presumably implying the victim was as silly as a young goose. The response would be: 'May Goslings past and gone. You're the fool for making me one!'

ALL FOOL'S DAY

On 1 April it's traditional to play practical jokes on friends, and recently it has become quite the thing for the media to invent outrageous hoax news stories especially for the day. According to the 'rules', anyone fooled on April Fool's Day (as it became known) has to take it all in good spirit since it's bad luck not to do so, but hoaxes can only be carried out before midday – any carried out in the afternoon bring bad luck to the perpetrator.

You might wonder how such an extraordinary 'day' came about. It all started in 1752 when England and Ireland changed from the Julian calendar to the Gregorian calendar we use today, in order to bring the calendar back in synch with the solar year (Scotland made the change much earlier, in 1600). Eleven days were 'lost' in the process, which caused a big upset. At the same time, New Year's Day, which had previously been celebrated on 1 April, was shifted to 1 January so it really *was* the start of the new year. People were, however, used to celebrating New Year on 1 April, so it became a custom to try to trick people into thinking 1 April was still the start of the year, and the habit of perpetrating hoaxes grew from there. Interestingly, the financial year still starts on 1 April, though it has to be said that old traditions which were fun tended to pass the test of time, and those involving abstinence were often dropped.

GUY FAWKES NIGHT

'Please to remember the fifth of November, gunpowder, treason and plot' goes the old rhyme. Guy Fawkes Night, or Bonfire Night, is an old tradition that's probably as popular today as it ever was. The event commemorates the Gunpowder Plot which took place on 5 November 1605, when Guido Fawkes and others attempted to assassinate King James I, along with his entire government, by blowing up the Palace of Westminster with gunpowder that had been placed in the cellar. Their aim was to return the Catholics (who had been kicked out by Henry VIII) to the throne. They failed. Guy Fawkes was caught red-handed and executed on 31 January 1606. However, his effigy was still being burnt on bonfires when I was a boy;

we had great fun collecting old clothes (Dad's work overalls and his old tweed jacket) and suitable stuffing, then hauling the guy round the streets on a home-made bogey made of old pram wheels and floorboards collecting 'A penny for the Guy' and using the money to buy fireworks.

On Bonfire Night itself we'd eat treacle toffee and parkin (sticky ginger cake) standing round the fire and setting off our sputtering Roman candles and Golden Rain fireworks, nailing Catherine wheels to the shed and getting Dad to free them with his gnarled finger while they were still alight if they got stuck instead of spinning and spewing out their liquid sparks. We'd light and then throw down 'jumping crackers' that snapped their way through the crowd, making them leap out of the way (no-one ever caught fire as I recall), and wrote our names in the air with sparklers.

Rockets were a waste of money. The only ones we could afford went 'whoosh' but produced no stars or spangles since they were only a shilling. There was better value in 'penny bangers', which could be lobbed in the direction of friends, or 'threepenny canons', which were fatter and louder and gave great delight when strapped to the back forks of your bike. You could pedal down the road and the back wheel would be lifted off the ground by the force of the bang.

Oh, it's all very non-PC these days, now that bangers, jumping crackers and bonfires are frowned on, but a lot of families still treat Guy Fawkes Night as a good excuse for a get-together, with a barbecue and a few sparklers, or a night out at a big organised public firework display.

HARVEST FESTIVAL

It must have come as a great relief to ancient farming communities when the harvest had been safely gathered in "ere the winter storms begin', knowing that their food supplies for the winter were secure. The event was celebrated by a harvest festival service at the village church; it was still quite a big event when I was a lad and even today our village church has an altar groaning with produce. There are special glossy loaves shaped like sheaves of corn, eggs from 'home-grown'

TOP: Nowadays a home-made guy is hurled straight onto the bonfire, but it used to be wheeled around the local streets to raise money for fireworks.

LEFT: No Guy Fawkes Night is complete without a roaring bonfire.

ABOVE: Traditional food such as breads, cheeses, pies, and the plum puddings shown here, would be brought in procession to the town hall for the harvest festivities.

chickens, and local gardeners bring baskets of fruit and veg to decorate the church. Afterwards, all the food is distributed among those who need it, such as local hospitals and old-folks' homes.

Corn dollies are still a traditional feature in some country homes, but their origins go back a long way. The spirit of the corn was said to be driven into the very last of the crop to be harvested from the final field, so instead of being cut as usual, it was collected and made into a life-sized model of the female form and dressed in flowers. This was carried from the fields and kept through the winter to ensure next year's corn crop prospered and gave another good harvest. Today's plaited corn stalk decorations are tiny symbols of the same sentiment.

HALLOWEEN

Halloween is short for All Hallows' Eve, and falls on on 31 October, the night before All Souls' Day, when the souls of the dead passed on from purgatory to their final resting place. The ghoulish costumes and masks were meant to frighten off the spirits that were believed to wander the earth on this particular night, but nowadays it's a good excuse for a party or spot of dressing up and larking about.

The pumpkin lanterns that we carve today aren't as old-traditional as you might think; the custom originated in the USA, where pumpkins have been a big part of its gardening and cookery culture for a long time, and only caught on here in a big way in the 1980s. Long before that we used hollowed-out swedes to make 'turnip lanterns'. I can still recall the odour of swede burnt by a stub of candle from the lantern we stood in our front window.

The traditional drink to accompany Halloween celebrations was originally 'lambswool', a beverage made from ale and roasted apples, flavoured with sugar and spices. Today we are more likely to make mulled wine; it needs to be something warming when you're outdoors, especially if you indulge in the traditional festive sport of bobbing for apples. It's still sometimes done today. The idea is to float several apples in a large bowl of stone-cold water (better still, use an old tin bath), then everyone in turn kneels down with their hands behind their back, plunges their face into the water and tries

to pull an apple out using only their teeth. The trick is to push your face right into the water to trap the apple against the bottom of the container, before sinking your teeth in to lift it out. A successful participant always gets soaked. But in times gone by, bobbing for apples had a slightly more serious purpose – for predicting the future. The young ladies of the village would carefully peel the apple they'd snagged, taking care to make one long complete peel, which they then threw over their shoulder. The shape it made when it landed would reveal the initial of their future husband. (As a result most girls went around looking for a man whose name began with a 'C' or an 'S'. The Toms and the Arthurs were not so lucky.)

It wasn't just girls who liked to know what their romantic future held; the lads had their own Halloween tradition. They'd go blindfold into a garden and pull up the first cabbage plant they felt, then take a good look at it. The shape showed how their future wife would look: plump or skinny, short, crooked or shrivelled. The taste of the heart predicted her character: sweet, bland or bitter.

CHRISTMAS

In medieval Britain, Christmas was a 12-day feast that lasted from Christmas Eve until Twelfth Night (6 January). It occurred at a time of year when the nights were long and there wasn't much work to do in the fields, so farm workers – which was just about everyone – could legitimately spend their time indoors feasting and making merry. The time was also filled with traditional activities.

Christmas decorations were put up on Christmas Eve; it was thought unlucky to put them up sooner. In ancient Britain branches of evergreens were brought indoors and hung round the walls as perching places for the spirits of the forest, since it was considered lucky to invite them in to share the family celebrations. In return these spirits would bring prosperity to the household and ensure crops and livestock gave high yields. The yule log would also be brought indoors on Christmas Eve; this was a large chunk of slow-burning oak which was burnt straight away in the hearth. Tradition states the fire should be kept alight continuously until Twelfth Night. The word 'yule', which is now synonymous with Christmas, comes from the Anglo-Saxon word for the midwinter solstice; these celebrations were pagan in origin. Evergreens continue to be popular decorations today, perhaps as swags or garlands, a wreath for the front door or sprigs of holly tucked behind picture frames. Today's yule log is more likely to be a chocolate-clad Swiss roll decorated with artificial leaves, served up for tea. But it's the thought that counts.

The Christmas tree and decorations with which we are familiar today are a relatively recent tradition. They were first introduced by Queen Victoria's husband, Prince Albert, who brought some over from his family home in Saxe-Coburg-Gotha (now part of Germany) to enliven a party for the estate workers at Windsor Castle, but the idea quickly caught on. Albert also introduced the wrapping of presents and the practice of displaying them under the tree. The original tree decorations were fairly basic – candles, nuts, fruit, sugar plums, ribbons and small gifts – but soon imitation fruit and fir cones made of glass were being imported from Prince Albert's old homeland. The first mass-produced Christmas tree baubles started appearing towards the end of Queen Victoria's reign in the late 1800s, made by F.W. Woolworth. When 'everyday' homes began to be connected to electricity, candles were swiftly replaced by fairy lights – far safer, but for anyone who's seen a Christmas tree lit by real candles, it's a never-to-be-forgotten experience.

At midnight on Christmas Eve, animals are said to kneel (as shown in traditional crib-side nativity scenes). No-one told the story more delightfully than Thomas Hardy in his poem 'The Oxen' in 1915:

'Christmas Eve, and twelve of the clock.
"Now they are all on their knees,"
An elder said as we sat in a flock
By the embers in hearthside ease.

We pictured the meek mild creatures where
They dwelt in their strawy pen,
Nor did it occur to one of us there
To doubt they were kneeling then.

So fair a fancy few would weave
In these years! Yet, I feel,
If someone said on Christmas Eve,
"Come; see the oxen kneel,

"In the lonely barton by yonder coomb
Our childhood used to know,"
I should go with him in the gloom,
Hoping it might be so.'

MISTLETOE

Mistletoe has been strongly associated with midwinter festivities since pagan times. Druid priests considered it to be magical, and used it in various rites and medicinally. So powerful was it believed to be that *only* Druid priests were allowed to cut the plant – with a golden sickle whilst wearing a white robe. The priests sent a sprig to their followers every year to celebrate the start of the new year. Kissing under the mistletoe began in Scandinavia, where mistletoe was under the care of their goddess of love, who called on everyone passing underneath to kiss. After Britain became a Christian country, mistletoe was banned from churches due to its strong pagan associations.

The Boxing Day meet is as much a festive tradition in Britain as a Christmas tree and stockings hung over the fireplace.

Some even said that animals develop the power of speech for a short time at Christmas, but according to ancient tradition, humans should attempt to watch either event at their peril.

For more contemporary children the big attraction is the arrival of Father Christmas, who delivers gifts down the chimney, arriving at homes on a sleigh, and fills stockings left on the mantelpiece. Custom declares that he should be left a mince pie and glass of sherry for refreshment and a carrot for his reindeer. Father Christmas is the modern incarnation of St Nicholas, a fourth-century Turkish bishop who was well known for his charitable habit of distributing alms to the poor. Not so many years ago, it was only the very wealthy who received luxury gifts at Christmas; for most families it was the time to get new clothes, shoes and similar essentials that today we just buy when we need them. When I was a lad, it was still very common for children to be given home-made toys such as a doll's house or a toy farm or fort.

Boxing Day is the day after Christmas when 'boxes' (we'd call them 'tips' today) were given to tradesmen and errand boys as a seasonal bonus for giving good service through the rest of the year. It was *de rigeur* in large Victorian and Edwardian households. The tradition still continues up to a point today if you give the milkman, the dustbin man and the postman a little thank-you for services rendered. (Though today the tip is best given just before Christmas since on Boxing Day they'll be having a lie in and you're unlikely to see some of them again before the New Year!)

But the big Boxing Day tradition for centuries was the hunt. The Boxing Day meet was a large event that was as much a social occasion as anything. The hunt would meet outside the squire's house and stirrup cups (sherry or something stronger) were drunk in the saddle to brace riders for the coming chase.

Twelfth Night (6 January) was (and is) the time to take down the decorations; it was thought to be unlucky to leave them up longer, or indeed to take them down sooner. Twelfth Night was also the traditional time to go wassailing (the word, which is unfamiliar to most schoolchildren today, still appears in some Christmas carols). It was when people took to the orchards to frighten off evil sprits with loud noise and drunken revelry to ensure a good harvest next autumn. After the invention of guns, it became part of the custom to fire a shotgun into the top branches of the trees to frighten off demons. Wassailing is still done in some parts of the country today, notably the West Country, and indeed is an old tradition that's being revived. It is a good way to end the long Christmas holidays.

CHRISTMAS FOOD

Being a feast, Christmas was always the time for enjoying rich food, and lots of it. A good deal of meat was traditionally eaten since it was a treat which didn't feature all that much in the daily diet of ordinary country folk throughout history; even though they usually kept some livestock of their own. But only essential breeding stock could be kept through the winter, since winter feed was scarce, so a lot of animals would be slaughtered just before winter set in seriously, which meant that Christmas was usually a time of plenty.

Victorian cottagers would invariably raise a pig in a sty down the garden and kill it in time to produce hams for Christmas, but birds were the preferred dish for Christmas dinner. In medieval times a lot of wild birds were used: swans, crane, heron or bustard were favourites. Goose was the traditional Christmas dinner for centuries, since geese were easily kept in backyards and were cheap to produce because they lived on grass. Turkeys were introduced from the New World in Tudor times but they didn't become popular as *the* Christmas bird until comparatively recently, when factory farming made them more economical.

Christmas was also a time when ordinary people indulged themselves with luxury foods such as sugar and currants that were far too expensive for everyday use, so the seasonal treats were figgy puddings (a sort of Christmas pudding made with dried figs instead of currants) and rich fruit cakes. Mince pies were originally made with real minced meat and currants, with sugar-icing on top – the suet that's still part of the recipe today is all that's left of the meaty origins. Today we eat mince pies to fill any gaps left after another huge meal, but originally they were considered to be lucky. Each mince pie you ate was thought to give you one month's worth of good luck for the following year (hence the custom of eating twelve of them before Christmas), and to refuse a mince pie was unlucky.

NEW YEAR

Celebrating the New Year was always a big thing in Scotland, but it has only recently caught on in the same way across the rest of the UK. The Scots would traditionally 'see the New Year in' by partying until long after midnight on New Year's Eve ('hogmanay' – first recorded as 'hagmonay' in 1604); the chimes of midnight are the occasion to sing 'Auld Lang Syne', and tradition has it that the first person over the threshold after that time brings luck with them, so it's customary to go out 'first footing'. The ideal 'first footer' should be male, tall and dark-haired (and according to tradition, he should also have flat feet and eyebrows that meet in the middle). He should also be carrying a gift to ensure the prosperity of the household; today's first footer usually carries a lump of coal, but originally it could just as well be a coin or a loaf of bread instead. And if you want to follow the old tradition to the letter, the first footer is meant to come into the house via the front door, wish everyone inside a happy New Year, go into every room in the house and then leave by the back door.

SAINTS' DAYS

The church calendar is filled with saints' days dating back to the time when Britain was a Catholic country. (These were originally 'feast days' held in honour of the saint.) Individual saints also have their own special flower, which acts as their emblem. This tradition began in the Dark Ages, when monks cultivated a wide range of flowers and herbs in their gardens, often for medicinal purposes, and particular flowers became associated with the saints on whose feast day they flowered. In medieval times, churches were strewn with certain plants or decorated with particular flowers for every saint's day. Nowadays only a small number of saints' days have remained in popular culture.

ST VALENTINE'S DAY (14 FEBRUARY)

St Valentine was a fourth-century Roman martyr who was put to death for taking pity on Christian prisoners on a cold night. He doesn't seem to have any connection at all with lovers or even 14 February; the best explanation available seems to be that in medieval times, 14 February was the date on which birds were observed to start pairing off. St Valentine's Day as we know it today started roughly 200 years ago, when 'nice young ladies' were heavily chaperoned. They'd be sent posies of flowers with hidden meanings by their secret suitors; each flower was 'code' standing for various romantic little messages. In the language of flowers, myrtle, lavender and rosemary signified faithfulness, while roses had a huge range of precise meanings depending on the variety, the colour, or even whether the flowers were in bud or full bloom. Today you can still buy books that list the message that tallies with each species.

Greetings cards didn't become popular until Edwardian times, but red roses became the standard decoration for Valentine's cards, which traditionally aren't signed, since it's assumed the recipient will know – or can guess – who they come from. Today, besides cards, real flowers are called for, and *the* top Valentine's day flower is the red rose, ideally a big bunch of them. (It's unfortunate that 14 February is about the worst time of year possible for supplying fresh roses – most of those sold nowadays are imported from flower farms in Africa.) But the very latest Valentine's Day trend is to have an exotic designer bunch of flowers from some top florist's firm delivered to your loved one's desk while they are at work; it does wonders for one-upmanship among their friends and colleagues. Otherwise I can recommend a bottle of champagne, a hearts-and-flowers themed lunch or short break to some romantic destination such as Paris or Rome.

To my Sweet Valentine

Postman CUPID
has a letter
And a rather
large one too,
Which I've told
him to deliver;
To-day without
delay to you.
The envelope
is rather thin
So everyone can see
It just contains a simple heart
A gift to YOU from ME.

ST DAVID'S DAY (1 MARCH)

The patron saint of Wales was a fifth-century bishop of an area now called St David's, who died in 601. The Welsh emblem, the leek, is dedicated to him. On St David's Day, daffodils or leeks are traditionally worn by patriotic Welshmen.

LEFT: St Patrick in all his glory, and (RIGHT) a less beatific modern-day representation of St George.

ST PATRICK'S DAY (17 MARCH)

St Patrick was the son of a Romano-British deacon, who was abducted by pirates at the age of 16 and taken to Ireland and sold – presumably into slavery – during the fifth century. After escaping to France several years later he became a monk, eventually being consecrated as a bishop. Pope Celestine I sent him back to Ireland as a missionary, where he started converting the local tribal chiefs to Christianity. The shamrock is worn on St Patrick's Day; according to legend, Patrick used the three-leaved plant to preach about the Holy Trinity.

ST GEORGE'S DAY (23 APRIL)

St George was a Palestinian martyr who is believed to have been put to death on 23 April in the year 303. The origins of the story about his famous fight with the dragon are unknown. He is the patron saint of chivalry and of both England and Portugal. It was once traditional to wear blue on St George's Day in honour of his flower, the pale blue harebell. Shakespeare's birthday is celebrated on this day, since his real date of birth has been lost in the mists of time. (It also happens to be the day on which he died.)

ST ANDREW'S DAY (30 NOVEMBER)

The patron saint of Scotland was one of Christ's twelve apostles; he preached the gospel in Asia Minor and was later crucified on the orders of the Roman Governor. He is also the patron saint of Russia.

THE PATRON SAINT OF GARDENERS

It's not often known that gardeners have their own patron saint – St Fiacre. He was born in Ireland in the year 620, became a priest and later moved to Seine-en-Marne in France to start a new life as a hermit. In the grounds around his cell he built a hospice for the sick, and developed a reputation for miracle cures when Louis XIII recovered from a serious illness after his wife prayed for his recovery at Fiacre's gates (women weren't allowed inside). After his death in 670, a village named Saint-Fiacre sprang up on the spot and miracle cures continued to occur around his shrine. His feast day is still kept in some parts of Europe, but opinion is divided as to exactly which day it is – 30 August or 1 September. St Fiacre is also the patron saint of taxi drivers.

VILLAGE LIFE

Local activities continued to form the heart of community life well into the 1950s, and they still live on in smaller towns and villages across Britain despite competition from modern telecoms, computer games and TV. There are still lots of good people today running local Scouts and Guides groups, taking keep-fit classes, running play groups, and organising tea-and-bun afternoons for pensioners, as well as lots of more old-traditional activities. Those who live in cities frequently make the mistake of assuming that such times are long gone. In many cases they live on.

SUMMER FÊTES

Fifty years ago vicarages were large, rambling houses with huge grounds, whose lawns were the venue for the annual garden fête which was organised to raise money for the church. Or there'd be a village fête, run in the grounds of a nearby country house courtesy of the local landowner. It was something we all looked forward to; there'd be stalls selling all the usual jams, cakes, handicrafts, garden produce and plants that you find today, but there'd also be a picnic tea on the lawn, perhaps a coconut shy or skittles, and going back some years there'd also be a stand where you could go bowling for a pig – which was a piglet that whoever won then took home to rear. At a big affair – and never a church event – there might be a fortune-teller's tent with a 'genuine' gypsy hunched inside over a crystal ball, and a beer tent where the men could retire for refreshments. There'd also be children's races, games and various strange competitions – for knobbly knees, bonny babies, or the dog who looked most like its owner. Oh, it was a big day out, and everybody dressed up and enjoyed themselves.

THE VILLAGE SHOW

The village flower and produce show is an old tradition that dates back to the eighteenth century, when large landowners were worried about their farm workers neglecting their families or turning to drink, so they introduced village produce shows with cash prizes as an incentive to get the men growing fruit and veg competitively. The idea blossomed, and the village show grew to become a regular part of the social calendar for rural communities, continuing long past the First and Second World Wars. Extra classes were gradually introduced for cakes, bread, scones, home-made jams and country wines, honey and all sorts of arts and crafts. Nowadays you'll also find classes for photography, flower arranging and needlework.

To encourage participation from all the family, most shows include a children's section – one of the most popular classes is for making a miniature garden in a seed tray, which involves lots of ingenuity to create fairy-sized garden implements, greenhouses, rockeries and water features alongside tiny real flowers and lawns made of moss. Today the cash prizes are only a few pence, and the real appeal is the chance to 'have a go' – plus the opportunity to carry home one of the silver cups, many of which date back decades. Winners traditionally have their name engraved on the cup, which they are entitled to keep until the same time next year, when they have to bring it back.

Nowadays shows are usually run in the village hall, but traditionally they took place under a big canvas marquee set up on the village green, and the atmosphere inside was amazing, with a heady scent of bruised grass, flowers and freshly cut veg. These would be ranged out in serried ranks along trestle tables and prize cards propped up alongside winning entries when the judges had finished doing their rounds.

TOP: Sweet stalls of yesteryear – as pretty as their produce.

BOTTOM: *The Village Fête*, by Jean Charles Meissonier, shows how much fun these local events were in the late nineteenth century.

THE WOMEN'S INSTITUTE

The Women's Institute is an organisation *of* women, *for* women. It first began in Canada, but groups started being set up in this country from 1915; the first was in Wales.

The WI (as it is usually known) caters particularly for women living in the countryside who were originally isolated from activities such as theatre visits, etc., that people in towns could enjoy. Each regional organisation holds monthly meetings in its village hall throughout the country (though there are also WI groups in towns – and even central London). Members are entertained with talks and demonstrations on domestic crafts and social affairs, as well as outings to stately homes, gardens and other places of interest. Originally 'Jerusalem' was always sung at the start of every meeting, and some groups still do this today.

During the Second World War, the WI was invaluable in passing on thrifty domestic skills such as jam-making, fruit bottling and vegetable cookery, which were useful to housewives during times of rationing and severe food shortages. The WI has its own college – Denman, in Oxfordshire – where members can go to learn traditional crafts and skills.

Today the WI is a force to be reckoned with; it is well known for championing good causes, acting as the voice of common sense and upholding traditional values on social issues.

GARDEN SOCIETIES

Today most cities, towns and large villages have their own gardening club, and there are also quite a few specialist societies catering for gardeners with an interest in a particular group of plants such as cacti, orchids, alpines, or hardy plants. Some of these have been in existence for over a hundred years. But both local gardening clubs and specialist societies have their roots in the florists' societies which started in the seventeenth century and reached a peak in the eighteenth century.

At that time the word 'florist' had a slightly different meaning; it wasn't a shop selling flowers, but an enthusiast who collected, bred and showed a particular type of flower. The best-known florists' flowers were show auriculas, gold-laced polyanthus, pinks and carnations, which were introduced by the Huguenot weavers who came to Britain in the late seventeeth century to escape protestant persecution in the Low Countries and brought their favourite 'hobby' plants with them. The challenge for florists was to breed new varieties with absolutely perfect round flowers, with symmetrical patterns, in new colours or colour combinations. Other classic florists' flowers, such as *ranunculus*, hyacinth, tulips and anemones, rose to prominence a little later.

Florists' societies didn't meet at the village hall for a talk and slide-show, like a modern gardening group, but instead gathered at an inn for a meal and drinks. On arrival they'd place their newest

members. Some societies loan large or specialist items of gardening equipment such as lawn spreaders or fruit presses to members; some incorporate a trading section with special prices for gardening supplies, and others incorporate sidelines from wine circles to bridge nights into their activities for the benefit of non-gardening spouses. Many more set up sales tables at meetings where members can trade their surplus plants and seedlings, or they'll make special arrangements with local nurseries or garden centres to give members a discount on goods. A garden society can also coordinate a single bulk order from its members, enabling them to get large discounts on purchases from several of the big seed firms. So although the reasons for joining have changed enormously over the centuries, it still pays to be part of a community.

plants on a table for other members to see, and later they'd swap or sell plants amongst themselves. Florists' societies were still in existence in Victorian times, when the ranks of florists' flowers had been stretched to include dahlias, violets, pansies and others, but interest was declining in spite of the fact that gardening in general was by then an up-and-coming hobby for the rising middle classes. The Norwich and Norfolk Horticultural Society is one of a handful in the country whose history can be traced directly back to an old florists' society. It was founded in 1829, is the oldest regional gardening group that's still in existence and is still flourishing.

Today, local gardening clubs meet regularly through the winter for talks and slideshows; some also arrange visits or shows in the summer, and all sorts of extra activities are added for the benefit of

OPPOSITE: The knowledge and skills of the members of the Women's Institute made a huge difference to morale on the home front during the Second World War.

THE ROYAL HORTICULTURAL SOCIETY

The RHS, to which many gardening clubs are affiliated today, started its life as the Horticultural Society of London in 1804, when John Wedgwood and six of his contemporaries met over Hatchard's bookshop in Piccadilly. Thanks to Queen Victoria's royal charter, it became the Royal Horticultural Society in 1861 with Prince Albert as its president. Today it is *the* authority on anything to do with gardening. Its website (www.rhs.org.uk) is a fund of gardening information, and also hosts 'The Plantfinder', allowing visitors to look up the nurseries who supply more than 70,000 varieties of plants, many of which aren't commonly available in garden centres. The RHS runs all the major gardening shows throughout the country, including the Chelsea Flower Show, and has show gardens at Wisley in Surrey, Harlow Carr in Yorkshire, Hyde Hall in Essex and Rosemoor in Devon. Its highest award is the Victoria Medal of Honour, conferred on those who have given 'outstanding service to horticulture'.

SUPERSTITIONS

Medieval people were highly superstitious. It's understandable; since there was no rational explanation for everyday woes, from illness and accidents to bad weather, infertile livestock and crop failure, it was easiest to blame such happenings on fate, witchcraft or other evil influences. Clearly anything folk could do to stock up a little luck was all to the good, so they took out 'insurance' in the form of lucky charms or ritual words or actions. And even though modern science has answers for most problems, some ancient superstitions have become habits, customs or 'old wives' tales'. Half the time we don't even know why we do them ... but sometimes it seems like tempting fate *not* to.

CROSSING YOUR FINGERS FOR GOOD LUCK

What you are actually doing is making the sign of the Christian cross, to ward off evil. When I was at school, kids would cross their fingers behind their backs when telling a fib, as if crossing their fingers somehow meant it didn't count. They'd also cross their fingers and yell '*pax*' (Latin for 'peace') to ward off a thumping from a bigger kid whom they'd annoyed.

NAILING A HORSESHOE OVER A DOORWAY

Horseshoes have long been associated with good luck, though it's not really known why. It's considered lucky to find a horseshoe lying on the ground after it's been cast by a passing horse; a horseshoe with seven nail-holes in it is claimed to be the luckiest of any. It's also lucky to walk through a doorway with a horseshoe over it. Some people claim the horseshoe should be fixed with the rounded end downwards to stop the luck running out, while others claim it should be hung upside down over the very top of the doorway so the good luck showers down on people passing underneath. Today, the lucky horseshoe shape still appears on wedding invitations and confetti.

REFLECTIONS

Reflections – in water or in glass – were once believed to capture part of your soul, so breaking them, or a mirror, was a damaging experience. Seven was considered to be a magical number, and major life events were thought to run in multiples of seven years, so breaking a mirror would bring seven years bad luck unless you practised the 'antidote' – burying the pieces in sacred ground or throwing them into a river. (No, please don't.)

LUCKY BLACK CATS

Black cats were once thought to be the 'familiars' of witches – their animal assistant who helped them to work charms and weave spells. The good luck came from the fact that the cat was, by association, thought to be able to cure ailments. A black cat walking towards you was thought to be lucky, but if it crossed your path it was unlucky. It was also thought witches had the power to turn themselves into animals on occasion, and when they did so they usually appeared as black cats. A witch was believed to be able to take on cat form nine times, giving rise to the nine lives cats are said to have.

MAGPIES

Magpies were thought to be messengers, particularly of bad luck, since they were the only creatures that didn't go into Noah's ark. The number of magpies seen at any time conveys the 'message' via the old rhyme, 'One for sorrow, two for joy, three for a girl and four for a boy, five for silver,

six for gold, seven for a secret never to be told'. A magpie perching on the roof of a house was meant to foretell a death in the family. Country people seeing a magpie would take off their hat and bow to it, to keep in its good books. I'm afraid I still have to salute a magpie and wish it and its family good luck so that ill luck does not befall mine. There are more magpies about than when I was a lad – I do a lot of saluting…

CUCKOOS

According to country lore, when you heard the first cuckoo of the season, turning over the loose change in your pocket was meant to ensure prosperity for the rest of the year.

OWLS

A barn owl flying in front of you is said to signify a birth. Whose is not clear.

BEES

Beekeepers dutifully stood by their beehives and told their bees of any death in the family, and if the beekeeper died then another member of the family had the job of informing the bees that their master was dead, after first tapping respectfully on the hive to attract their attention. This is often still practised in the country. Some families also tell the bees about family weddings or other major events. The idea originally was to keep the bees happy so they wouldn't abandon their hive, a vital precaution at a time when the honey represented an important part of the family food supply.

It was also bad luck to *sell* a swarm of bees; you were meant to swap them for something else so no money changed hands, probably because money was scarce and the 'vendor' never knew when they might want to get a swarm of bees back themselves without parting with cash. 'A swarm of bees in May is worth a load of hay; a swarm of bees in June is worth a silver spoon; a swarm of bees in July is not worth a fly'. The reason? Bees re-housed in July do not have sufficient time to build up a food supply that will see them through the winter.

SNEEZING

It's still customary to say 'Bless you' when someone sneezes, but the habit began in the fourteenth century when the Great Plague, or Black Death, was rife. Since anyone showing any symptoms of illness – of which a sneeze was the most obvious – might be coming down with the disease, people would say 'God bless you' to ward it off.

LEAP YEAR

The tradition that women were only allowed to propose on 29 February was said to have been a concession granted by St Patrick at the request of fellow Irish saint, St Brigid, who took pity on girls kept waiting by their beau. Since 29 February only occurs in leap years, every four years, a woman wouldn't have to wait any longer than that before taking matters into her own hands.

SPILLING SALT

Spilling salt was thought to be very unlucky, dating from the days when salt was an expensive household essential, needed for preserving food supplies (such as hams) for the winter. Every grain of salt wasted by being spilt, it was thought, represented a future tear shed. Salt was also thought to repel the devil and his works, so the antidote to the bad luck brought on by spilling salt was immediately to throw a pinch of it over your *left* shoulder – where the devil was thought to perch.

FAMILY SUPERSTITIONS

I'm sure every family has its own superstitions, some of them of unaccountable provenance. My own father, a Northern plumber who could never be described as fanciful, had a few of his own that have passed down to me. Some were hard to fathom: if he took his socks off during the day, they had to be go back on the same feet – right on right, left on left. If he fastened his belt and it was twisted, it stayed that way all day. Oh, and he'd never pass a person on the stairs. In answer to your question – yes, I now do the same…

COUNTRY SAYINGS AND EXPRESSIONS

'Sayings' are snappy one-liners that are easy to remember, but carry a nugget of genuine country wisdom. They've come about over hundreds of years, starting way back in ancient history. But all sorts of 'old saws' and other expressions have been passed down through the ages.

NE'ER CAST A CLOUT BEFORE MAY IS OUT

This weather warning reminds people not to cast off their heavy outer clothing while the weather could still take a turn for the worse. It's often assumed to mean that you shouldn't do so before the end of the month of May, but some folklore fans think 'May' actually refers to the flowers of the hawthorn tree – meaning you shouldn't cast your clouts before the May blossom is out. This seems much likelier since hawthorn flowers open several weeks earlier or later, depending on the warmth of the spring.

SPARE THE ROD, SPOIL THE CHILD

This was all to do with discipline. Medieval villages weren't the place for spoilt kids or stroppy teenagers – no-one had an easy ride in life. Farmers and tradesmen needed a male workforce accustomed to doing what they were told in all weathers regardless of personal discomforts, and girls had to grow up with good household and gardening skills and to *know their place* – their whole future lay in landing a good husband, and a willing nature and pleasant demeanour depended on it. The rod (or switch or strap) was regularly employed on those who stepped out of line.

AN APPLE A DAY KEEPS THE DOCTOR AWAY

Before the NHS came into being, people had to pay for every trip to the doctor so they'd try anything to avoid being stuck with a bill, and apples were reputed to have healthy properties. (And unlike other things that were good for you, they were free since they grew on the tree that most people had in their back garden.) It's clearly a long-held belief since apple trees and their fruit feature in all sorts of Greek, Roman and Norse legends as 'health-giving'. As a boy, I used to think it was all just a 'tale' designed to persuade us to eat fruit, but modern food science tends to bear out the beneficial properties of apples: they are full of fibre, minerals, pectin and other beneficial phyto-chemicals that between them lower cholesterol and stabilise blood sugar, making regular eaters less likely to have problems with their heart, diabetes and even colds. A trial at a Canadian university showed that students who ate apples regularly made a third fewer trips to the doctor than non-apple-eaters.

BEING FULL OF BEANS

To say that someone is full of beans means they are full of energy, which doesn't immediately seem to make a connection with beans. The saying comes from the Twelfth Night celebrations in medieval Britain. Twelfth Night was the last day of the 12-day feast of Christmas, when one last big blow-out meal was held to end the holiday. A special Twelfth Night cake was made containing – not a threepenny bit for luck, as our Christmas puddings always used to – but one pea and one bean. The man who found the bean in his slice would be crowned King until midnight and he'd naturally be quite pleased with himself and therefore be a little merrier than usual – or 'full of beans'. (A woman who found the pea would be his Queen, and was presumably pretty cheery about it too, though apparently she wasn't said to be full of peas.)

TO RING THE CHANGES

This phrase means to change the order of things, for variety, and comes from the ancient art of campanology – better known as bell-ringing. 'The changes' were the various sequences of musical notes that could be made up from the particular set of bells in the church tower; bellringers would run through all the possible sequences to 'ring the changes'. When the number of bells in larger churches and cathedrals increased from three to five or more, sometime in the seventeenth century, it became possible to ring a lot more 'changes' from the number of notes available. Most bell towers have a ring of eight bells, larger cathedrals as many as sixteen.

'THAT RINGS A BELL'

Church bells have acted as memory joggers at various times in history. In medieval times they'd be rung at a certain time of night to remind

householders to put their fires out before going to bed, and during the last war church bells remained silent since their chimes were the signal that would warn people of the start of the invasion. Traditionally they ring on Sundays to tell people it's time for church; this dates back to the days before ordinary people owned clocks and watches.

DONKEY-WORK

Donkeys were often used to do repetitive monotonous work, such as turning tread wheels to raise water from wells, or pulling carts of manure to be spread on the fields, since donkeys were cheaper to buy and cost less to keep than horses.

UNDERDOG

In medieval times tree trunks had to be sawn up into planks by hand. The trunk was placed over a deep oblong hole in the ground known as a saw pit and cut up using a very long saw operated by two men (known as sawyers), one of whom stood at each end of the blade. To saw up the tree, one man had to stand at ground level just outside the pit, and he was known as the top-dog; his was by far the better job. The other chap had to work standing down inside the pit where he was constantly breathing in sawdust and covered in 'bits'; he was known as the under-dog, the one who came off worst.

NEST EGG

The term nest egg goes back to the seventeenth century. Hens used to be encouraged to lay their eggs just where the owner wanted them by making a cosy nest-box containing straw arranged in a dish-shape, and an artificial egg made of pottery (known as a nest egg) would be placed inside to give them the idea of adding the rest of the clutch to it. (Chicken keepers were still doing this using a white china egg when I was a boy.) The same term was later shifted to savings, the original idea being that once you made a start at saving money you'd add to your nest egg, in the same way that the hens did. Today it's usually understood to mean money you save for the future or keep for emergencies.

STRIKE WHILE THE IRON IS HOT

This means picking the best possible moment to do something. The expression originates from medieval blacksmiths' forges, since iron must be worked while it is red hot and therefore at precisely the right temperature to be shaped into tool blades, horseshoes or fancy scroll-work brackets, etc. A blacksmith would keep several pieces of ironwork heating up at any time, so he could work on them in turn as they each reached the right temperature, without wasting time. But a smith who had *too many irons in the fire* was trying to do more work than he could handle all at once.

A PIG IN A POKE

Medieval markets contained some notoriously dodgy traders. It was common practice to place a piglet on display and, having found a buyer, to switch it for a stray cat when putting it into a sack (or poke) for the buyer to take home. Buying a pig in a poke became a euphemism for being daft enough to buy something without looking at it carefully first. But anyone who had the foresight to open the bag before parting with his cash would be 'letting the cat out of the bag' so the traders dirty little secret would be out in the open.

TAKING POT LUCK

In medieval homes ordinary people cooked over an open fire, in a large iron cooking pot slung from a long metal bracket fixed to the wall. The pot was kept boiling constantly, and contained the usual monotonous everyday diet of gruel made from oats flavoured with whatever was available at the time. This might be a few pot-herbs from the garden or a nearby hedgerow, a handful of dried beans, or on 'good days' there might be a bit of meat, fish or fowl as well. Unexpected visitors had to take pot luck, meaning they'd be offered whatever happened to be in the cooking pot since no special meal could be prepared for them.

PAYING ON THE NAIL

To pay on the nail means to pay immediately. The term comes from medieval markets where buyers and sellers would regularly cheat each other, so money that was changing hands in payment for goods was placed on top of short pillars known as 'nails' so that passers-by could see fair play.

BELOW: In medieval times you had to take a chance on what was going to end up in your supper dish...

FOLKLORE AND ♘
OLD WIVES' TALES

Medieval life revolved round the countryside, the annual farming cycle, the state of the crops and the health of the livestock. Country families were virtually self-sufficient; they grew, preserved and stored all their own food, so crop failures were disastrous. To avoid this, these people learnt from their own experience and the wisdom that was handed down through the generations. All this ancient knowledge was passed on by word of mouth in the days before printed books were available to ordinary people, and some of it still has a toe-hold in modern life. Though some plant lore and old wives' tales might sound a bit strange on first hearing, there's often more common sense or even science behind them than meets the eye.

OLD WIVES' GARDENING TIPS

SOWING SEEDS

In bygone days it was so important to get seeds off to a good start that there was masses of ancient wisdom to help. Where a modern gardening book might tell you how thickly or otherwise to sow seed, the 'old wives' said it in verse – 'one for the rook, one for the crow, one to die and one to grow', meaning they expected only one in four seeds to germinate and reach fruition. They were talking about seeds of hardy vegetables and grain crops sown directly into the ground out in the open, of course, but it's still reasonably good advice today, even if today's seed-thieves are more likely to be mice and pigeons.

Today, however, when you're sowing large seeds such as courgettes, peas or beans, tomatoes, cucumbers or melons under glass or in some other protected environment, you'll get virtually every one up, since modern seeds are tested and have to meet certain minimum germination standards. And it has to be said that modern seeds are packed in airtight foil and supplied with full instructions, unlike medieval seeds which were home-saved, stored in damp conditions and passed round the community.

Timing and temperature were vital. One piece of advice was to sow seeds during a waxing moon, rather than a waning one, and there are still people who believe in this method of 'lunar gardening'. (You can buy calendars and guides from specialist organic gardening catalogues.) Some advice recommended sowing certain crops in the nude; parsley in particular. I don't know if this was a means of gauging the correct temperature and weather conditions generally when it was propitious to sow seed, but another old idea was to drop your trousers and sit on the soil to tell if it had reached the right temperature for sowing. (It works rather like testing the baby's bathwater with your elbow.) Nowadays a soil thermometer does the trick nicely and saves embarrassment, though it's usually sufficient to follow the timings given on the back of your packets of seed, remembering, as my Yorkshire mother reminded me, to add on a month for colder parts of the country.

FEEDING PLANTS

Old wives' tales advocate using all sorts of unusual items for feeding plants, and (with a few small reservations) it's quite okay to follow the same advice today. People were told to bury banana skins or old cooking fat round their roses. Banana skins supply potash when they decompose, and fat provides phosphate and trace elements; since roses are heavy feeders, anything of the sort would have been very welcome. (But today we might draw the line at burying fat, since it attracts foxes, which will come and dig up the garden, as well as rats.) Horsehair, feathers, human hair and nail-clippings were all once recommended as natural fertilisers, and indeed they all break down in the soil after a time, releasing nitrates – all very useful for leafy crops in the veg garden.

Used tea leaves and teabags are still often recommended today for spreading round camellias; used tea leaves act as a mulch that helps retain moisture round these notoriously shallow-rooted plants, while the tea supplies a good many trace elements as it breaks down. (I suspect a lot of the reason behind this particular advice was that tea itself is a member of the camellia family.) But tea had other uses. Fifty years ago country people were still using cold tea left behind in the bottom of the teapot to use as liquid feed for their houseplants. The trace elements would certainly have helped, but the big benefit was that boiling the water to make tea precipitated the chalk out, so the plants benefited from soft water – it was as good as rainwater without the bother of going outside to the water butt.

Many country folk still pee on their compost heap, and an Irishman once told me that when I planted a grape vine, I should bury underneath it 'tree dead dogs'. I have never been in a position to do so.

PEST AND DISEASE CONTROL

Old wives' tales often advised planting certain plants close together to ward off pests or even diseases, and nowadays this idea has come back into fashion with organic gardeners, who know it as 'companion planting'. Garlic, parsley or chives are recommended for planting under roses to deter pests such as greenfly, and some enthusiasts think it also helps control diseases. Veg growers are advised to sow rows of onions between carrots; the smell of onions deters carrot fly, which can ruin the crop by tunnelling into the roots. Another tip is to plant certain flowers with veg crops to deter pests; marigolds (tagetes) with tomatoes is the best-known one. This seems to work because the nectar-rich marigold flowers attract hoverflies whose adults and larvae both feed voraciously on aphids, but the root exudation of the marigolds may also help, provided they are planted so that their roots intertwine with those of the tomato.

Today organic gardeners will also plant other annuals such as *Phacelia campanularia* and poached egg plant (*Limnanthes douglasii*) in or around their veg patch to attract beneficial insects to patrol their crops instead of using chemical sprays. And to treat a sickly or ailing plant, the old wives' tale advised planting chamomile next to it, since chamomile is reputed to heal anything near it – herb enthusiasts sometimes refer to it as 'Doctor Chamomile' for this reason. Another beneficial plant combination was strawberries and borage, though in this case I think it's probably that the borage attracted bees which pollinated the strawberries, so they produced a bigger, better crop. (Strawberries that haven't been well pollinated produce small, stunted and misshapen fruit.)

A multitude of sage advice was on offer for keeping unwanted wildlife out of gardens. For moles in lawns, it was advised you put moth balls down the holes. I suggest you powder them first, or the moles may just push them out with their noses. Toy windmills often discourage them on heavier soils where the vibration carries down the stick. A row of them can be advanced and will send the moles into retreat – I've seen it work! Some also suggest sinking transistor radios, musical cards or half-buried milk bottles into the tops of molehills so the underground sounds frighten them off. If deer break in to gardens, old wives' suggest hanging bundles of human hair round the boundaries, hoping the smell of humans will frighten them off. I didn't find them so easily scared when I had a deer problem at Barleywood, though dabs of now unavailable creosote on top of fence posts was more effective. High fencing plus a screen of trees they can't jump over is best, but even then there's no guarantee.

HARVESTING

Old wives' tales said that you shouldn't pick blackberries after Michaelmas Day – 29 September, the feast of St Michael and All Angels – as they are cursed by the devil (who pees on them) after that date. In fact, the last of the crop is usually small, soggy and bitter tasting due to bad weather, so they aren't worth having anyway.

FLOWER AND PLANT FOLKLORE

In medieval times, the entire lifestyle of country families relied on their ability to make everything they needed to run the household out of things they grew in the garden or picked wild from the hedgerows, so plants naturally played a very important part in everyday life – far more so than today. In a superstitious society, it was only natural that certain plants also came to be credited with 'special properties'. Those beliefs, and the rituals associated with them, have been filtered down through generations, and what's left now is folklore. Cynics may scoff at the apparent obscurity of these old customs, but some of them are based on underlying truths which are not always immediately obvious.

WARDING OFF WITCHES OR EVIL SPIRITS

Certain plants were claimed to have properties that would ward off witches or evil spirits, so growing them in or round the garden was a good insurance policy. Betony was one (it was also said to cure nightmares), and angelica another (that's the same plant whose green candied stems decorated trifles at tea-time when I was a lad).

Ash and rowan trees (below) both had the reputation for undoing spells. And anyone wanting protection from witchcraft carried a piece of rowan wood in their pocket as a lucky charm; certain plants including vervain, dill and St John's wort were also believed to do the same job.

WEATHER PREDICTION

According to superstition, if it rains on St Swithin's (or St Swithun's) Day (15 July), it'll rain for the next 40 days and 40 nights. St Swithin was the Bishop of Winchester who died in 862. He was a very humble man, and when he was dying he insisted on being buried in the graveyard outside his church, the same as his congregation. A few years later the authorities thought it more appropriate to give him a more prestigious resting place so his remains were moved to a tomb inside. The job was scheduled for the 15 July, but work was halted by 40 days of continuous rain.

A less well-known bit of weather lore states that if the sun shines on Candlemas Day (2 February) a second winter is about to start. In the past, Candlemas Day was thought to mark the halfway point between winter and spring; sunshine on that day indicated that spring had started too early so winter would return for another six weeks – i.e. a second one following the first.

The behaviour of animals, birds and plants were all 'read' at one time as signs of weather prediction. Watch for trees coming into leaf: 'Oak before ash, we shall have a splash – ash before oak, we shall have a soak'. Look at the flowers of scarlet pimpernel; they are said to close when it's about to rain – this plant was often known as poor man's weatherglass for this reason. And study seagulls; as children we were always told that seagulls fly inland when there's bad weather at sea, though these days a lot of seagulls have moved inland almost full-time to enjoy the free meals to be had at rubbish dumps, and some are even nesting on flat roofs in cities which they regard as man-made cliffs. An old country rhyme you don't hear often nowadays says 'swallows flying high, no rain in the sky – swallows flying low, 'tis likely to blow'. This is thought to be due to barometric pressure causing the tiny insects swallows feed on to be held close to the ground or swept up into the air. But when I was a lad the ones we all watched were cats and cows. We were told if a cat is seen washing itself, or cows lie down, it's shortly going to rain. And if cats get frisky and dash about wildly with a stiff tail and 'mad' staring eyes, wind is on the way.

GOOD LUCK

The best-known natural good-luck charm is a four-leaved clover. You can very occasionally find one in a grassy field or lawn containing the usual white clover. According to tradition it's lucky to pick it, but not just for novelty value – a four-leaved clover was believed to protect its owner from witches. Some said its magical properties came from the fact that the four leaves form the shape of the Christian cross; others thought it was due to the elves that lived where four-leaved clovers grew. But there's more: carrying a four-leaved clover was thought to bring success, and if you put one in your loved-ones' shoe it would ensure that he or she always came back to you.

There's another, less well-known lucky charm: an even ash leaf. That's to say an ash tree leaf that has an even number of leaflets instead of the usual uneven number. If you find either leaf, the best way to keep it safely is to press and dry it to preserve it.

LOVE LIFE

Ordinary white daisies – the sort that grow wild on your lawn – were once used by girls to see if their beau was equally fond of them. They'd pick a daisy and chant 'he loves me, he loves me not' as they plucked off each petal in turn; the last petal to come off gave them their answer. It's thought to date back to Victorian times, but it clearly caught on because girls were doing this when I was at school. But back in the distant past, a crafty girl didn't leave things to chance. She'd visit a 'wise woman' to obtain a love potion. A number of plants were used to make these, including cyclamen tubers and several wild orchids, but *the* plant for love philtres was mandrake. Its roots were said to be shaped like a man or woman, and had so many mystical properties that – rumour had it – the plant shrieked when pulled out of the ground, driving all who heard the sound mad. It could only be harvested by tethering it to a dog who did the pulling.

A couple who'd already wed and just wanted to promote long-lasting true love were advised to both eat periwinkle leaves. It was known as sorcerer's violet.

Mandragora fœmina. Chelidonium minus.

Catherine Middleton's bouquet included myrtle, which may or may not have come from Queen Victoria's plant at Osborne House

WEDDINGS

Confetti is traditionally made up of a mixture of paper good luck symbols including horseshoes, and is thrown to shower the happy couple with good luck for their future life. In medieval times it was common practice to throw wheat at weddings, to symbolise fertility.

The tradition of catching the bride's bouquet was meant to reveal who of the unmarried wedding guests would be next to wed – with most brides aiming the flowers squarely at their older bridesmaids. Originally a cutting of the evergreen foliage used in the bridal bouquet was taken home and rooted by the bridesmaid; it was usually myrtle. If it died she'd remain an old maid, but if it rooted she'd be next to wed. The plant grown from the cutting would in turn be used to provide the sprigs of foliage for her wedding bouquet. In keeping with the old tradition, myrtle rooted from a sprig taken from Queen Victoria's wedding bouquet was grown at her holiday home, Osborne House on the Isle of Wight, and sprigs from it have been included in several royal wedding bouquets since.

FORTUNE TELLING

In times gone by, the fortune teller was always a great favourite at village fêtes. It was always a lady – usually of mature years, wearing a flamboyant gypsy costume with huge dangly earrings – sitting in a tent, who'd read your palm or peer into a crystal ball with a good deal of amateur dramatics. It was great fun for your penny (even when it went up to sixpence), although you took her findings with a large pinch of salt, especially when you knew her to be the lady behind the counter at the local post office or the bacon counter at the grocer's shop.

Behind closed doors, you'd hear of people who foretold the future by means of tarot cards or by 'reading the runes' or other means. And even today, a good many people who scoff at the idea of fortune-telling read their horoscope in their daily newspaper or weekly magazine. But reading tea leaves was somehow more respectable and it has a very long history. The ancient art of tasseography, or reading the tea leaves, began in ancient China – well, they were the people who grew tea and first made it into a beverage. From there both tea-drinking and reading tea-leaves travelled round much of the civilised world via itinerant gypsies. (Authentic Romany gypsies in brightly painted horse-drawn caravans had great reputations as fortune tellers, and a few of them still travel our roads today.) When I was a lad, 'reading the tea leaves' was often practised by respectable elderly ladies – my Auntie Alice among them – who'd upturn their cup into the saucer to check out what the future held – for themselves or any visitor who stopped for afternoon tea. To them it was more interesting than the six o'clock news.

NATURE'S LIGHTNING CONDUCTORS

An elder bush was believed to be a safe place to take cover during a thunderstorm because witches and elves were believed to shelter beneath its branches, so it was protected from being struck by lightning. At home, growing houseleeks (*sempervivums*) on your roof was also believed to safeguard the house from lightning strikes.

HOW TO READ TEA LEAVES

...

FIRST YOU NEED the right sort of tea. Naturally it must be proper tea made with a teapot and tea leaves, not a teabag, and you need a wide, shallow tea cup, not a mug – ideally white inside, or a light colour, and without any pattern. Make the tea in the usual way, but when pouring it out *don't use a tea strainer*, since you want lots of tea leaves in the bottom of the cup. You can add milk and sugar as usual. After the subject has drunk their tea, leaving the dregs in the bottom, the fortune teller tells them to hold the cup firmly in their left hand, swill it slowly round three times in an anti-clockwise direction, then tip the cup smartly upside down into the saucer. While it's still resting in the middle of the saucer, they should push it across the table to the fortune teller. Starting with the handle of the cup pointing directly towards the subject, she turns the cup round three times, also in an anti-clockwise direction, before lifting the cup and turning it over to look at the leaves left on the inside.

INSIDE THE CUP, there are two things to look for. The first is groups of tea leaves that form obvious shapes such as aeroplanes, cars, or letters of the alphabet – these show the events. Next take note of the part of the cup they are in, which tells where and when the events will occur, and how they affect the subject.

SHAPES DEPICTED IN TEA LEAVES don't always represent exactly what they look like; the symbolism used is the same as that for interpreting dreams. An aeroplane, train or anchor means a journey, a gallows shows bad luck is coming, stairs mean going up in the world, and a pair of lips means hearing something to your advantage. A loaf of bread indicates freedom from money worries, while a fence means hurdles to cross, and a shark shows approaching danger. An envelope shows good news is coming by post – if there are dots near the envelope that means money is coming. Letters of the alphabet may be the initials of a person coming into your life, or causing trouble – depending on what symbol they appear next to. Numbers may show how many months or how many children, or whatever it may be; it all depends on the nearest pictorial symbol to the number.

BUT THE MEANING OF SYMBOLS can change depending on the position of that particular group of tea leaves inside the cup. Tea-leaf shapes close to the rim of the cup foretell events that will happen in the very near future; the closer to the bottom of the cup they come, the further ahead in the future they'll occur. The area close to the rim is the 'happy' part of the cup, while the bottom of the cup spells worry, sadness and tears. The quadrant of the cup that includes the handle – which should still be pointing at the person whose fortune is being told – refers to events happening close to home and within the family, while the opposite quadrant reveals events away from home or involving strangers.

BUT IT'S NOT JUST A CASE OF REMEMBERING all the different meanings of dozens of different tea-leaf 'pictures'; tea-leaf reading is a means of channelling the fortune-teller's natural psychic powers (which by all accounts have to be developed by training and practice, just like any other talents), so if you don't have the gift you can only make an educated guess. I imagine dozens of Edwardian-era aunts did just that, for the amusement of their friends at afternoon tea. And I'm sure that Auntie Alice meant well...

WORKING THE LAND

CHAPTER 2

Today there are still some lucky people who, because they love the countryside and the traditional way of life, combine their everyday job with running a smallholding. Others keep livestock as a hobby. It might even earn them a few pounds. This is the deep end of being a countryman, and there's more to it than just 'liking the life'.

The secret of a successful smallholding is hard work and attention to detail. Livestock needs looking after 24/7, and it's not all Beatrix Potter (though she was a woman who knew what it was all about, running her own flock of championship Herdwick Sheep on the Lakeland fells). What I mean is that you've got to be realistic about it: there's a lot of manure to shovel, worming and ear-tagging to do, matings and births to supervise, unexplained deaths to investigate and, worst of all if perhaps you've become friends, animals to send off to slaughter. Livestock is also a tie; it's not easy to find someone to take over for a few weeks if you want to take holidays or even go away for a few days. But if you're prepared for the reality, running a smallholding is very rewarding – at least, spiritually speaking.

Unlike large-scale farmers who have to operate with ruthless efficiency and factory-like methods in order to keep their business profitable, smallholders and crofters can set their own agenda, which might mean an idyllic lifestyle in lovely countryside or pursuing a passion for rare breeds. A good many smallholders breed livestock (including exotic poultry or novelties such as llamas and alpacas) to exhibit at agricultural shows round the country, and sell surplus young stock to other breeders or to families as pets. For anyone downsizing to a quiet life in the countryside, it's possible to produce a lot of your own fruit, veg, chickens and eggs, with a small surplus to sell, from half an acre of land. Even if you aren't wholly self-sufficient, it'll boost your lifestyle and it's hugely enjoyable. What follows here is a handy guide to the sort of things you will need to know and take into consideration when endeavouring to live off the land.

THE LEGAL/ADMIN SIDE

· · ·

YEARS AGO, ANYONE could keep a few animals in their own grounds and sell anything from honey to home-made cheese at the local market without any 'red tape', but nowadays these areas are all increasingly bound by rules and regulations which change frequently, so it's vital to keep up to date. Although it takes time – and it has to be said money – to meet the rules and regulations, the reasons behind them are sound. When bodies such as DEFRA (the Department for Environment, Food and Rural Affairs) know which livestock is where, it's easy to contact owners if there's a sudden animal health alert (such as in the case of a foot and mouth outbreak, or bird flu being found in the wild bird population that requires poultry keepers to keep their flock under cover).

THERE ARE ANIMAL HEALTH AND WELFARE requirements, and also rules regarding animal movements. For instance, you can't just turn up at a slaughterhouse with a couple of pigs or sheep; you need a proper permit to move them, and they need to be booked in well ahead of time and arrive with all the right paperwork.

YOU ALSO NEED TO KEEP DETAILED RECORDS; some types of livestock must have births registered and the young are issued with passports which stay with them for life. Most livestock also needs to be identified by means of ear tags which they wear throughout their life, and there are rules and regulations covering disposal of fallen or dead stock which apply to any animal or poultry considered to be 'livestock' (i.e. a farm animal), even when it's kept as a pet.

ANYONE THINKING OF TAKING ON A SMALLHOLDING or croft, or starting their own from scratch, is well advised to do their homework first; smallholding magazines, their websites, and smallholders' shows, are all good places to start. You can find local smallholders' groups by searching the Internet, or looking for details in smallholders' magazines or at shows. There are also special-interest organisations for beekeepers or particular breeds of livestock, many of which also have local groups.

THE GOVERNMENT'S DEFRA WEBSITE (www.defra. gov.uk) isn't the easiest to fight your way around but it does have all you need to know about registering a smallholding, or registering as a beekeeper, animal health, ear tagging, etc., and lots of useful information about the rules and regulations surrounding everything to do with keeping livestock. If you prefer to phone, they have a helpline which will pass you to the right department. Call them on 08459 335577.

THE NATIONAL FARMERS' UNION offers legal advice and insurance to members.

THE COUNTRY LAND AND BUSINESS ASSOCIATION offers members free professional advice, also a guide to issues regarding the rights and responsibilities that even small-scale landowners should be aware of regarding their land.

IF YOU EXPAND INTO THE FOOD BUSINESS, perhaps by selling produce or making it into chutneys, pies, etc., to sell at markets, then you need to register with the Environmental Health Department of your local council, who will send someone out to inspect your kitchen and advise you how to comply with all the legislation that affects you, and you'll have to take a food-handling course and display your certificate on your stall.

A LOT OF FUSS AND BOTHER? Yes, but it's worth it.

SMALLHOLDING OR CROFT – WHAT'S THE DIFFERENCE?

According to the dictionary definition, a croft is a small rented farm, usually in Scotland, with a house and an area of arable land plus the right to use common pastureland for livestock. A smallholding is similar in size – an agricultural holding smaller than a farm – but south of the border, and without any rights to common pastureland. It's often owned and run by the smallholder. Both crofts and smallholdings are worked predominately by the tenant or owner, and their families, rather than paid farmhands.

In some parts of the country, ancient grazing rights still exist – older homes within the New Forest automatically have 'commoners' rights' which pass to successive owners and allow them to keep livestock such as ponies, donkeys or even pigs in the forest. It's not a great way to keep your riding horse or pony on the cheap, since the rights mean the livestock run free over a huge area, so it might take you rather longer than you'd like to find your mount. The livestock is rounded up at particular times of year, and the New Forest pony roundup, when foals are separated from their mothers, marked and sold or selected to return for future breeding stock, is a great tourist attraction every autumn.

RARE BREEDS OF LIVESTOCK

The types of livestock that we know as rare breeds today were once standard commercial breeds of pigs, poultry, sheep and cattle, decades or even centuries ago, that have simply been superseded by modern advances. Their numbers have fallen to very low levels and some are at risk of extinction – many have already vanished forever. Why? Today, rare breeds are mostly kept going by enthusiasts, smallholders and country parks; some rare breeds of cattle are used for 'conservation grazing' on nature reserves. Rare breeds look picturesque, though they'll cost more to keep than modern commercial breeds since they produce lower yields and take longer to mature – the very reasons why they were superseded – but they have bags of character and their owners enjoy the novelty value and their usually very tasty meat or eggs, not to mention the glow that goes with doing their bit to preserve a little corner of countryside history.

POULTRY

'Poultry' is a catch-all term covering all sorts of farmed birds; not just chickens but also ducks, geese, turkeys and more unusual fowl too. Poultry are ornamental, inexpensive and (as livestock goes) fairly low maintenance, yet they give quick returns in the form of eggs or meat, which, depending on how you house and feed them, can be free range and/or organic. Poultry are fun to keep – I've kept a few chickens for twenty years or more now – and compared to commercial intensively-produced poultry, it's good to know that they enjoy a happy life and are well fed. Their great advantage over other types of livestock is that if you go away on holiday, it's relatively easy to find a friend or neighbour to stand in and take over the feeding and watering temporarily, in return for the eggs.

CHICKENS

For most people embarking on keeping livestock, chickens are an obvious way to start, and compared with sheep and pigs, goats and cattle, they are relatively easy to accommodate.

HOW TO KEEP CHICKENS

Chickens are easy to keep on a very small scale; anyone with a large lawn can keep two to six birds in a portable ark which is moved daily. I've had great success with those neat plastic 'Eglu' runs, which are easy to maintain and to move. For a larger number of hens, you'll need a freestanding hen house fitted with perches and nest boxes. Perches should be placed as high up as possible, at waist level or above. Nest boxes should be the shape and size of an orange box, and fixed a handy hen's-leap above ground level (which means roughly knee-high); they should be partly filled with bedding such as straw or wood shavings, which needs replacing once or twice a week. Since the eggs must be collected daily, it's best to buy the type of henhouse that has nest boxes built into the sides with hinged 'lids' that can be opened from outside; it makes the job quicker and easier, and you won't be disturbing the hens. A henhouse also needs a securely fenced run around the outside. If the run is large enough it can be grassed over, but hens will soon scratch up the grass in a small run and reduce it to mud, so it's best surfaced with wood shavings or straw.

Hens need to be shut in at night. Henhouses usually feature a 'pop-hole', which is a hen-sized hole fitted with a sliding 'door' that can be secured in the open position by day and then lowered at night. Hens lay almost all of their eggs before about 10 am, so keeping them in until then makes certain the eggs are laid in nest boxes and not outside in the run, where they get dirty. If you have to leave for work early, then you'll need to open the pop-hole before you go and trust to luck that you can find them! Eggs laid outside may not be very fresh by the time they are discovered – they'll also attract egg thieves such as magpies and crows.

You can keep chickens in even a small garden; just make sure they've got a safe hut to sleep and lay their eggs in, and a space to run and scratch around in, and they'll reward you with delicious fresh eggs.

Hens will happily eat grain – usually whole wheat, though the addition of kibbled (broken-up) or flaked (flattened) maize makes for eggs with deeper yellow yolks, and, if you are raising them for meat, chickens fed a fair percentage of maize produce better-flavoured flesh with a rather golden colour. (This is what the supermarkets and butchers mean by corn-fed chickens.) This is all my chickens are given, plus whatever they can get from scratching around under the damson trees in their grassy run. For maximum egg yields, many people feed layers' mash or layers' pellets, either alone or mixed with a little wheat and/or maize.

Although it looks rustic to throw feed onto the ground for chickens, it is wasteful (and, given hens' toilet habits, rather unhygienic), so the feed is best tipped out into a hopper first thing each morning where the birds can help themselves any time. If possible, keep the hopper under cover to prevent feed being taken by sparrows or ruined by rain. Hens also need flint grit, which helps them grind up hard grains so they are digested properly, and oystershell grit, which provides the calcium that ensures their eggs have strong shells. Both types of grit should be available to the birds at all times. Even when they can run around outside, they won't find enough naturally. Hens also need to be able to peck at greenery, both for their health and because it improves the quality of their eggs or meat, so if they don't have access to a grassy run or veg patch, hang up a bunch of greens for them. While we're thinking of their welfare, give them logs or branches to jump around on; the exercise does them good, keeps them amused, and it's fun to watch. Mine love foraging in the compost heaps behind their run!

A henhouse needs cleaning out regularly so it doesn't smell and to prevent pests or disease; it also means the hens' feet stay fairly clean so they don't tread muck into their nest boxes and dirty the eggs. Even so, do replace the straw in the nest boxes every week. Both this and dirty straw or wood shavings from the floor of the henhouse can be added to a compost heap; fresh hen manure is high in nitrogen so it makes a good activator that helps a heap rot down quickly – don't dig it straight into the ground, as it is so 'strong' it can scorch plants.

STARTING WITH CHICKENS

Most people start chicken-keeping by buying 'point-of-lay pullets', which begin laying eggs within a couple of weeks of being introduced to their new home. (Most hens can be reckoned to start laying at the age of 20 weeks.) 'Growers' are young birds which cost less to buy but need feeding for several weeks before they start laying. Both commercial breeds of hens and rare breeds can be bought either as point-of-lay pullets or growers, but rare breeds can set you back something like £25 per bird for good breeding stock.

Experienced poultry-keepers will sometimes buy young or even day-old chicks, which are far cheaper, but they need special facilities to keep them warm day and night, and they take a good deal of care and attention. The youngsters take several months to reach egg-laying age and some losses are inevitable on the way, so it's not always as cost-effective as it appears. It's also sometimes possible to buy fertile eggs which need to go under a broody hen or into an incubator to hatch, but this needs a bigger investment and more skill.

The cheapest and perhaps most satisfying way to start is to re-home retired battery hens. Several organisations save 'old' chickens from battery farms, when they'd otherwise be culled. A rescue chicken is normally 'retired' from commercial flock at one year old, but it will keep laying for another three years or more, often starting from within a few days of being re-homed, yet it costs considerably less to buy than a point-of-lay pullet. Because rescue chickens are not used to outdoor life, they need to be kept shut into the henhouse for a short while after their move, but once allowed out they quickly start wandering cautiously outside and soon begin to scratch around, flapping their wings, pecking greenery, and doing all the things that hens do in natural surroundings. They soon replace lost feathers and bald patches; some specialist animal feed firms supply special feeds for rescue hens, which provide extra calcium and minerals to help them make stronger bones, joints and feathers after life in battery cages where they get no exercise. It's a joy to watch them recover and take on a new lease of life. If you have to introduce new hens to an existing flock, pop them into the henhouse at night when the birds have gone to roost – it makes for a calmer form of integration.

CHICKENS IN THE KITCHEN GARDEN

Hens are very good at clearing up. They can be allowed to run around in an orchard or even – out of season – in a fruit cage. If you have a kitchen garden, you can let the hens out into the area when the crops are finished; they'll peck away at old cabbage leaves, weeds and weed seeds, soil pests and caterpillars, and they'll turn the ground over by scratching around, and manure it at the same time. Some keen veg gardeners deliberately position their chicken house in between two or four fenced veg plots in order to let the hens out into whichever patch is 'free' at the time. However, it's no good letting hens out into growing crops in the hope that they'll weed between rows or clear pests; they'll just eat your plants and scratch up your seedlings.

HOW MANY HENS DO YOU NEED?

If you're buying hens with egg production in mind, first work out exactly how many birds you'll really need.

A hen in its prime, well fed and kept free from stress, will usually lay an egg every day, although productivity does decline in winter due to low light levels. Mine tend to lay daily between January and October, then go 'off lay' for about three months. Some hen-keepers cheat and leave a low-wattage electric light on in the henhouse for a few hours on winter nights to 'top up' the natural daylight to a total of 16 hours per day, which triggers the birds to keep laying year-round. If you're going to follow suit, use a timer and readjust it regularly to take account of changing day-length, to save electricity.

For most families, two or three hens will provide as many eggs as you can comfortably use up; if you keep more you'll be spending out needlessly on feed. But out in the country a lot of poultry-keepers sell their surplus eggs at the garden gate, with an honesty box.

WHICH CHICKEN BREED?

Anyone intent on producing eggs reasonably seriously usually chooses one of the high-yielding, hybrid, commercial kinds, which lay far more eggs than pure breeds. But if you are keeping hens for home consumption and fun as much as for gain, choose one of the handsome unusual or rare breeds.

1 Wyandottes: available in various colours including white, lavender, black, buff and blue, but silver-laced and silver-pencilled are particularly showy.

2 Leghorn: the classic farmyard hen with a sleek shape, chestnut breast and dark grey back and tail.

3 Maran: handsome chunky chickens barred dark grey/black and white, which lay deep brown eggs.

4 Light Sussex: popular traditional breed of white hens with a black lacy collar round the neck, and also at the tip of the tail; lays white eggs.

5 Rhode Island Red: popular, traditional breed of warm-brown hens laying brown eggs.

6 Buff Orpingtons: big and fluffy with foxy-orange feathers. Often go broody, which may be an advantage if you want to raise your own chicks.

7 Corals: those in my arms on the back cover of the book, are white speckled with cream, very friendly.

8 Bantams: these small breeds eat a bit less than full-sized chickens and lay slightly smaller eggs, but plenty of them. Some breeds are very good-looking, and some lay eggs with unusually coloured shells – such as green – which taste the same and have the same culinary uses as chickens' eggs. Bantams tend to 'go broody' a lot, and since they make excellent mothers, are often used to hatch the eggs and rear the young of other birds, especially exhibition chickens and ducks. The most popular bantam breed is the Silkie; these strange shaggy birds – usually white – have feathery feet and lay blue-green eggs. My favourites are Lavender Pekins, with blue-grey feathers and feathery feet.

DO YOU NEED A COCKEREL – OR NOT?

Hens will lay without a cockerel being present; the eggs will simply be infertile so they'll never hatch into chicks. Some chicken-keepers like to keep a cockerel as he looks big and showy with his large red comb and wattles and a long arched tail. If you're counting the costs, you might feel he is just an extra mouth to feed, but a cockerel keeps a close eye on 'his girls', giving audible warning and often going on the attack if there's a predator about, but in built-up areas, alas, some neighbours are not very keen on the sound of a cockerel crowing as he tends to be noisiest around the crack of dawn.

If you want to rear chicks then you'll have to keep a cockerel, so the hens will lay fertile eggs. The only slight drawback with having fertile eggs is that if you don't collect them daily, keep them in a cool fridge and use them fairly promptly, they'll often start to develop a red spot in the centre, which is an early chick embryo. Although an egg in this state is still okay to eat or use for cooking, a lot of people find it a tad off-putting.

POULTRY PROBLEMS

Hens need to be wormed to kill internal parasites; it's also possible to use a product to kill worm eggs on the ground in the hen run.

Hens also get mites; affected birds are irritable and don't lay well as they are under stress – it's a dead give-away if eggs have tiny spots of blood on them. Ideally use a mite-repellent product on perches or on the floor of runs before birds are affected; some products also contain disinfectants that protect against infections including E. coli, salmonella and listeria. You can also get mite powder to apply directly onto the birds. This is the reason I have 'plastic' hen houses – the mites are very difficult to get rid of in a wooden house with lots of crevices.

Various products to treat everyday ailments and for use as precautions, including natural chemical-free ones, are sold at pet shops, animal feed centres and agricultural stores and are also advertised in poultry-keeping and smallholding magazines. The firms also take stands at shows. But always consult a vet in case of problems.

BROODY HENS

'Going broody' is natural for hens; it's what happens when a hen decides to sit on a clutch of eggs and hatch them instead of laying more. Broody hens look listless, go off their food and spend all their time sitting in a nest box – they can be aggressive with other hens who try to use the nest boxes, and may peck at humans who try to shift them to collect the eggs. Broodiness happens most with bantams and pure breeds of chicken, least with commercial hybrids, and can happen even when hens aren't kept with a cockerel. If a hen turns broody, either pen her on her own for a week or so until she gets over it (fresh air and very little comfort is what she needs) or let her sit on a clutch of eggs and raise chicks. Either way, lift her twice a day to make sure she eats and drinks.

RAISING CHICKS FROM EGGS

A broody hen doesn't have to hatch her own eggs; indeed, if you don't keep a cockerel there's no point in trying as they won't be fertile – you can obtain fertile eggs of a different variety from a breeder, or even use a broody hen to hatch bantam, duck or turkey eggs, since bantams make particularly good mothers.

A broody hen won't be happy in the usual henhouse with other hens around. Move her and her clutch of eggs into her own nest box in a separate run, and leave her to sit on them until they hatch (it takes 21 days). Duck or turkey eggs take a few days longer to hatch, but most broodies will keep sitting for the extra time it takes. During the whole time a broody hen is sitting on eggs, you'll need to lift her carefully off them daily and take her to food and water, otherwise she may not bother to feed, and give her the chance to relieve herself – she won't do so while she's sitting on eggs. Then let her go back. Once the chicks have hatched, she'll look after them automatically. Within a day or so of hatching they'll be wandering round with her looking for food and water so you'll have to lay in a stock of chick crumbs. (This is very fine dried food that their tiny beaks can manage and which contain all the nutrients they need.) Good hygiene is vital, so make sure food and containers are cleaned daily, and clean out the pen they are kept in extra well and more often than usual.

CLIPPING WINGS

Despite their seemingly un-aerodynamic shape, chickens can fly – at least enough to flutter clumsily over a fence round their run – so most owners clip their wings to stop them getting airborne. It's easily done with a strong pair of gardening secateurs. Have an assistant to hold the chicken firmly but gently, and stretch out one wing. Snip through the large, long flight feathers at the tip of one wing, cutting them off at least a couple of inches from their base, so you are cutting through the 'quill' – this way, you won't draw blood and it won't hurt the bird. It's best just to clip one wing, since this unbalances the bird so it feels less inclined to try to fly – if it has a go it's very lopsided so it soon gives up. Since chickens moult regularly, you'll need to repeat the process a couple of times each year. Usually the first sign you get that it's time to clip wings again is when you spot hens trying to take off and fluttering a bit higher than usual, or you see a lot of cast-off feathers in their run, showing that they have started to moult.

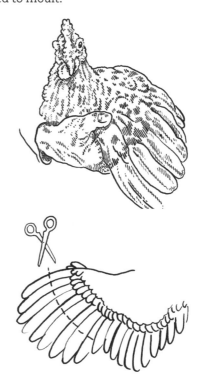

DUCKS

While some folk keep ducks just for their egs and meat, others simply enjoy their company and their antics, which are guaranteed to make you smile.

HOW TO KEEP DUCKS

Ducks are just as easy to keep as hens, but if you keep both don't keep them together – give them separate accommodation.

Ducks don't need perches or nest boxes, so their house can be a lot lower than a henhouse. A small hut will do, but a custom-made duck house is usually triangular in cross section, with a pop-hole fitted with a sliding door (since, like hens, ducks need to be shut in at night) and a roof that lifts open for cleaning out and for collecting eggs. The house needs plenty of straw bedding on the floor – this is where they'll lay their eggs, so it needs to be changed regularly to keep it clean, and ducks make a heck of a lot of mess.

They also need a run, which needs to be bigger than a hen run. Ducks soon foul a small area of land so they need plenty of room; allow at least 1.4 square metres (15 square feet) per bird. Better still, make a second run adjacent to the first, so that one area of ground can be 'rested' for a few weeks while the grass recovers, before the birds are moved back. Alternatively, ducks can be allowed to roam freely in a farmyard or orchard during the day, but they must be shut up in a hut at night, and protected from foxes and rodents.

While ducks don't absolutely have to have access to a pond, they really are happiest when they do – even a small one is enough for them to bathe and splash about in. Make a small duck pond in the same way as you'd make a garden pond, by digging out a dish-shaped hollow, but if you take my advice, instead of lining it with butyl, line it with concrete. I've found that since ducks foul the water very quickly, a concrete pond is easier to keep clean – sweep out the water every week with a stiff broom and replace it with fresh. Whatever you do, don't try to introduce ducks to a decorative garden pond. Oh, they'll love it, but in no time at all they'll have eaten all the plants and the fish, and turned the

Ducks are an idyllic sight splashing around on a pond; these birds are easy to keep and happy as anything with a little water, space to roam and a warm, safe hut away from foxes.

Ducks will find a lot of their own food if there's space to roam, but they will appreciate a bowl of pelleted food and one of fresh water.

DUCK EGGS

Ducks' eggs are quite different from hens' eggs; they are slightly larger in size, with large yolks and glutinous whites which make them brilliant to use in baking – they make moist, rich cakes and puddings – but, for some people, too slimy for omelettes or boiled, fried or scrambled for breakfast. Ducks start laying at roughly 16 weeks of age, and continue for about three years before the yield starts declining badly. A good laying breed should produce roughly 6 eggs per week, but production falls off slightly in winter when light levels are low. It's vital to collect ducks' eggs daily since they'll often lay them outside or in dirty, muddy places, and as the eggs cool, the porous shells can soak up bacteria from their surroundings. (This is why it's a good idea to cook ducks' eggs very thoroughly, especially when you don't know where they've come from.) Even if ducks lay eggs inside their house, the birds tend to bring a lot of muck back in with them from their pond or a muddy run so it's vital to keep the bedding clean and replace it regularly.

surroundings into a sea of mud. They'll also foul the water and turn it murky and smelly. No, keep them to a pond of their own, which is inside their run and fenced off from the surrounding area so they can't get out into the garden or your veg patch. If there's no room for a pond, then give ducks a large tub that's sunk into a hole in the ground that they can splash about in. It's most important they can get their heads under water. Their eyes and beaks need to be rinsed frequently in clean water; if you're using a container make sure it's regularly cleaned out and refilled.

As well as water for splashing about in, ducks need clean drinking water at all times, so provide them with a separate bowl (one that's too small for them to get into) and change it daily. Ducks can't drink from the same sort of water dispenser as chickens since their wide beaks prevent them dipping into the narrow trough area.

Ducks will find a lot of their own food if they have access to a large field or orchard in which to forage; they are especially good at clearing slugs and snails from land used for growing vegetables after the crops have been harvested (since they'll also eat plants) and if you can cope with their feet flattening the ground. But they do need something more solid as well; ducks do well on a home-made mixture of whole wheat, barley, crushed oats and flaked maize (special pellets are available). The food can be scattered on a clean bit of ground (which can be difficult to find in a duck run) or else tipped into a trough which needs to be cleaned out regularly. Since their wide beaks mean they can shovel their food down quickly (unlike hens, which are forced to peck daintily) they'll clear a meal quickly and keep eating until they can hardly walk, so instead of using the sort of help-yourself hopper that's used for hens, give ducks as much food as they can eat within 20 minutes, and do this twice a day – morning and evening.

In spite of the fact that they take rather more time and effort to look after than hens, ducks are fun to own since they are great characters. A few breeds are kept for both eggs and meat, though mostly separate breeds are used for each job, and there are several ornamental breeds that are popular for showing.

BREEDS OF DUCK

The type of duck you choose will depend on whether you want your birds for eggs, meat or ornament.

1 Muscovy ducks: large heavy-looking deep-grey/black-and-white ducks with a reddish 'knob' on top of the beak, often kept as ornamental waterfowl on duck ponds. They are also known as Barbary ducks, which are favourites for meat; they fatten rapidly and are usually killed at 10 weeks old for the table. Muscovies make the best broody ducks.

2 Aylesbury: the classic 'table' ducks. These large, deep-chested white birds have orange beaks and also lay about 100 eggs a year, making them a useful dual-purpose breed.

3 Indian Runners: very tall, striking, upright ducks, usually white or brown but also available in various colours, mostly kept as pets or for showing, though they do produce around 180 eggs per year.

4 Khaki Campbells: again of upright demeanour, dull, light brown ducks, the favourite egg-laying breed, and very productive, yielding 300 eggs per year. White Campbells are equally good. They rarely go broody, so if you want to raise more of your own it's best to put fertile Khaki Campbell eggs under a broody bantam.

REARING DUCKS FROM EGGS

Domesticated ducks are very poor mothers, so though it may be fun once in a while to allow a duck that looks so inclined to sit on a clutch of eggs, it's far better to give a clutch of fertile eggs to a bantam to hatch. (Beatrix Potter's Jemima Puddleduck was not all fiction!) You will need to splash the eggs with water daily to dampen them slightly, since a duck does this naturally but a bantam won't. Even though duck eggs take slightly longer than hens eggs to hatch (28 days instead of 21), a bantam foster-mother will keep sitting until they do, then she'll take on the job of looking after ducklings despite her obvious concern at their tendency to take an 'unhealthy' interest in water. Feed the ducklings with chick crumbs and make sure they always have access to clean drinking water, as well as a wide, shallow bowl of water in which to bathe and – if it's deep enough – swim around in.

GEESE

For a long time after turkeys first reached Great Britain, a goose was still the standard Christmas dinner for 'ordinary' people, but after a long period of unpopularity, it's fast becoming the upmarket choice for folk who've grown tired of mass-produced turkeys.

Geese are also the easiest poultry of all to keep, for anyone with plenty of grassy space available. A small flock of geese is a good way to keep an area of rough grass cropped without the need for mowing, since they'll graze it short, and when grass is growing vigorously they can live on it without supplementary feeding, which keeps feed bills down. The only slight downside is that their droppings make a mess of the grass, especially if they are confined to a small area, so they need to be kept off your garden lawn if it's used for family games, sunbathing and barbecues.

Geese need a good-sized grassy area in which to wander by day, and ideally it should be fenced to protect them from foxes. They need a hut for shelter, with straw or wood shavings on the floor, and a pop-hole since they need to be shut in at night. Like ducks they don't need perches, though it's worth having a nest box area along one side, at ground level, in which they can lay their eggs, since this keeps them far cleaner than leaving them on the ground. It's far quicker and easier to collect the eggs if the lid of the nest area opens from the outside, and there's no risk of a close encounter with a disgruntled goose in a confined space. A hut for geese needs a higher roof than a duckhouse, since geese are clearly much bigger, taller birds.

Geese appreciate access to a pond, which they can share with ducks, though they can be kept without one as long as they are given a deep trough or tub of clean water that's changed regularly; it's essential they can plunge their heads under water completely to rinse their eyes and beaks properly. When there isn't enough grass to keep them well fed (usually in the winter and during dry summers), geese should be fed whole wheat and barley grains twice daily – morning and late afternoon – in a trough or thrown over a clean patch of ground. They'll also enjoy fresh greens, so put out old cabbage, kale, broccoli and Brussels sprout plants to strip, and give them any lettuce plants that have run to seed, or let them into your veg patch in winter to clear the ground after the crops are finished. They are generally fairly problem free, though (like any poultry) they should be treated regularly for internal parasites.

GOOSE EGGS

Geese lay the biggest eggs of any domestic poultry, weighing roughly half a pound apiece. A single one is equivalent to four large hen's eggs – enough for a whole omelette. Adult birds start laying in February or March and continue until roughly midsummer, and over that time each bird will produce approximately 70 eggs. You can sometimes sell a few goose eggs at the gate, or to local farm shops, but they aren't well known to the general public so you'll probably end up using most of them yourself. But perhaps the best way to use surplus eggs is to allow a goose to hatch a clutch and rear the young for their meat.

RAISING GEESE FROM EGGS

Rearing geese from scratch is very simple as the mother goose does most of the work. Allow her to sit on a clutch of up to 14 eggs, ideally in a separate enclosure of her own where the other geese won't bother her. She'll need constant access to water, as she'll use some to splash the eggs with daily, or they may well not hatch – and you'll need to bring her food and water since she won't want to wander far. Keep her well fenced in because foxes find a sitting goose and her eggs a very appealing target; rats will also make a beeline for the eggs so take anti-rodent precautions (see page 50). It's possible to hatch goose eggs under a broody hen, but you'll need to splash them with water daily and turn them – mark one side with a pencilled X so you know which way they are meant to be, since they are too heavy for the hen to turn.

Goose eggs take 30 days to hatch. When the goslings emerge, they'll appreciate some shallow water to splash about in if they don't have a pond, and you'll need to feed them on chick crumbs. They'll soon start to eat grass and once they are doing well on their own you can stop supplementary feeding as long as there's plenty of grass. If you want to hurry them along to reach slaughter size fast, continue feeding them; give them whole wheat and whole barley, mixed in roughly equal quantities. Traditionally, goose was never eaten until Michaelmas (29 September) at the earliest, with most kept for Christmas. It's well worth doing; even a small oven-ready goose weighing 3½–4kg (8–9lb) costs around £60 in the shops. As a bonus, goose fat makes the best roast potatoes ever, and each bird produces a big bowlful.

Geese are sparky, characterful creatures that will happily mow your lawn in return for some pretty large eggs.

1

2

3

BREEDS OF GEESE

1 Embden: the typical farmyard goose, large and white with bright orange bill, legs and feet, which produces the biggest carcass – look no further if you want roast goose on the menu.

2 Toulouse: a thick-set goose with a shorter neck; white-shaded brown feathers, also good for meat, and barely smaller than the Embden.

3 Chinese: a rather unusual goose with a slightly swan-like shape, in white or light brown with a barred pattern. This breed is less hardy than more popular kinds; it needs more shelter from bad weather, and lays 40–50 eggs every year.

LIVING SECURITY GUARDS

Geese are handy creatures to have around a smallholding or large country garden; their loud honking gives advance warning of approaching visitors, dogs or foxes, and their feisty behaviour tends to ward off unwelcome callers. The security value is especially high if you have a small flock of six or more geese with a gander, who is bigger and fiercer than the females in his harem. During the breeding season, in spring, a gander can be a bit nasty, so it's worth taking care even at feeding times.

TURKEYS

Of all poultry, turkeys are the trickiest to keep. They are susceptible to the cold and wet so they need a good-sized hut with deep bedding as they won't go outside much in bad weather, though it's a good idea to give them access to a large outside area (a grassy field or orchard is ideal – so when conditions allow it they can get out for some fresh air and exercise – they like to scratch about a bit).

Turkeys are also very prone to disease, so good hygiene is a must. Besides cleaning them out and replacing their bedding regularly, it's essential to keep feed and water containers scrupulously clean. Don't allow them to share living accommodation or outdoor grazing with other poultry because there's a risk they'll pick something up from their neighbours. Feed them on whole grain or special pellets for turkeys (available from animal feed merchants).

Though the females do lay eggs sometimes, turkeys are mainly kept for meat. Commercially, white hybrid turkeys are the usual choice since their flesh is light-coloured; they are fast to fatten and can reach 4kg (9lb) in 12 weeks or 7kg (15lb) in 16 weeks. But when you rear your own on a small scale you can go for a tastier alternative – the traditional Norfolk Black, which produces darker, richer meat, sells for a premium, especially if its kept free range and fed organically. The turkey cock is a splendid-looking beast in full plumage with long red wattles, and its 'gobbling' sound will make you smile – at first!

Breeding turkeys is the trickiest part of the exercise, so ideally when starting out you should buy young birds to rear. However, if you can get hold of some fertile turkey eggs, give them to a broody bantam – they take 28 days to hatch – and feed the young hatched birds on specially formulated turkey crumbs (or chick crumbs, if not available) until they are big enough to start taking the usual whole grain or pellets.

For advice on anything to do with turkeys, visit the Turkey Club website www.turkeyclub.org.uk.

Not the most beautiful of birds, nor the easiest to keep, but if you want a succulent homegrown turkey on your Christmas table, the hard work and attention they need may be well worth the effort.

GUINEA FOWL

Guinea fowl are second only to geese when it comes to easy upkeep. They are most attractive, almost exotic-looking, birds, in white, lavender or dove-grey, patterned with dots and flecks and a strange head-dress. They are slightly smaller than bantams, but belong to the pheasant family. Guinea fowl are thought to originate from the Guinea coast of Africa, and they've been kept throughout Europe since ancient Greek and Roman times. In Britain they were once known as Tudor Turkeys.

Like geese, guinea fowl are happiest when they are allowed to run around freely by day (ideally in an area fenced against foxes and other predators) and they need to be shut into a suitably sized hut at night. Provide clean water and feed them twice daily on whole wheat grains with some kibbled maize or game bird pellets. If they're given a large area to roam in, they will find quite a bit of their own food while they are scratching around – they are very handy for clearing up a veg patch. The birds can be a bit noisy and rather nervy, and unless you keep their wings clipped they'll fly up into trees to perch or roost. Guinea fowl make good pets, but they're usually kept for meat; a young bird is ready for the pot at 10 weeks old, weighing half a kilo to a kilo (1½–2lb).

If you want to raise your own from scratch, guinea fowl don't make good mothers so it's usual to give fertile eggs to a bantam to hatch. Eggs take 28 days to hatch, just as for ducks' eggs.

These petite and pretty birds make great pets if you don't want to rear them for their meat.

QUAIL

Wild quail are now very rare in this country; these small dumpy birds migrate here for the summer from southern Europe and are usually heard rather than seen, since they creep about amongst tall crops and only take to the air when really pushed.

However, domestic quail make an unusual alternative to other forms of poultry. They are ideal for keeping on a small scale, mainly for their eggs, though sometimes for their meat. Quail lay well; when kept indoors, birds start laying at 10–12 weeks old and commercial producers get 200–300 eggs per year from each hen. Even when kept outside they'll still be very productive. Four hen birds will give you more eggs than you need in spring and summer.

When kept for meat they mature quickly, and are ready for the pot at six weeks old, but the final carcass is so small – only 22g (½lb) – you really wonder if it's worth the effort of plucking, as it takes two birds to make a meal for one person. (When you rear your own, it might be worth treating them the same way a lot of country people treat wild pigeon: simply cut the breast off each side of the breastbone and discard the rest of the carcass, which has virtually no meat on it.)

My quail have a 'winter' home in what looks like a rabbit hutch with a wire-netting front and a side compartment filled with straw where they can go to lay their eggs. On cold nights I lower a double sheet of bubble wrap over the front since the birds are not quite as hardy as chickens. Some folk keep quail in this kind of 'rabbit hutch' all year round, but I like to move the birds to a wire-netting-covered outdoor run from spring to autumn – it has a wire netting floor, too (to keep out vermin) and sits on grass. Alternatively, it can be set on clean bark chippings or sand (which needs replacing regularly). Some logs or leafy branches to investigate and hide among will be appreciated. If they don't have a hen-type house to go into, give them a slightly screened off corner for shelter. (Don't use an open-topped run or your birds may fly away!)

Quail don't need perches or nest boxes and they lay their eggs on the floor – anywhere! – so they need collecting frequently.

Those kept for meat are usually housed in a shed or similar outbuilding as they'll grow faster, but ideally give them access to an open-air run during the day as they like to go outside, unless the weather is poor. They need cleaning out often. Like any poultry, quail need clean water at all times. Special ready-mixed quail feeds are available but can be difficult to find if local livestock feed suppliers don't have any other quail-keepers amongst their customers, in which case give them crumb-sized feeds formulated for turkeys or game birds – if you can't get these, use chick crumbs.

Quails' eggs are a real delicacy, much loved by foodies. These little birds lay well, saving you trips to the deli.

PIGS

The last time there was a great self-sufficiency boom, in the 1970s, goats were the most popular form of livestock for smallholders, but today pigs top the bill. Pigs are very efficient meat-producers – in the 20 weeks from birth to butcher, a pig can put on 95 kilos (15 stone) in weight. People will often buy one or two weaners (young piglets that have just stopped being fed by their mother, aged roughly 10 weeks old) and fatten them for ten weeks, by which time they'll be the right size for the freezer. That way it's possible for a 'backyard farmer' to keep themselves in meat without the usual year-round ties that usually go with keeping livestock; when you come home from your summer holidays, simply buy another weaner or two (pigs are happiest kept in company) and start again. It's not necessary to keep your own breeding stock; but if you do, a lot of smallholders like to go for rare breeds instead of the usual commercial varieties beacause they are great characters and look good in an orchard, paddock or pen. But sows have large litters, so instead of just rearing a couple of piglets you'll be looking at full-time care of up to 16 individuals!

HOW TO REAR WEANERS

You can rear young pigs in the open, given an ark for shelter, or in a concrete sty with a covered area and an outdoor run. They'll need plenty of straw bedding in their shelter – it needs topping up regularly – and they'll have fun rearranging it and sorting through in case there's anything interesting to eat that they've missed. Pigs are intelligent and appreciate something to do; some smallholders give them a football to play with. Pigs kept in the open will find a damp area to turn into a mud-patch to wallow in; they'll also like to have a big tree for shade as pigs (especially pale pink hairless breeds) can get sunburnt on hot summer days. When they are kept in a sty, pigs will need cleaning out daily; they are naturally clean animals that will keep using the same corner as their loo. Between different batches of weaners, clean the living area thoroughly, disinfect it and rinse it well, and replace all the bedding entirely.

As for food, the old days when wartime smallholders collected food scraps from schools and householders to make into mash for fattening pigs are long gone – it's now illegal; there's just too much risk of diseases such as foot and mouth. (The 2001 outbreak was traced back to the use of untreated waste food.) You can, however, feed your pigs fruit and veg from your own holding, as long as you don't operate a catering business, and you can also feed surplus milk from your holding to pigs if you register with DEFRA. (But regulations change, so it's worth checking the current rules with your local Animal Health Divisional Office.)

When you only keep a few weaners, the easiest option is to use ready-made pelleted feed sold in bags; it can be bought in bulk and will keep for quite a long time if the bags are stored in a clean, dry, rodent-free place. Pellets are clean and easy to handle, and quick to feed. Give weaners two feeds each day, morning and late afternoon/early evening, in a trough, which must be cleaned regularly. As a rough guide to consumption, at eight weeks old each weaner will need 700g (1½lb) of feed a day, rising gradually to 1½kg (3lb) a day by the time they are ready for slaughter at 20 weeks old, when they'll be the perfect size for pork. (If you're using weaners from a rare breed such as Tamworths, they'll grow more slowly than modern commercial pigs, so expect them to take 26 weeks to reach slaughter size.) In cold weather pigs use more energy keeping warm, so if you keep yours outside in winter, be prepared to increase their rations

slightly to compensate. If you have surplus fruit and veg or milk, then they are best used as 'treats' to supplement their normal 'concentrated' feed; if you try to treat them as free food in place of part of their usual rations, they won't fatten so quickly.

HOW TO BREED PIGS

A breeding sow will grow to a surprising size and get to know her keepers. Rare breeds in particular are great characters. Breeding sows, especially old and rare breeds which were bred for the job, are happy to live outdoors in a securely fenced grassy field, with an ark to shelter in. Several sows will happily share the same space if it's a reasonable size, with each sow having her own ark to retreat to and have her piglets in. They enjoy rooting around together, and they'll turn muddy patches into wallows, where they can take cooling mud baths (which protects against sunburn in strong sun). You can also move them around during the year; in an orchard they'll eat windfall apples, or can be turned out into a field that's grown feed crops for other livestock (such as kale or mangolds) or the veg patch at the end of the season. They'll do the land a power of good since they turn it over, eating roots and soil pests and manuring it naturally as they go.

But you can keep breeding sows in traditional-type sties, one in each. A sty needs to have an enclosed sleeping area plenty big enough for her to turn round easily in, with room for a litter of 14 piglets, and an outdoor run. To keep sties clean these are usually both floored with concrete, so deep straw bedding is necessary.

Whichever method you opt for, be prepared for the amount of water they'll need – an adult sow can drink up to 10 litres (17½ pints) a day, so it's worth investing in some drinkers of the type that refill themselves from a built-in storage unit, or if you're keeping breeding sows with litters, then use drinkers that are connected to a permanent plumbed-in water supply, which will save you carting an awful lot of buckets of water about. But check drinkers daily, since they can get blocked, and pigs will soon suffer if they go short.

BACON AND HAMS

If you intend rearing weaners to produce bacon and hams, they need to be kept longer than pork pigs so that they produce a larger carcass – bacon pigs are usually kept until they are about 32 weeks old. Naturally this means extra expense since they'll eat more and need more straw, not to mention labour for cleaning out, etc. Some smallholders prefer to keep old breeds of pigs that lay down far more fat than is acceptable for a modern porker, especially for bacon and ham production, since the flavour is in the fat. Traditionally, weaners for bacon and hams were bought in spring and fattened until shortly before Christmas.

Sows kept outside on grassy fields, in woods or orchards will find some of their own food by digging about with their snouts, but they still need proper feeding. You can use barley meal moistened with water to make a mash, or specially prepared pelleted feed for pigs. In sties, they live almost entirely on concentrates.

A sow can produce two litters of piglets per year, and a young female pig, known as a gilt, can breed from the age of 6–8 months. To start the ball rolling you need a boar, but only a fairly large-scale pig breeder will go to the expense of keeping their own – most people hire or borrow one from a fellow pig-keeper. Boars are bigger than sows, and aren't always the best tempered of animals, so they need handling with extreme caution, especially when you don't know the individual animal well. After mating, the sow will produce her litter exactly three months, three weeks and three days later. Two weeks before the expected birth, clean out a special farrowing pen well and put in a particularly deep layer of clean straw, then move the sow into it. Shortly before giving birth the sow will make a 'nest' in it, which is a sure sign that farrowing will start shortly. Unlike a good many farm animals, sows will get on with it for themselves, especially when they are given a natural stress-free

environment in which to do so. The farrowing pen should be fitted with a strong metal bar that keeps the sow out of part of it, and here the piglets can lie in straw under a 'creep lamp', which keeps them bathed in warmth. When the piglets are three days to a week old, the whole family can be moved back to their field and put into an ark with deep straw inside, provided the weather is warm enough.

Once she has piglets to feed, a sow will need more food herself – the rule of thumb in country families was to give her daily as many pounds of barley meal as she had piglets, plus an extra two pounds. She can be very defensive of her piglets, so keep dogs, small children and visitors safely on the other side of the fence. As the piglets grow older they'll continue to suckle but they'll start rooting around in the field and also take some of their mother's feed, until they are weaned at roughly 8–10 weeks, when they need feeding with concentrates of their own.

PIG BREEDS

Commercial pigs are usually hybrids, specially bred to fatten fast on the minimum of feed, but although they take longer to reach slaughter size, rare breeds are more fun to keep.

1 Tamworth: a handsome medium-sized pig covered in reddish-brown hair, and rather wild-boar-like in shape. A popular breed with smallholders.

2 Saddleback: very traditional-looking pig, black with a pale pink band round the middle and pale pink front legs.

3 Gloucester Old Spot: another favourite smallholder's pig that's also popular as a 'paying pet'; it is large, rather block-shaped and heavily marked with black spots and blobs of varying sizes on a pale pink background.

4 Large Black: all-black pig with lop-ears, valued for producing particularly tasty meat.

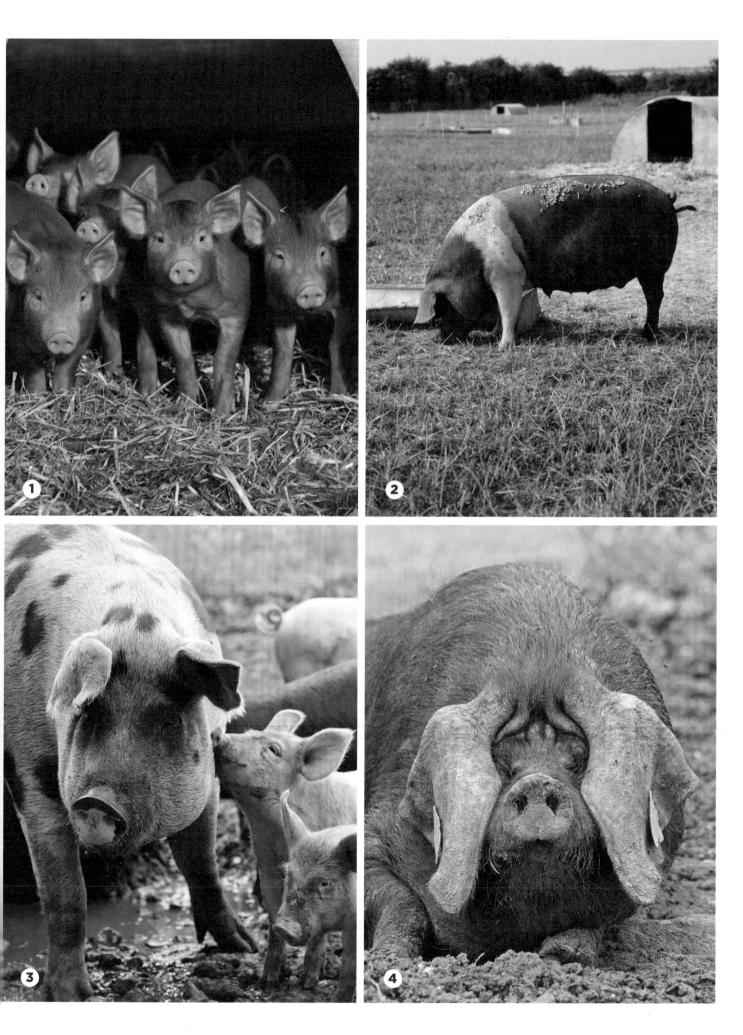

GOATS

Goats were the 1970s smallholders' must-have, and they've been popular as 'paying pets' ever since. Being so much smaller than a cow, a goat is docile and easily handled by people who don't have a lot of experience with livestock. A nanny will yield between two and three and half litres (four and six pints) of milk a day over two milkings – morning and evening – which is quite enough for the average family, with some over for making yoghurt and soft cheese. A cow, by comparison, costs considerably more to buy initially, and more to feed. It also needs a larger area of land, is bigger and harder to handle, and will produce far more milk than a family can use so, inevitably, a lot goes to waste unless you can feed the surplus to pigs or convert it into ice cream, yoghurt and hard cheese.

Goats' milk is slightly different in character to cows'. The cream is distributed evenly through the milk itself, which means it won't rise to the top, so you can't make goats' milk into butter. But it is more easily digestible than cows' milk, and so often it is recommended for children who suffer from eczema or for anyone allergic to, or intolerant of, cows' milk.

HOW TO KEEP A GOAT

Goats are great characters and easy to keep. They aren't keen on being kept on their own and will go to great efforts to get out or cause mischief; however, if you don't want to keep a second goat they are quite happy to have a pony, donkey or other large livestock as a companion. (Though if you want continuity of supply, it's a good idea to keep two nannies together so that one is producing milk while the other one is pregnant.)

You'll need a hut large enough for the animal or animals to move around in freely, as they'll need to be shut in at night and during spells of bad weather. The hut needs to be high enough so the animals have plenty of headroom, as they'll sometimes stand up on their back legs with their front feet against the wall. If the hut has a window, use clear polycarbonate instead of glass so there's no risk of breakage. Put a layer of deep bedding on the floor; straw is best but wood shavings are a good substitute – and clean the hut out frequently. Ideally the hut is best situated inside a large, open

pen, with the door left open during the day so the goats can return to it if they need to shelter from the weather. The pen can be grassed if it's big enough, otherwise cover the ground with straw and put a few large branches inside for goats to browse on – they'll enjoy munching the twigs and chewing the bark, so replace them every so often. They'll also enjoy having a whole bale of straw to jump onto, and if you cut the strings they'll break it open and push it around in case there's anything good to eat inside. A bucket of clean water to drink is essential at all times.

If you have a securely fenced grassy paddock, goats can be turned out in it to roam loose with other livestock (including poultry). Give them a field shelter they can go into if the weather turns inclement, but put them back inside a proper hut at night so they can be shut in.

Because goats are browsers rather than grazers, they particularly enjoy being turned out into a rough area full of weeds and brushwood – they eat far more semi-woody and weedy wild food than grass. But don't imagine you can use goats to clear wasteland for you; contrary to popular belief they are very selective feeders and will merely take what they fancy and leave everything else. They will, however, strip the bark from young trees, eat whole saplings and nibble at hedges, so it's no good introducing them to a newly planted 'conservation area', and it's risky keeping them in an orchard unless it's an old established one with very large trees, since goats will eat any twigs within reach. If you don't have a paddock or an enclosed pen to keep them in, goats can be tethered from a collar round the neck to a short metal 'post' with an 'auger' at the base that is screwed into the ground; in this way the animals can be moved from one area to another to ensure grazing is evenly used and to make use of small unfenced areas that otherwise couldn't be grazed. But don't just leave them out and forget about them; you'll need to take them a bucket of water and bring them in if the weather turns bad – and always at night.

Besides what they gather for themselves by browsing, goats need to be fed on hay, which is best secured in a hay net and fixed to the top of a fence post or a ring in the side of their hut, or else placed in a wooden hayrack fixed very slightly above a goat's head height inside their hut, so they have to reach up. If you feed them loose hay on the ground, or put it where they can pull it down, they simply trample it into the dirt, whereupon they won't eat it. Pregnant and milking goats also need extra rations, so give them a mixture of rolled oats and flaked maize, divided into two feeds, morning and evening. Resist the temptation of giving milking goats old brassica plants from your veg patch to browse on as they can make the milk taste slightly 'cabbagey'. But since the animals can't always get the full spectrum of minerals they need from their regular feedstuffs, it's vital to provide a mineral salt-lick that the animals have access to all the time. This is best placed inside the hut where it won't be dissolved by rain, fixed securely to the wall of the building at roughly a goat's head height.

The best way to start goat-keeping is to buy a pregnant nanny; once she's had her kid she'll start to produce more milk than the kid needs, so let the two continue living together until the kid is weaned and simply take the nanny aside to milk her twice daily, morning and evening. If she's used to being handled she should behave quite well, but secure her with a halter to a ring in the wall, and as 'bribery' it pays to give her a bucket of concentrated feed to distract her. You can milk a goat while she's standing on the floor if you don't mind crouching down, but people with several goats construct a solid 'table' on which the animal stands, so the owner can milk from a more comfortable position, standing upright.

Goats have a perhaps undeserved reputation for being a handful, but these entertaining animals are great fun to have around.

HOW TO MILK A GOAT

...

TAKE A CLEAN BUCKET, ideally stainless steel, which you've sterilised by scalding the inside well with boiling water. Ensure your hands are perfectly clean; wash them thoroughly with soap and hot water immediately before milking.

SIT THE BUCKET UNDER THE GOAT'S UDDER. Ensure she is quiet or she'll very likely kick the bucket over or step into it and spoil the milk.

GENTLY GRIP A TEAT IN EACH HAND, holding it with your thumbs uppermost. Use each hand in turn. Use the thumb against the side of your index finger to nip the top of the teat closed, then slowly and gently close the remaining fingers in turn to squeeze the milk from the teat. Then release your grip so more milk flows down, while you repeat the process with the other hand on the other teat. Continue until no more milk is let down. Er…it's a knack!

MILK TWICE A DAY, morning and evening, at as near as possible the same time each day. This way the goat will come to expect the attention, and the meal that goes with it, and – especially if you are gentle – she'll cooperate. Some goat keepers find it helps to talk quietly to the animal as they work.

STRAIGHT AFTER MILKING, transfer the milk to a clean, sterilised container or glass bottles and put it in the fridge so it cools down quickly.

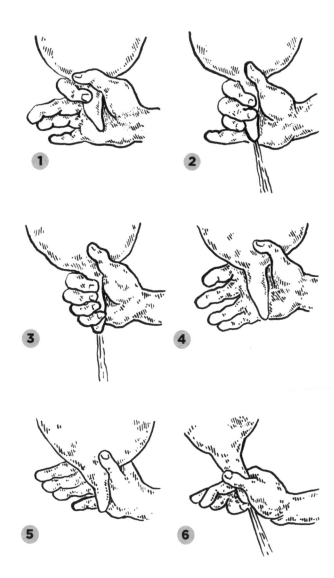

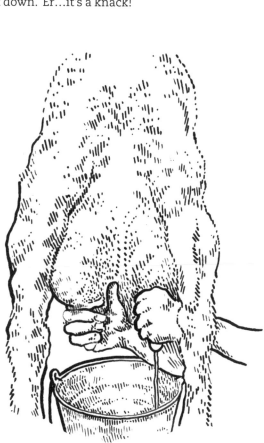

GOAT MYTHS

Goats smell.

Not true, or at least, not the nannies and kids; it's mature billy goats that smell, particularly in the breeding season. But unless you go in for breeding on a large scale there's no need to own your own billy – simply take your nanny to visit a local male owned by a breeder.

Goats eat anything, from cardboard boxes and paper to weeds and rubbish.

Not true; goats are quite fussy eaters, and though they'll nibble at certain weeds that take their fancy, they won't touch mouldy or poor-quality hay, or concentrated feed that isn't as good as it should be.

Goats love warmth.

Up to a point; they can stand cold but they hate damp, wet, wind and draughts, so don't tether them outside in poor weather or leave them in a field without shelter, and make sure their hut is quite weatherproof.

Goats are great escape artists.

In fact this is not a myth. Some climb or jump over fences, while others force their way though tiny gaps and any weaknesses in hedges. If you don't have really good fences round fields, keep goats in a run round their hut where it's easier to keep them in, or else keep them tethered.

The milk smells and tastes 'goaty'.

Not true. If the milk smells or tastes odd, it may be because the goat has eaten something that's given the milk a slight taint (usually brassicas), but most often it's because the bucket used for milking wasn't thoroughly clean or the person doing the milking hadn't washed their hands properly. If milk is stored in open containers in the fridge where there's strong-smelling food such as cheese, that can also impart a taste or smell to the milk.

BREEDS OF GOAT

Meat, milk or fleece? You can have any of the three depending on the breed of goat you choose.

1 Angora: a dual-purpose goat that looks like a faintly aristocratic, curly-coated sheep with horns. It gives useful amounts of milk and has a valuable fleece with very soft, fine, high-quality wool, better known as mohair. The animals can be sheared twice each year to maximise returns.

2 Anglo-Nubian: a favourite milking breed as it's a high yielder with rich milk that's good for cheese-making. A very distinctive-looking goat with lop ears and a Roman nose.

3 Toggenburg: brown goats with white markings and a rather pretty deer-like face with a white stripe down each side.

4 Boer: relatively new to Great Britain, a rather chunky goat originally from South Africa with a barrel-shaped body, bred for its meat which is naturally low in cholesterol. It is starting to find a ready market as kid, for roasting, and it's also popular with ethnic communities who enjoy curried goat. Roasted kid tastes a lot like lamb.

COWS

In the past, large country families often kept their own 'house cow'. Guernsey and Jerseys were especially popular as they are (at least, compared to many breeds) relatively small, docile (usually!) and easy to handle, but the big 'plus' was their very rich milk, which besides being delicious for drinking, produces plenty of cream, ideal for making butter, ice-cream, cheese and other dairy products.

A cow is a very different proposition from a goat; it costs more to buy, it needs a bigger field shelter or a proper stall inside a well-built outbuilding, and a larger supply of straw for bedding. It also takes more land to support a cow since it eats a large amount of grass – allow at least an acre, but ideally two and a half. But a cow also needs a lot of extra feed. It eats a bale of hay per day in winter, when it's not out to grass (you'll need on average a ton of hay per cow each winter), and if you don't have enough grass you'll need to feed some hay all year round. A cow also needs feeding with concentrates in the form of sugar beet pulp and rolled oats or barley, or proprietary cattle cake, which needs to be calculated on the basis of how much milk it is giving – if you don't feed enough, the milk yield declines.

To keep costs down many owners grow an area of winter kale or mangels to supplement concentrates, though a cow can also be given potatoes if you have a surplus from the veg patch, and she'll also enjoy outer leaves from brassica plants when you've picked your cabbages, sprouts, cauliflowers and broccoli. You'll also need to provide a mineral salt-lick to avoid nutritional deficiencies which can cause all sorts of health problems. Ideally this needs to be kept under cover, somewhere the cow can get at it whenever she wants. Another essential requirement is plenty of water – a cow drinks getting on for 90 litres (20 gallons) every day when it is producing milk, so you need a proper trough connected to a mains water supply.

Once she's calved, a cow will produce milk for up to ten months, and she needs milking twice a day. (You can get away with doing it once if you leave the calf with the cow, since the calf will take what you don't for the rest of the day.) If it's for your own use, you can milk the cow out in the field, though it's easiest to put a halter on and bring her into a stall or tie her up to a metal ring in the side of a building, so she has a wall along one side of her, to stop her moving about too much. Since hand-milking takes time, it's most comfortable for the milker if they sit on a small stool. Use a scrupulously clean stainless steel bucket that's been scalded with boiling water to make sure it's perfectly hygienic, and give the cow a bucket of concentrated feed to keep her occupied while you do the deed. It's also a good idea to follow the same routine each time you milk, as it relaxes the cow. Cows are quite sensitive and develop a bond with their regular handler, so to keep the animal calm and stop her fidgeting, fretting or kicking, experienced milkers behave confidently, handle the cow without tickling, and talk quietly to the animal during the process. If she is upset she's likely to kick the bucket over, step in it, or refuse to let you near her. Good stockmen have a 'way' with livestock that comes from behaving quietly and treating them kindly.

HOW TO MILK A COW

Wash the udder gently using a cloth and warm soapy water. Sit on a stool and press the top of your head into the cow's flank – this establishes contact, acts like her calf, and gives you advance warning of any bad behaviour. Milk a cow like you would a goat (see page 77); the four teats (or 'quarters') need to be completely emptied. A cow produces up to 18 litres (4 gallons) of milk a day; roughly one large bucketful morning and evening. Chill the fresh milk immediately.

Naturally, in order to produce milk a cow has to have a calf, so rather than dispose of this in order to concentrate on maximum milk yields, smallholders will often raise the calf themselves – a heifer can be sold later as a house cow or to join a dairy herd, but a bull calf can be reared for beef.

When choosing a breed to farm, check out the conditions in which that particular breed does best, since some were originally developed for lowland pastures with mild climates, and others for hardier surroundings in hills – they don't thrive in the wrong set of conditions.

REARING STORE CATTLE FOR MEAT

Instead of keeping a dairy cow and raising their own calves from scratch, a lot of people with some spare grazing land will instead buy a few 'store cattle' (the proper term for half-grown young bullocks) to fatten for meat, in much the same way as rearing your own pork from weaners. Turn them out in a well-fenced pasture with a stream or a water trough that can be kept filled (ideally connected to a mains water supply so it's self-filling), though a lot of small-scale farmers rent saltmarsh fields for this job as they are cheaper than top-class pasture – and 'saltmarsh beef', as it's known, is especially sought after in food-lovers' circles. Buy store cattle in spring and by the autumn you can turn them into cash or put them in the freezer.

GOOD DUAL-PURPOSE HOUSE-COWS FOR SMALLHOLDERS

The popular milk breeds, Guernsey and Jersey, aren't known as great beef producers, so most smallholders choose a dual-purpose breed that gives them the best of both worlds – a reasonable milk yield plus a good saleable meat carcass.

1 Dexter: an unusually small, almost miniature black cow, with short, upright horns. Needs less input and produces less milk than larger breeds, so popular with smallholders. Can be a tad feisty.

2 Gloucester: a very old rare breed with short, forward-curving horns, in black or brown with white markings and a white stripe down the back, white tail and white belly. This dual-purpose breed is now being used for conservation grazing. (The Gloucester Cattle Society www.gloucestercattle.org.uk)

3 Dairy Shorthorn: the top choice for smallholders and small family farms shortly after the war, when besides rearing the bull calves for meat, the old dairy cows would also be eaten – after lengthy stewing – which made them earn their keep several times over. Now a rare breed; these brown and white cows with short horns are good for keeping outside.

4 Red Poll: a rare breed that lives happily outside with just a field shelter, and on a home-grown diet of roots, cereals and hay with oats or barley. A good-looking cow with a rich, red-brown coat, with the big advantage of being naturally hornless. Originally from East Anglia, it was a dual-purpose breed, but nowadays is mainly kept for meat.

5 Jersey: a lovely-looking smallish cow with big, soulful eyes and a pale golden-tan colour, with a normally very docile temperament. Jerseys produce the richest, creamiest milk of all – even more so than Guernseys – but they're from a mild climate and need housing indoors in winter and ideally at night in summer too. Butchers don't like the carcasses of the bull calves, so they don't sell well, but they do produce good meat – you'll just need to raise them for home consumption.

SHEEP

Sheep look idyllic roaming in a grassy paddock, and a tiny flock is a popular way to keep the grass short on a large country-garden lawn. By dividing the grass into strips with temporary fencing, the sheep can be confined to one area at a time so the grazing is used efficiently. If you're using your lawn, it's advisable to keep the animals off a 'best' area close to the house as they'd soon ruin it with their cloven-hoof-prints and manure.

A good many people keep a few decorative rare breeds, such as Soay, as pets that double as lawnmowers; smallholders sometimes breed them on a small scale for show and for sale as pets, with the bonus of fleeces that can be used for country crafts such as spinning and weaving, plus the occasional carcass for the freezer. But they are smaller than modern sheep so though they're useful to have at home, they don't sell so readily to butchers.

HOW TO KEEP SHEEP

Sheep are cheap to keep as they live outdoors, mainly on grass, with hay in the winter when the grass isn't growing, and a little concentrated feed to improve their condition just before the start of the breeding season. They also need a regular supply of water, and access to a mineral salt-lick at all times. This is essential to their welfare since a deficiency of copper (a mineral they particularly need that's usually lacking in the grass on their pasture) causes pregnant ewes to abort and eventually even adults may die as a result.

Sheep don't need a field shelter, since they'll huddle behind a hedge to escape bad wintry weather or for shade from the sun in summer, but at lambing time you will need to provide a temporary structure that you bring them into, so you can supervise the proceedings and intervene if need be. A lot of larger-scale sheep farmers will bring their ewes into a large permanent barn to lamb in cubicles divided up by straw bales or hurdles – this is particularly worthwhile because they rely on producing lambs very early in the year when the conditions outdoors are still harsh, since early lamb makes the best prices. On a small scale

it's far easier to arrange things so your flock lambs a bit later in the season when the weather is better and there's plenty of young grass for the new growing lambs to eat. And if you choose a very hardy hill breed, they can often be left to get on with lambing all by themselves, out in the field – though to avoid losing lambs that could easily have been saved, it's still worth going out regularly to keep an eye on things.

However, sheep aren't quite as trouble-free as they might look. You will need to move them to fresh pasture regularly over the summer so they can't re-infect themselves with internal parasites, as well as to 'rest' the grass and give it a chance to re-grow. If you only have access to one field, this means dividing the area into strips with temporary fencing and allowing the sheep to graze only one strip at a time.

Sheep have quite a few problems that have to be treated or averted, too, so owners need to hone-up on shepherding skills such as foot trimming (to avoid foot rot which makes sheep lame), drenching (administering liquid medicines via a tube to kill internal parasites), shearing (to stop them getting too hot in summer and also to produce a woolly fleece for sale), dipping (done after shearing, to kill external pests living in and on the skin) and dagging (to remove dirty wool round the backside so that flies' eggs don't hatch out into maggots that burrow into the sheep).

You also need to borrow a ram every year to start the breeding cycle again. If your flock is big enough to justify it, then buy your own – but you will need to sell him or swap him every year or two so that he isn't fathering offspring from his own daughters, which often results in weak, defective or sub-standard lambs.

THE LAMBING YEAR

AUTUMN

Get ewes and the ram ready for the breeding season early in the autumn by feeding them concentrates (cereals or sheep nuts) for a few weeks to boost their condition. Check their feet at the same time, since sheep feel less like mating if they are lame or their feet hurt due to overgrown 'hooves' or infection between the two 'toes'.

The gestation period for sheep is 146 days, so time the introduction of the ram so that the first lambs will be born to coincide with decent spring weather and the first flush of good grass growth in your area. Commercial sheep farmers put a harness on the ram with a coloured marker on his chest, which will dab a blob of colour onto each ewe he mounts, so the farmer knows which should be pregnant and which won't be. Don't assume all your lambs will be born 146 days after introducing the ram, since the ewes only come into season intermittently; lambing continues over several weeks once it has started.

WINTER

Sheep will continue grazing, but since the grass isn't growing and the quality is fairly poor during the winter, it needs to be supplemented; anticipate each ewe needing roughly 230kg (500lb) of hay. Ewes will only need concentrates such as cereals or sheep nuts if the winter is particularly harsh, and they shouldn't be too fat at lambing time or the births can be difficult, which creates a lot of extra work and extra expense if the vet has to be called in.

SPRING

Construct a temporary shelter in the sheep field made from hurdles and straw bales, so ewes can be brought inside for the last day before lambing is due, in case they need assistance. A roof of corrugated iron or clear plastic sheet makes conditions more comfortable for the lambing assistant, though the sheep don't need it. And if there's no electricity available for lighting you'll need a powerful torch, since sheep invariably choose to lamb between early evening and on through the night till early morning. The signs to look for, when a birth is imminent, is a ewe that lies down , 'star-gazes' (raises her head with nose pointed upwards) and groans and strains. Most ewes will lamb perfectly well on their own; at a normal birth the nose faces towards the tail end of the sheep and the two front legs appear first, with the head in between. After a good push, the whole lamb emerges; all you need do is make sure its nose and mouth are clear of mucus so it can breathe straight away, then the mother will clean it up.

After an hour or so it should be strong enough to stand, so come back and check that it's started suckling – if not, it needs a helping hand to find the right place. There may be one or even two more lambs still to come, so watch out for further signs of labour. Sometimes you will need to intervene; if a ewe seems to be struggling for some time or seems distressed it may be that the lamb is the wrong way round, its forefeet are tucked back instead of pointing forwards, or multiple lambs may be tangled together. In this case the shepherd needs to reach inside and sort the problem out, or assist the lamb with a gentle pull on the forelegs. If for any reason a ewe rejects a newborn lamb, the shepherd needs to persuade another sheep to foster it – usually a ewe that's only had one lamb of its own – or else rear it in a warm indoor pen themselves. (Traditionally sheep farmers left this job to their wives, who often used the warm farmhouse kitchen to rear orphan lambs in front of the Aga.)

New lambs and their mums are usually kept in their shelter for a few days to make sure all is well (especially if the weather is a bit rough at the time or it's been a difficult birth) before turning them back out into the field with the other sheep. The lambs are fed by their mother for a time and start nibbling grass before grazing full-time. While they are still very young, male lambs being reared for meat rather than kept as breeding stock are castrated using proprietary rubber rings. It's also usual for sheep (at least commercial flocks) to have their tails docked using a similar method, since the tail stores fat, which means the animal doesn't reach slaughter size so fast.

SUMMER

Dag the sheep to remove messy or excrement-laden bits of wool that might spoil a fleece, then before the weather gets too hot, shear and shortly afterwards dip or otherwise treat them against pests in the wool or skin. For reasons of cleanliness and convenience, it's also worth dagging sheep with mucky backsides before you introduce the ram in autumn, or in spring shortly before the start of lambing season.

'CASTING' A SHEEP

One of the essential shepherding skills is knowing how to hold a sheep securely so you can trim its feet or administer medicine as a 'drench', and it's the first step towards keeping it still for shearing. It needs practice.

First catch your sheep; do so with as little stress as possible. Keep her calm and handle her gently. Hold her by the wool of the throat, and with a hand on the rump gently push her down so she's lying on the ground. Then roll her round on her rear to up-end her so she's left sitting on her bottom, with her back against your legs with your feet about a foot apart so you can grip her gently with your knees. This holds her firmly so she's less likely to wriggle or get away.

SHEARING

Sheep need to be shorn every summer, otherwise the animals become far too hot, and also at great risk from blowflies which lay their eggs in dirty fleece – the maggots that hatch out burrow into the sheep causing infections and great distress. It's often said that some of the more ancient rare breeds of sheep shed their own wool naturally without needing to be shorn, but that's not advisable. Unlike more modern breeds, they tend to cast their old wool off in large clumps which get pulled off their body when it snags on brambles or barbed wire, but as a general rule responsible owners prefer to shear these too. The only sheep that don't need to be sheared are lambs under a year old.

Shearing is usually done in May, June or July, depending on which part of the country you live in, but it's the state of the coat, not the calendar, which determines the timing. Wait until the old coat starts to lift away naturally on top of the new coat that's starting to grow through underneath. You don't have to do the shearing yourself; you can hire in a team of itinerant sheep shearers, 'gangs' of whom often come over from Australia to find work when their own shearing season is over. Several neighbouring small-sheep-owners will often group together to share their services for the day. If you are close to an agricultural college, you might be able to arrange for a lecturer to demonstrate the skill using your sheep on your premises, or for final-year students to do the job under supervision.

If you decide to do it yourself, have a training session with an expert or at the very least an experienced sheep-owner who does their own shearing. You'll need hand-operated sheep shears which are worked with one hand, leaving the other free to control the sheep, or electric clippers which are rather like a large chunky electric razor, which clearly have to be close to a power source. It's easiest to shear sheep in a large outbuilding, after rounding all the sheep up and corralling them in a temporary holding pen.

To go about shearing, remove an individual sheep from the holding pen, take her to a place where there's plenty of elbow-room and 'cast' her, so she is in a sitting position against your legs (see page 87), then kneel down so both knees are on the ground, with the sheep belly-up over your knees and its head under your non-shearing arm. This way you can control her so she can't move, and if you are firm rather than hesitant she'll realise it's not worth fighting. Again, it takes practice!

First, clip away the wool from the stomach, which is usually dirty and tangled, full of burrs and weed seeds etc., and discard it. Then turn the sheep slightly so one side is uppermost. Clip the side of the sheep from the newly cleaned belly outwards, up the sides towards the spine, including the front and back leg, going right up the side of the neck. Then turn the sheep so the other side is uppermost, and repeat the process as before, but this time working down the side from the spine. The entire fleece will 'peel away' as you work.

An experienced shearer can strip a whole fleece in a few minutes without nicking the sheep, but a beginner can't always avoid the odd tiny cut, and if so, dab wounds with Stockholm tar applied straight from the tin with a twig. This stops the bleeding and cleans and disinfects the cut, preventing it becoming infected.

SHEEPDOGS

...

SHEEP NEED A LOT OF ROUNDING UP, whether it's to move them to a fresh strip of grazing or to a different field, or to bring them in for shearing, medication or foot-trimming, and it's sometimes necessary to separate a particular sheep from the flock. If you've only got a few sheep you can do it yourself with the help of an assistant, but most owners of larger flocks find a good sheepdog invaluable, since it saves a heck of a lot of running around.

SHEEPDOGS ARE ALMOST ALWAYS BORDER COLLIES, though in other parts of the world other breeds are also used, especially if they also have to round up cattle. Most Border Collies from working parents will instinctively have the urge to round up sheep, so they are relatively easy to train to lie down, move forwards, or go to their right or left. Since instructions from their handler have to carry across large wide-open spaces in all weathers, the commands are given by voice (which is used more at closer quarters) or as a series of whistles, using a special whistle that's kept inside the mouth to make a conspicuously different sound for each manoeuvre. (It takes a bit of practice to use an in-mouth sheepdog whistle so as to produce the specific sounds that the dog understands, so new sheepdog handlers need to practise in private to avoid confusing their dog.) Not all sheepdog handlers use exactly the same commands for each manoeuvre, but they are usually fairly similar.

'WALK ON' (two short blasts on the whistle) tells the dog to walk quietly up to the sheep, so as not to frighten them away. 'Come here' (*phwee phwee phweet*) calls the dog to its handler. 'Come by' (*phweet pheeoh*) tells the dog to move off to its left and circle the sheep in a clockwise direction, 'away' (*phwee phwoo*) tells it to move off to its right and circle the sheep in an anti-clockwise direction. 'Lie down' (one long blast of the whistle) means stop still and lie down, and it's often used just to tell the dog to slow down – the dog knows which from the tone of voice and if the command is repeated. 'Go back' (*phoo hee hoo*) is used to send a dog back to find sheep that are standing behind it, and 'get out' (*phweet pheeoo phweet phweet*) is used to send the dog further away from the sheep to avoid panicking them. 'Take time' (four short staccato blasts) slows the dog down when it's running too fast, and 'that'll do' (also four short staccato blasts) means the dog must stop whatever it's doing and come straight back to its handler. But when a flock of sheep is being driven by the dog cross-country, the command 'that'll do' is also used to keep the dog between the handler and the sheep, so the flock moves ahead of the shepherd. It all takes a deal of practice for both dog and handler, but the end result can be magical to watch.

SHEEPDOG TRIALS are a traditional country pursuit that's since proved hugely popular with audiences on TV. For these competitions, the best dogs are trained to obey a larger and more complicated range of commands than a basic working dog and then put through their paces. Each team of dog and handler is given a small flock of sheep that have to be herded into a small open-fronted pen, which is then closed by the shepherd at the end of the exercise, all is done against the clock.

DUE TO THE BORDER COLLIE's in-bred willingness to do as it's told, dogs that prove inadequate with sheep often find a new lease of life as well-behaved family pets that easily learn tricks. They also excel at obedience trials, retrieving dumbbells, running obstacle courses, etc., which are also popular features at country fairs and agricultural shows.

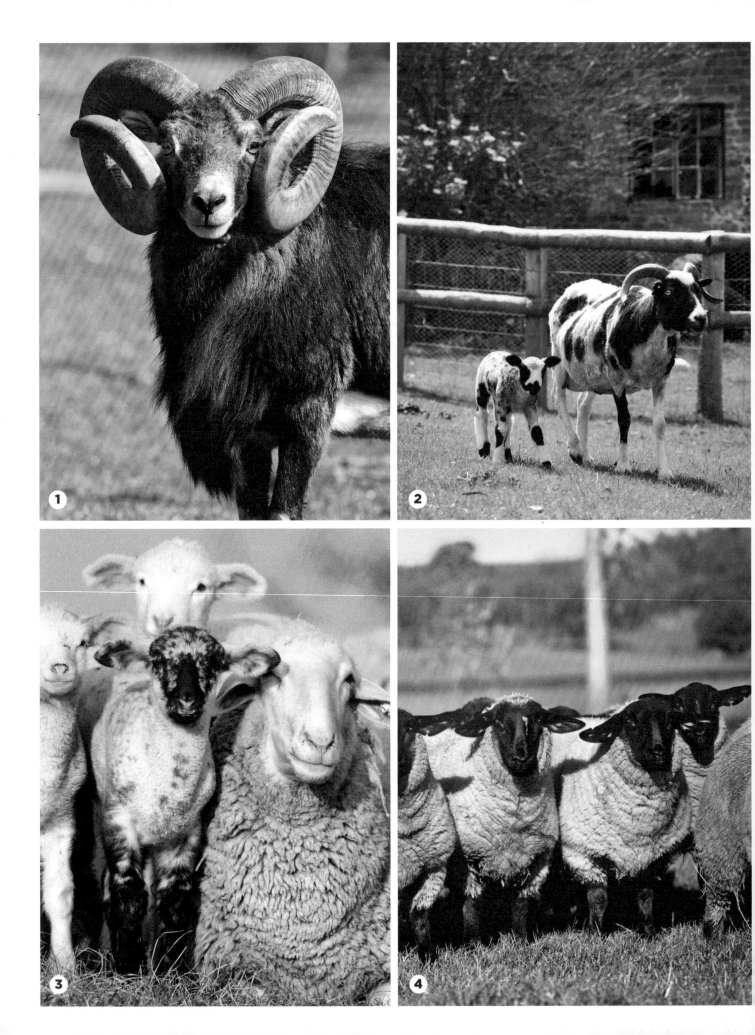

BREEDS OF SHEEP

Some types of sheep are best for meat, others for wool – it's rare to find one that is good for both purposes. Some breeds have been developed for rich lowland pastures and others are adapted to life at higher altitudes with harsher weather and rougher grazing, so choose one that suits the area in which you plan to keep them.

1 Soay: a very ancient breed of small brown sheep originally only found on the island of Soay in the St Kilda group in Scotland. Both sexes have horns. Soay sheep are popular as pets and 'lawnmowers'. Lambs are slow to mature; it takes a year before they are ready to send off for slaughter, and even so produce a very small carcass. They are a dab hand at escaping, so make sure fencing is secure!

2 Jacob: good-looking, small, brown-and-buff patterned sheep; both sexes have curving, backswept horns. The wool is popular for using, undyed, in crafts such as spinning and weaving, and the sheep are a great favourite as pets and 'lawnmowers'.

3 Merino: widely kept in Australia, this breed produces the finest-quality wool used for weaving into cloth for suits and overcoats. A large, impressive-looking sheep.

4 Suffolk: solid sheep with black faces, kept for meat – the wool is poor quality. Needs lowland grazing.

SHEEP MEAT

Lamb comes from young sheep under a year old; the very best lamb is spring lamb, slaughtered at about three months old, when weighing roughly 3 kilos (75 pounds) and sold before about June; lambs need to be born as early as possible in spring (actually late winter). The cuts are quite small but the meat is very tender.

Hogget is older than lamb but younger than mutton, usually around 12–18 months old. Being older it's a tad tougher and needs a bit more cooking, but it has more flavour, and the cuts are larger, which is better for bigger families.

Mutton is coming back into fashion, with good reason. It is meat taken from older sheep, technically two years or older, but often from ewes that have produced several lambs or which have proved barren. Mutton needs a lot longer and slower cooking than lamb, but enthusiasts find the meat much more tasty – and the cuts are larger. The Prince of Wales is a great champion of mutton.

DIRTY WOOL

Dirty wool that you've gathered when 'dagging', or the wool from the belly of the sheep removed before you start shearing, is called 'shoddy'. It has no commercial value, but years ago it was once highly prized by gardeners as a soil conditioner, so it's worth putting on to your compost heap or digging straight into the bottom of a trench in your veg patch. It holds moisture and breaks down slowly, releasing nitrogen and trace elements into the soil, and any manure it contains is a bonus. But only save dirty wool before dipping, not afterwards, to avoid introducing unwanted chemicals.

Llamas (left) are slightly larger than their relatives, alpacas, but if you have the space, they make good pets. If you're keeping them for their fleece, alpacas are a better bet.

LLAMAS AND ALPACAS

Some of the very latest livestock to appear on smallholdings and in paddocks at country gardens are llamas and their smaller relatives, alpacas. They belong to the camel family, but since they originate from the harsh mountainous regions of South America, they are very hardy; they don't need lots of expensive feed, elaborate housing or special care. They are good-looking curiosities, great for keeping the grass down, and if you keep sheep, a male llama will 'adopt' the flock and protect them from intruders and predators just as they'd guard their own ladies.

Since llamas and alpacas are relatively new to UK livestock keepers, there's a good demand for them, both as 'paying pets' and for breeding stock, but this means animals are expensive to buy. Breeders advertise in smallholders' magazines, and many offer training for potential new owners.

Llamas, being large, can be worked; they are sometimes used for llama-trekking, where the animals carry light loads (waterproof clothing, rugs, picnics, etc.) and accompany walkers who lead them on halters. However, both llamas and alpacas are also kept for their fleece. Like sheep, they need to be sheared annually. The fleece from llamas has limited uses as the fibre is rather coarse. Alpaca fleeces, though, are high quality – soft and silky – and much in demand for making yarn used for fabrics by the tailoring business, for making posh overcoats and suchlike. But neither animal is easy to shear, it's not something an amateur can easily get to grips with – a professional can do the job much faster, and without causing the animal too much distress. If the animals are being kept as pets rather than for fleeces, instead of shearing, owners will sometimes keep the animals' coats groomed to remove loose strands and avoid loose wool becoming matted and tangled as it's shed naturally, or they'll cut the wool on the backs, flanks and rump to about an inch long with strong scissors each spring.

Both llamas and alpacas are happy to live outside all year round since they eat grasses and wildflowers living in the turf, and they'll also browse on trees and shrubs. Their paddock needs very secure fencing at least 1.2 metres (4 feet) high (ideally 1½ metres/ 5 feet for llamas) to keep them in. (Avoid barbed wire; 10 centimetre/4 inch square woven wire is best, with a strand of electric fencing along the top if necessary.) They don't need a huge area; you can happily keep two llamas or four alpacas in a half-acre paddock – they are herd animals and prefer to be kept in small groups rather than singly – but you'll need to pick up the poop daily when they are kept in a relatively small area of pasture. They'll appreciate a large tree for shade, though it's not essential, but they will need a three-sided field shelter for protection from bad weather, and this should have straw bedding on the ground – it also makes a good place to feed the animals. Though they live on grass for most of the year, in winter, and any time the grass isn't growing well, they need hay as well. Concentrated feeds are available for llamas and alpacas, but normally only used for expectant females. The animals also need access to clean, fresh water at all times.

Since they occasionally need individual attention, it's advisable to have a small catch-pen in one corner of the field where animals can be enclosed. Llamas and alpacas don't like being handled; their camel-like nature means they tend to spit and kick if annoyed, so it's usually necessary to restrain them with ropes. Adult animals need to have their teeth ground down, otherwise they can become so overgrown that they can't eat; they need to be wormed, and they also need to have their horny toenails cut regularly because soft fields don't keep them worn down the way rocky hillsides do in the wild.

If you're keeping them in a small way, as pets, it's worth pointing out that they aren't the easiest animals to find 'sitters' for when you're away on holiday. Serious breeders usually have helpers or live-in family members who can take over.

BEES

Beekeeping is a most genteel occupation, typical of an English country garden behind a traditional olde-worlde cottage. A row of beehives looks wonderful in an orchard, a single hive sits well near an herbaceous border, and the sound of bees working in the flowers adds another dimension to a wonderful sunny summer day. Bees do invaluable work by pollinating crops, and at the end of the season there's the honey harvest to look forward to – not to mention all the 'extras' that beekeepers can make out of the by-product, beeswax.

Bees look as if they take care of themselves, but it actually requires a fair bit of knowledge and equipment to be a beekeeper. It's all best obtained through a local beekeepers' club, where you can also get training and advice, and find a supplier of bees and equipment.

The first essential is a hive, which consists of a series of stacked chambers inside a weatherproof outer shell. Between two of the chambers a queen excluder is fitted; this is a thin slatted layer that acts like a 'filter' to keep the egg-laying chamber (where new bees are produced) separate from the honey chambers or 'supers' where worker bees store the honey. Without the 'filter', bees would mix cells containing bee larvae in the same combs as honey, which doesn't make for a pleasant end-product. Each super is like an open-ended box that contains a number of frames which slot into it a small distance apart; it's inside these frames that the workers make the hexagonal wax 'cells' that form the honeycomb in which they store honey, which is produced as food for the bee larvae. At the very top of the hive is a roof, which lifts off for access, and at the bottom the base of the hive has a 'landing strip' projecting from the front, just below an opening where bees go in and out of the hive.

You can't just plonk a hive anywhere there happens to be room. A beehive needs a sunny, sheltered space, ideally with a hedge or fence along the back and a wide, open area in front, on the sunny side. (Some beekeepers also rent their hives out to local fruit farmers or veg producers to pollinate crops, and this involves transporting the hives and the bees inside to a new location for the summer.)

The bees to occupy the hive are bought as a surplus swarm from another beekeeper in summer. To work with bees without being stung you'll need a complete set of protective clothing including head-gear and veil. You'll also need a smoker, which burns bits of old dry cloth or hay to generate smoke, and some basic beekeeping tools.

Bees were originally kept in dome-shaped straw 'skeps'.

Any time you need to open the hive, wear full protective gear and check there are no gaps where bees could get in. Have your hive tools on hand and your smoker lit and working, so you can minimise the time you'll need to have the hive open. Make sure there's no-one else in the surrounding area while you do this.

Waft plenty of smoke round the hive; the bees sense danger to the hive and gorge themselves on honey, which makes them rather 'dozy'; they'll then be less aggressive and less likely to sting. Prise the lid off with the hive tool and puff several generous squirts of smoke inside. Then do whatever you need to: remove supers to add the queen excluder, or put new supers on top, or remove supers filled with honey if you're harvesting. Waft a few more puffs of smoke over the interior every few minutes, especially if there seem to be more bees about than before, or you feel they are getting more assertive. After closing the hive, keep your protective gear on until you are reasonably well clear of the area, then leave the hive alone for a day or two afterwards so the bees can settle down again.

THE BEEKEEPER'S YEAR

The queen bee is one of the few inhabitants of the hive that survives the winter; she is larger than the other bees and quite distinctive-looking. In early spring she starts laying eggs in the brood chamber of the hive.

As spring flowers appear, the numbers of worker (female) bees starts to build up rapidly. The hive needs to be opened; put a queen excluder above the brood chamber to keep the queen 'downstairs' so all the bee larvae are contained in their own special area of the hive, and above this place one super, filled with frames. Use new frames each season, since bees won't re-use old or dirty ones. To give the bees a base to work onto, beekeepers slot a thin flat sheet of hexagonal patterned wax into each frame as a foundation to get them started. The frames are slotted into the super so they don't quite touch, and the exact size of the gap between adjacent frames is crucial, or the bees won't fill them properly – a special tool is used as a spacing guide.

Since bees tend to 'glue' shut any gaps in their hive with wax, you need to use a special hive tool for prising the lid off without damaging it. (Bees tend to abandon a damaged hive.) By the time the

SINGLE-FLOWER HONEY

Most honey is made from nectar and pollen from a mixture of different kinds of flowers, but when there's one particularly prominent flower in bloom in the area, the bees will make honey largely from that one type. The predominance of one species gives the honey a characteristic flavour. (Some beekeepers will move hives of bees out to moors for the heather or to pastures for the clover, deliberately to produce single-flower honey.) As soon as that particular flower has finished blooming, the beekeeper will then collect the honey from the hive, before any more can be added from other sources, so he can sell it as heather honey or clover honey. The hive is then restocked with new frames, so the bees can start again. Wildflower honey is another favourite, from hives kept out in the countryside close to a wide range of natural species.

BEE PLANTS

Medieval cottagers relied on a hive of bees down the garden to supply the honey that was their only form of sweetening, since sugar was imported and only affordable to wealthy homes. To ensure a plentiful supply of nectar and pollen for the bees to work on, cottagers made sure their gardens supplied plenty of suitable flowers during the main bee foraging season – spring till autumn. Today it's still a good practice for beekeepers. Good bee plants include lavender, sedums, Michaelmas daisies, *buddleia* (butterfly bush), also old-fashioned annuals such as calendula marigolds, poppies and sunflowers, and flowering herbs – particularly borage, rosemary, marjoram, and Greek oregano (wild marjoram).

big flush of early summer flowers is out, bees will probably have filled the frames in the first super, so open the hive and add another super full of vacant frames, prepared as before, on top of the one that's already been filled.

As summer progresses, more supers may need to be added to cope with the volume of honey the bees are generating. There's no point in putting all the supers into a hive at once, because the bees won't fill them properly – they'll just dot cells of honey around in partly empty combs. An experienced beekeeper knows when another super is needed without opening the hive to check, basing his judgement on the density of bees flying around the hives, the weather, and the number of flowers in bloom at the time. It's all part of the skill and the knowledge. Fields of oilseed rape in the immediate area are a big draw to bees, which will temporarily desert garden flowers while rape is in bloom.

Around midsummer the workers 'bring on' a few bee larvae especially so they turn into queens instead of more workers. When a new queen bee finally emerges from the hive, she'll be followed by a large number of workers that go with her, forming a swarm. This flies off in a 'cloud' and settles somewhere nearby, perhaps in the branch of a tree, with the workers gathering tightly round the new

HOW TO EXTRACT HONEY FROM A HONEYCOMB

...

UNLESS YOU USE ALL THE HONEY you collect as unprocessed honeycomb, you'll need special equipment for separating honey from the comb – this is usually done using a mechanical centrifuge. You'll also need strainers to remove any 'bits' from the liquid honey, and a supply of clean, sterile, glass honey jars with your labels on them.

REMOVE THE WAX CAPPINGS from each frame of honeycomb by running a long knife across it, using the wooden edges of the frame as the guide, then place it into the centrifugal extractor which flings the honey out of the cells, so you can collect it all. Small-scale beekeepers often manage without, simply by removing the cappings and standing the frame on edge so the honey runs slowly out – but this leaves quite a bit of honey still inside. On a commercial scale, honey is heated to make it runnier so it comes out of the honeycomb faster and more efficiently, and to ensure a larger haul of honey, but enthusiasts think that cold-extracted honey is of a higher quality as it's entirely unprocessed.

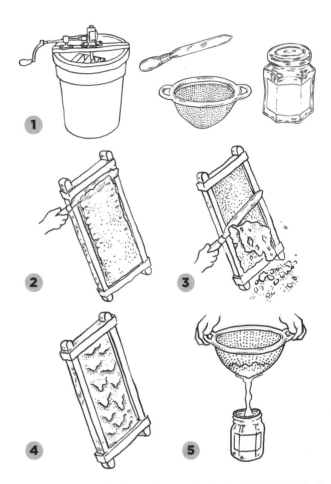

BEESWAX

When you keep bees, the process of extracting honey from the frames in which it's stored by the bees in the familiar 'cells' leaves you with a quantity of beeswax. Wash any remaining honey off the beeswax with warm water, then allow it to dry as much as possible before melting it – heating it will drive off any remaining water as steam. If you don't have any immediate use for melted wax, pour it into moulds to make small solid bars to store until you are ready to use it. Some can be used in making face cleansers, lotions, hand creams and other toiletries, also candles (see Chapter 4) and furniture polish.

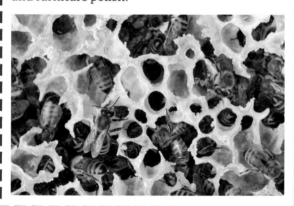

VARROA MITE

In recent years bee colonies have started to decline or disappear completely, leaving empty hives at a time of year they should be very busy, and although it's likely that several factors are responsible, one of them is the varroa mite. This tiny insect can sometimes be spotted on infected bees, looking like minute specks of dust. Mites sap the bees' strength by feeding from their bodies, which weakens them so they can't work well and they die prematurely; this means hives don't work as efficiently as they should – fewer worker bees are raised, so less honey is stored. Mites build up inside the hive so bees are infected when they return to it, if they weren't already. Due to the threat posed by varroa mites, beekeepers are having to take strict precautions by checking their hives any time they are open for routine jobs, and using suitable treatments, especially in winter. Treatments and advice regarding varroa mites change frequently as more is found out about the problem, so for the latest advice consult the British Beekeepers' website or a local beekeeping group.

queen, who by now will have met up with a few drones (male bees), one of whom will have mated with her. Collecting swarms is a useful way for beekeepers to increase their number of hives for free. Handling a swarm of bees, transporting them safely and introducing them to a vacant hive back home is a skill that needs to be learnt from an experienced beekeeper. Someone who's kept bees for years can usually tell when a swarm is likely to emerge by the restless behaviour of the workers, so they'll follow its path and be ready to 'take' the swarm as soon as it settles.

By late summer the hive is carrying a full load of honey, ready for collecting. This is when wasps may attack the hive to steal the crop; beekeepers keep a watch for wasps' nests in their catchment area and try to destroy them before this happens.

To collect the honey, open the hive, and insert a special board between the brood chamber at the bottom and the honey-bearing supers at the top; this lets worker bees come out of the honey chamber but it doesn't let them get back in, so 24 hours later, with luck, there should be very few bees inside the part of the hive you are interested in. Bees won't take kindly to having their honey stolen, so remove the supers quickly and take them somewhere the bees can't follow to extract the honey.

As autumn proceeds, the number of worker bees falls as fewer nectar-rich flowers are in bloom. Some beekeepers leave a few frames of honey inside the hive to feed the queen and the few worker bees that remain during the autumn and winter. Others take all the honey and feed the hive with a solution of sugar or syrup instead. If you choose to feed artificially, don't do so during the day; do it in the evening when bees have returned to the hive for the night, since they'll then be naturally quiet and sleepy and there's less risk of getting stung.

GROWING GRASS AND HAY

When you keep livestock, you need grass for grazing and also hay for winter feed. Good grassland doesn't just contain one species; it contains a mixture of grasses but also a sprinkling of wildflowers, which don't merely look good (though they do) but also contribute to the nutrition of livestock. If you're starting new grazing or hay meadows from scratch, agricultural suppliers can provide suitable seed mixtures. Grassland and hay meadows aren't just lawns on a large scale, though, they need to be managed properly to produce good-quality, productive crops.

PASTURE FOR GRAZING

Secure fencing is vital, and it needs to be suitable for the type of animal you plan to keep since some are great escapers. Don't allow livestock to have access to the whole area all at once; unless you have several fields in which you can rotate livestock, divide the grazing up into strips and turn the animals out into one patch at a time. (Electric fencing is often used, powered by a car-type battery, or the cheaper nylon ribbon fencing which consists of long white 'ribbons' hooked onto loops in the top of slender metal poles knocked into the ground.

Both are easily moved.) This allows the remaining pasture to grow and recover from trampling, for manure to be broken down by soil insects such as dung beetles and absorbed back into the ground, and for any parasites to die off.

Pasture needs to be walked over regularly so that any undesirable weeds can be removed by hand. Ragwort is the chief offender as it's very poisonous to livestock. Don't just chop it down; pull it out and remove the remains from the field since dead ragwort is even more attractive to grazing animals to eat than live ragwort, and just as poisonous.

Some weeds are merely a nuisance; livestock will normally graze round a dense patch of thistles or nettles since there's normally nothing worth eating in the patch, so it just spreads and takes up space that could have been used by decent grass. Weeds like these can be controlled by cutting them down regularly with a mower or scythe, which is preferable to using weedkillers. Dock is another useless weed that spreads quickly and wastes space, but it needs to have the thick tap root dug out rather than being chopped down, ideally before it can shed seed, to stop the next generation taking hold.

But some wildflowers are well worth having as they contribute to the nutrition of the animals grazing on them. Yarrow, dandelion, wild chicory, white clover, burnet and ribwort are often present in existing pasture. If you're growing a new meadow from seed, it's worth obtaining a mixture that already contains a selection of suitable wild flowers and herbs, otherwise buy the seeds separately and add them to a standard agricultural grassland mixture before sowing. If you need to turn livestock outside in winter, it pays to include meadow fescue in your mixture, since it stands up better than many grasses to harsh winters.

Whilst a lot of smallholders graze a mixture of different types of livestock in the same field at the same time, it's far better to rotate them over a period of time in order to make the most of the available grazing. The first animals to introduce are those that can eat long grass – cattle and horses – and then turn out sheep and goats which trim the grass shorter. (The goats will eat a lot of weeds and light scrub that cows and horses won't touch.) Geese will eat even shorter grass than sheep, so they can be turned out last of all, and hens will also enjoy scratching around. This way of 'rotating' pasture is also good practice when it comes to keeping livestock parasites under control, since the parasites of one species of livestock can't live in a different host.

On a large scale, commercial farmers use a fair bit of fertiliser to keep grassland growing strongly to provide as much rich grazing as possible, but you can avoid doing so by not overstocking (i.e. not keeping too many animals on a given area of land), by rotating the livestock so pasture is rested in rotation, and by including clovers and trefoils in the sward. These useful plants have nitrogen-fixing nodules on their roots where beneficial bacteria 'trap' nitrogen from the air and release it into the soil, where it helps to feed the grasses growing round them entirely naturally and for free. My own organic wildflower meadow, while not producing a massive crop of hay, still manages to produce a useful annual yield without the need for artificial fertilisers.

My pleasure in pasture comes from its summer beauty – the hay is a bonus.

HOW TO MAKE HAY

The same mixture of grass and wildflowers used for pasture also makes a good hay meadow. It's not essential to keep two separate fields for grazing and hay; if part of the field used for grazing is sectioned off with electric fencing till June or so, you can often cut a crop of hay from it before turning livestock back onto it later.

It's still worth dealing with weeds, even in a hayfield. The presence of dried docks, thistle and above all, ragwort, lowers the quality of the hay, and dead ragwort is still poisonous. When it's cut for hay, grass must not be lush and green. Wait until mid to late June when it's flowered and seedheads have started to form, by which time the stalks will just be starting to dry out naturally. Choose a time when the weather forecast suggests you'll have a week or ten days of continuous fine dry weather. Cut the grass off a couple of inches above ground level, by hand using an old-fashioned scythe, or using a mechanical rotary scythe if you don't have an area big enough to justify a tractor-powered hay cutter.

Leave fresh-cut hay lying on the ground for a few days to dry before turning it. It's worth turning it (an operation known as 'tedding') several times so that the sun and wind can air it thoroughly, to prevent it going mouldy when it's baled and stored. On a small scale you can simply rake it around to turn it or use a pitchfork, but on a larger scale a tractor-mounted implement with two rotating circular rake-like tines is used. When the hay is well dried it's baled; to use the baling machine the hay first needs to be raked up into rows, so either use an old-fashioned wooden hay rake or use a tractor-mounted hay turner (by adjusting it, it'll also throw the hay into rows).

Since bales of hay quickly absorb moisture if they're left standing on damp ground, it's best to get them shifted under cover and stacked in

 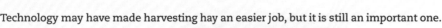

Technology may have made harvesting hay an easier job, but it is still an important one.

a dry shed or barn as soon as possible, ideally on the same day the crop is baled. If possible, raise the bottom course of bales up on old wooden pallets so some air can circulate underneath, otherwise there's a risk of condensation forming so the bottom bales start rotting – this can happen even on concrete floors.

If you only have a small quantity of grass to cut for hay, or you don't have the facilities to bale it, it is possible to store loose hay – the old-fashioned haystack (which is rarely seen nowadays) was just that. It was made of loose hay piled up in a circle, with each new layer raked as it was piled up, so the stems all ran in the same direction; the top rose to a central peak and was then thatched to keep the rain out. It's rather a lost art, but today it's possible to keep loose hay under cover in a dry barn, but it's essential that it doesn't get damp, If it does, the hay turns musty so livestock either won't eat it or if they do, it doesn't do them any good.

SMALL-SCALE FARMING EQUIPMENT

There's only so much land you can work by hand; an area about the size of an allotment is usually plenty for most people. But a larger smallholding or croft will normally need some mechanical help – to pull a trailer and cultivate land at the very least. These days there are all sorts of miniature tractors available new or secondhand. Another option is to buy an old (well, vintage, really) small second-hand tractor such as the little grey 'Fergie' (as the Ferguson TE20 is affectionately known), and the equipment, such as ploughs and cultivators, to go with them. Two-wheeled tractors, also known as rotavators, can also be used for turning over soil, and these, too, can be coupled to a small trailer. All this type of equipment is available from specialist dealers who take stands at shows and advertise in smallholders' magazines, and from private individuals in the small ads. When it comes to the more specialist equipment that you might only need once a year, or expensive kit that it isn't worth buying when it's going to sit around for most of the time, then most people either hire it temporarily or call in contractors to do jobs like baling hay.

LIVING OFF THE LAND

Can you live off the land? It's the dream of a good few folk who head into smallholding or crofting. But however self-sufficient you are, there's always the odd bill that can only be paid with real money – council tax, utility bills, petrol or diesel for vehicles, vet's bills, livestock feed, seeds and fertilisers, plus any food or household goods you can't make or grow – quite apart from mod-cons and holidays that the family won't want to do without.

You can certainly make some income from sales of honey, eggs, fruit, veg, salads or herbs, at the garden gate or to local shops or hotels, particularly where the proprietors are very clued up and have a name for sourcing local fresh/organic produce, which is increasingly in demand these days. But however high the quality, many shops and restaurants need regular supplies all year round and may not be interested in irregular or purely seasonal purchases. Farmers' markets can be another good outlet for produce, as can organisations that run 'box schemes' where a selection of seasonal fresh fruit and veg is delivered regularly to participating householders.

If you raise livestock and/or poultry, you'll be able to sell surplus young stock to other breeders or as pets, and any meat you can't use or put in the freezer yourself can usually, by prior arrangement with the slaughterhouse, be sold or used to offset the cost of slaughter and butchery.

Most smallholders and crofters, however, need alternative sources of income; there are several that fit in nicely with a country lifestyle, but developing any kind of income stream usually needs extra investment to get it off the ground.

Running a B&B is a favourite choice for sociable people who enjoy looking after guests, and a well laid out smallholding, especially one stocked with rare breeds of livestock or pretty poultry, is an extra 'draw'. To do B&B takes a large house, with space to provide a guest breakfast room. You'll need to bring guest bedrooms up to scratch – these days a bedroom with a TV and an en-suite bathroom is almost essential, as well as a high standard of decoration and furnishing, and a lot of guests prefer self-contained accommodation in an annexe that has its own front door so they can come and go as they please. You'll need to publicise yourself by paying for space in B&B guides and/or advertising in magazines, and be inspected to ensure that you comply with fire regulations and other legislation. The overnight rate you can charge will vary with your location and the rating you achieve with the tourist board, which is based on the facilities and standard of accommodation you offer.

If you have a talent for country arts and crafts and want to sell your wares to the public, one of the best ways to do so is by taking stands at countryside shows. You'll need to take plenty of stock along (which means having a lot of storage space at home), plus a stand with whatever leaflets, posters or point-of-sale material you have, and a suitable vehicle for delivering off-road. You'll need to plan your sales strategy and book stand-space at shows well in advance – often a year ahead. Alternatively, you might sell direct to the public from local craft shops – who will want to take a commission on every sale they make on your behalf – or from a dedicated studio/workshop at home.

It's also possible to turn your specialist hobbies or interests into money-making opportunities by teaching. All sorts of organisations need specialist speakers and tutors, from adult education centres and local groups to craft centres who hold short courses, though for some it's essential to have a formal qualification. If you start doing talks or teaching, it's also worth taking some training in public speaking to learn how to project your voice and organise your material, to give a professional presentation that comes across well.

Another option is to open your smallholding to the public, either for individual special 'days' (such as 'Farm Sunday') or for more regular visits from schools or local groups. (There's currently a stewardship scheme called Educational Access, which is run by the Countryside Stewardship and Environmental Stewardship Schemes – see the Defra website.) Opening to the public involves a lot of red tape, especially regarding hygiene and extra insurance. If you're organising special days for the general public you'll be competing with other tourist attractions so you'll need to lay on more than just a guided walk-round to make a success of it – perhaps cream teas, plant sales, displays or demonstrations, and you'll need to rent portable loos and provide adequate car parking, signposts, and leaflets to assist visitors, besides arranging publicity for the event.

But one of the newest sources of additional income is from power generation. Without making a big investment yourself, it's possible to obtain rent from hosting a wind turbine or solar power plant on your land. (For more information, visit www.energysavingtrust.org.uk.)

COMMUNITY-SUPPORTED AGRICULTURE

If you're interested in the good life but can't or won't take on a smallholding of your own, a good alternative is to share in other people's efforts under the various community-supported agriculture schemes. Here the general public can invest in small farming projects by taking out an annual subscription, or perhaps sponsoring a fruit tree in an orchard, or even contributing labour in return for a share of the crop. Investors can often attend farm walks or other organised events to keep in touch with their 'share'. Schemes currently under way include both arable crops and livestock; there's one where members loan money against the price of dairy cattle and take their return as cheese, there's a rent-a-vine scheme that yields wine, an orchard that rewards investors with perry, and a livestock scheme that returns a whole sheep. (Small farmers can get advice about setting up CSA schemes from the Soil Association www.soilassociation.org.) Alternatively, consider becoming an investor/ participant in someone else's scheme as a way of obtaining local produce that you don't raise yourself.

MANURE COLLECTING

If you keep a lot of livestock on a relatively small area of land, instead of waiting for dung beetles to bury the manure that's deposited, go round every few days with a rubber trug and collect it up to put on the compost heap in your veg patch. The grass recovers faster, and your compost will rot down quicker given the free 'starter'.

THE COUNTRY HOME

CHAPTER 3

(AND GARDEN)

In the past, the one thing farm labourers' cottages, farmhouses and full-blown manors had in common was a highly productive garden. It provided them with more than just fruit and veg. Country folk produced their own honey, preserves and drinks such as beer, mead and country wines. They also had the skills to convert garden produce into a huge range of household essentials from furniture polish and soap to candles and herbal remedies. In the days before village shops or when money was short (which was often) country folk had to be very self-reliant – if not fully self-sufficient – since there was no alternative; anything they couldn't make for themselves they generally did without. Today all sorts of old country crafts are being rescued from the past by modern families wanting a better lifestyle.

HOME CRAFT SKILLS

HOME-BREWING

For centuries, country people made their own beer, mead, cider and country wines at home. Well, they were free, which was what attracted me to them when my wife and I were first married! The ingredients grew on the doorstep; they were either picked from the countryside or grown in the garden, and mead (which is 'wine' made from honey) would have come from the householders' own hives. Some people still enjoy doing a little home-brewing today, to save money, avoid additives, or make good use of a surplus of garden produce – though one or two 'extras' sometimes need to be bought.

BEER

Beer is made from malted barley, which is basically whole grains of barley that have been moistened and allowed to start germinating, then dried and 'cracked'. This process alters the flavour quite considerably; it also causes the starch in the grains to turn to sugar, which feeds the yeast that makes the alcohol.

In commercial breweries that make 'real ale' today, malting, as it's known, is all done in highly controlled conditions where temperature and humidity are monitored to ensure the perfect brew. Old-fashioned ale or stout is made from malted barley alone, but to make beer, hops are added for flavouring – they give beer its bitter taste. The finished product is then sent out to the pubs in barrels, which were traditionally transported by horse-drawn drays. On delivery, the landlord puts his beer barrels down into his cellar and lets them settle for a while before connecting them up to the pipes that deliver the beer, a glassful at a time, to the pumps on the bar. Today a few giant breweries make most of the beer that's sold, but in the past most local pubs used to brew their own 'out the back', and until fairly recently you could find a few country pubs that still did.

But before Victorian times it was very common for farm labourers to make their own beer at home.

KEEP IT CLEAN

All the equipment you use for any sort of home-brewing should first be thoroughly cleaned and then sterilised (buy suitable products from homebrew shops) to ensure unwanted bacteria don't find their way in by accident. They'll ruin your brew.

It was very weak, but since there was no piped water at the time and wells or pumps might be contaminated, beer was far healthier than water, since the water used for making it had to be boiled first, thus killing off any 'bugs'. Beer also provided lots of calories and B vitamins, which bolstered an otherwise poor diet, since many farmhands lived on little more than bread and beer. (William Cobbett, the nineteenth-century agriculturalist, pamphleteer and traditionalist, despaired of the rise of tea for the way it deprived farmhands of their beer and replaced it with a nutritionally empty drink, besides ranting about the waste of time occupied in tea-making by their wives who, he thought, had better things to do. Such as brewing beer?)

HOW TO MAKE BEER

…

TODAY MOST PEOPLE wanting to brew their own beer buy a kit and just follow the instructions, though real enthusiasts will buy the ingredients separately from homebrew shops and do it themselves from scratch. There are various recipes but all follow similar steps.

SOAK PLAIN BARLEY GRAINS (as harvested from the field or sold specially for brewing, not pearl barley used for cookery) in warm water for four days, then drain and spread out the plumped-up grains thinly on a clean surface. Keep them at a temperature of between 18°C and 29°C (65°F and 85°F) for roughly ten days, spraying occasionally with tepid water and turning them regularly. By now the grains should have grown very short shoots, so 'kill' these by putting them in a cold oven and heating it up to 50°C (120°F). Check regularly, and when the barley is dry and brittle (test it between your teeth) turn the temperature up a little – by no more than another 10°C (20°F), for a quarter of an hour. It should now have a roasted, malted smell. Then 'crack' it; use a rolling pin or a heavy duty blender. Aim to just break the grains up a bit, you don't want them turning to powder.

TIP 12½ KILOS (27½ POUNDS) OF THE MALT, as it's now called, into a large clean plastic bin (a brand-new swing bin or plastic dustbin is ideal – you'll need to insert a plastic bung with a tap a few inches from the bottom). Into this, mix 23 litres (5 gallons) of water that's been boiled and left to cool down to 66°C (150°F), so it makes a 'mash' – this looks something like old-fashioned pig swill. Cover it with a clean cloth and leave it overnight to settle.

THE NEXT MORNING OPEN THE TAP and allow the *wort* (as the liquid that runs off is called) to drain out of the bottom of the bin into a large saucepan or jam-making pan. As you do this, drizzle boiling water from a kettle over the mash that's still in the bin to 'rinse' the grains; you'll need to collect 23 litres (5 gallons) of wort altogether. Then put the saucepan onto the stove and add 225 grams (8 ounces) hops tied up in a muslin bag or cotton pillowcase, plus a little sugar if you want to make a stronger beer. Boil for an hour. Cool the

brew as quickly as possible, perhaps by standing the container in a bath of cold water, till it reaches 16°C (60°F).

WHILE IT COOLS, PREPARE YOUR YEAST. Take out a jugful of wort, and cool it separately until it reaches roughly body temperature, then stir in a sachet of brewer's yeast and stand it somewhere warm (in the airing cupboard, or by the Aga perhaps) so the yeast can develop. When the rest of the wort has reached 16°C (60°F), add the jug of yeasty 'starter', stir well and transfer the whole lot to a fermentation vessel. (Homebrew shops sell large plastic buckets with lids especially for this job, but a brand new and entirely clean plastic dustbin is fine.) Cover it with a cloth, or put the lid on, to keep out flies, since they carry bacteria which will ruin your brew.

AFTER THREE DAYS a thick, foamy, yeasty crust develops over the surface, which needs to be skimmed off. This can be used as the 'starter' for the next batch of beer if you are going into production seriously, or it can be used as live brewer's yeast for making bread.

A WEEK LATER THE BEER IS READY to be siphoned off into a clean barrel, which produces traditional flat beer. Avoid stirring up the sediment in the bottom of the container, and leave the barrel to settle in a cool place for at least two to three days so it's in the best condition before you start drinking it – don't try to keep it too long or it goes past its best. If you want gassy beer, use thick bottles capable of withstanding the pressure without exploding, and get the beer bottled as early as possible while it's still fermenting a tad. Don't use normal screw-top bottles that soft drinks are sold in, buy proper beer bottles with clip-down flip-tops (the sort that are like old-fashioned ginger beer bottles) and reuse them for subsequent batches. The finished beer can be tasted any time onwards.

A LOT OF WORK? Yes, but if you're feeling creative and enterprising there's a lot of satisfaction – and a lot of decent pints – in it!

1

2

3

4

5

6

CIDER

When you're used to commercial bottled or draft cider, you're in for a shock when you experience the homemade kind – it's more like scrumpy: cloudy, flat and not at all sweet, but it's the real thing and a great way to use up surplus apples. You can use whatever apples you have (a mixture of cooking and eating apples – and even a few crab apples – is best), though in cider orchards, traditional cider-apples are grown, which are small, sour, and often grotesquely misshapen. The important thing is that the apples should be really ripe; it doesn't matter if there are a few bruised, bird-pecked or maggoty ones in with them. It also does no harm at all if, after being picked, the apples hang around for a few weeks before you start turning them into cider – if anything, it helps them develop more sweetness.

Perry is the same sort of thing, only made with pears; again you can use whatever you have but perry orchards use perry pears, which are very hard – you wouldn't want to try eating them.

HOW TO MAKE CIDER

First turn your fruit into juice. To do this you need a fruit press; some gardening groups or wine circles own one that they hire or lend out to members, otherwise it's probably best for several friends or neighbours to club together and share one as it's a fairly expensive bit of kit you only need for a day or two every year. It looks like a large bucket with handles at the top and a 'lid' which you screw down to exert pressure on the fruit inside to squash it flat, and the juice comes out of a chute in the base.

Roughly chop the fruit so it's a bit broken up, otherwise it's almost impossible to squash. As a rough guide, expect to get 4½ litres of juice from 5½ kilos of apples (a gallon from 12lb). The dryish pulp that's left behind after pressing was traditionally fed to the pigs; this and letting the animals forage for windfall fruit under trees in the orchard resulted in sweet, tasty pork. If you don't keep pigs, then hens and other livestock will enjoy it – otherwise put it on the compost heap.

There's no need to add anything else to your freshly squeezed apple juice; no sugar or yeast is

required, because the fruit comes complete with all that's necessary. (You can certainly leave out the traditional dead rat, which was once thought essential for 'real' farmhouse scrumpy.) Pour the juice into a large clean container or some buckets covered with several layers of muslin or other cloths. For the first few days fermentation is fast and furious, then, when it's calmed down, perhaps a week later, pour the liquid into a clean wooden cask or a few well-sterilised glass demijohns (the containers that are normally used for making homemade wine) and fit fermentation traps to them. Keep the containers at a steady temperature and out of direct sun, and when the fermentation has stopped you know all the sugar has been turned to alcohol, and the cider is ready for tasting. Since the yeast is still alive, the brew will usually still be naturally slightly fizzy.

Cider will keep for a while, but like beer, the character of it will change slowly the longer you leave it. However, it's the simplest form of homebrew you can have, and the best one to 'cut your teeth' on, assuming you have a good supply of free apples. If you don't grow your own fruit, look out for people offering surplus fruit for free at the side of the road, or check out farmshops who sometimes sell off second-best, bruised or damaged fruit very cheaply.

MAKING APPLE JUICE

If you don't want the bother of making cider, simply extract the juice from sweet eating apples and use it fresh, just as it is, as pure apple juice. You can use a fruit press to do the job, but if you only have small quantities to do, it's easier to use an electric juice extractor. This works by grating the fruit finely and then centrifuging it to remove the juice, which is dispensed into a separate container from the pulp. Juice extractors are available from most electrical stores for about the same price as a coffee-maker.

Any juice you can't use straight away can be frozen for another time. Pour the juice into polythene containers with sealable lids and pack them into the freezer; frozen fruit juice keeps for six months to a year, and as it defrosts it's ready-chilled.

Don't expect home-grown apple juice to be just like the apple juice you buy in cartons at the shops. Home-pressed apple juice looks a tad cloudy, but that's as it should be – it hasn't been pasteurised or pressure-filtered or treated in any way. It's also a slightly different colour; freshly pressed apple juice quickly turns a slightly amber shade due to oxidisation, because it doesn't contain preservatives. This doesn't spoil the quality, but if you want to keep the original colour, stir the juice of half a lemon or half a level teaspoonful of vitamin C powder to each pint of freshly squeezed juice. This also gives a slight 'bite' to the flavour, which makes very sweet apples more tangy.

MAKING VINEGAR

Almost any beer, cider or wine will turn itself into vinegar naturally if it's left uncovered during the brewing stage so that fruit flies (also known as vinegar flies) can get in. They tend to fall in and drown, which doesn't look too attractive, but at least the presence of bodies warns you what's happened. If you aren't too squeamish, you could simply strain the bodies out and bottle the liquid when it's finished fermenting, rather than let it go to waste.

But any batch of homebrew cider or wine can be deliberately turned into vinegar; it's a good way to use up a batch that's 'gone sour', perhaps because equipment wasn't properly sterilised, or bacteria has found a way in somehow or, if you prefer, you can make vinegar from perfectly good red or white wine, or cider.

Soak some clean birch twigs in good-quality 'bought' vinegar for a few hours. Then drain them off and pack them loosely into a funnel, which is stood in the neck of a cleaned and sterilised bottle. Pour ready-made red or white wine, cider (or sherry, for a particularly posh vinegar) or a batch of homebrew cider or wine that's 'gone sour', slowly through the funnel so that it runs all over the vinegar-soaked twigs, and picks up the vinegar bacteria from them en route. Cap the bottle securely. It should very soon start to taste acidic, like a bought vinegar, but you can test it by pouring a little over a slice of cucumber (just enough to cover it) and leaving it out in the kitchen for a couple of days. If it goes mouldy your vinegar isn't acid enough, so it won't keep for long (maybe only for a week or two in the fridge), though if it tastes okay it may well be fine to use over the next week or two in salad dressings.

COUNTRY WINES

Winemaking was a huge craze in the 1970s, when affordable package holidays to the continent gave people a taste for wine-drinking, but the recession made it hard to afford off-license prices back home. So homebrew shops sprang up, selling demijohns, fermentation traps, corks and cans of concentrated grape juice so that anyone could make their own.

But rural people had been making country wines for far longer, using all sorts of locally sourced ingredients instead of grapes. They used wayside flowers (cowslip, dandelion or elderflower), berries from the hedgerows (elderberry, blackberry), or fruit from the garden (gooseberries, etc), and also more unlikely ingredients such as wallflowers, oak leaves, pumpkins or pea pods. It has to be said, some country wines proved to be rather an acquired taste (pea pod in particular). Even today results can be rather variable and usually improve significantly with practice – and with keeping. Many a novice has abandoned several bottles of country wine at the back of the shed when their first taste proved a bit 'iffy', only to find years later that the stuff had matured very well – this is particularly true of elderberry, which really needs to be 'laid down' for several years before you drink it.

Nowadays I can't advocate picking wildflowers to make wine, but surplus garden fruit and any bought cheaply at a farm shop are all good wine-making ingredients, plus dandelions from your lawn (just don't pick them if they have been doused in weedkiller or other chemicals). Rosehips make a particularly good wine, which isn't over-sweet (a common fault with many country wines). One of the great successes, when you can pick the flowers from your own garden or nearby hedgerows, is elderflower champagne (or, as we should probably call it nowadays, sparkling elderflower wine, which doesn't have quite the same ring).

Although home winemaking has taken a big dip in popularity over the last twenty years, you can still find specialist home-brewing supply shops that sell the equipment needed. (Search the Internet, or look in local business directories.) It doesn't take much to get started. But if you *aren't* using winemaking 'kits', you need to find a good book for advice on how to brew your own because there isn't one standard formula you can apply to every fruit, flower, berry (or pea pod) to produce good wine.

OTHER TRADITIONAL COUNTRY DRINKS

Wine isn't the only way of converting surplus fruit or hedgerow crops into drinks. You can use elderflowers to make a country cordial which is very tasty and entirely non-alcoholic. When I was a lad, a lot of families brewed their own ginger beer and kept what they called a 'ginger beer plant', which wasn't horticultural at all, but rather a yeast culture that was kept going and used in batches.

Now that fruit growing is the latest gardening craze, all sorts of people are looking for novel ways to use surplus crops – one of which is to make your own liqueurs. Sloe gin is an old country favourite that's enjoying a comeback and is easily made using either sloes (the fruit of the blackthorn bush), or their close relatives bullaces, or damsons. The same basic technique of immersing fruits in spirits can be used to make plum brandy, or mulberry, quince, cranberry or raspberry vodka, and so on. It's a great way of using smallish quantities or unusual fruit to make something a bit special.

HOW TO MAKE ELDERFLOWER CHAMPAGNE

...

START AS IF YOU WERE MAKING ELDERFLOWER WINE. Take a one-pint jug and loosely fill it almost to the top with fully open fresh elderflowers, snipped from their stalks. Weigh them – this volume should give you 75 grams (3 ounces); if not, pick a few more.

PLACE THE FLOWERS IN A LARGE POLYTHENE bucket (the sort sold especially for winemaking, which can withstand heat) or a large heavy-based saucepan. Boil 4½ litres (1 gallon) of water, then pour it over the flowers and add 1.5 kilograms (3½ pounds) white sugar, 250 grams (½ pounds) chopped raisins – old ones left over from Christmas are fine for this job – and the juice of three lemons.

LEAVE THE MIXTURE TO COOL, and when the temperature drops to 21°C (70°F) – which is when you can comfortably stick a finger into it – add wine yeast, one teaspoonful of grape tannin and some yeast nutrient (buy this from any good winemaking supply shop). Cover the container with a lid or a thick, clean cloth and set aside in a warmish place.

AFTER A WEEK OR SO, WHEN VIGOROUS fermentation takes place, funnel the liquid into a clean, sterilised demijohn and fit it with an air-lock (fermentation trap). Stand it in a warmish place where the temperature stays fairly even. When the liquid clears, siphon it into a second demijohn, leaving the sediment behind. You'll need to do this a couple more times over the next 2–3 months until the wine is ready to bottle.

NOW, YOU COULD WAIT UNTIL IT'S completely stopped fermenting, and no more sediment sinks to the bottom, then simply bottle it up as elderflower wine. But to turn it into champagne, you need to catch it while it's still forming a little light sediment (showing that the yeast is slightly active) and siphon it off into thick bottles designed to withstand the pressure that builds up inside.

(YOU COULD SAVE UP USED CHAMPAGNE bottles to re-use, but be aware that these are very tricky to secure – you need to wire the tops of the corks down to stop them being blown out by the pressure inside. Alternatively, use strong, thick, flip-top bottles, of the sort that are sold for making beer or ginger beer. Larger versions with clear glass are available for a variety of uses in homebrew shops.)

STORE THE BOTTLES ON THEIR SIDES in a wine rack for the next six months. The results are not terribly predictable, but that's part of the fun. The contents of some bottles will be flat like normal wine, whilst it's not unknown for the odd bottle in a batch to explode if the contents start fermenting too vigorously again – so be warned and keep them out of harm's way.

HOW TO MAKE ELDERFLOWER CORDIAL
...

PICK SEVEN LARGE HEADS OF ELDERFLOWERS, shake them to remove any bugs and 'bits', and put them in a large bowl.

USE A POTATO PEELER TO REMOVE THE RIND from one small lemon in thin strips (after scrubbing it first); add this to the elderflower heads, then thinly slice the peeled lemon and add that to the bowl of flowers too.

IN A SAUCEPAN, heat up half a kilo (one pound) of white granulated sugar with 1/3 litre (2/3 pint) of water, and when the sugar has dissolved, set it aside to cool.

ONCE COOL, POUR THE SYRUP OVER THE flowers and fruit, and stir well to coat them in the liquid. Some recipes call for 20 grams (¾ ounce) citric acid to be stirred in at this stage; it acts as a slight preservative but for my taste it makes the mixture too acidic.

If you prefer to leave it out, add more lemon juice instead, to taste.

COVER THE BOWL SECURELY with a large plate or several thicknesses of clean cotton cloth and put the bowl in a cool place for 24 hours, then strain and pour it into a clean, sterilised bottle.

THE CORDIAL IS READY TO USE straight away; dilute the 'neat' cordial with water to taste.

ELDERFLOWER CORDIAL KEEPS IN THE FRIDGE for several weeks. It can also be frozen in small portions in an ice-cube tray, and then a couple of the still-frozen cubes can be dropped straight into a glass of chilled sparkling water to make a brilliant instant summer drink.

HOW TO MAKE MEAD
...

MEAD IS ONE OF OUR OLDEST COUNTRY WINES. It is honey wine, which was traditionally made by cottagers who kept their own bees. Some eighteenth-century authors advised adding herbs and/or spices to turn basic mead into a more invigorating tonic drink.

TODAY MEAD IS SOMETIMES FOUND for sale at country shows and food fairs, though it's not very popular – people are usually worried that it's going to be terribly sweet. It's rather extravagant to make if you have to buy the honey, but beekeepers still make their own to enjoy during the winter.

ADD FOUR POUNDS OF HONEY to a gallon of water in a large saucepan or jam-making pan, bring it to the boil, and when it cools down, stir in the juice of a lemon and an orange, add a teaspoonful each of yeast, yeast nutrient and pectin enzyme, then funnel the lot into a clean demijohn and fit an air lock. Wait until it stops bubbling, showing that fermentation has stopped and all the sugar from the honey has been converted to alcohol, so the wine won't be too sweet. Then bottle it, and 'lay it down' for at least a year – it improves with keeping.

HOW TO MAKE SLOE OR DAMSON GIN

• • •

PICK 1.5 KILOS (3 POUNDS) OF SLOES, bullaces or damsons, prick them thoroughly all over or put them in the freezer for a few days so the cells break down enough to let the juice leak out. You'll also need 1½ kilos (3 pounds) of white granulated sugar.

TAKE A LARGE GLASS SCREWTOP JAR (an old-fashioned sweet jar is about the right size) and fill it with alternate layers of fruit and sugar until you have filled it right up to just below the top, then top it up to the rim with gin. (It takes roughly a litre/1¾ pints; there's no need to buy a fancy kind, supermarket own-label is fine.)

SCREW THE LID ON THE JAR AND STAND IT in a cool, dark place for 3–4 months, turning it gently every day (but don't shake it) until all the sugar dissolves, then strain off the gin into a clean screwtop bottle.

DRINK THE GIN 'NEAT' AS A LIQUEUR, or add a shot to sparkling wine or homemade elderflower champagne for a fresh-tasting cocktail. Meanwhile, the 'spent' fruit left behind in the jar can be used to make delicious and faintly alcoholic pies or crumbles. For me damson gin (which we make every year) is the best since it is not quite so 'dry' as that made from sloes.

HOW TO MAKE ROSEHIP WINE

• • •

THIS IS A GOOD WAY TO MAKE USE of the large, plentiful hips of *Rosa rugosa* if you grow the plant as a hedge in your garden, but it's also very good made with wild rosehips picked from the countryside – just avoid places close to busy roads because of the traffic fumes and dust.

PICK THE ROSEHIPS AFTER THE FIRST FROST if possible, or else store them in the freezer until you're ready to use them – this helps break the cells down so the juice is released more easily, though it's not absolutely essential. You'll need 1 kilo (2 pounds) of hips to make 4½ litres (1 gallon) of wine.

PUT THE ROSEHIPS THROUGH a coarse mincer, or crush them up a bit in a bucket using a piece of wood, then place them in the bottom of a large brewing bucket. Add 1½ kilos (3 pounds) of white sugar, then pour 4½ litres (1 gallon) of boiling water over the top and stir well. When it's cooled enough to comfortably stick a finger in, add a teaspoonful each of yeast, yeast nutrient and pectin enzyme (all available from winemaker suppliers).

PUT THE LID ON THE BUCKET OR COVER THE TOP with a thick clean cloth and keep it in a warm place, stirring once or twice a day, until the vigorous fermentation calms down, then strain it into a demijohn.

THREE MONTHS LATER, SIPHON IT INTO A clean demijohn, leaving the sediment behind in the bottom of the old one, and repeat this process again after a further three months. Bottle and cork.

Damson gin is my favourite fruit gin. We make a big batch every year.

PRESERVES

The traditional way of preserving sudden gluts of summer fruit was by turning it into jam or jelly. Then in midwinter, when Seville oranges (the rather ugly-looking, bitter-tasting sort) came into season, country housewives would also make marmalade. Although home preserving reached its peak during the last war and immediately afterwards, when all sorts of luxury foods were in short supply, it is making a comeback today, now that so many gardeners are growing fruit again.

Since all fruits are different, you can't simply use a standard formula for everything; there are thousands of different recipes. All sorts of fruits and berries can be used to make traditional jams or jellies to use on toast, bread and butter or scones, or as ingredients for desserts, but some of the sharper-tasting berries, such as cranberries, make jellies that are traditionally used as accompaniments to

meat, poultry or game. And if you only have small quantities of several different fruits, it's quite okay to blend them to make a mixed fruit jam.

Jam-making is quite scientific; the sugar acts as a preservative, and the pectin plus natural acids present in the fruit 'set' the jam or jelly when it has been boiled long enough. Fruit that's naturally low in pectin (such as strawberries and blackberries) needs to have pectin added. You can buy it in bottles at supermarkets and specialist cook shops, or buy special jam-making sugar which has already had pectin added. Otherwise the recipe needs to include some apples or redcurrants which are naturally rich in pectin, and if the fruit is not very acidic (again, strawberries spring to mind), the recipe may also call for lemon juice.

To make jam you need a preserving pan (which is a large, squat, metal bucket with a large handle and a lip for pouring), a jam-maker's thermometer and a wooden spoon with a very long handle so that you can stir without risk of boiling jam splashing up onto your hand. Prepare a supply of clean jam jars, which can be secondhand but must be well washed and sterilised just before you need them. (The best way to do this is to heat them slowly in the oven or a large saucepan of water for 20 minutes to kill any germs. The jars need to be hot when you put the molten jam in them, otherwise the glass would crack.) You'll then need some jam-pot covers with elastic bands to hold them in place, also a supply of the waxed paper discs that sit on top of the jam before the cover goes on, and perhaps some stick-on labels on which to hand write in order to identify the finished jars. The basic technique for making jam is to boil the fruit with just the right amount of sugar (usually ½kg/1lb of fruit to ½kg/1lb of sugar), stirring all the time so that the bottom of the pan doesn't burn, and regularly removing the scum that comes to the top. A jam thermometer gives a good indication as to when the right temperature has been reached, and this needs

Nothing beats the flavour of home-bottled preserves.

to be maintained until the mixture reaches the point when the jam will 'set'. The traditional test is to drop a spoonful of boiling jam onto a cold plate then push it gently with your finger; if the jam forms a surface-skin that wrinkles, it will set when it's put into jars. (If jam is put into its jars before it's been boiled long enough, it won't set, so it always stays soft and runny. It still tastes nice, and makes a good sauce to pour over ice cream, or to use in cooking, it just isn't *proper jam*.) Nowadays microwave ovens have revolutionised the art of jam-making, as all sorts of jam can be 'thrown together' in minutes and kept in the fridge. But traditionalists still prefer doing it the 'old way'.

Jelly is like jam, but without any bits of fruit in it. It is made by cooking the fruit in water, then the mixture is tipped into a jelly bag (a large reusable bag made from very fine plastic mesh) which is suspended from a special frame – or sometimes hung from a hook in the ceiling – so the juice drips down into a pan while the solid fruit, skins and pips are kept out. It's important not to be tempted to squeeze the bag to force more juice out because this makes the juice cloudy, which means murky jelly later. (Mum hung her crab apple jelly bag at the bottom of the cellar steps and woe-betide us if we touched it!) The juice is then measured and the right amount of sugar added (usually 1¾ litres/a pint of juice to ½kg/1lb of sugar), then it's boiled until the correct temperature is reached, and the setting point is achieved as for jam. Some fruits are

traditionally made into jelly rather than jam; redcurrants in particular, since the small pips are irritating when they get stuck between your teeth. Apple jelly is the basis of traditional mint jelly, eaten with lamb – only here the fruit is cooked in a mixture of water and white vinegar instead of plain water. The same recipe can be adapted to use with other herbs such as thyme, rosemary or sage or a mixture of your favourites.

A conserve is something different again; correctly speaking it's a thick, sweet fruit syrup rather like a jelly that's not quite set properly, with whole pieces of fruit suspended in it – it's very rich and unctuous. Conserves are traditionally eaten on scones with clotted cream, or used as tart fillings, though they are also brilliant spooned over ice cream. Raspberries and strawberries are the fruits most often used in this way, but if you grow something special, such as mulberries or Japanese wineberries, it's worth using the same recipe for those – but using only the most perfect fruit.

Marmalade is often thought of as 'orange jam' – at least, by people who aren't British. The original marmalade was quince marmalade, but it was nothing like the spread for breakfast toast that we know today. It was thick and chewy, more like fruit-flavoured rubber, which was sliced up and eaten as sweets for special occasions, rather like us having a box of chocs today. Quince marmalade arrived in this country when Edward I was king (1272–1307), all because his Spanish wife, Eleanor of Castile, missed her traditional taste of home. Quince trees were brought over and grown especially for the job in the grounds of the Tower of London, which was a royal residence at the time. Orange marmalade as we know it today is thought to have come about as a result of another royal marriage. Catherine of Aragon, Henry VIII's first wife, missed the oranges from her native Spain and since fresh oranges didn't last long enough to reach Britain in good condition (due to the lengthy overland and sea journey involved), they were preserved specially for her benefit – and marmalade was invented. It's basically orange jelly with 'bits' of coarsely chopped or thinly sliced cooked orange peel added. You can also make lime marmalade, or indeed use any citrus fruit you fancy.

HOW TO MAKE MARMALADE

. . .

TAKE 900 GRAMS (2 POUNDS) OF SEVILLE oranges and one lemon; remove the peel thinly, making sure you don't take any of the bitter white pith with it (use a potato peeler). Slice the pieces of peel into thin strips, then cut the fruits in half and squeeze them to remove as much juice as possible.

INTO A PRESERVING PAN, put 1.9 litres (4 pints) of water, plus the juice and peel of all the fruit. Tie the pith and pips up in a piece of clean white cotton cloth and drop that into the pan too. Bring the mixture almost to the boil then let it simmer for two hours without a lid.

AT THE END OF THAT TIME THE PEEL should feel soft if stabbed with the tip of a knife. (If you like a darker, stronger flavoured 'Oxford'-type marmalade, keep boiling the mixture for longer, until it's as dark as you want, but don't let it burn.) Then lift the parcel of pips and pith out of the liquid and stir in 1¾ kilos (4 pounds) of sugar. Heat gently and stir well.

WHEN THE SUGAR HAS COMPLETELY DISSOLVED, skim off any scum that's formed on the surface, bring the mixture to the boil, and continue to boil rapidly (still stirring and removing any scum) for about fifteen minutes. Test to see if it 'sets' in the same way as jam (see page 124).

WHEN THE MARMALADE IS READY, leave it standing – off the heat – for about fifteen minutes, and stir it well before putting it in clean, sterilised pots so that the shreds of peel are mixed evenly. Pot, cover and label it the same way as for jam.

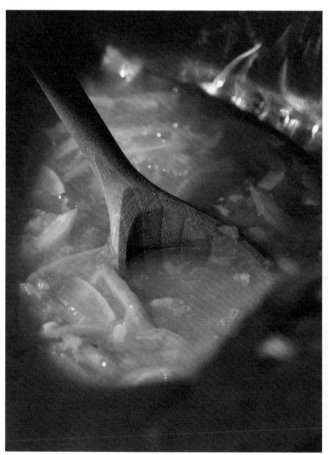

HOW TO MAKE ROSE PETAL JAM

...

THIS IS A REAL LUXURY OF THE SORT that can't be bought in shops; it was once a great favourite with Victorian ladies and it's very do-able when you grow your own roses. Dark red, strongly scented roses are the favourites for this job.

PICK THE ROSES WHEN THEY ARE JUST FULLY OPEN, ideally early in the morning before they dry out too much in the sun. Pull the petals from the heads, then use scissors to remove the white bit at the base of each petal, as it tastes bitter. You'll need 225 grams (8 ounces) of petals, which looks like quite a lot.

PUT THE PETALS IN A BOWL and sprinkle them with the same weight of caster sugar, then cover the bowl (cling film is ideal) and leave for eight hours so the scent of the roses flavours the sugar.

PUT 1.2 LITRES (2 PINTS) OF WATER and the juice of two lemons in a large saucepan, then add 225 grams (8 ounces) of sugar and heat the liquid gently so the sugar dissolves slowly. Stir in the rose petals and all the sugar that's with them, and simmer gently on a low heat for twenty minutes.

TURN UP THE HEAT AND BRING THE MIXTURE to the boil, then let it boil vigorously until it thickens, which takes about five minutes, stirring constantly to stop it sticking to the pan.

WHEN COOL ENOUGH, POT THE MIXTURE INTO small, clean, sterilised jars. A pot of rose petal jam with a pretty label makes a very attractive gift, and with any luck the recipient will appreciate all the trouble you took!

HOW TO MAKE STRAWBERRY CONSERVE

TO MAKE A CONSERVE YOU NEED fairly small, fully ripe fruit that's all the same size and is perfect in both shape and condition. The strawberries then need the green hulls pulled out along with the plug that goes down into the centre of the fruit.

USE 450 GRAMS (1 POUND) OF FRUIT to the same quantity of sugar. Place alternate layers of strawberries and sugar in a bowl, cover with a clean cloth and leave for 24 hours, so the sugar draws a lot of the juice out of the fruit.

PUT THE LOT INTO A LARGE SAUCEPAN and bring it slowly to the boil, then boil rapidly for five minutes, stirring all the time so the jam doesn't stick to the bottom of the pan. Return the jam to the bowl and leave it in a cool place for another 24 hours.

RETURN THE COOLED JAM TO THE SAUCEPAN, heat slowly to boiling point then boil rapidly for ten minutes, again stirring all the time. This time, leave the mixture to cool slightly then pot it up into clean, sterilised jars the same way as for jam.

YOU CAN USE THE SAME TECHNIQUE FOR MAKING conserves from other berries, such as blackberries and loganberries, but this is an especially good way to use up surplus raspberries.

THERE IS SIMPLY NOTHING TO COMPARE with home-made strawberry conserve and clotted cream spread on a warm, freshly baked scone. Heaven!

HOW TO MAKE CRAB APPLE JELLY

THE TRADITIONAL FAVOURITE CRAB APPLE variety for this job is 'John Downie', whose large, red-flushed, flask-shaped fruits produce the most delicious aromatic pink jelly, but any crab apples can be used; use all one variety, or a mixture.

HALVE 900 GRAMS (2 POUNDS) of washed, ripe crab apples, then bring them to the boil in 1.2 litres (2 pints) of water in a large saucepan or preserving pan and simmer gently until all the fruit is tender (but don't be tempted to mash them, or the juice, and later the jelly, will become cloudy).

TIP THE COOKED FRUITY GOO INTO A JELLY BAG and leave it to drip over a bowl for several hours to collect the juice. Strain the collected juice to remove any bits.

MEASURE THE STRAINED JUICE AND weigh out 450 grams (1 pound) of sugar for each 600ml (1 pint) of juice. Put the juice and sugar back in the pan and heat gently until the sugar dissolves. Raise the heat and boil the liquid until a blob of the syrupy mixture 'jells' when dropped onto a chilled plate.

ALLOW THE JELLY TO COOL SLIGHTLY, then pour it into sterilised jars and cover it in the same way as for jam.

THIS JELLY IS BRILLIANT ON BREAD AND BUTTER or on toast, though a spoonful also goes well with pork or cold turkey.

HOW TO MAKE LEMON CURD

LEMON CURD IS A GREAT COUNTRY favourite that's not often made at home today. It is traditionally used as an alternative to jam on bread or toast, or as a filling for a Victoria sponge cake, or in lemon curd tarts. But unlike jam, lemon curd does not keep for long – only a month – so it's a good idea to make small quantities and store it in a cool place, and once a jar has been opened, keep it in the fridge.

PUT THE GRATED RIND and juice of two large lemons into a heatproof bowl with 225 grams (8 ounces) of caster sugar, 100 grams (4 ounces) of butter, and three beaten egg yolks.

STAND THE BOWL IN A SAUCEPAN of hot water kept over a low heat so that it barely simmers, and stir constantly.

AS THE SUGAR DISSOLVES, the egg yolks will gradually thicken the mixture. When it's thick enough to coat the back of a spoon and all the sugar has dissolved completely, strain the mixture through a sieve and pot it up into small jars in the same way as jam.

HOW TO MAKE MINT JELLY

ROUGHLY CHOP 1.3 KILOS (2½ POUNDS) of cooking apples (don't bother peeling or coring them, but cut out any bruises or bad bits).

PUT THEM INTO A LARGE SAUCEPAN or preserving pan with 600ml (1 pint) of water and a few sprigs of mint (spearmint or apple mint are best – or try eau de cologne mint for an unusual, fragrant twist). Bring to the boil, then reduce the heat and leave to simmer for 45 minutes, stirring regularly so the mixture doesn't stick to the bottom of the pan. Add 600ml (1 pint) of distilled white vinegar and bring back to the boil for five minutes.

TIP THE MIXTURE INTO A JELLY BAG set over a bowl and leave to drip overnight. Measure the juice you've collected and put it back in the preserving pan with 450 grams (1 pound) of sugar to every 600ml (1 pint) of juice.

HEAT IT SLOWLY, stirring all the time to help the sugar dissolve, until it reaches boiling point, then boil it rapidly for 10 minutes. Test a spoonful using the cold plate method to see if it's ready to set, then skim the scum off the top with a slotted spoon and stir in four tablespoons of fresh chopped mint.

IF YOU LIKE YOUR MINT JELLY to be green all the way through, the same as the 'bought' version, add three or four drops of green food colour, then cool and put in sterilised jars.

PICKLING

Before it was possible to bottle, can or freeze surplus summer crops, they were often preserved by pickling. Country people have traditionally pickled all sorts of vegetables in vinegar, as a means of storing them to use in winter. Pickled onions, pickled red cabbage, pickled beetroot and pickled gherkins (which are special varieties of miniature cucumbers) are old favourites. In the West Country it was traditional to pickle apples. But anyone whose garden yielded a surplus of assorted vegetables would often make piccalilli to preserve them in a distinctive bright yellow spicy-mustard-flavoured sauce, and at the end of the summer a glut of unripe tomatoes would be turned into chutney. Well, it was just another way of making sure that crops didn't go to waste, especially after all the hard work of growing them.

The principle of pickling is that the acidity of the vinegar kills off bacteria. Any vinegar can be used. Malt vinegar is the cheapest and often sold at farm shops in autumn alongside nets of shallots or small pickling onions at the end of the summer, but it has rather a harsh, astringent taste for some people's liking. Distilled vinegar, which is clear, has less of the strong vinegary taste, and doesn't 'colour' the finished pickles. But enthusiasts often prefer the finer flavour of white wine vinegar; if you make homemade wine, you could make your own wine vinegar (see page 114).

Most pickle-makers like to flavour the vinegar they'll use for pickling with spices; make spiced vinegar a month or so before making pickle so the flavour has time to intensify. Simply add the whole spices (a cinnamon stick, 6 cloves, 6 peppercorns, a bay leaf and a teaspoonful each of mustard seeds and allspice berries to a 1.2 litre (2 pint) container of vinegar) and leave for 4–8 weeks, then strain the spices out before proceeding with your favourite pickle recipe.

To make pickles you'll need a large saucepan with a tight-fitting lid and a supply of clean screw-top jam jars that need to be sterilised in the same way as you do when making jam (see page 120). Country people always used to do their pickling in an outhouse down the garden, but when you can't,

it's a good idea to shut yourself in the kitchen with a window or the back door open when you have a pickling session. Boiling vinegar is a never-to-be-forgotten smell that will percolate the whole house and linger, given half a chance.

HOW TO MAKE QUICK PICKLED CUCUMBERS

THIS IS A GOOD WAY to use up a sudden glut of cucumbers during the summer; the result is very much like gherkins.

PEEL A COUPLE OF CUCUMBERS and cut them into 'fingers' 7.5 cm (3 inches) long or else make long, slanting slices about 5 mm (¼ inch) thick.

POUR 600 ML (1 PINT) OF SPICED VINEGAR into a large saucepan and bring to the boil; cider vinegar is a good one to use for this job. You might like to add a teaspoonful of sugar to make a slightly more sweet-and-sour flavour, and/or add a sprig or two of fresh dill.

DROP THE CUCUMBER PIECES INTO THE PAN, making sure they are all completely covered. (If they don't all fit, use the same pickling liquid to make two or three batches, one after another.)

BRING THE VINEGAR BACK TO THE BOIL and boil gently for 4–5 minutes, until the cucumber turns slightly 'glassy' looking, then remove with a slotted spoon and do a second batch (if you have more cucumber pieces left).

PACK THE CUCUMBERS TIGHTLY into a large wide-necked jar (the sort that 'bought' gherkins come in is ideal) that's been sterilised in hot water then, while the jar is still hot, top it up with the hot spiced vinegar, screw the lid on and leave to cool. When cold, keep the finished pickles in the fridge and use within two weeks.

HOW TO MAKE PICCALILLI

CUT UP A MIXTURE OF VEGETABLES into uniform bite-sized pieces; you can use cauliflower, cucumbers or gherkins, onions, white cabbage, marrows, celery, broad, runner or French beans, peppers or green tomatoes; you'll need 1.5 kilos (3 pounds) in total. (Make double the quantity if you have enough veg.)

MAKE UP A BRINE SOLUTION by dissolving 225 grams (8 ounces) of cooking salt in 1.9 litres (4 pints) of water; put this in a large jar or bucket and put the prepared vegetable pieces into it, pressing them down well. Put a plate with a weight on top to keep them immersed, and leave them overnight to soak.

THE NEXT MORNING, rinse the veg in fresh water and leave them to drain. Meanwhile mix one and a half teaspoons of ground turmeric with two teaspoonfuls of dry English mustard powder, two teaspoonfuls of ground ginger, and 150 grams (5 ounces) of white sugar; stir this into 850 ml (1½ pints) of distilled vinegar and add the prepared vegetables; bring to the boil and allow to simmer for 20 minutes.

USE A SLOTTED SPOON to transfer the veg to clean, sterilised, hot jars, then stir 25 grams (1 ounces) of cornflower into a teaspoonful of cold vinegar and stir this into the hot vinegar mix remaining in the pan. Stir it while you bring it back to the boil for a few minutes; this will thicken it slightly.

LET IT COOL SLIGHTLY BEFORE POURING it over the veg in the jars, filling them up to the rim. Screw the lids on straight away; store in a cool place (a pantry is perfect) and let it stand for at least six weeks before starting to use the pickle, so the vegetables can absorb the spicy flavours – they should still remain slightly crunchy.

HOW TO MAKE GREEN TOMATO CHUTNEY

Chop around a kilo (2 pounds) green tomatoes, ½ kilo (1 pound) of cooking apples and ¼ kilo (8 ounces) of onions into small pieces, then add ¼ kilo (8 ounces) sultanas (whole or minced, or a mixture of each). Put them in a large saucepan with 300ml (½ pint) of spiced vinegar. Tie up 15 grams (½ ounce) of whole, mixed pickling spices in a piece of muslin or clean white cotton cloth, and throw that into the mixture. Bring slowly to the boil, then add ½ kilo (1 pound) of brown sugar and another 300ml (½ pint) of vinegar. Boil gently until the mixture is thick enough to leave a depression when you run your wooden spoon through it. Remove the pickle parcel, then ladle the chutney into hot, sterilised jars and screw the tops on while hot.

DAIRY WORK

Large country estates had their own dairy, but that wasn't the place where cows or goats were milked – it was a naturally cold, stone-floored room kept spotlessly clean, where the dairymaid turned milk into cream, butter or cheese for the 'big house'.

But today you can do dairy work in your kitchen at home. A lot of people do if they keep a goat or have neighbours whose smallholding produces seasonal surpluses of milk. It's really very easy to make cream, soft cheese, yoghurt and ice-cream, and if you're prepared for a bit more time, effort and equipment, you can even make butter and hard cheeses. If you don't have access to surplus milk, you can always use cartons of milk bought from a supermarket.

The big secret when working with dairy produce is to keep all the utensils sterile and pay great attention to detail; a small error in temperature is enough to allow the wrong kind of bacteria to thrive while the right one doesn't. But with patience and a bit of practice, you can achieve very good results. There are also various electrical gadgets that take away a lot of the hard graft and guesswork.

MILK FOR MAKING DAIRY PRODUCE

Cream is the starting point for producing butter. Traditionally, anyone wanting to make butter would keep a breed of cow that was well known for producing milk with a high fat content, (ideally Jersey or Guernsey), since this naturally produces a lot more cream, though any cows' milk will produce some cream.

Goats' milk can't be used for making cream or butter, however, because the globules of fat it contains are too small and too evenly distributed to separate out in the same way as happens with cows' milk. It can be used to make other dairy products such as soft cheese and yoghurt instead.

CREAM, BUTTER AND ICE CREAM

Cream is the fat-rich part of the milk which floats to the surface. If you had bottles of gold-top Channel-island milk delivered to your doorstep, years ago, you'll remember the cream forming a layer at the top of the bottle – where it was often collared by bluetits who pecked through the foil lid to pinch it. Dairymaids of the past did much the same thing on a larger scale. To collect cream they poured whole milk into a wide shallow bowl and left it to stand in a cool place – the dairy. The cream rose to the top and was then skimmed off with a special spoon with holes in it to retain the cream but let the milk drain through. Today you could do it the same way or else use a mechanical separator, which works by centrifugal force; devices of this sort are sold by smallholders' supply shops, and they'll extract almost twice as much cream from a given volume of milk as you could by hand.

The cream collected from the top of the milk can be used just as it is. Double cream is the thickest and has the highest fat content; this floats to the very top of the bowl. Single cream is thinner in consistency as it contains rather less fat, so it's usually the second layer to be skimmed off. Clotted cream is cream that's had a special culture added to thicken it (available from smallholders' suppliers).

What's left behind after all the cream has been skimmed off is skimmed milk or semi-skimmed milk, again depending on the percentage of fat it contains. In the past this was usually fed to the pigs, but today there's a big demand for it with health- and diet-conscious folk.

If you have enough cream you can use it for making butter and ice cream, but it takes a lot of milk to do so, since even the richest full-fat milk only contains about 5 per cent cream, by volume.

Commercially, butter is made by adding a lactic acid culture to cream, but at home you can simply save up cream that's been separated from the milk over several days, keep it at room temperature, and add each new batch to it every day. By then the original cream will be quite 'ripe' due to the natural bacteria that develop, which helps give butter its distinctive flavour. Wait for 12 hours after adding

HOW TO MAKE YOGHURT

...

IF YOU'RE USING HOME-GROWN MILK, as against 'bought' milk from a carton, start by boiling it for a few minutes to kill off any unwanted bacteria. Use a thermometer to follow progress as it cools; at between 25°C and 35°C (77 and 95°F) stir in a 'starter'. You might be able to buy a freeze-dried culture of yoghurt bacillus, but the easiest way is to use 2–3 teaspoonfuls of *live*, natural (i.e. plain, unflavoured) yoghurt. (Live yoghurt is sometimes available from health food shops.)

THE MIXTURE THEN NEEDS TO BE KEPT at a steady temperature for several hours, until the milk has thickened and turned to a creamy constituency. (The exact timing is a tad variable, depending on whether you want a thinner, milder tasting yoghurt or a thicker, stronger one, and how warm you keep it. About 21–25°C/70–77°F is ideal.) There are various ways to keep the cultured milk at the right temperature. Some people leave it in a bowl covered with a close-fitting lid in the airing cupboard, or you might prefer to use an electric yoghurt maker, which consists of several pots that sit inside a covered, temperature-regulated container (and which comes with full directions). But one of the simplest ways is to use a wide-necked stainless steel thermos flask; fill the interior with boiling water and leave for five minutes to kill germs etc, then tip the water out and after a minute or so (while it's still warm), pour in enough of the cultured milk mixture to fill it up to *just* below the top. If you do this early in the evening you'll have yoghurt ready for breakfast next morning.

ONCE YOU HAVE A BATCH OF YOUR OWN LIVE YOGHURT, it will keep for several days in a bowl in the fridge – mix it with fresh or stewed fruit to taste, or use plain yoghurt as the basis for dishes such as tandoori chicken, or raita and tzatziki (grated cucumber in yoghurt, eaten with curries or Greek food).

BUT BEFORE YOU DO ANYTHING ELSE with a fresh batch, take several spoonfuls from it to use for starting your next batch. Don't, whatever you do, try to use fruit-flavoured yoghurt (or indeed any yoghurt containing any other flavourings) as a 'starter', as whatever you've used will introduce unwanted bacteria or mould, which will ruin the yoghurt.

your last lot of cream, before churning it to make butter. You could use a genuine antique butter churn, though it normally needs quite a large quantity of cream to operate properly; smaller hand-operated versions that look like a glass jar with a paddle inside are available from smallholders' supply shops. Otherwise you could use a food mixer with the blades set to a fairly low speed, since all that's necessary is to agitate the cream fairly vigorously and continuously.

When you start churning, nothing happens for a while, then suddenly the fat in the cream 'clumps together' forming yellowy globules floating in buttermilk. At this point drain off the buttermilk, leaving the blobs of butter behind, then put some cold water into the churn, and churn the lot again. This washes all the milk out of the butter, which stops it tasting sour or turning rancid. Keep replacing the dirty water with clean cold water and churn again until the water stays completely clear. Then tip your lump of butter onto a clean board, sprinkle it lightly with a little salt and use traditional-type wooden butter pats (which look rather like small wooden paddles) to mix the butter up. The idea is to make sure the salt is distributed evenly throughout and to squeeze out any remaining water. After working it for a while, bash it into a rectangle and wrap it in waxed paper – the saltier the butter, the longer it keeps – but if you don't want over-salty butter, or you aren't sure you've pressed all the water out, then play safe and store it in the freezer, where it keeps in perfect condition for a year or more.

BUTTERMILK

Buttermilk has a very characteristic flavour; it is basically skimmed milk (since all the fat has been taken out in the form of butter), but with a richer, more buttery flavour due to the lactic acid it contains. Some people like to drink buttermilk, but it's brilliant for making scones and can also be used in other forms of baking. Traditionally any surplus buttermilk was fed to pigs or poultry.

HOW TO MAKE REAL ICE CREAM

ICE CREAM IS SOMETHING we take very much for granted today, and until quite recently no one would ever have thought of making their own. But nowadays electric ice cream makers have revolutionised the process – just follow the directions and the device simultaneously freezes and churns the ingredients to produce perfect ice cream effortlessly. What's more, you can incorporate your own homegrown fruit, or experiment with ideas of your own. (Most machines also make sorbets, too.)

THE ICE CREAM WE BUY in the shops today is mostly water ice, but anyone who has their own Channel Island house-cow and a well-stocked henhouse can experience *real* ice cream, the way Mrs Beeton made it (just don't count the calories!).

BOIL 600ML (1 PINT) OF CREAM and 300ml (½ pint) of full-fat milk with half a vanilla pod for a few minutes, then stir this into a bowl containing the yolks of four eggs that have been beaten with 100 grams (4 ounces) caster sugar.

TIP THE LOT BACK INTO THE SAUCEPAN and heat it very gently over a low heat until it thickens. Strain, add a few drops of vanilla extract if needed to intensify the flavour, then pour into a freezerproof container and freeze.

REMOVE FROM THE FREEZER several times to stir the layer of frozen crystals that form round the inside of the container into the unfrozen mixture in the centre, until it is all even.

CHEESE-MAKING

Soft cheese, also known as curd cheese, is by far the easiest and fastest sort of cheese to make, and the one that's most practical for people to make at home. It doesn't keep for very long, so aim to use it within a few days. You can use either cows' or goats' milk for this.

Hard cheeses take a lot more time, equipment and skill to 'get right'; most smallholders stick to cream cheese and yoghurt and leave the more technical stuff to specialist cheese-makers (who, it has to be said, need to comply with a lot of hygiene standards and legislation if they want to sell their produce). It takes about 4.5 litres (1 gallon) of whole milk (i.e. milk that includes the cream) to make 450g (1lb) of cheese, but if you are interested, this is how it's done.

First the milk is curdled by adding rennet (an enzyme extracted from the stomach of a calf, though vegetarian rennet is also available). Most cheese-makers will also add a starter of lactic acid bacteria (from cheese-making supply firms, or a culture obtained from a fellow cheese-maker). When the milk sets firmly, it's cut into 2cm (¾in) squares and the whole lot is warmed very slowly to 38°C (100°F) and stirred, before being left to ripen slightly. The acidity is tested regularly, and at just the right stage the mixture is strained to separate the curds from the whey. The curds are then broken up into pieces the size of walnuts, and salt is added at 25g (1oz) salt to every 1¾kg (4lbs) of curd.

Next comes the cheese mould. This is a cylinder of metal or wood which looks something like an old-fashioned cake tin with a removable base, but deeper. This is lined with cheesecloth, leaving the surplus fabric hanging over the outside of the container, and packed full of pieces of curd. When it is full to the top, the overhanging edges of cheesecloth are folded back over the top and pressure is applied. Regular cheesemakers use a proper cheese press, but if you're having a go at home it's possible to put a plate the right size to fit inside the top and stand half a dozen bricks on top. Six hours later, the weights are removed, then the cheese is taken out and unwrapped. The cheesecloth is rinsed out in clean water, then the

cheese is turned upside down, rewrapped, and replaced in its mould. More pressure is applied this time, up to a hundredweight (112lbs). After two days the cheese is turned again and the pressure increased to half a ton (if using a cheese press) or as much as you can balance on top. After another two days, the cheese is removed, wrapped with strips of clean cotton held in place by a flour-and-water paste (which will eventually form the rind), and sat on a slatted shelf in a well-ventilated cheese room (at home, a pantry is ideal) at a temperature of 13–16°C (55–60°F) to dry and mature.

Cheeses are turned upside down every day for a week, and after that twice a week, while they mature. If the outside starts to turn mouldy, it is brushed clean. After two weeks, whole cheeses are sometimes brushed all over with melted wax to help them 'keep' more reliably. Professional cheese-makers have their own recipes for producing a range of blue-veined cheeses, Cheddar-like cheeses and such like.

HOW TO MAKE CURD CHEESE

FIRST YOU NEED TO TURN THE MILK SOUR; in warm weather it'll often do this all on its own, due to bacteria present in the air, but to help things along add a spoonful or two of live natural yoghurt.

LEAVE THE MILK IN A WARM PLACE (the airing cupboard or the cupboard that encloses the central-heating boiler is ideal); it will take between one and four days to thicken – the exact time will vary according to the warmth and other conditions.

WHEN THE MILK HAS SET SEMI-FIRM (wobble the container slightly to see how it's doing, it should behave a bit like a jelly), pour the whole lot into a large sieve lined with a couple of thicknesses of muslin, cheesecloth or clean cotton fabric that's previously been sterilised by boiling for a few minutes, and stand the whole thing over a bowl to catch the drips. If you're only doing a small quantity, stand it in the fridge to 'stop' the cheese ripening any more while it drips, otherwise keep it in a cool place – this would traditionally have been done in the dairy.

THE CLEAR LIQUID THAT RUNS THROUGH the cloth is whey; feed it to pigs or hens as it doesn't have much other use. The milk solids left behind in the cloth are basic curd cheese.

WHEN IT IS THOROUGHLY DRAINED, which takes a good 12–24 hours, add chopped fresh herbs, garlic or ground black pepper (or any combination of your favourites to taste) to make a herby soft cheese, or simply leave it plain.

CURD CHEESE DOESN'T KEEP FOR LONG, so aim to use it within 2–3 days. It's good on toast or in sandwiches (especially with cucumber and Marmite, or smoked salmon), but it makes brilliant homemade cheesecake.

IF YOU ARE FEELING FLUSH or you have a neighbour with a house cow, follow the same recipe but use double cream instead of milk – this makes cream cheese, as against the more economical and everyday curd cheese.

Making curd cheese can't be rushed; first the milk needs to thicken, then semi-ripen, before it can be tipped into a sieve lined with muslin to catch the delicious curds.

COUNTRY COOKERY

If you visit ancient buildings that have been restored and opened to the public at open-air museums (like the one at Singleton, near Chichester in West Sussex), you'll see how country people cooked hundreds of years ago. Originally everything was cooked in an iron cauldron over an open fire in the centre of a room. As living conditions improved and chimneys became commonplace in most homes, much of the cooking was still done over the open fire, but now there would be a bread oven built into the chimney breast at a convenient height above the fire, or slightly off to one side. At slightly more superior houses, there'd also be a higher 'hatch' in the chimney where meat or fish could be hung to smoke, at the lower temperature required for this. (In the past this wasn't done to produce gourmet food, it was an important method of preserving food for winter use at a time long before refrigeration, when all but essential breeding livestock was slaughtered each autumn due to lack of grazing and shortage of winter feed.)

The kitchens of grand stately homes would have a stand-alone bread oven, of the same sort found in medieval bakers' shops in towns. Inside this a fire was lit, and after the interior was heated up, the ashes were raked out and the trays of bread slid inside. The rest of the cooking was done on an enormous cast-iron range which would have been fuelled by logs at first, but later coal. Smaller versions of these ranges later became the norm in town houses and country cottages (we still had one in our Northern terraced house until the mid-1950s!), and after a rush to have modern electric cookers when power was laid on to country communities, the fashion has moved back to range-style cookers, although today they are powered by gas or electricity rather than solid fuel.

Nowadays a lot of people are in love with their Aga (or similar device), and besides doing the cooking these stoves will heat the hot water and sometimes run several radiators as well. The great beauty of this type of cooking is that the oven is on all the time, so the kitchen always stays cosy. Farmers' wives traditionally raised orphan lambs in front of the solid fuel cooker; it was also the ideal place to put bread dough to rise, or sit in a chair to warm up when you came indoors on a cold day. (Yup, I'm an Aga man – I love being warmed up after a winter morning in the garden!) Laundry would be dried on a wooden clothes horse in front of the range, or by hanging the clothes up on wooden racks suspended just below the ceiling that were lowered on ropes and pulleys. (You can still buy them through adverts in magazines devoted to country living and traditional kitchens – 'sheilas' they are called, and they are very effective, making good 'green' alternatives to tumble driers.)

But for keen cooks, the great advantage of having an oven that's on all the time is that you don't think twice about cooking things that need long cooking times. It's very practical when you like to do lots of baking, it's a great way to cook casseroles using tough game, stewing steak or dried beans, and to make jams and other preserves. Well, you might just as well make the most of it, since the cooker and its hobs are always hot and ready to go.

THE OLD-FASHIONED PANTRY

IN THE DAYS BEFORE FRIDGES and freezers, country kitchens always featured a pantry. This was like a walk-in larder, built into the coldest corner of the house – facing north – with a grille to let in cold fresh air, and marble or slate shelves and a concrete floor so it stayed as cold as possible inside. Here, housewives kept fresh produce such as eggs, milk, cream and cheese, and even meat could be kept for several days.

SINCE THE PANTRY WASN'T TOTALLY blue-bottle-proof, jugs of milk and cream were kept covered with a circle of muslin weighted down round the edges by glass or metal beads, cheese was kept on a china cheese dish which had its own matching china lid, and meat was kept in a meat safe – a box with sides made of perforated zinc or very fine mesh. Dishes of cooked food were protected by sitting fine mesh covers, looking like large muslin tea cosies, over the top.

THE PANTRY WAS ALSO A GOOD place to store fresh fruit and veg from the garden until it was needed, as the temperature of the 'room' was very similar to that of the salad drawer at the bottom of a modern fridge – and it was brilliant for keeping apples and pears, since conditions were like those inside a proper apple store – which only gardens of large country estates had. People also stored all their jams, pickles and jars of salted beans on the higher shelves.

ANYONE WHO KEPT HENS would also keep surplus eggs in a bucket full of isinglass (a gelatin-like material obtained from the internal organs of certain fish, which looked like wallpaper glue). In this way they'd stay fresh for quite a long time – isinglass was traditionally used for storing fresh eggs to use in the winter, when hens 'went off' lay.

DIY HOT-SMOKING OF MEAT OR FISH

· · ·

COLD SMOKING, which produces smoked salmon, requires precise temperature control, so it's best left to a commercial smokery. Keen trout or salmon fishermen will often know of one that they can take their own catches to, to be smoked professionally and then returned to them.

HOT SMOKING, however, is something you can do at home without too much trouble.

TAKE A LARGE, DEEP, HEAVY FRYING PAN, saucepan or wok and line the base with several layers of tin foil. Mix a couple of teaspoons of brown sugar with a couple of handfuls of rice and place this in the bottom of the pan, then sprinkle a couple of teaspoons of dry tea leaves (ideally Earl Grey) over the top – these are what will create the smoke, which will be pleasantly flavoured and nicely scented. Wedge a wooden rack or several criss-crossed wooden chopsticks in place an inch or so above the tea, rice and sugar mixture. Choose the food to be smoked (it's usually sections of salmon fillet, or whole chicken or duck breast, but you

can try other meat or fish) and sprinkle it fairly generously with salt for half an hour before you start to smoke it. Before putting it into the pan, brush off as much of the salt as you can but don't wash the food. Place it on the rack, and if smoking several pieces, space them an inch apart so the smoke can circulate. Place the lid on the pan – it needs to be a fairly close fit so the smoke stays inside – and stand it on a fairly high heat (use a hob indoors, or else a barbecue, or put it over the chimney of a chiminea in the garden) for 20 minutes. By then it'll be cooked, with a nice smoky flavour. For a more economical version or simply to create a different flavour, use oak sawdust or hickory chippings to smoke the food over.

IF YOU DON'T WANT THE BOTHER, or you like to do a lot of food-smoking, various ready-to-use smokers are available from kitchen shops. There are self-contained electric models also ones that look like large metal trays with lids, heated by methylated spirit burners or tea-lights underneath, which use oak or hickory sawdust to generate the smoke.

HOW TO SWEEP A CHIMNEY

⁘

IN CHARLES DICKENS' DAY, large country houses were heated entirely by open fires and huge inter-connecting chimneys which had to be swept by small boys climbing up inside them. Cottagers meanwhile swept their own chimneys by tying a bundle of holly stems to a stone, climbing up on the roof, and dropping it down the chimney, where it found its way into the hearth below, producing clouds of soot which drifted all over the room.

SINCE THEN, MOST PEOPLE who still had open fires employed a chimney sweep to come round with his own set of dust sheets, rods and brushes to sweep their flues annually, every autumn. But you can save the fee by doing it yourself, and it's not half as difficult – or as messy – as you'd think.

YOU NEED A SET OF RODS and a traditional-type circular, flat flue brush; DIY centres sell them with several different heads for rodding drains as well. If you have a wood-burning stove you'll need a special head for sweeping inside the flue-liner; this is bullet-shaped and only about 10–15cm (4–6 inches) wide.

SPREAD A DUST SHEET ALL ROUND the hearth as a precaution and hang one from the mantelpiece – draping it over the opening to prevent it flying into the room. Fit the brush head to the first rod and push it up into the chimney, underneath the overhanging dust sheet. Screw the next rod in place and keep pushing, using a slightly up and down motion so the sides of the chimney are scoured thoroughly as you go. You also need to twist the rods slightly in the direction that tightens them up as you push. (This is important because if you twist the wrong way or even if you don't twist at all, it's just possible that a rod or the brush head will get unscrewed and end up stuck up the chimney, where it takes a lot of shifting.)

CONTINUE ADDING MORE RODS and pushing the kit up the chimney; when you get to the last two or three rods in your bundle send an assistant outside to look at the top of the chimney to see when the brush pokes out. It won't matter too much if you push the brush out of the top of a chimney that's open to the air, but if you have a cap on top to stop birds or rain getting in, you can easily knock it off, and you need a long ladder and a head for heights to replace it. There's always a risk that a dislodged chimney-cap will fall through the conservatory roof or dislodge several roof tiles on its way down.

ONCE THE BRUSH IS VISIBLE AT THE TOP, start pulling the whole assembly back down again, still using the same twisting motion that tightens up rather than unscrews the rods. If you do it fairly slowly you won't bring a huge rush of soot down into the hearth all at once, it'll descend as a gentle trickle. Unscrew each rod in turn until the last length with the brush on top has been safely returned, then have a good clean up and vacuum, leaving the fire good to go for another year.

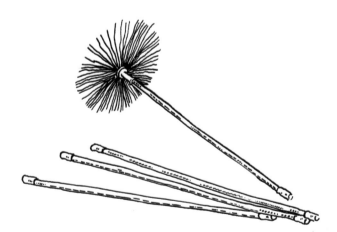

STILL-ROOM SECRETS 🌿

In medieval times country people relied on their gardens for the ingredients to make a vast range of household products. As recently as early last century, a good few farm-workers and other people living on low wages were still making some of their own everyday household goods whenever it was practical. Today a lot of old country crafts are making a comeback as creative hobbies, which can be very satisfying, cost-effective and fun to do.

HERBAL REMEDIES

Herbs contain an enormous number of natural substances that the plant uses for its own protection from sun, insects, disease or predators, some of which, it turns out, also have medicinal uses when applied to humans. The medicinal properties of certain plants must originally have been discovered largely by trial and error and observation, and these discoveries were passed on down the generations by monks – the doctors of their day – and 'wise old women' in villages.

In some cases ancient herbal medicine has given us modern drugs that were used until synthetic replacements or improved modern drugs became available; for example, digitalis obtained from foxgloves was used for a long time to treat heart conditions.

But the big problem with using herbs medicinally is that the active constituents present in plants can vary from season to season, or with different growing conditions, so – unlike modern pills – it is difficult to predict accurately and precisely how much of the active ingredient you are taking.

Today, using herbs for serious medicinal purposes is best left to properly trained herbal practitioners, who usually have conventional medical training as well. However, herbs are increasingly being used at home in herbal teas, home-made toiletries and face creams, etc., (which are often believed by enthusiasts to be every bit as effective and considerably cheaper than over-packaged high-street brands) as well as for treating minor ailments and as basic first aid. A well-stocked herb garden can provide ingredients for a wide range of purposes.

One of the most useful 'herbs' for first-aid is a succulent, *Aloe vera*, sometimes known as the burn plant. It's a typical aloe, making a symmetrical, upright rosette of thick, fleshy leaves. It's ideal for growing in a pot on a sunny windowsill indoors, though it can be kept outside on the patio in summer. The leaves contain a thick, sticky gel which is easily squeezed out if you cut a whole, or part of, a leaf off, slice it in half lengthwise, and press it flat against a wooden chopping board with the flat of a knife. The gel can be applied 'neat' to burns, scalds, sunburn or cuts, where it forms a protective seal as well as encouraging the area to heal. The gel can also be added to home-made hand creams, etc. Houseleek (*Sempervivum*) leaves can be used in much the same way; they are a far older burn and scald remedy that was readily available to early cottagers as the plants often grew wild on their roofs and in nooks and crannies of rough stone walls, where rosettes had been scattered by birds.

For anyone wanting to cut down on salt in cooking, dried dill seeds, freshly finely ground and used in small quantities, makes a good substitute without raising the blood pressure.

Herbs were also once used as a tonic, supplying valuable vitamins and/or minerals. Hardy annual herbs such as chervil, parsley, sorrel and common orache (*Atriplex hortensis*) are naturally high in vitamin C. They were often used as spring salads by medieval cottagers for the tonic effect they produced; this was badly needed at the end of a long winter when people had lived for months on a diet of dried or otherwise preserved food which was always low in vitamin C, as they'd often be suffering from scurvy-like symptoms by then. Dandelion contains a good supply of other vitamins and minerals as well as vitamin C – the young leaves make a good salad ingredient, especially if the whole plant is blanched under a bucket for a few days before picking. Nettles, too, are rich in both vitamins and minerals; young leaves can be made into nettle tea, cooked like spinach, or made into soup. (Make a potato and onion soup using chicken stock and add a handful of chopped young nettle tops per serving when cooking, then put the mixture through a blender.)

Warts were traditionally removed by smearing them with the sap from pot marigold (*Calendula officinalis*) or houseleek and leaving the 'gel' to dry. Results took a while and several applications were usually recommended.

For flatulence, caraway seeds were chewed before meals; today caraway is often recommended for cooking with cabbage since the slightly aniseedy flavour goes well with it and quells any tendency to windiness. Other herbs share the same reputation: dill leaves and seeds, coriander (fresh leaves or ground seeds, which are used as a traditional curry spice), also lovage seeds. But if you want to give them a try, save seeds from your own plants or use seeds bought for culinary purposes – don't use packeted seeds intended for growing since they've often been treated with fungicides.

For hiccups, try dill tea. Dill is one of the major ingredients of gripe water, which is traditionally given to babies with 'colic'.

Various oral disorders respond to herbal remedies. Treat bad breath by chewing whole dry dill seeds, or use rosemary tea as a mouthwash. To neutralise the smell of strong food, particularly garlic, on the breath, chew fresh parsley. For mouth ulcers and sore gums, use wild strawberry leaf tea (*Fragaria vesca*) as a mouthwash.

To help you sleep, try borage tea made by pouring a cup of boiling water over three teaspoonfuls of chopped fresh borage leaves; add a slice of lemon or a few drops of lemon juice and honey to taste. Or fill a small pillow case with dried hop flowers to make a hop pillow; inhaling the scent is meant to help you nod off. Dried lavender heads have the same reputation; you can use them in a pillow or just have a big bowl of freshly dried flower heads in your bedroom. They make the place smell nice, anyway.

For colds and sore throats, chew a stick of natural dried liquorice root; this was once sold loose from glass jars in old-fashioned sweet shops for children to eat on their way to school (it also turned our tongues an attractive shade of yellow!). Alternatively, sit with a towel over your head above a saucepan of freshly boiled water containing juniper berries, and breathe in the steam for a few minutes. Two other good old-fashioned cold remedies are sage tea and home-made onion soup – both of which are also good for laryngitis – or make an even more potent brew by mixing the two together. Warm thyme tea, used for gargling, is good for sore throats.

For catarrh and blocked sinuses, add horseradish or chilli to a dish to make your eyes and nose run.

To improve the memory, use rosemary (for remembrance, as Shakespeare so wisely observed), or take lemon balm as a herbal tea.

For insect bites and stings, rub the affected area with sap from a bruised houseleek leaf, or use pennyroyal leaves. Rub crushed leaves of summer savory on bee stings. For a natural insect repellent, rub pennyroyal or basil leaves onto bare skin.

Chamomile is one of many flowers that has long been famed for its restorative properties.

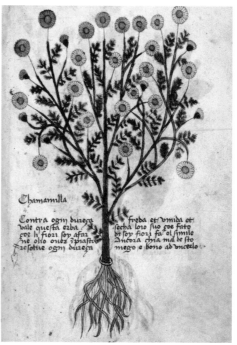

HERBAL TEAS

...

HERBAL TEAS ARE CAFFEINE-FREE ALTERNATIVES to everyday tea or coffee, which often have added health benefits. Regular favourites for frequent drinking are chamomile, mint, fennel or nettle. Use freshly chopped herbs whenever possible; if using dried herbs, halve the amount.

CHAMOMILE TEA: grow Roman chamomile (*Chamaemelum nobile*) or its double form 'Flore Pleno', which is a more compact and rather prettier plant. Add a heaped teaspoonful of fresh flowers (stems removed) to a cup of boiling water; infuse for 3–5 minutes then strain and add a slice of lemon and honey to taste.

MINT TEA: use spearmint (*Mentha spicata*) for a pleasant everyday drinking tea, as against black peppermint (*Mentha* x *piperata*), which is an indigestion remedy. Pour a cup of boiling water over a heaped teaspoon of roughly chopped fresh leaves and infuse for 3–5 minutes until it's a comfortable temperature to drink. Add honey or sugar if you prefer your tea sweet. (The mint tea you are given in North Africa is made by adding a lot of fresh mint to normal tea leaves and leaving the lot to brew; it's traditionally drunk strong with a lot of sugar. Some herb firms supply a special variety of mint especially for this use, otherwise use spearmint or peppermint.)

FENNEL TEA: use plump, pale green, dry fennel seeds for the best brew. Pour a cup of boiling water over a heaped teaspoonful of dried seeds and leave till it's a comfortable temperature for drinking – put a lid on the mug to keep the liquid hot for longer, which extracts more of the flavour. Strain, and add a slice of lemon and a little honey if you like; it's nice on its own unless you have a very sweet tooth.

Thyme makes a refreshing tea; just steep a teaspoonful in hot water. Lemon thyme is particularly fragrant.

NETTLE TEA: use freshly picked nettle tops; chop fairly finely and pour a cupful of boiling water over a heaped teaspoonful, then leave to stand till it's the right temperature to drink; strain first. It doesn't need honey or lemon as, surprisingly, it's very pleasant on its own – it tastes rather like newly mown grass smells, if you know what I mean.

DANDELION COFFEE

IN WARTIME, WHEN IMPORTED COFFEE was almost unavailable, people made their own dandelion coffee substitute. It still has a small following today as a natural, do-it-yourself, healthy, caffeine-free hot beverage that's low in calories. Dandelion roots are rich in minerals, as they reach down deep into the soil, so it's also quite good nutritionally.

CHOOSE STRONG, HEALTHY PLANTS growing in part of the garden where there's no risk they'll have been contaminated by chemicals, especially weedkillers. (Although dandelions grow in the lawn, they are regularly beheaded so the roots are unable to grow as big and strong as dandelions left to grow in open ground.) Ideally cultivate a short row in the veg patch especially for the job. (Save seeds from dandelion 'clocks' during the summer, or use cultivated dandelion seed, which is also sometimes available from specialist herb-seed or wildflower-seed firms.)

DIG UP THE PLANTS IN AUTUMN, when the roots are at maximum size. Trim off the longest, thickest roots to use; wash them well and steam them for a few minutes until the white sap stops leaking out of the cut surfaces. (Don't boil them, or the goodness will leak out.)

CUT THEM INTO 1CM (½ INCH) LONG PIECES, spread them out thinly on baking trays, and keep them in a warm place to dry until they snap cleanly without bending. Then put them in the oven and roast them at 200°C/400°F. I'd suggest doing a few at a time while you gain experience, since the colour and flavour of the finished dandelion coffee will vary according to how lightly or deeply you roast the roots. They'll turn pale yellow when lightly roasted, and a darker, almost coffee-colour when they are more heavily roasted.

LET THEM COOL COMPLETELY when you take them out of the oven, so all the steam has dispersed, before storing the whole roots in airtight jars to preserve their flavour.

WHEN YOU WANT TO MAKE YOUR 'COFFEE', grind a few roots especially. Use an electric coffee grinder or the spice mill attachment on a food processor. Add boiling water and milk or honey, if required; you'll soon find the right strength to suit your personal taste.

HOW TO MAKE TRADITIONAL LAVENDER-SCENTED BEESWAX FURNITURE CREAM

USE A LARGE SAUCEPAN OF HOT WATER with a big, clean, tin can standing inside as a make-shift double-saucepan; in this melt 100 grams (4 ounces) of beeswax in 600 ml (1 pint) of turpentine (this must be real turpentine, the sort artists use for thinning oil paints, and not the turps substitute used for cleaning decorators' paintbrushes). Turpentine is very inflammable so this job needs doing carefully.

YOU'LL ALSO NEED ANOTHER SAUCEPAN; in this, bring 300ml (½ pint) of water to the boil and then stir in 16½ grams (2/3 ounce) of soft soap. Leave both panfuls to cool down, then stir the liquid soap-water into the beeswax and turpentine mixture a little at a time, mixing it well as you go, just like making mayonnaise. It should take on a thick, creamy consistency.

AS SOON AS YOU'VE MIXED THE TWO LIQUIDS together, add a few drops of lavender oil, or use rosemary or a mixed herb oil if you prefer a slightly different fragrance. Pour it into a suitable container (maybe an old polish tin you've saved) to cool, when it should semi-set.

(NOTE: YOU CAN MAKE YOUR OWN LAVENDER or herb oil by filling a small jar loosely with fresh lavender flowers, rosemary or mixed fresh herb leaves, and covering it with olive oil – leave it on a sunny windowsill for at least two weeks for oil to take on the fragrance of the plant material. Strain the oil before using.)

HERBAL INSECT REPELLENTS

Fly repellents

Grow pennyroyal (*Mentha pulegium*) or your favourite culinary mint close to the back door of the house and also near dustbins or other areas at risk from flies. A bunch of mint in a jar in the kitchen, or a pot of sweet basil – the small leaved one – also helps. Greek oregano (*Oreganum vulgare*) deters flies and mosquitoes.

Ant repellents

Rub fresh pennyroyal leaves over doorsteps or round the edge of a path or patio; ants hate the strong minty scent and won't cross the line. The task needs repeating regularly.

Moth deterrents

Make up sachets of equal quantities of dried southernwood or wormwood, lavender flowers and spearmint to hang in the wardrobe. Instead of real lavender, you can use cotton lavender (*Santolina incana*), for a slightly different scent.

Otherwise (even though you can't grow the ingredients), hang up sachets impregnated with patchouli, the essential oil of an oriental plant called *Pogostemon cablin*, which was originally used by silk traders to prevent moths damaging their cargo on its long journey to Europe.

MAKING SOAP

···

SOAP IS MADE BY BOILING ANIMAL FATS or vegetable oils with a strong alkali. The original source of alkali was lye, extracted from wood ashes, but later caustic soda was used, and nowadays this element is normally sodium hydroxide.

MAKING SOAP FROM SCRATCH isn't something many people (other than a few real hobbyists) do at home, but you can 'customise' bought soap very easily. Grate a whole bar of unscented soap (or if you are feeling thrifty and it's for your own use, save up the equivalent amount of scraps of almost-used bars that you'd otherwise have thrown out, after letting them dry out till they are completely hard).

WEIGH THE SOAP FLAKES and to every 125 grams (4½ ounces) of flakes (the weight of an average bar of soap) you need to add 200ml (8 fluid ounces) of water. Put the soapflakes and water in a bowl and warm slowly over a pan of hot water until the soap melts.

THEN STIR IN two tablespoonfuls of almond or olive oil and ten to fifteen drops of your favourite essential oil to perfume the soap, and mix thoroughly.

FLOWER SCENTS SUCH AS ROSE OR LAVENDER are always popular, but you could try citrus scents or herbs such as rosemary; a huge range of oils is available in chemists and health food shops. If you want a prettier soap, stir in a few dried dark red rose petals or some dried calendula marigold petals at this point.

POUR THE MIXTURE INTO SOMETHING that will act as a mould, or make a block of soap in a loaf tin and when it's set hard cut it into suitably sized slices.

'HOME-MADE' SOAP MAKES GOOD ARTISAN-STYLE gifts, wrapped in brown paper and tied with raffia, or floral paper and ribbon. A real fag? Yes, but it's good to know just what goes into a bar of soap!

DIY HERBAL TOILETRIES

SKIN LOTIONS

AN INFUSION OF FRESH CHERVIL in water makes a lotion that cleanses and tones the skin, and is said to discourage wrinkles. (An infusion is basically a strong herb 'tea' made by pouring a cup of boiling water over a handful of whatever herbs and or flowers you want to use, then leaving it to stand for 10 minutes and straining it when cool.) Make fresh every day and store in the fridge up to 24 hours – it doesn't keep.

MARIGOLD FLOWERS INFUSED in water make a lotion that's traditionally used to clear the skin by reducing enlarged pores and healing spots. The healing properties of marigolds make the flowers popular for using in hand creams.

TO FADE FRECKLES or to keep a pale complexion fair, use fresh strawberry juice, made by mashing and straining ripe fresh fruit , and apply 'neat' or mix with finely ground oatmeal to make a face pack. For more instant use you can also apply a cut strawberry straight to your face; it's also comforting for mild sunburn.

HAND AND BODY CREAM

MELT SOME BEESWAX (it won't matter if there's still a little honey attached) and slowly beat in about five times the volume of olive oil or almond oil, over a low heat. Make an infusion of marigold flowers, lavender heads and/or herbs such as rosemary, sage or thyme.

WHISK A FEW DROPS OF THE HERBAL infusion at a time into the wax/oil mixture; allow it to cool. The mixture should be soft but not runny; add more oil or herb infusion as needed.

STORE IN A SCREW-TOP JAR and use within a couple of months; it keeps best in the fridge.

BATH ADDITIVES

FOR A SOOTHING, RELAXING, fragrant herbal bath, use a few fresh leaves of culinary bay (*Laurus nobilis*), rosemary, sage, scented-leaved geraniums, eau de cologne mint, horsetail, lemon balm, lemon-scented verbena, lavender flower heads, or blend a mixture to suit yourself.

THE HERBS CAN BE THROWN STRAIGHT into the hot water. but when you don't want to share your bath with a lot of floating 'bits', put the herbs in the centre of a square of muslin or cotton and tie the corners together to make a bag. Hang it under the hot tap when you run the bath.

ALTERNATIVELY, MAKE A STRONG 'TEA' from a mixture of herbs such as thyme, sage and rosemary (all of which have antiseptic properties as well as a fresh, clean fragrance) and pour a couple of teaspoonfuls into the hot water just before you step in.

DEODORANT

LOVAGE ACTS AS A NATURAL DEODORANT. It can be taken internally (eaten as a culinary herb it tastes like celery and can be used in soups or stews or as a leafy green vegetable).

LOVAGE CAN ALSO BE ADDED TO bathwater, on its own or with other herbs, to make a deodorising herbal bath. For smelly feet, place a few lovage leaves in the bottom of shoes such as trainers.

HAIR PRODUCTS

MAKE YOUR OWN NATURAL SHAMPOO from soapwort (top right) (*Saponaria officinalis*). Simmer two handfuls of chopped, fresh soapwort stems in 750ml (1¼ pints) of water in an old saucepan for 20 minutes, strain when cool and use as needed. (The same soapwort liquid can also be used for hand-washing delicate woollen and silk fabrics.)

CHAMOMILE FLOWERS (bottom right) make a pleasantly scented herbal rinse for enhancing blonde hair; it's like making chamomile tea but on a larger scale. Pour 1 litre (1¾ pints) of boiling water over a handful of fresh chamomile flowers and leave it to 'brew' for half an hour. When it's cooled, strain and use. For dark hair, use a similar infusion of rosemary as the final rinse after shampooing.

NETTLE 'TEA' MAKES A GOOD CONDITIONING hair rinse that's said to treat dandruff. Bring a bunch of nettle tops (15 centimetres/6 inches long and as big as you can hold in one gloved hand) to the boil in 60ml (1 pint) of water and simmer for 20 minutes. Store unused rinse in a bottle in the fridge, but use it within a few days.

HERBAL TEA MADE FROM HORSESTAIL (*Equisetum arvense*) makes a good hair conditioner for strengthening weak or brittle hair, and it's also a good nail-strengthening treatment due, it's thought, to the silica and other minerals that this deep-rooted plant collects and stores in its stems. Bruise eight fresh stalks of horsetail and cover with 600ml (1 pint) of boiling water to infuse. When cool, strain the liquid.

TO USE AS A HAIR RINSE, wash your hair as usual then apply as much horsetail tea as it holds without dripping everywhere, put a shower cap on and leave for ten minutes before rinsing it off with plain water.

TO USE AS A NAIL TREATMENT, sit for 20 minutes with your fingertips resting in a bowl of comfortably warm horsetail tea. You'll need to do it fairly regularly to really reap the benefit.

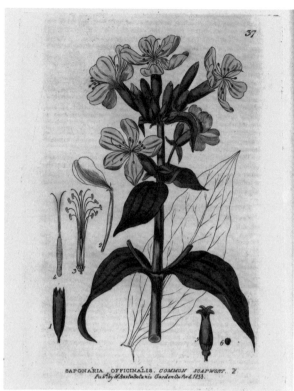

SAPONARIA OFFICINALIS. COMMON SOAPWORT.

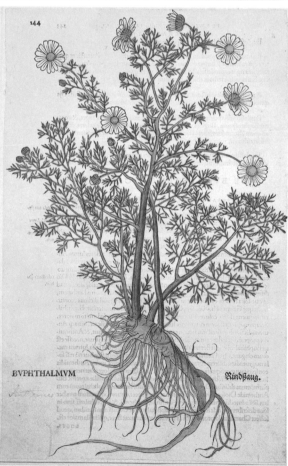

BVPHTHALMVM   Rindßaug.

COUNTRY GARDENING

Well-stocked gardens have been important life-support systems for country people for centuries. Medieval peasants and farmhouses had self-sufficient gardens that were more like smallholdings, complete with fruit, veg and herbs, bees for honey, and a variety of livestock plus a small pond for ducks. In Victorian times, rural farm workers relied on the gardens round their cottages to feed the family, and besides a kitchen garden they'd keep hens and rear a pig or two each year, feeding it on all the kitchen scraps and veg-garden waste that we put on the compost heap today. In wartime, when food was scarce and rationed, people turned their back gardens over to food production, keeping chickens and rabbits as well as growing fruit and veg.

Now, after decades of largely ornamental gardening, folk are realising the benefits of growing edible crops. For a lot of people, kitchen gardening is a lifestyle choice, intended to yield superior-quality food that's dew-fresh, organically grown with no food miles or packaging involved, using 'green' techniques. Also, a lot of folk have discovered how much 'growing your own' can contribute to a hard-pressed household budget, especially if you concentrate on raising more exotic and unusual crops that are expensive to buy. For anyone with enough space, a kitchen garden provides opportunities to raise the raw materials for country crafts such as flower arranging, home-brewing or making herbal potions and lotions, and even growing firewood to fuel wood-burning stoves.

KITCHEN GARDENING

You don't need green fingers to have a successful kitchen garden; the secret is a sheltered situation, good, fertile soil, and attention to detail. Edible crops make more demands than any other plants, so to get a decent crop it is important to limit yourself to what you can grow *well* in the time and space available. The mistake most novices make is to take on far more than they can manage. The tastiest, most tender crops are those that have had an easy life, so they grow quickly and steadily; any checks in growth can make them run to seed or become tough and tasteless.

Soil preparation is really important; more so for vegetable growing than for any other kind of gardening. Edible crops take an awful lot out of the ground (water, major nutrients and trace elements) because you are constantly removing what you grow and eating it, so it's vital to put plenty of goodness back. Fertiliser is only part of the story; a kitchen garden needs regular inputs of organic matter; this keeps the soil soft and 'fluffy' so roots can penetrate easily, and it keeps the soil aerated and well drained, besides housing a thriving community of beneficial soil bacteria. The goal of soil improvement is to create good growing conditions where hard-working crops can get on with the job.

Start preparing the soil in autumn and continue over the winter whenever the weather allows, so that the ground is ready for planting come spring. If you're starting a new kitchen garden plot from scratch, clear the ground completely of turf or perennial weeds first; don't dig them in as they always re-grow. (Annual weeds can be turned in if they are not bearing seeds, otherwise pull them out, too.) Improve the soil of an existing plot a little at a time, as the ground becomes vacant when winter

crops are cleared. Spread a barrowload of well-rotted organic matter per square yard, and dig it in to evenly incorporate it. You can use garden compost, manure, spent mushroom compost – whatever you can get hold of in quantity, cheaply and locally.

Once the groundwork has been properly done, kitchen gardening is all about timing and keeping up to date with routine work. It's vital to do key operations such as sowing and planting on time – you can find full details and instructions for individual varieties on the backs of the seed packets. And keep on top of regular weeding, watering, feeding, and pest and disease control; it's the only way to produce perfect crops that everyone wants to eat. Standards need to be high; now that everyone is used to the perfect crops bought from shops and supermarkets, people tend to be squeamish about the odd slug, insect or suspicious hole in things they are going to eat.

The vegetable garden is the one place where annual soil cultivation and the addition of well-rotted organic matter is essential.

MAKING A COMPOST HEAP

• • •

A PRODUCTIVE KITCHEN GARDEN needs regular supplies of well-rotted organic matter to improve the soil and then maintain the fertility, but it's easily produced for free by recycling your own garden waste and suitable kitchen scraps via a compost heap.

USE LAWN MOWINGS, soft hedge clippings, weeds, fallen autumn leaves, old bedding plants pulled out at the end of the season, crop remains from the veg patch, veg trimmings, fruit peel and used teabags from the kitchen. You can also use plain white paper (such as kitchen paper that you've used for mopping up spills) and discarded cotton or woollen fabrics, including old clothes.

DON'T USE SYNTHETIC FABRICS or printed paper, woody plant remains (since they take several years to rot down), weeds that have run to seed, roots of perennial weeds, or diseased plant material (since you'll spread the infection all round the garden when you use the compost). Avoid meat scraps and tasty morsels such as bread or cooked food as they'll attract rodents.

MAKE A COMPOST CONTAINER to keep a freestanding heap tidy; knock four 1.2–1.5 metres (4–5 feet) posts into the ground, forming a square that's at least 90cm (3 feet) by 90cm (3 feet) – anything smaller won't heat up enough. Nail planks or wire netting all round to enclose it and stop compost material falling out; make sure the front can be easily removed to extract the finished compost in due course. Fork the soil over at the base to loosen it and improve drainage.

START ADDING SUITABLE COMPOST INGREDIENTS; mix them together, if possible, to avoid concentrations of materials such as lawn mowings, and for every 15cm (6 inch) deep layer, sprinkle on a little soil or fresh animal manure to stop green waste drying out and act as a 'compost starter' by adding beneficial bacteria that help the other ingredients rot down.

SPREAD NEW COMPOST INGREDIENTS out so the top of the heap stays fairly flat, and firm each new layer down as much as you can. If the new compost ingredients are dry, damp them with the hose to help the rotting process begin.

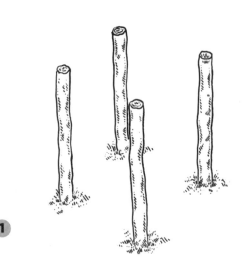

①

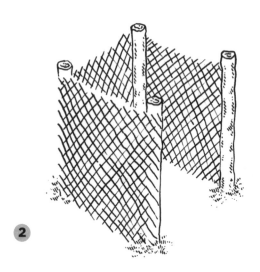

②

WHEN YOU'VE FILLED THE CONTAINER to the very top, cap it with a 15cm (6 inch) layer of soil and if possible cover the whole heap with an old tarpaulin or sheet to keep the warmth and moisture in and stop the outer layer drying out in the sun or growing weeds.

AFTER THREE MONTHS (summer) or six months (winter), fork the contents out and re-stack it so that the dry or uncomposted material from round the edge of the original heap goes to the bottom and centre of the new heap, while the most crumbly well-rotted material goes over the top and sides. After another three or six months, depending on the time of year, the whole heap will be full of ready-to-use compost that looks brown and crumbly, with few visibly identifiable ingredients. If you're in a hurry for some useable compost, cheat and take the well-rotted stuff to use straight away, then pile fresh compost ingredients on top of the older, unrotted material, dampen, cover and start the ball rolling again.

IF YOU ONLY HAVE SMALL QUANTITIES OF GARDEN rubbish to dispose of, instead of a compost heap use a compost bin with solid sides. It composts green materials faster since it holds the heat and moisture better, and because it works more efficiently you don't need to 'turn' the compost – it rots evenly all the way through.

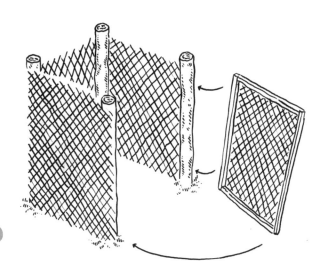

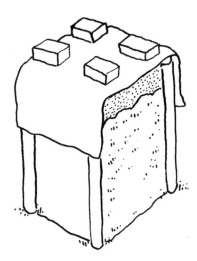

PLANNING A KITCHEN GARDEN

The traditional way to plan a kitchen garden was for ease of management. I'd still recommend it today for anyone with a large kitchen garden or an allotment.

Long-term crops that occupied the same ground for many years were kept quite separate from things that needed replanting annually. Fruit trees were grown in grass in an orchard, which traditionally had livestock grazing underneath to manure the trees and keep the grass short without mowing. Soft fruit was grown in a fruit cage to keep out birds, herbs were grown in a geometric-shaped herb garden with paths for easy access in all weathers, since evergreen kinds might be needed year-round, and asparagus was grown in a bed of its own so it could be given its own yearly cultivation regime without the tall, leafy 'fern' getting in the way of other crops.

Short-term crops that came and went within a year were grown in the veg patch. This was divided into three or four rectangular plots, each used for a particular type of crop that needed the same soil preparation, to make the best use of resources and avoid carry-over or pests or disease peculiar to that type of crop. Each year the crops would be grown in a new patch – a technique known as 'crop rotation'.

Crop rotation is still considered good gardening practice, though we've tended to adapt the original rotation scheme to take account of the sort of crops people want to grow today.

Now that gardens are so much smaller, newer and more intensive means of growing crops are more practical for most people. Deep beds or raised beds allow crops to be grown at closer spacing than usual (about two-thirds the traditional spacing) so you can produce more from a limited space, and there's less work involved because the rows of vegetables soon meet in the middle and cover the ground completely, so they smother out weeds.

If space is very limited, you can restrict yourself to a small salad bed, which still yields useful crops as they are so fast-growing. Even when a tiny plot makes it difficult to practise traditional crop rotation, it still pays to avoid growing the same crop in the same patch of ground in successive years, so simply move crops round every year so you don't grow the same thing in the same patch of ground two years running.

The alternative for small gardens is to grow suitable crops on the patio in growing bags or containers filled with potting compost and simply rotate the soil instead; start each season off with new growing bags or compost, and recycle the used stuff by digging it into the garden as mulch. The most suitable crops for growing in containers include salads and annual herbs, courgettes, climbing beans, early potatoes and outdoor tomatoes, though in a particularly warm sheltered spot (and given a good summer) it's also worth trying a few heat-loving peppers, chillies and aubergines.

GROWING HERBS

Herbs were traditionally grown in a separate garden of their own. This was usually laid out in a geometrical shape, with brick or gravel paths providing easy year-round access to a big concentration of useful medicinal, household and culinary plants. Today the most popular culinary herbs are often grown in tubs on the patio, or as borders round a kitchen garden, to make the best use of limited space. They fall roughly into two camps when it comes to cultivation.

Mediterranean herbs are mainly aromatic, evergreen shrubby perennials; the most popular are rosemary, sage, bay, oregano and thyme, but you can also add lavender. These need plenty of sun, warmth and shelter with well-drained soil, and they are good for patio containers, courtyards and sunny corners. Traditional wisdom always advised not to overfeed them, as fertiliser was thought to encourage strong lush growth that was lacking in the vital oils that give these herbs their flavour and fragrance, but in practice they do need feeding little-and-often, especially when grown in containers.

Traditional British herbs such as tarragon, mint, chives, marjoram, parsley, chervil, sorrel and borage are happiest in more normal garden conditions. They like rich, moisture-retaining soil and a situation with plenty of light and sun for part of the day, but not strong, scorching midday sun.

PROTECTING CROPS WITHOUT CHEMICALS

EVEN GARDENERS who don't think of themselves as 'organic' generally prefer to avoid using chemicals on crops they are going to eat, so instead of spraying, use a combination of organic techniques to protect crops from pests and diseases.

WHEREVER POSSIBLE, CHOOSE VEG varieties that have been bred to resist disease and certain pests (these are identified in seed catalogues and on seed packets).

USE ORGANIC REMEDIES such as copper strips round a raised bed or saucers of beer instead of slug pellets, and cover veg crops with fine, insect-proof netting to protect them from sun, wind and unwanted visitors.

AVOID SPREADING CHEMICALS all round the garden; then all sorts of beneficial insects will start to build up in numbers – they will patrol your crops and help themselves to aphids, small caterpillars or soil pests.

BENEFICIAL INSECTS

Ladybirds: both adults and larvae feed voraciously on aphids all summer; adults are easily recognised but learn to identify the larvae, which look like tiny, charcoal-grey dragons.

Lacewings: pale green insects with large, translucent, gossamer-like wings usually folded over the top of the body (it must be difficult to get them packed back again, which is probably why they don't often take off); they're aphid-eaters, mostly seen in late summer.

Hoverflies: both adults and larvae are large consumers of aphids; adults are also attracted by nectar-rich flowers such as old-fashioned annuals, so grow a row or two in with veg to encourage them to your plot.

Centipedes: rather flattened and chestnut-coloured (as against the largely vegetarian, i.e. plant-damaging, millipede, which is black and tubular); feeds on numerous small soil pests and their larvae, tiny slugs and slugs eggs, also vine weevil larvae.

Spiders: several kinds live in gardens; wolf spiders sunbathe on leaves with two pairs of forelegs extended out in front of the body and chase insect prey; garden spiders make the large webs you see sparkling with dew early on autumn mornings, which trap flying prey, and tiny money spiders are invaluable hunters of aphids.

Black beetles: several kinds live in gardens and feed on small soil pests such as cabbage root fly, young vine weevil larvae, slugs eggs, etc., so they are invaluable; use old-fashioned tarred felt collars around brassica stems to encourage friendly beetles to stay where you want them to work and to prevent cabbage root flies laying their eggs.

Earwigs: disliked by exhibitors of dahlias and chrysanthemums since they'll nip holes in petals, but very useful for clearing up greenfly.

Wasps: more valuable to gardens than you might think, since in late spring and for much of summer they remove masses of small green caterpillars and aphids to take back to their nests to feed their own larvae; it's not till late summer, when worker wasps stop being fed sticky secretions back at the nest, that they turn elsewhere in search of sticky soft drinks, fruit and sweet food, earning themselves a bad name.

Some of the herbs in this group are perennials that die down each winter, including mint, chives and tarragon. These can be planted in spring or summer. Dig up and divide them every few years, and move mint to a new patch of ground every two years as it is so 'greedy' it quickly exhausts the ground. Planting it in a sunken bottomless bucket will restrict its rampant spread. Others are either annuals or are treated as such for convenience; they include marjoram, chervil, parsley, sorrel and borage. With these, you'll need to sow a new batch each spring, or buy pot-grown plants from a garden centre. All of the traditional British herbs need to be watered in dry summers to keep them fresh and leafy, and when grown in containers they also need regular liquid feeding.

Nowadays several more unusual or exotic herbs are also proving popular, and these are best treated individually. Leaf coriander is an annual, grown in the same way as parsley, in pots on a kitchen windowsill indoors, or outside in patio tubs or a herb garden in summer. Scented-leaved pelargoniums need growing in the same way as normal zonal pelargoniums – in pots, which can be put outside in summer but need bringing inside for winter since they aren't frost-hardy. A huge range of varieties is available from specialist nurseries, with scents that range from pine to peppermint, citrus, apple, and rose – they are brilliant as natural air fresheners, can be used in potpourri, in the bath, and a few are good for baking in cakes. Basil (which now includes various exotic forms such as lemon basil, purple-leaved basil, etc.) is a tad delicate and does best in pots on a kitchen windowsill. If you do grow it outside, choose a sheltered patio tub during a fine summer. Genovese basil and the large lettuce-leaved basil are the two recommended for making pesto sauce.

CROP ROTATION

...

THIS IS A MODIFIED FORM of the traditional four-course rotation, designed to suit the sort of crops modern gardeners want to grow.

DIVIDE THE PATCH INTO FOUR PLOTS, treat each one to its own special cultural routine and move the crops on to the next plot the following year.

PLOT 1: GREEDY CROPS

Soil preparation: well-rotted organic matter plus general fertiliser.

Crops: follow early potatoes with outdoor tomatoes, courgettes, pumpkins. Sow salads in any gaps.

Routine care: after planting, weed once or twice (earth up potatoes as the young shoots emerge) until crops cover the ground, then the dense foliage will smother out annual weeds. Add more general feed and a scattering of chicken manure pellets before planting summer crops (tomatoes, courgettes, etc.) and use high-potash liquid tomato feed for tomatoes (also courgettes and pumpkins for best results).

Benefit: the dense potato foliage creates heavy shade that smothers out germinating weed seeds, which is why potatoes are well known for 'cleaning' the ground, leaving it relatively weed-free for the next crop.

PLOT 2: PEAS AND BEANS

Soil preparation: well-rotted organic matter plus general fertiliser.

Crop: peas, mangetouts, sugar or snap peas, runner beans, broad beans, French beans, beans for drying for winter use.

Routine care: put up a framework of rustic poles or canes for beans to grow up, and use netting or twiggy pea sticks to support peas. Make several sowings over the season to keep yourself continuously supplied; sow early varieties in pots under cover and transplant, then sow later batches directly into shallow drills where you want them to crop, and for a late crop to be picked in autumn, sow early varieties of peas and dwarf French beans in July, or sow in early August and cover the crops with cloches in autumn. After pea and bean plants have finished cropping, cut the plants down leaving the roots in the ground. Use any vacant space in the plot for fast-growing summer and autumn salads, and follow with overwintering onion sets planted in October.

Benefit: peas and beans feed the next crop; the plants 'fix' nitrogen from the air via bacteria living in nodules on their roots which break down, releasing it into the soil.

PLOT 3: BRASSICAS

Soil preparation: lime (but no organic matter – the two antagonise each other so must always be applied separately; lime also 'locks up' fertiliser to some extent so it's a waste of money to use it with lime).

Crop: any members of the cabbage family, including Brussels sprouts, calabrese, sprouting broccoli, swedes and kohl rabi (which, though a root crop, belongs to the brassica tribe).

Routine care: sow seeds in an especially well-prepared seedbed in March, April, May according to variety (see instructions on the back of the seed packet) then thin out seedlings to an inch apart and after another few weeks when they've become strong young plants, transplant them to their cropping positions at the correct spacing. The exception is swedes, which need sowing in May, then thinning – don't transplant.

Benefit: brassica plants use up the nitrogen left in the ground by the legumes grown last year, and the lime helps avoid club root disease, besides keeping the pH of the soil at the right level for growing vegetables, when it's used once in four years.

PLOT 4: ROOT CROPS

Soil preparation: general fertiliser only, no organic matter.

Root crops: carrots, onions, onion sets, shallots, beetroot, parsnips, celeriac, leeks, spring onions. For large exhibition onions, keen exhibitors use lots of manure, too.

Routine care: sow in April; transplant leeks for best results, but sow other root crops (except celeriac) where you want them to grow as they don't transplant well. For late crops, sow early carrot varieties and baby beetroot in July. Sow overwintering spring onions in September, for picking next spring. Sow celeriac in March/April indoors, prick out seedlings into small pots and plant outside in mid-May.

Benefit: by following brassicas that don't have organic matter added to the soil and which take a lot of nitrogen out of the ground, conditions are made ideal for sowing root crops which tend to grow 'fanged' or deformed, if there's too much nitrogen or fresh organic matter in the ground.

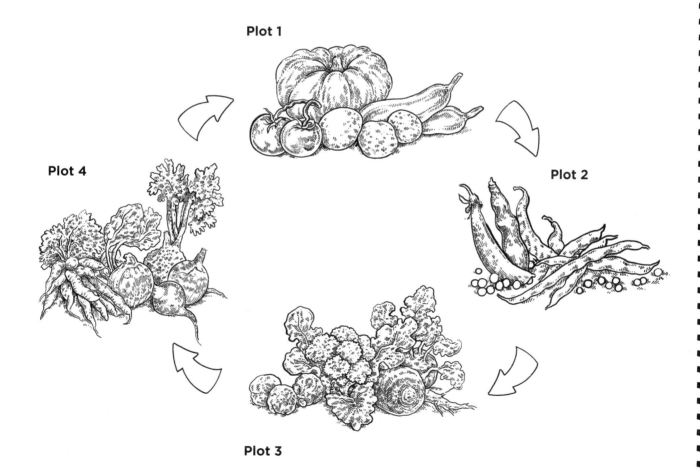

Plot 1

Plot 2

Plot 3

Plot 4

GROWING CUT FLOWERS IN THE VEG PATCH

COTTAGERS FROM VICTORIAN TIMES ONWARDS often grew a few rows of flowers for cutting in their veg patch to sell at the garden gate to make 'pin money'. Today the veg patch is a good place to grow sweet peas or other annual flowers when you don't want to risk ruining flower borders that are 'on show' from the house.

PREPARE THE SOIL WELL; work in lots of well-rotted organic matter, and shortly before sowing or planting, rake in a dressing of general fertiliser such as blood, fish and bone meal.

SOW HARDY ANNUALS IN ROWS where they are to grow, and thin the seedlings out to a few inches apart when they are big enough to handle. Good kinds include calendula marigolds, larkspur and cornflower.

SWEET PEAS, ALTHOUGH HARDY ANNUALS, have large seeds often stolen by mice or pigeons when sown straight into the garden, so they are usually sown in pots in a cold frame in November (for the earliest flowers) or March/April for later summer blooms.

HALF-HARDY ANNUALS NEED TO BE SOWN in March or April on warm windowsills indoors; prick the seedlings out into trays when they are big enough to handle and grow them on at 10–15°C (50–60°F) until planting time, after the last frost, from mid-May onwards. Good kinds for cutting include statice, cosmos, stocks and zinnia.

DAHLIAS ARE VERY GOOD CUT FLOWERS but are not frost-hardy; plant dormant tubers in late April or early May, or plant rooted cuttings from mid to late May – they'll form tubers by the autumn. Dig the tubers up in autumn after the first frost blackens the foliage; cut the stems down to about 10cm (4 inches) above the tops of the tubers. After drying off thoroughly, store the tubers in nets or stacking trays in a frost-free shed for the winter, before replanting them again the following year.

GROW YOUR OWN LIQUID FEEDS

LIQUID COMFREY

Grow Russian comfrey, and in summer, when growth is at its maximum, cut the stems and press them down tightly into a plastic dustbin or similar large watertight container, packing it to the top, then add water to the rim. Put the lid on and leave for at least four to six weeks. When the leaves have turned black and are well decomposed, remove the decaying plant material and use the liquid (be warned – it looks dirty and smells foul) diluted to about one-part to six or eight of water, as a high-potash feed for tomatoes, courgettes and pumpkins.

LIQUID NETTLES

Follow the same method only using freshly cut nettles. This makes a high-nitrogen feed that's good for leafy veg and salads. Dilute it in the same way.

MANURE 'TEA'

Fill a hessian sack or an old plastic, mesh-net onion bag from the greengrocer's with well-rotted manure, and place in a dustbin, then fill to the brim with water. After six weeks, lift out the sack and dilute the liquid manure in the same way as for liquid comfrey. This is a useful general-purpose liquid feed for 'greedy' plants all round the garden, especially rhubarb, brassicas, courgettes and pumpkins, but it's also good in the flower garden for roses and clematis.

Note: It's not a good idea to use any of these on plants growing in pots or other containers, since you can't be sure of the dilution rate in the way that you can when using bottled feeds and following the instructions.

GROWING FRUIT

Fruit trees (apples, pears, plums, cherries) are traditionally grown as large standard trees, with a trunk topped by branches that radiate out all round forming a crown, but increasingly they are being grown on dwarfing rootstocks to keep them compact and trained into more space-saving forms to suit smaller modern gardens.

Apples and pears are often grown as single cordons; these are merely straight trunks about 1.8–2.4m (6–8ft) long with short twiggy 'spurs' growing out along their length that bear the fruit. Cordons can be upright or inclined – grown at an angle of 45 degrees to the ground, which allows you to grow a longer trunk and yet still be able to pick its entire length without a ladder. Spaced 45 cm (18in) apart and supported by posts and two rows of horizontal wires, a row of cordon trees makes a very pretty and productive 'fruiting hedge'.

Horizontal cordons are also available; known as step-over trees, they are ideal for edging a path or a border. Espalier-trained trees look like an upright trunk with two or three tiers of horizontal 'arms' growing out from each side of it to make a flat tree, which can be grown against a south-facing wall or fence. This is the best way to grow the fussier varieties of pears, which need more warmth to develop fully and ripen reliably in our climate, but one or two espalier-trained fruit trees supported by a row of posts and horizontal wires makes a productive and decorative way to screen off a veg patch from the ornamental part of the garden. You may occasionally find cordon-trained plums or cherries in the catalogues of specialist fruit nurseries, but they aren't often seen in garden centres. It's more usual to grow these fruits as fans against a south-facing wall. (The sour-cooking 'Morello' cherry is one of the few fruits that thrives on a north-facing wall.)

More exotic, and unusual, fruit trees are also being cultivated thanks to the newfound interest in kitchen-gardening; nowadays people are trying nectarines, peaches and apricots, which are especially successful grown as fan-trained specimens against a south-facing wall. (Apricots are the most reliable of the three when you don't have a sheltered garden; in the south of England they'll even produce ripe fruit when grown as freestanding trees as long as you choose a warm, sunny, sheltered spot.) Where space is really short, go for genetically dwarf versions sold as 'patio peaches' or 'patio nectarines'. These are ultra-compact and extremely slow-growing miniature trees, ideal for growing throughout their lives in large pots or tubs, yet they bear full-sized fruit.

If you are buying fruit trees by post from specialist nurseries which issue annual catalogues, they are usually sent out with bare roots (to save postage and production costs) and despatched in winter. They need planting straight away, but if that's not possible, 'heel them in' temporarily to keep the roots moist until you have time to plant them properly. Pot-grown fruit trees are available all year round from garden centres and some nurseries; though the choice is far more limited, you can plant them at any time of year – even when they are in flower and fruit – but they'll need to be kept well watered for all of their first summer.

Since trees will stay put for many years, it pays to prepare the ground very well before planting. Dig a hole about twice the size of the pot, or three times the size of the root system of a bare-root tree. Work a good bucketful of well-rotted compost or manure into the bottom and mix in a handful of blood, fish and bone meal. Knock a strong stake into one side of the hole to support the trunk after the tree has been planted. It will need to protrude from the ground as far as the lowest branch of the tree. If you're planting a bare-root tree, spread the roots out well in the bottom of the hole and use a mixture of topsoil and well-rotted compost to fill the hole, firming the soil gently with your foot as you go.

If planting from a pot, gently bang the container down to loosen the plant and lift it out. If the rootball is packed solid with tightly coiled roots, carefully ease a few of the larger ones loose from the mass so they can spread out into the surrounding soil once they've been planted instead of staying stuck in their rootball. (If this happens, the tree doesn't 'take off'.) Use improved topsoil to fill the gap between the rootball and the sides of the planting hole, and again firm down gently. After planting, secure the tree to the stake using two proprietary tree ties – one 15cm (6in) above the

ground and the other about 2½cm (1in) from the top of the stake.

Since most fruit trees are grown on dwarfing rootstocks, they must be staked for life. For the first year after planting, keep fruit trees well watered any time the ground starts to dry out, and don't expect much – or indeed any – crop in the first year. It usually takes two or three years for fruit trees to get into their stride. Check the ties regularly to be sure they aren't constricting the trunk.

Soft fruit, which includes strawberries, fruit bushes such as gooseberries and blackcurrants, and cane fruit such as raspberries and blackberries, are sold in pots at nurseries and garden centres all year round, or in winter as bare-root plants by mail order from the catalogues of specialist firms. It's usual to plant soft fruit in rows inside a fruit cage, or else at one end of the veg patch.

Prepare the soil as you would for a vegetable garden, by digging in plenty of well-rotted manure or garden compost over the whole area, and raking in general-purpose fertiliser, then plant straight into the chosen positions. No staking is needed, but cane fruit (blackberries, raspberries, etc) need a row of posts with two or three strong horizontal wires stretched between them for support. (The exception is autumn-fruiting raspberries, which don't need supporting because they don't grow as tall as the usual summer fruiters.)

Strawberries are normally planted in beds of their own, or grown in large tubs on a patio, since they are relatively compact but also need replacing every four years, as old plants aren't very productive. (Save a few of the strongest runners each summer to replace an entire row and save the cost of buying new plants.) Rhubarb is usually grown in a bed of its own – or more often an odd corner somewhere in the garden – for convenience. It enjoys rich but well-drained soil.

Soft fruit such as strawberries, gooseberries, plums and blackberries are easy to grow and taste delicious plucked from the plants, still warm from the sun.

STRAWBERRIES

Strawberry plants have a useful working life of roughly four years, after which they need replacing. It's easy to raise your own replacements by pegging down a few strong, healthy 'runners' produced by older plants in summer into small pots of potting compost sunk into the ground around them. Do this is in August and you'll have sturdy young plants to plant out the following spring. Dig up and dispose of old plants, and refresh the soil with well-rotted organic matter and some general fertiliser such as blood, fish and bone before replanting. Don't propagate diseased or unhealthy-looking strawberry plants – if they don't look good, buy new runners or pot-grown young plants to start a fresh row. Virus-infected plants (identifiable by their distorted or yellow-mottled leaves) will produce fewer fruits.

HEDGE VEG

Victorian farm labourers started selling their surplus veg, eggs and honey at the garden gate to raise 'pin money' to buy things they couldn't grow or make for themselves, and in time they began growing cut flowers such as dahlias especially to raise a little extra spending money. When I was a lad the tradition of garden gate sales was still going strong; when you drove through a small village or past a lone farm out in the country, there'd always be a homemade stall that looked as if it had been knocked together from old bits of second-hand timber bearing an array of homegrown produce with a handwritten price list and an honesty box for the money. Maybe it's a sign of the times but you don't see so many garden gate sales in mainland Britain today, but the tradition still continues at a cracking pace over in the Channel Islands, where they're known as 'hedge veg'.

AFTERCARE OF FRUIT

After planting and staking, water new fruit trees and bushes in well and give them a good mulch to seal in the moisture. Each year in spring, top up the mulch with a fresh 2½–5cm (1–2in) layer of well-rotted organic matter after applying a generous sprinkling of general-purpose fertiliser.

Water newly planted fruit during dry spells, and if there's a long, dry summer, even after the plants are well established, be prepared to water soft fruit bushes, fruit canes and trained fruit trees on dwarfing rootstocks while they are carrying a crop, or the fruit may be shed prematurely before it has had a chance to ripen.

Fruit trees, bushes and canes need regular pruning. Each type of fruit and all the various trained forms have their own particular set of pruning requirements (look them up in an illustrated pruning guide, or keep the instructions on the back of the label that comes with the plants when you buy them). Pruning will either need doing in summer, straight after the fruit has all been picked, or in midwinter.

Summer pruning is mostly done for cordon fruit and espaliers – each 'arm' is treated like an individual cordon. To prune these, cut this year's shoots back to a couple of buds from their base, or two leaves beyond a developing fruit. Summer-fruiting raspberries, also blackberries and their relatives, are all pruned by cutting back the stems that carried this year's crop shortly after you've picked the last of it, then the young unfruited canes are tied in to the supports ready for fruiting next year. (Autumn-fruiting raspberries are treated differently; all the stems are cut down to just a couple of inches above ground level in February each year.)

Winter pruning is used for standard fruit trees. With these, simply thin out branches that rub, cross or are overcrowded, and remove what horticultural students know of as 'the three Ds': dead, diseased or damaged wood. It's much the same for freestanding soft fruit bushes, except the aim in pruning these is to remove older stems that have carried a crop or two, leaving younger stems that will crop well in future.

Stone fruit (peaches, nectarines, apricots, plums and cherries) shouldn't be pruned in winter as they are at risk from silver leaf disease, so it's advisable to buy well-shaped trees with regularly spaced branches in the first place and then leave them alone (if you simply must cut something out, do it in early summer). If the tree is grown as a fan, rub out unwanted shoots while they are fat buds and you can do so without making an open wound where airborne infection can enter.

HEDGEROW FRUIT

Old cottagers traditionally grew several suitable species of fruit in the mixed hedge round their garden, where they provided a useful crop without making any work or taking up space. Good fruit for growing this way include sloes, bullaces, damsons and greengages, crab apples, brambles, elderberries and even rosehips, all of which had several culinary uses from jams and jellies, puddings and pies, to country wines. Apart from damsons and greengages, most hedgerow fruit would not have been deliberately planted; plants usually grew naturally from seeds dropped by birds. Crab apples usually grew up from pips in discarded apple cores (these days you often see apple trees in the countryside where they've grown from cores thrown out of windows of passing cars). Today, a deliberately planted mixed country hedge containing fruit and berries makes a good wildlife resource, even if you don't harvest the fruit to use yourself.

GROW YOUR OWN FIREWOOD

Most country gardens will generate a small amount of waste wood that's suitable for burning on an open heath or in a wood-burning stove. Fruit trees need regular pruning, and even ornamental trees sometimes need crown lifting (removing lower branches to make it easier to mow and walk underneath) or crown thinning (thinning out the main branches to reduce shade). And once in a while a whole tree needs taking down when it grows too big, or you need to make room for other things. Don't waste them by putting them on a bonfire.

Instead cut them into suitable lengths to fit comfortably into your hearth or the interior of your wood-burning stove, then stack them to 'season' so they become fit to use as fuel. (See page 170. Use only hardwoods; conifer trees produce a lot of tarry materials that build up quickly inside the chimney.)

It's not only thick branches and whole trunks that are worth saving. Small twigs, such as those shed regularly underneath birches, make good kindling for lighting the fire, and dry fruit and vine prunings are also excellent for starting barbecues. They are all so much more pleasant-smelling and eco-friendly than petro-chemical firelighters.

But when there's space to plant a few trees especially, or you have a small patch of woodland, then it's very feasible to grow and harvest your own crop of firewood. Unless you have several acres, you won't be self-sufficient in central heating, but every little helps – and there are all sorts of other uses for woodland by-products, such as bean poles (usually hazel), posts (such as sweet chestnut) and peasticks (birch and hazel). You can even earmark a particularly handsome stump or 'character' log to bring indoors on Christmas Eve as a Yule log.

GOOD LOGS TO GROW AT HOME, FOR BURNING IN GRATES AND WOOD-BURNING STOVES

Ash: one of the best logs for burning, and unusual in that it can be burnt 'green', without the need to season it first. The logs have light brown bark with green striation.

Hazel: not a classic log, and probably not one you'd buy from a log merchant, but good for growing at home since the fast-growing tree takes kindly to being coppiced, which produces a regular supply of slim logs of an ideal size for wood-burning stoves (leave them to season for a year first), also long straight poles suitable for using as bean poles. The twiggy smaller stems and tops of longer poles make good pea sticks. Once established, hazel can be cut every 10–15 years (more often if being harvested smaller for bean poles, etc).

Birch: good-looking logs that burn fairly quickly but can be burnt when only partly seasoned, often ready six months after cutting. Trees take roughly 25 years to reach harvestable size, but many of those planted in gardens are cut down when they grow too big, so this puts them to good use.

Apple and pear: not planted specifically for producing logs, but when you have to cut down an old tree it yields good-quality logs for burning, which yield fragrant smoke. Season for at least one year first.

Hawthorn: good to burn when you have to remove a tree from a hedgerow, the narrow trunks are easy to cut up and produce small but solid logs. Season for a year.

SEASONING LOGS

. . .

BOTH HOMEGROWN WOOD and any logs that you buy need to be 'seasoned' before they are fit to burn. This is because freshly cut wood contains a good deal of sap and resins that prevent the wood burning well or yielding maximum heat, but they also cause deposits that build up inside the chimney where they can eventually create a fire risk and can block the narrow steel chimney liner used with wood-burning stoves.

STACK LOGS AFTER THEY'VE BEEN CUT to a suitable length for your fireplace or stove. Slim branches can simply be cut to length, but whole trunks and thick branches need to be split, which helps them burn more readily.

CHOOSE AN AIRY, OPEN PLACE that's reasonably well sheltered from rain – some people stack logs against a wall, or they'll build a wooden structure that has a roof with open or slatted sides backing onto a wall or outbuilding. Make sure log stacks are well supported at each end, as logs shift slightly as they dry out and a stack can collapse, especially if it's nudged by passing garden machinery or people.

IT'S A GOOD IDEA TO STACK WOOD that'll be ready to use fairly soon, such as ash or birch, separately from logs of beech or oak, which need to be left much longer. Most logs need to stand for a year; beech and oak need two years to season since their wood is so dense.

YOU CAN TELL WHEN LOGS ARE PROPERLY seasoned since they crack, producing a pattern like spokes radiating out from the centre, and they also feel far lighter than freshly cut logs. If you prefer a more scientific approach, you can test logs by pressing a commercial damp meter (the sort surveyors use on walls or woodwork) up against them; on properly seasoned wood it should register 'low', or below 30 per cent moisture.

BUYING LOGS

...

OAK AND BEECH LOGS are the best value for money as the wood is very dense, so they burn longer and more slowly than other kinds, yet they put out more heat. However, they take two years to season properly, so you need plenty of storage space to stack them.

BIRCH AND ASH are good for starting a fire in the first place as they burn fast, and they can be burnt from as little as six months old. A lot of people buy nothing but birch or ash as they are easily available and don't need to be stored for long before they are fit to use, so less storage space is needed.

EVEN IF YOU BUY LOGS described as 'well seasoned', you may still need to stack them for a while before they dry out enough – it's advisable to order logs in spring or early summer to use the following winter.

WHEN BUYING LOGS, FIND OUT in advance what size they are. For a wood-burning stove you'll need shorter logs than most people could accept for burning in an open hearth; it's worth specifying that you want them for a stove when ordering.

LONGER AND THICKER LOGS take longer to burn once they've got going, and they're capable of keeping an open fire going overnight. Really huge slabs of tree trunk are only suitable for burning in a large inglenook.

IN THE PAST READY-CUT FIREWOOD was sold by the cord, which was 128 cubic feet. (Imagine a solid stack measuring 1½ x 1½ x 1½ metres high (5 x 5 x 5 feet) – that's just a little short of a cord.) Today logs are mostly sold by the trailer or truck-load, meaning the back of a pick-up truck. Since the size is by no means standard, it's worth having a look at a delivery first; word of mouth is the best way of finding a good supplier.

FOR SMALL-SCALE USERS, plastic sacks filled with cut logs are sold in garage forecourts, garden centres and at country general stores.

IF YOU WANT TO ECONOMISE, you may sometimes be able to buy whole logs and cut and split them yourself for rather less than the price of ready-cut logs. You may also be able to make agreements with farmers, other gardeners, or parish councils, etc., to obtain fallen tree branches or remove dead trees (with suitable insurance), doing the job of clearance for free in return for the timber. However, you can't just help yourself.

BURNING WASTE TIMBER, INCLUDING OLD PALLETS, old fencing slats and the like, is false economy since, like conifer wood, the chemicals they contain can tar-up your chimney and cause blockages that are expensive to rectify, besides stinking out your neighbourhood when you burn them.

THE WILD GARDEN

CHAPTER 4

A lot of people think a wild garden is just a patch of ground that's left to run wild, but nothing could be further from the truth. It's more like your very own miniature wildlife reserve, but one that's been designed with looks as well as habitats in mind. A real wild garden is properly managed to provide a series of wildlife facilities; it looks natural – not too manicured – but it's not overgrown. Easy to create? Well, no, but with the right approach it can be one of the most rewarding forms of cultivation.

Wild gardens are fashionable, eco-friendly and low-maintenance; they tick all the boxes for a lot of busy, 'green' modern families, and for anyone with young children a wild garden is fun, entertaining and educational, too. But you don't need a meadow, or huge garden for this – don't underestimate the value of even small 'natural-style' gardens to wildlife. Between them they help to make up for the increasing loss of natural habitat out in the countryside (even a tiny wildlife area within a conventional small garden makes a significant difference). This has shrunk due to intensive agriculture and the demands of modern life, and as a result, millions of acres of land have been turned over to concrete or bricks and mortar. Today, gardens contain significantly higher populations of hedgehogs, newts and other amphibians similar to those you would expect to find in the countryside.

You can pick-and-mix from a selection of typical wild garden features and choose the ones that most appeal to you or that can be incorporated easily into the space you have. These include long, shaggy grass, native species of trees, shrubs and wildflowers, a mixed country hedge, a wildlife pond, or a 'loggery' or 'stumpery' of dead wood landscaped with wildflowers. If you don't want to go quite so wild you could legitimately include borders of plants loved by butterflies and bees, bird-feeding stations and 'bramble thickets' made from species roses with bee-friendly single flowers and rosehips for the birds. The ultimate goal is to create a haven of biodiversity that houses insects, birds and small mammals, and possibly even amphibians or reptiles, all supported by a wide range of plants that provide a variety of food, shelter and breeding sites for all the various types of wildlife.

Besides the satisfaction of 'doing your bit' for wildlife, there's a huge fringe benefit, too. A lot of wildlife perform useful services in the more cultivated parts of your garden, from pollinating fruit trees to providing ever-present biological control of pests in your veg patch and flowerbeds. So they are well worth encouraging.

If you have a large garden, the natural place to put a wild garden is down the far end of your patch, so the area close to the house stays neat and tidy, with the landscape becoming steadily more 'relaxed' the further away you go. If your garden is surrounded by countryside, woods or farmland, a wild garden is a great way of helping the house merge gently into the landscape instead of standing out like a sore thumb.

Downsized wild features can be slotted into small gardens; simply opt for a shallow watery 'scrape', a mixed wildlife hedge or a wildflower border for more conventional features. You can even create wildlife containers using butterfly and bee plants instead of bedding; they work well even on balconies and roof gardens several storeys up. If you want a totally laid-back, easy-care garden, then it's perfectly possible to turn a whole small garden over to a natural style of planting that looks stunning but needs far less upkeep than normal.

You can start making a wild garden at any time of year, but when you have a fair amount of construction or ground preparation to do (for instance, if you are making a pond or planting hedges), the best time to start is during the winter, any time from October to March, when there's a lull in routine gardening work. The winter is, in any case, the only 'window of opportunity' for planting bare-root plants, which is the way most native trees and shrubs, and many hedging plants, are sold.

GARDENING WITH NATIVE TREES AND SHRUBS

When you want to encourage wildlife to visit, native species provide food such as fruit, seeds and berries, while their foliage and bark harbour insects which are food for birds and other creatures. Some truly wild species also have closely related ornamental versions that are good for wildlife, and some purely decorative garden trees and shrubs look at home in wild surroundings and are worthwhile wildlife resources. However you play it, a few trees and shrubs are of great value; besides food they provide birds with perching, roosting and nesting places, out of the way of predators. Don't worry about giving trees or shrubs the 'right' spacing (after all, self-sown plants don't follow 'rules'), just pack a lot into a small space. Grow three trees in the space of one, with a large shrub underneath and climbers up it – it looks more natural anyway.

BIODIVERSITY

This is the big ecological buzz-word these days. Basically all it means is a wide range of different species of plants, flowers, insects etc., that directly or indirectly support the larger creatures higher up the food chain. Biodiversity is a good thing to build into a wildlife garden as it makes the area part of a larger life-support system that's good for individual species but also – loosely – the health of the whole planet.

STAG BEETLES

If you live in certain parts of the country (mainly London and the South East), then your wild garden may house a very rare creature: the stag beetle.

It's quite unmistakable: a big black beetle (it's the biggest in Britain), over 2.5cm (1 inch) long. The male has a pair of fearsome nippers sticking out at the front, which he uses for fighting with other male stag beetles, which push and shove rather like real rutting stags, rather than nipping as such. The female has a body the same size but without the nippers.

Adult stag beetles only live for a month – you might spot a few flying around on warm evenings any time between June and August – but they don't eat during that time, as their main purpose in life is to find a mate, breed, and then die.

Stag beetles are attracted to dead wood, which they use as a crèche to lay their eggs in; the larvae then feed on the rotting wood for *three years* before emerging as the next generation of adults. This being the case, you are most likely to find stag beetles in heavily wooded gardens or in a garden within a wooded area, especially if it's a bit neglected. Unfortunately, modern forestry and woodland management tends to remove fallen trees so there's little or no rotting wood for these and other beetles to feed on, which is probably the main reason for the decline in their numbers. A loggery, however, provides just the right conditions.

GOOD NATIVE TREES AND SHRUBS
FOR WILD GARDENS
...

1 Birch (*Betula pendula*): slender, upright, deciduous tree growing to 10 metres (30 feet) with small, heart-shaped, pale lime-green leaves forming a light canopy that allows other plants to grow underneath, and conspicuous, shining white bark patterned with black streaks and triangular or diamond-shaped patches. In mature trees the bark peels off in horizontal strips. Birch was one of the original trees to colonise much of Britain after the Ice Age; it is very rugged and tolerant of poor soil and exposed conditions. Birch twigs were once used to beat miscreants to drive out evil sprits, and the process continued as a punishment known as 'birching' until relatively recently.

2 Wayfaring tree (*Viburnum lantana*): large deciduous shrub growing to 5 metres (15 feet); the big, heart-shaped leaves have white felty undersides and are arranged in pairs that grow opposite each other along the branches. The stems are tipped with elder-like, tightly packed domes of small white flowers in May/June, followed by clusters of red berries which ripen to black in late summer/early autumn.

3 Hazel (*Corylus avellana*); medium-sized deciduous tree growing to 10 metres (30 feet) with long, yellow, 'lamb's tail' catkins dangling from bare branches in February, followed by large, rough, heart-shaped leaves, and hazelnuts in autumn, which are eaten by squirrels, jays, mice and sometimes pheasants.

Hazel is a traditional tree of managed woodlands, which were coppiced (see page 180) to provide flexible poles for wattle and daub panels in medieval house construction, and hurdles – temporary fences for enclosing livestock (see pages 231–233) . Nowadays they are handy as a source of bean poles and pea sticks in country gardens. Hazel leaves are one of several food sources for green shield bugs.

4 Blackthorn (*Prunus spinosa*): small, bushy, deciduous tree growing to 4 metres (12 feet), whose densely packed prickly stems and branches are popular as safe nesting sites for birds. It is good for early blossom; the large bunches of small white flowers wreathe the bare branches in March. Blackthorn blossom often coincides with a period of bitterly cold easterly winds, giving rise to the name 'blackthorn winter' for a cold spring. The fruit, known as sloes, are small (1cm/½ inch), round and ripen to blue-black in autumn, and are traditionally picked by country people for making sloe gin. The leaves are the food plant for caterpillars of the brown hairstreak butterfly. A few more decorative garden varieties are available, including *Prunus spinosa* 'Rosea', which has pink flowers, and 'Purpurea' with purple leaves, but avoid any of the double-flowered forms in a wild garden as they won't bear fruit.

5 Holly (*Ilex aquifolium*): slow-growing evergreen growing to 10 metres (30 feet) with prickly leaves and red berries ripening around Christmas time, later turning soft so they can be eaten by birds. Self-sown plants often arrive as seed deposited through animal or bird droppings; dig up small seedlings carefully and pot them up to transplant later wherever you want them to grow. Hollies are good for exposed situations or poor soil, but dislike soil that stays wet; one or two trees look good growing up through a country-style hedge. Caterpillars of the holly blue butterfly feed on holly flower buds in spring.

6 Dogwood (*Cornus sanguinea*): named 'dogwood' because the straight stems were cut by medieval butchers to use as skewers which were called 'dogs' at the time. Deciduous shrub growing to 3 metres (10 feet) with deeply veined leaves arranged in pairs growing opposite each other along the branches. The young stems are bright red and show up well in winter after the leaves have fallen. Inconspicuous greenish white flowers in June attract insects, and are followed by clusters of black berries ripening between August and September. Grows on downland and other areas of chalky soil, and hosts caterpillars of the green hairstreak butterfly.

7 Wild cherry (*Prunus avium*): handsome and potentially large and fast-growing deciduous tree growing to 10 metres (30 feet), with rich, brown, semi-shiny bark that peels slightly in horizontal strips. White blossom in April appears on bare branches, followed by small red cherries in July which birds enjoy (we can also use them as sour cherries for culinary purposes). In autumn the leaves take on red tints. Wild cherry is a useful timber tree, used for wood-turning and furniture-making.

8 Guelder rose (*Viburnum opulus*): large deciduous shrub growing to 4 metres (12 feet) with rather maple-like leaves arranged opposite each other in pairs. The stems are each tipped by a head of greenish-white flowers rather like those of a lacecap hydrangea – a flat circle of small fertile florets surrounded by a collar of larger, showier, infertile flowers with petals. These are followed by clusters of soft red berries in autumn, which birds love, and often attract flocks of whitethroats stocking up for their long migration. The leaves then turn dull red before falling. A good shrub for wet or boggy situations. The cultivated form with double flowers, known as the snowball tree, looks showier but lacks berries.

9 Rowan or Mountain Ash (*Sorbus aucuparia*): medium to large deciduous tree growing to 11 metres (35 feet), tolerant of poor soils and windy sites, with compound ladder-like leaves. The clusters of pale cream flowers in May are followed by bold bunches of bright red berries, which ripen in late summer in a hot dry season, or early to mid autumn in a 'normal' year. Birds love them.

10 Elder (*Sambucus nigra*): large, craggy-looking deciduous shrub or tree, potentially growing to 10 metres (30 feet) but usually very much smaller. It has compound leaves arranged in pairs opposite each other along shoots tipped with large, flat clusters of elderflower (traditionally used to make elderflower champagne, see page 116) and later large, drooping bunches of berries that ripen to a deep, rich purple-black, and are eaten by birds or traditionally harvested for elderberry wine.

Self-sown plants are almost a weed in many country gardens, where birds drop the seeds after eating elderberries in surrounding hedgerows; dig up seedlings and transplant to a wild garden area. Self-sown trees often push up through a country hedge, which is perhaps the best place to grow them.

COPPICING

Coppicing has been carried out as a means of managing woodlands for many centuries. Hazel and sweet chestnut trees have traditionally been the favourites for coppicing, though at one time other species, including oaks, were also treated this way. The idea of coppicing is to cut down a growing tree to a stump, which then regenerates producing several long, straight shoots instead of a single trunk. The process can be repeated regularly every seven to fifteen years, and continued almost indefinitely. It does the trees no harm at all, in fact quite the reverse; coppiced trees are some of the oldest still alive today.

Coppicing was originally carried out to produce long, straight poles used in medieval house construction (thick poles were used as supporting uprights and roof timbers, and thinner stems were used for the wattle-and-daub wall panels). Coppiced stems also provided fencing and firewood; the thin trimmings were trussed into sheaf-like bundles called faggots that fuelled medieval bakers' ovens. Sweet chestnut is still coppiced to provide certain types of fencing materials today.

From a wildlife point of view, coppicing is good practice because it lets light into areas that would otherwise become increasingly shady as the canopy of branches met overhead and cut out the sun. By letting light back into the woodland, all sorts of wildflowers that have been 'dormant' are able to emerge and carpet the copse floor. A flush of wild orchids often occurs in ancient copses a year or two after they've been cut, but all sorts of wildflowers pop up shortly after coppicing and gradually disappear again over the next ten years, as the canopy thickens, cutting out more light.

At home, you don't need your own woodland to make good use of the old art of coppicing; it can also be done to one or two individual trees or shrubs in a wild garden to keep them a convenient size. If you have several suitable species (hazel is particularly useful) and cut them in rotation, you'll always have a home-grown supply of bean poles, pea sticks and small logs for firewood or for making a 'loggery', and you'll maintain the light shade that provides a great woodland habitat for wildflowers and all the creatures that rely on them. But many other native trees and shrubs respond well too – birch and Guelder rose, for instance, and coppicing can also be used to control and enhance some of the strong decorative shrubs used in wild gardens, such as ornamental elders, willows, dogwoods and buddleia.

COPPICING WITH CARE

Coppicing or even hard cutting-back is not a technique to use for most decorative garden trees and shrubs. It can often kill them. If you cut grafted trees or shrubs down hard you'll eliminate the named variety and leave only the rootstock behind, which grows strongly but isn't half so decorative. Hard cutting-back also 'forces' trees and shrubs to go vegetative and they'll usually stop flowering for several years afterwards. It's not a technique to use in your decorative garden to make big shrubs fit a small space – it often proves the truth in the old saying 'growth follows the knife'.

HOW TO COPPICE A TREE

...

COPPICING IS DONE IN WINTER, between leaf fall in autumn and bud burst in spring, when the trees are bare and dormant. An established tree with a single trunk first has to be cut down to a stump 15–30cm (6–12 inches) above ground level, and then in the following years several strong shoots grow up from the stump. When they are thick enough for the job they are needed for, after 7–15 years, these poles are ready for harvesting, which again is done in winter.

USE A PRUNING SAW to cut off all the stems to within a few inches of the 'stool' (as the stump is now known). Stack the poles and leave them to season for the winter, then trim the thicker pieces to length to use all round the garden as rustic fencing, for beanpoles (2.2 metres/7 feet is ideal) or for staking perennials and dahlias (1½ metres/5 feet). When you are trimming poles, save the twiggy tops to use as pea sticks (which need to be 1½–2 metres/5–6 feet long). Tie them in bundles with string for easy handling and prop them up against a shed wall to dry out; they usually last a couple of seasons before turning brittle.

THE SHORTEST BITS, well dried out and stored in plastic sacks, make good kindling for starting barbecues, open fires and wood-burning stoves.

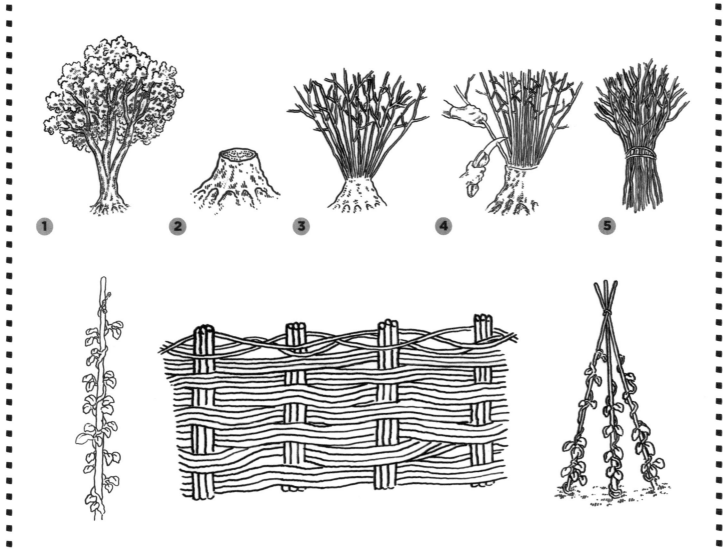

MAKING A STUMPERY OR LOGGERY

• • •

A STUMPERY IS A GREAT wildlife feature. Think of it as a wild rockery, but made from dead tree stumps instead of rocks. Stumperies were once popular in grand Victorian gardens; they were created on a huge scale by setting dead stumps artistically in a mound with soil packed in between them, and used to provide a naturalistic setting in which to grow a collection of those great Victorian favourites, ferns.

TODAY A LOGGERY MAKES A GOOD alternative for a wildlife garden created on a small scale, and its main purpose is to make a habitat for wildlife. As the name suggests, a loggery is simply a stack of logs (the small ones sold in bags at garages for firewood are fine), with some soil packed in between them to 'cement' them together. Add dead autumn leaves, bracken or sticks too, which will create pockets of varied habitats inside, and plant it with ferns, wildflowers or ivy to create a more natural look.

ALL SORTS OF SMALL CREATURES WILL soon move in to the vacant nooks and crannies within the logs. You might have a hibernating hedgehog and the odd field mouse or family of shrews, possibly even a weasel, but the main residents will be beetles and 'creepy crawlies' such as centipedes, which help to maintain the natural balance of a wild garden. Learn to love your creepy-crawlies – they are a valuable link in the food chain and also a good indicator of the overall health of a garden.

WILDLIFE HEDGES

A good way to make the best use of limited space, at the same time as increasing your garden's biodiversity, is by growing a mixture of native species in a row as a wildlife hedge. It can be kept fairly tidy, given just one clip per year to keep it roughly in shape and a suitable size, but it doesn't have to look too suburban – you can allow one or two trees to grow up above the hedge line and add a few climbers so it resembles the picturesque hedgerows you see lining ancient country lanes and byways. Take a trip to Devon and admire the wonderful hedgebanks there – they are every bit as spectacular as an herbaceous border and far more useful to wildlife.

PARENT BUGS (*Elasmucha grisea*)

If you grow birch, look out for an unusual species of shield bug called the parent bug, which lives and feeds on the plant's leaves. (It is also sometimes found on brambles.) The bugs are flat, shield-shaped and a dull grey-brown or yellowish-brown. What makes this species remarkable is that it is one of the few insects that cares for its eggs and young, which it stands over protectively.

PLANTS FOR TRADITIONAL COUNTRY LANE HEDGEROWS
...

1 Field maple (*Acer campestre*): rarely seen as a full-grown tree, but popular for hedging in the southern half of England. An attractive maple with small, typically maple-shaped, light-green leaves growing in pairs opposite each other along the stems; the foliage turns an attractive shade of amber each autumn. Small, inconspicuous, lime-green flowers grow in loose clusters, followed by bunches of small, neat winged keys. Two- or three-year-old stems have corky outgrowths. The timber is 'birds eye maple', which forms the veneers in some antique furniture and was used for making violins, and it's still popular with woodturners for making bowls.

2 Hawthorn (*Crataegus monogyna*): probably the favourite species for hedging fields of livestock in much of the country, ever since the Enclosures Acts of the eighteenth century, when the patchwork of fields that characterise today's countryside was created. If you see rows of tall hawthorn trees growing alongside lanes, they are usually what's left of old hedgerows that have become overgrown. Today, thorn or 'quick' hedges (as hawthorn is often locally known) are often planted round country gardens or wild areas, with a few individual trees left unclipped to stand out above the hedge-line; it is only these, and not close-clipped hedges, that bear the flowers and berries that are so valuable to wildlife. The red berries (known as 'haws') are late to ripen and persist for much of the winter; they are some of the last to be eaten by birds. The dense, prickly branches provide good nesting sites and cover for birds, and the foliage is host to numerous species of caterpillars while the flowers are visited by many kinds of insects. Hawthorn is home to the hawthorn shield bug (*Acanthosoma haemorrhoidale*), which is shaped like the shield carried in battle by a knight-of-old, but about a centimetre (half an inch) long and half that width, in dull green with red trim forming the shape of a triangle in the middle of its back. It feeds on the leaves and haws of hawthorn, but it is also sometimes found on other trees.

3 Wild privet (*Ligustrum vulgare*): semi-evergreen shrub which loses a lot of its leaves in a very cold or windy winter. It was used as formal hedging in Elizabethan gardens, but in early Victorian times it was superseded by a more reliably evergreen Japanese privet (*Ligustrum ovalifolium*) which fast became the popular kind for suburban garden boundaries and is still used today. The native species has the narrower leaf of the two. Privet has short spikes of fragrant white flowers in July, followed by black berries which ripen in the autumn. It is a food plant of the privet hawkmoth.

4 Dog rose (*Rosa canina*): the name is nothing to do with dogs; 'dog' was the medieval term for something inferior or worthless. The common wild hedgerow rose has prickly stems whose downwardly arched thorns are used as grappling hooks for clawing their way up through branches of other plants; the leaves are compound, with five leaflets. The flat flowers are single, pale pink, and are followed by small oval hips that ripen to orange-red.

5 Bramble, wild blackberry (*Rubus fruticosus*): a large, fast-growing, untidy, sprawling shrubby plant that climbs using its hooked spines to clamber over other plants, often appearing out of the tops and sides of hedgerows. The flowers are produced in clusters at the tips of the shoots for much of the summer and may be white, pale or fairly bright pink, followed by fruits that turn from green to red and finally ripen to black in September. Though often considered a pest, due to its habit of spreading by self-rooting stems and from seed, brambles host a huge range of wildlife: several kinds of butterfly feed on the nectar, and many caterpillars feed on the leaves, while birds, small rodents and foxes feed on the berries. Rabbits often make burrows beneath bramble thickets to ensure safety from predators.

6 Ivy (*Hedera helix*): an evergreen climber that rambles through the base of a hedge, or climbs up trunks of trees growing up above the hedge-line, and forms thickets of foliage in the crown. It is one of the food plants for caterpillars of the holly blue butterfly. (Holly Blues produce two generations each year, one feeding on ivy flower buds in autumn and the other on holly flower buds in spring.) The clusters of small, greenish ivy flowers open in late autumn and are rich in nectar, which attracts small flies that wrens feed on. The berries ripen from green to black in late winter and persist in early spring, providing late food for birds. The dense foliage of ivy is a popular nesting place for small birds. If allowed to roam unchecked into the canopy of trees it can kill them, but poses no threat if its territory is restricted to the trunk. It is not a parasite, merely an opportunist.

7 White bryony (*Bryonia dioica*): a widespread and strange-looking hedgerow wildflower that dies down in winter and rapidly grows back in summer to cover large areas of a hedge. The long, weak, pale green stems climb using wiry green tendrils that are tightly coiled like springs, and cling tightly round any twig that they touch. The leaves are rather sparse, small and fingered with five lobes. Bryony has small and rather inconspicuous greenish-white flowers from June to September, shortly followed by small berries that ripen from green through yellow and orange to red. Even after the plant has died off in winter, the berries remain hanging like beads on the dead thread-like remains of the stems. All parts of the plant are poisonous, but particularly the berries.

8 Woodbine, wild honeysuckle (*Lonicera periclymenum*): a large climber growing to 6 metres (20 feet) which twines clockwise round branches and trunks. It also sends out stems along the ground to reach new uprights to increase its territory; these often take root as they run. The exotic-looking, highly fragrant flowers appear from June to September; these are whorls of amber and white tubes that flare out at the tips, and are followed by small clusters of red berries that birds love. Honeysuckle is one of the first plants to come into leaf in spring.

9 Wild hop (*Humulus lupulus*): the wild ancestor of the hops grown for beer-making. It's a large climber, growing up to 6 metres (20 feet) with tiny hooks all along the long, slender stems which allow it to scramble up and over a hedgerow; hop stems twine round in a clockwise direction when they encounter an upright trunk, bare branch or pole. Hop plants have elegant, three-lobed, light-green leaves which in July and August are joined by insignificant greeny-yellow flowers, followed by the familiar clusters of papery green fruiting heads at the end of the summer. The whole plant dies down each winter and re-grows from the root next spring. A wide range of insects visit the flowers for nectar, and several caterpillars feed on the leaves.

10 Traveller's Joy (*Clematis vitalba*): wild clematis is a large, woody climber growing to 10 metres (30 feet) with insignificant greenish-cream flowers from July to August followed in late summer and autumn by the distinctive, fluffy seedheads that are its best feature. Like garden clematis, Traveller's Joy clings by twining its leafstalks round the twigs of supporting plants, enabling it to scramble over a hedge and up into low trees. It is a reliable indicator of chalky (alkaline) soil.

11 Hedge bindweed (*Calystegia sepium*): heartily loathed by gardeners, but in a wild garden hedge bindweed looks lovely, with its heart-shaped leaves and huge white trumpet flowers (which stay open on moonlit nights), but the best reason to grow it is that the flowers attract the *enormous* convolvulus hawkmoths. It grows from an entanglement of white roots that have resulted in the common name of 'devil's guts'.

GARDENING WITH WILDFLOWERS

Wildflowers are easy to accommodate in a wild garden without any conventional beds or borders, as they are usually happiest naturalised in grass. They can be scattered throughout a wildflower lawn or meadow, grown in drifts under trees, at the base of a hedge, or alongside a ditch or pond.

Most kinds are generally easy to grow as long as you match the plant to the growing conditions. Some, such as primroses and lady's smock, need damp soil, light shade and short grass, while others, particularly traditional hay meadow species, are happier in dryish conditions and taller grass. But the secret of growing wildflowers successfully is quite the reverse of what's advised for cultivated parts of the garden. With wildflowers, you *don't* use fertiliser and *don't* dead-head. Native plants need to self-seed to maintain thriving colonies, and if they are fed or grown in rich conditions they grow uncharacteristically lush and may not flower well.

INTRODUCING WILDFLOWERS

The best way to get wildflowers established is to let them arrive on their own. Seeds are distributed for free by the wind, shed by birds in their droppings, or introduced on the coats of animals. That way you are certain of obtaining species that thrive in the local growing conditions, and since they are self-sown they'll form a strong, wide-ranging root system so the young plants look after themselves without needing to be watered or tended. It's simply a matter of leaving them alone. You don't even need to thin them out, as a mixture of dense clumps and thinly scattered plants mixed with other species looks truly natural. The downside is that the sort of species that turn up for free tend to be the more common, unexciting kinds, and amongst them will be ones that you may not want to accommodate at all – the kind that need weeding out.

The best way to introduce new species that don't 'do-it-themselves' is by putting in a few clumps of young plants so they'll self-seed and spread. You can raise wildflowers yourself from seed, or buy them – as young plants, 'plugs', or flowering-sized plants in larger pots. Don't imagine that you can just scatter wildflower seeds over your lawn and turn it into a meadow. The established grass and lawn weed tapestry will quickly overpower the seedling plants and you'll have wasted your money (see page 188).

Planting large pot-grown plants gets you off to the quickest start, as the plants should flower and set seed in their first summer. Since you'll only buy a few large plants, it pays to group them in the centres of key places you intend to colonise. Treat them in much the same way as any (cultivated) plants you'd put into the garden. Loosen the soil with a fork, work in a bit of organic matter to improve the soil (but no feed) and keep new plants watered in dry spells until they are growing well. After the plants have flowered, leave them to set seed; their self-sown offspring are somehow better at taking care of themselves than those sown from a packet and will slowly keep the colony going from then on, always assuming you've given them the right place and conditions.

HOW TO RAISE WILDFLOWERS FROM SEED

...

AS A GENERAL RULE, wildflower seeds are best sown in autumn. In the wild, seeds of all species would be shed as soon as they are ripe and spend varying lengths of time on the ground before coming up when conditions are suitable. Be guided by the instructions on the back of individual packets if you want to be accurate about it.

FIRST FILL SUITABLE CONTAINERS with multi-purpose compost (this has low levels of nutrients, ideal for wildflowers). If you are sowing individual varieties, it's best to use a separate pot for each species of wildflower, as they'll all germinate and grow at different rates, so it makes them far easier to deal with later. If sowing a mixed packet of wildflower seeds, use a large tray and sow very thinly so there's room for slow-germinating species to push up through the faster-growing kinds. After filling the containers with compost, tap them down gently to consolidate the growing medium slightly, otherwise firm it very lightly using a presser – perhaps the bottom of a clean flowerpot. Sprinkle the seeds thinly over the surface of the compost and cover them with a very thin layer of horticultural vermiculite (for tiny seeds) or pea-sized shingle (for larger seeds). The idea is just to hold the seeds down so they won't blow away or be washed away by rain or watering, at the same time as letting some light reach them, since a lot of wildflowers need light to germinate.

LABEL EACH CONTAINER, then water carefully by standing the pots in a few inches of water for long enough to allow moisture to soak right up through the compost. You can usually tell when enough water has been absorbed since the surface of the compost changes colour slightly, but also well-watered pots feel far heavier than dry ones when you lift them.

ALLOW EXCESS WATER TO DRAIN OUT, then stand the pots in a safe place where they won't be knocked or blown over. A cold frame or cloche is handy, otherwise park them in a car port with a clear roof or a large enclosed porch where they'll have plenty of light but protection from drying wind, heavy rain and strong direct sun. If you don't have suitable facilities, simply slip the pots inside a large loose polythene bag and stand them outside in semi-shade. Don't worry about cold since most wildflower seeds need a short chilly spell to trigger them into growth.

WHEN THE FIRST FEW SEEDLINGS have germinated, start to acclimatise them gradually to the open air by making several holes in the polythene bag or ventilating the cloche on fine days so they don't grow leggy and weak. Remove the cover entirely as soon as weather conditions permit, but be ready to protect them from bad weather and any forecast frosts, and take regular precautions against pests, particularly slugs and snails. (If you happen to have space in a cold greenhouse or unheated conservatory, those are great places for bringing on seedlings early in spring while the weather is uncertain, but move them outside as soon as it's safe to do so.)

SEVERAL WEEKS LATER, when the seedlings are becoming nicely established, they'll need more space. Prick them out into seed trays or 'cells' (these are multiple trays made up of lots of small individual containers rather like yoghurt pots joined together) or small pots, again using multipurpose compost, and give them a week or two of intensive care while they rehabilitate.

FROM THEN ON THEY'LL NEED regular watering and protection from pests, birds and bad weather, but don't mollycoddle them since it's essential they grow tough rather than soft. Wildflowers that germinate in spring should be big enough to plant out later the same year. Any pots of seeds that don't come up till later that season, or even the following year, are best given some slight protection over the winter. (Some species *do* take a long time to come up, so don't rush to throw away pots where nothing seems to have happened.)

HOW TO PLANT PLUGS

Plugs or young plants are a better choice when you need a lot of plants to dot randomly over a large area of grass to create a wildflower lawn or meadow. Start in early spring, around March or April, depending on the weather. (It mustn't be too cold or dry – wait for mild, rainy conditions when new plants will 'take off' faster and become established better.) Cut the grass as short as possible, then start planting your young wildflowers straight away – before the grass has a chance to grow again. Use a trowel to remove 'divots' of turf. Work a handful or two of well-rotted garden compost or multipurpose compost from a bag into the planting hole, as it helps young plants root-in, especially when they've been raised in potting compost. Plant two or three 'plugs' or young plants in each planting station, then gently press the grass back round them. Do the entire area all at once.

When you have a large area to plant, or you want to save money and do it yourself, raising wildflowers from seed is the most economical (and satisfying) way of obtaining plants. It's very easy to do because you simply treat them as you would any hardy annual or perennial garden plants that you'd normally raise from seed. You don't need a greenhouse or any heat – just raise them in pots or trays in a sheltered corner outdoors somewhere it'll be convenient to look after them. And when they are big enough to plant out, treat them exactly as those you've bought as plugs or young plants.

'NUISANCE' WILDFLOWERS

Not all wildflowers are the small, pretty kind; some of the large, invasive perennial kinds that give gardeners nightmares are amongst the most valuable to a wide range of wildlife. But even they can be incorporated into a wildlife garden, with care.

Large spreading climbers, stragglers and creepers such as white bryony, wild hops, bindweed and bramble are best grown through a mixed country-style hedge; otherwise let them ramble along a post and wire fence, which they'll soon cover attractively. Alternatively, train them over a large or tall branching tree stump, bank or soil mound, where they make more of a feature and are easier to control.

Thistles provide seedheads that attract flocks of finches, especially goldfinches, in autumn and early winter, but some of the more distinctive members of this family are useful without being a nuisance. Go for spear thistle (*Cirsium vulgare*), which is good for growing in grass, or milk thistle (*Silybum marianum*) and carline thistle (*Carlina vulgaris*), both of which are good for hot, sunny, dry spots, or marsh thistle (*Cirsium palustre*), which needs moist ground.

Nettles are invaluable butterfly plants since they house and feed several batches of caterpillars of four or five different species of butterfly over the summer. But alas one or two nettles aren't enough; you need a reasonably sized clump to do any real good. You can, however, stop nettles from spreading by sinking a vertical barrier of thick polythene all round the area allocated for your nettle bed. It needs to go down 30–45cm (12–15 inches) deep and stand out an inch or two above ground level to stop wandering rhizomes climbing over. Nettles need rich, fertile soil, so a spot close to a compost heap suits them well. At the end of the season, cut the tops down and add them to the compost to enrich it, but don't recycle the roots.

WILDFLOWER LAWNS AND MEADOWS

Wildflower lawns and meadows both contain a mixture of grass species and wildflowers; the big difference between them is the height. A wildflower lawn is relatively short, rather like a slightly longer and shaggier version of a domestic lawn with low wildflowers such as speedwell, cowslips, violets and primrose-sized plants growing in it. A meadow is taller, more like an old-fashioned hayfield, filled with long grass and tall-growing wildflowers such as ox-eye daisy, or traditional cornfield species such as poppy and corn cockle. In practice, the two need slightly different management, and while a wildflower lawn can be walked on and treated like a normal area of rough grass, a haymeadow must be *kept off* because if people push through tall grasses they'll leave a trail of bashed-down foliage in their wake, and it never springs back.

But there are other alternatives to creating solid areas of wildflower lawn or meadow that may prove more practical for some gardens. One is to use a mower to cut short paths through your wildflower lawn or meadow to walk round on. This idea is used by a lot of stately homes with large grounds to keep maintenance costs to a minimum, at the same time as providing reasonable access for visitors. Another possibility is to leave attractively sculpted 'drifts' of long grass within an area of short grass, or simply to mow round existing bumps and hollows in the ground, turning them into natural grassy features instead of hard-to-mow problem spots. Both methods are good ways to add detail to an otherwise plain area of grass without making extra work. But you can go one better by using drifts of wildflowers – either a mixture, or tall, showy individual species such as ox-eye daisy, cow parsley or rosebay willowherb – in particular places. By mowing round these areas, these striking plants stand out sharply against their background of short grass.

Both wildflower lawns and meadows look stunning combined with other naturalistic features such as willow sculptures, a thatched summerhouse, chunks of gnarled driftwood or a rustic bench to make a basically simple feature into a more upmarket, 'designer' wild garden.

MAKING A WILDFLOWER LAWN

If you already have an existing lawn or an area of rough grass, it's very easy to convert it to a wildflower lawn. You hardly need to do anything at all to make the transformation. (But, as I've said, don't take the 'obvious' route and sprinkle packets of wildflower seed about over existing turf – it doesn't work because the dense grass means the seeds can't get going.)

Simply stop using fertilisers or indeed any other lawn products (particularly weedkillers), and a mixture of desirable wildflowers will usually appear all on their own over the next season or two. First on the scene will be the 'usual suspects' that keen lawn fanatics try to eliminate: daisies, plantains, dandelions, trefoils and white clover. In a wildflower lawn they are welcome, within reason. (If too many appear, or they come up in large patches that start to swamp everything else, dig out the superfluous ones by hand so they don't take over.) Prettier species such as speedwell, violets, self-heal, and possibly birds-foot trefoil, take a bit longer to turn up. You may need to introduce anything you particularly fancy, such as cowslips or primroses, as young plants or 'plugs' in spring. Do so by removing a divot of turf and planting them while the grass is short. But it's a good idea to plant them in groups, and mark the places with sticks so you can mow round them while they find their feet.

If you're starting with a bare plot, the best way to grow a wildflower lawn is from seed in exactly the same way as a domestic lawn. You can sow in April or September, but September is best as it gives the flowers longer to establish before the grass starts growing strongly, and provides those that need freezing temperatures to trigger germination the impetus they require to grow. Buy enough ornamental ryegrass to allow twenty-eight grams (an ounce) per square yard (0.8 square metres) and choose packets of suitable, low-growing wildflower seeds to mix with it, or buy a ready-made wildflower lawn mixture.

First prepare the area. Dig the ground, level it well, firm it down evenly by trampling all over it with your feet, then rake again and sprinkle the seed mixture all over using a small clenched fist-full per square yard (0.8 square metres). Rake it in lightly if the area is small; if not, leave it alone and it'll still grow. If possible, sow grass seed when you're expecting rain within a couple of days, otherwise you'll have to water it. Wait till the grass is a couple of inches high before giving it its first cut – ideally by hand with shears, as a mower tends to pull a lot of it out, and mow as usual from then on.

Management of a wildflower lawn is very easy since you treat it very much like any area of rough grass. Mow it reasonably regularly, perhaps every two or three weeks throughout the growing season (April to October) and once or twice over the winter, always keeping the blades of the mower raised up as high as they'll go. Most of the flowers pass safely underneath; any that are beheaded will soon be replaced since the main body of the plant won't

have been damaged. Either way, enough plants will be able to set and shed seed that continuity will be maintained. (If you need the lawn to look smarter for a special occasion, simply mow it a bit shorter than usual to behead all the flowers, so it looks entirely grassy for a week or so, then it will soon return to normal.) But do use a grass box or rake up and remove the grass clippings after cutting. That's not just so the 'lawn' looks tidy and you don't bring grass indoors on your feet, but because any wads of dead grass left lying about will stop new growth coming through, and they can smother out delicate, low-spreading wildflowers.

The combination of not feeding *and* removing the grass clippings means that the levels of nutrients in the ground drop, so the grass grows less vigorously and the wildflowers do better. Thus the two soon reach a harmonious natural balance.

CLOVER

If there's one flower a wildflower lawn shouldn't be without, it's white clover.

Clover flowers attract bees, so you'll see many kinds of bumblebees, besides honeybees, visiting the garden to work in the flowers. If you keep your own beehive, white clover makes the most popular 'single flower' honey of all.

A good population of clover also keeps the lawn a lovely rich green colour even during a long, hot, dry spell in summer, since it has far better drought endurance than grass.

Clover also helps to feed the lawn naturally, since the nodules on its roots 'fix' nitrogen from the air and release it slowly into the soil without creating the sudden boost in growth that occurs when gardeners use proprietary feeds on 'posh' lawns.

WILDFLOWER TURF

Nowadays it's also possible to buy wildflower turf. It is too pricy to make an entire wildflower lawn from though, unless money is no object, in which case you can do that very thing.

The best way to use wildflower turf is to insert a few sections of it into existing grass. It is best to do this in spring.

Remove a few strips of turf from all over the existing lawn area to get a good 'spread' of flowers, and fork the soil underneath to loosen it up a bit.

Then fit the pieces of wildflower turf in place and firm them down. Once in, water the turves well to help them knit into the lawn.

Once established, the wildflowers you've introduced will do the rest of the work for you, spreading through the rest of the lawn from self-sown seed.

WILDFLOWERS FOR LAWNS

• • •

1 Dog violet (*Viola riviniana*): small, neat, perennial plants 2–15cm (2–6 inches) high with pale violet flowers that, unlike sweet violet (which in any case is a woodland plant) have no scent. The seedpods of dog violet are similar to those of a pansy or viola, and open out to three tiny pods of mini brown 'peas' arranged in a three-pointed star shape.

2 Bird's foot trefoil (*Lotus corniculatus*): low, spreading perennial 10–25cm (4–10 inches) high forming neat, rounded or slightly domed mats with small, clover-like leaves and flower stems topped by rings of slightly claw-like, yellow pea flowers from June to August. These sometimes have slightly rusty streaks, giving rise to the alternative common name of bacon-and-eggs. Prefers dryish grassland on slightly chalky soils. Several butterflies visit the flowers for nectar and it is host to caterpillars of the green hairstreak.

3 Primrose (*Primula vulgaris*): one of the first wildflowers to bloom – early in March and continuing till May. A small plant with 15cm (6 inch) rosettes of elongated-oval leaves which form a ruff round a loose posy of pale yellow, five-petalled, upward-facing flowers, which grow one per stalk. Prefers slightly moist, shady conditions; good for lawn edges close to hedges or in grass under trees and shrubs.

4 Cowslip (*Primula veris*): leaf rosettes superficially similar to primrose, with slightly longer and tougher leaves. The smaller, nodding, cup-shaped flowers – slightly brighter yellow than the primrose – are carried on longer, stronger stalks (to 23cm/9 inches) with a cluster at the end of each. Prefer a sunnier, drier situation than primroses (especially chalk downland), so are best in an open situation in the centre of a lawn.

5 Self-heal (*Prunella vulgaris*): small, spreading perennial forming low mats of foliage in turf from which arise short, straight stems 5–20cm (2–8 inches) high with paired leaves topped by tight clusters of hooded, lilac-purple flowers. Reputed to have wound-healing properties, and much used by medieval farm labourers and carpenters for treating cuts and gashes.

6 Germander speedwell or bird's eye speedwell (*Veronica chamaedrys*): low, creeping perennial, 10–15cm (4–6 inches) high, with paired leaves having scalloped edges, and small circular flowers made up of four petals with a white eye in the centre, flowering April to July.

7 Lesser trefoil or yellow suckling clover (*Trifolium dubium*): creeping perennial 5–7.5cm (2–3 inches) high, despised as a weed in well-kept lawns, but really quite pretty with low spreading mats of small clover-like leaves studded with tiny yellow 'balls' of flower from May to October. (**Black medick (*Medicago lupulina*)** looks very similar, flowering April to August, but the seedheads turn black when ripe.) Like clover, both medick and trefoil have nitrogen-fixing nodules that help return nutrients to grass, and all three remain a lot greener than grass in dry spells.

8 Harebell (*Campanula rotundifolia*): known in Scotland as bluebells. Delicate-looking plants with narrow, grassy leaves and thin, wiry flower stems 15–30cm (6–12 inches) tall and topped with a few nodding, pale bluebells, from July to September. Thrives in very poor, shallow, dry ground where the grass naturally grows rather weakly.

9 Snake's head fritillary (*Fritillaria meleagris*): a rare wildflower, sometimes available as pot-grown plants in flower at garden centres in spring. Grassy-like plants 20–45cm (8–18 inches) tall bearing large, nodding heads of lantern-shaped, chequer-patterned mauve/purple or creamy white flowers in April and May. Needs damp to moist grassland that's kept shortish in summer. Plant in groups and mow round them until the seeds have shed in late June.

10 White clover (*Trifolium repens*): a short perennial, 2½–15cm (1–6 inches) tall with creeping stems that root as they run along the ground. From these grow the familiar, three-lobed leaves and tiny white pea-flowers arranged in tightly packed spheres on stalks a few inches above leaf-level, from June to September.

TALLER WILDFLOWERS FOR 'DRIFTS' IN A WILDFLOWER LAWN

Cow parsley or Queen Anne's Lace (*Anthriscus sylvestris*): a tall, upright, clump-forming perennial at 60cm–1.2 metres (2–4 feet), with ferny foliage and a froth of flat-topped circular flowerheads made up of many tiny white florets, in flower April to June. Schoolboys used to use the hollow stems as peashooters; the flat flower head often used by red soldier beetles as a mating ground.

Teazel (*Dipsacus fullonum*): a tall, upright, clump-forming perennial to 90cm–1.8 metres (3–6 feet) with paired leaves and prickly stems branching near the top. Each sideshoot is topped with a large, bristly, green head ringed with a frill of tiny pink flowers, which dries out into a hard, almost fir-cone-like seedhead. The plants are very attractive to finches, particularly goldfinches, which feed on the seeds in autumn and early winter. The leaf bases wrap around the stems to form a reservoir for water where birds and insects may drink.

Rosebay willowherb (*Epilobium angustifolium*): a spectacular perennial with tall, 1.2–1.5 metres (4–5 feet) upright stems clad in long, narrow, paired leaves and topped by an elongated pyramidal flowerhead made up of many pinkish-mauve flowers with immature buds at the top. Commonly called 'fireweed' on account of its habit of emerging after fires on railway embankments. Flowers June to September.

MAKING A WILDFLOWER MEADOW

A wildflower meadow can be created in the same way as a wildflower lawn, by introducing young plants of suitable species to an existing grass paddock or area of rough grass in spring while it's short, but it's not ideal. Cultivated grass does not have the diversity of grass species of a proper wildflower meadow. It's also much harder for the flowers to establish themselves since grass in a meadow is left to grow tall, so young wildflowers are quickly swamped and smothered out.

No, the best way to grow a wildflower meadow is from seed sown where the plants are to grow. It's a job I've done twice now, and few tasks are more rewarding, provided you have a little patience. It's just like sowing a garden lawn, but far less preparation is needed. The best time to start is in autumn. Seed can be bought as wildflower meadow mixture (choose a mix that will suit your situation and soil type) or you can buy grass seed and suitable wildflower seeds separately and create your own blend.

First, clear the ground of any scrub, perennial weeds and other rubbish, then fork it over lightly or rotavate it and roughly level it with a rake. There's no need to firm it or fuss too much. Then scatter the seeds; a small handful per square yard (0.8 sq metres) should be enough. I used an old-fashioned seed fiddle the first time I sowed a two-acre meadow. The second time – sowing the same sort of area – it broke and I resorted to the 'bucket and chuck-it' method! I needn't have worried – the results were in fact very similar.

Don't worry about raking over the ground afterwards, but do choose a time when rain is likely to fall within a day or two, so the seeds are watered in. Then just leave them to grow until next spring.

From then on, maintenance of a wildflower meadow is very easy. Cut it twice a year, in spring and autumn. Do the first mow in early spring, cutting the entire meadow down to about 8cm (3in) high. Then leave both grass and wildflowers to grow to their maximum height, flower and set seed, and give it a second cut in the autumn, after all the seeds have been shed. This is vital to allow wildflowers to form stronger colonies and replace any short-lived kinds that have died during the summer.

Naturally, a normal lawnmower won't be able to cope, so you'll either need to use a rotary-line trimmer or a petrol-powered brush cutter, which is similar but uses a rotating metal blade to cut instead of a rotating nylon line. Otherwise hire a rotary scythe, or do the job by hand using the traditional father-time-style implement. There's an art to using a scythe – it needs to be kept razor sharp (buy a sharpening stone to go with it). Swing it rhythmically with the blade parallel to the ground, using a twisting action from the waist – it's good for keeping the figure in trim. It's probably best learnt from a practical demonstration and followed up with lots of practice.

But however you cut the grass, it's important to rake up and collect the 'hay' afterwards. This stops thick wads smothering new growth or clogging the cutting machinery next time round, but it also helps to remove nutrients from the ground, which in turn improves conditions for wildflowers at the same time as keeping the grass from growing too strongly. Long, cut grass is easiest to collect when it's been left to dry out for a few days, then use a traditional wide, wooden hay rake. The dry grass can then be added to your usual compost heap or piled up in a mound in a corner of the meadow and left to heat up naturally, providing breeding sites for grass snakes or hibernating places for insects, etc. during the winter. It can also be used to make hay; in this case turn the cut grass once or twice so it dries evenly, then store it in a dry shed. It won't be such good quality as properly made summer hay, but it's perfectly okay to use as bedding for small pets such as rabbits and guinea pigs.

YELLOW RATTLE

Yellow rattle (*Rhinanthus minor*) is an invaluable wildflower for any meadow and I grow lots of it in mine. It's quite attractive, with upright stems of large yellow 'dead nettle flowers' that contrast nicely with grasses. But its great value is that, being semi-parasitic on grasses, it stunts the growth of its hosts, which gives other wildflowers a far better chance of succeeding, so you achieve a better natural balance between grasses and flowers.

SEED MIXTURES

Garden centres and seed catalogues sell various grass seeds and some wildflowers, both as individual species and as mixtures. But specialist catalogues supply all sorts of mixtures of grasses and wildflowers to suit different situations: damp soil, shady areas, clay or chalk soil, plus butterfly meadow mixes which are ideal for creating conservation areas.

WILDFLOWERS FOR MEADOWS

...

1 Ox-eye daisy (*Leucanthemum vulgare*): tall, upright daisies, 38–75cm (15–30 inches) tall with a solitary, yellow-centred white flower at the tip of each stem, floating several inches above long grasses. Flowers June to August.

2 Knapweed or hardheads (*Centaurea nigra*): a tough, stiff-stemmed, upright, clump-forming, non-prickly perennial 38–60cm (15–24 inches), with long, narrow, lightly toothed leaves and solitary, thistle-like magenta flowers whose petals grow out of a hard knob like a tiny pineapple, one at the tip of each stem. Flowers June to September. **3 Greater knapweed (Centaurea scabiosa)** is similar, but with showier flowers and long, shaggy petals forming a whorl round each 'knob'.

4 White campion (*Silene dioica*): rather upright-growing perennials, 30–75cm (12–30 inches) tall, with pairs of slightly rough, bristly leaves and star-shaped white flowers, each emerging from what looks like a small 'purse' at the tip of the stem, flowering May and June.

5 Scabious: perennials with rather upright wiry stems bearing few slender leaves, each topped by a purplish-blue circular pincushion-like flower (the plant is often known as 'lady's pincushion'), from July to September. Grow **6 Field scabious (*Knautia aravensis*)** in drier conditions, and **7 Devil's bit scabious (*Succisa pratensis*)** in damper areas. Flowers of both species are very attractive to a wide range of butterflies and their foliage feeds and houses several rare species.

8 Meadow buttercup (*Ranunculus acris*): the familiar species that children held under a friend's chin to see if they liked butter (a faint yellow reflection on the skin said 'yes'). A spirited spreader, bordering on the invasive, 30–90cm (1–3 feet), flowering May to September. Don't plant it; it'll find you.

9 Field poppy (*Papaver rhoeas*): a 20–45cm (8–18 inches) annual with fragile, crumpled red flowers all summer, followed by small 'pepperpot' seedheads. The ground needs annual disturbance if it is to come up year after year, or it will fizzle out until cultivations recommence.

10 Wild carrot (*Daucus carota*): a tallish, rather cow-parsley-like perennial growing 30–90cm (1–3 feet) tall, with ferny foliage and upright flower stems topped by large, domed, composite heads made up of lots of tiny white flowers, backed by a distinctive green frill, flowering June to August. Does best on dry to average soil including ground that's sandy or chalky. In some years I have masses; in others not so many.

11 Meadow cranesbill (*Geranium pratense*): a 30–90cm (1–3 feet) perennial with elegant, deeply divided, almost lacy leaves and large, light blue to pale purple flowers, similar in appearance to a hardy cranesbill, to which it is related. Flowers June to September.

12 Clustered bellflower (*Campanula glomerata*): upright flower stems grow from a cluster of leaves at the base of the plant; the flowers are blue, upward-facing bells clustered round the tip of the stem from May to September.

13 Common vetch (*Vicia sativa*): not so common now; a member of the pea family with weak, straggly stems 30cm–1 metre (12–40 inches) tall with small, paired, ladder-like leaves and a pair of pale purplish-pink pea flowers at the tip of each stem from May to September. Lower on the stem you'll see pea-like pods that start green, ripen to brown, then split open to shed seeds.

14 Wild chicory (*Cichorium intybus*): a tall, upright perennial with a loose, shaggy rosette of dandelion-shaped basal leaves, from the centre of which grow the branching flower stems, 30cm–1.2 metres (1–4 feet) high, dotted along their length with showy blue, multi-petalled flowers from July to October. A good butterfly plant. Cultivated chicory is a subspecies.

15 Yellow rattle (*Rhinanthus minor*): an upright-growing perennial, 20–60cm (8–24 inches) tall with pairs of narrow, nettle-like (non-stinging) leaves. Towards the top of the plant large, pale yellow, dead-nettle-like flowers grow from a pale, buff-coloured 'purse', one per leaf axil, from May to August. The ripe seeds make a rattling sound (see page 195).

WILDFLOWER LAWNS AND MEADOWS

WOODLAND WILD GARDENS

Wild gardens don't have to be grassy, open places; any area that's shaded by a light canopy of trees can be turned into a natural-looking woodland garden using a wealth of shade-tolerant wildflowers that wouldn't grow well anywhere else. It's a wonderful way to make use of an area conventional gardeners have always regarded – with good reason – as 'difficult'. And it doesn't matter if the trees are wild species, ornamental garden trees or even street trees growing outside your property that simply cast shade over part of your garden; the conditions they create mimic those of the ideal woodland floor.

But gardening in woodland raises problems you don't find in other situations. The dense canopy of leaves overhead means the ground is plunged into darkness from early summer until autumn, and since the trees take up all the available moisture when they are in full leaf, the soil is also very dry during that time. That's why the great majority of wild woodland flowers are spring species, which complete their annual growth cycle while there's still enough moisture and light. Naturally this means that, in real wild woodland, there isn't much of interest from bluebell time onwards, but at home you can simply add other attractions such as natural sculptures, a loggery or rustic shack. Another good ruse is to open up small clearings for pockets of wildflowers within woodland, or to create wildflower areas round the edges where there's dappled shade. This habitat suits quite a few attractive summer wildflowers and also some butterflies.

MAKING A WOODLAND GARDEN

Real woodland has one big thing going for it that you won't find in most gardens: leaf-mould. When a dense stand of trees sheds its leaves each autumn over centuries, they rot down and a huge depth of rich, fertile leaf mould builds up naturally underneath. Leaf mould is unlike any other kind of soil; it has a uniquely spongy texture that makes it well-drained but moisture-retentive. In winter woodland plants aren't waterlogged so they won't

rot, and in summer when most of them are dormant, their roots, bulbs or tubers won't totally shrivel up.

In gardens, you're unlikely to have a layer of leaf mould covering the ground under trees, but if you have a good source of well-rotted organic matter such as garden compost, manure or mushroom compost, you'll find it helps a lot when you're trying to get new plants established. You won't be able to work it in due to the tree roots that fill the soil, so instead spread a layer several inches deep all over the area that you want to plant.

Keep the layout as natural-looking as possible. For practical reasons as well as for looks, it pays to plant informal 'drifts' of wildflowers between trees and create well-defined paths in between them. Paths can be merely well-trodden soil which will eventually grow a carpet of moss, or you can make a more non-slip finish by spreading bark chippings. For greater effect, outline the paths with long, dead tree trunks or branches, or a row of stones that show up well in the shade.

Plant a woodland garden in two phases. In early autumn, put in spring bulbs such as bluebells since that's when they are dormant and offered for sale. (Snowdrops – *Galanthus nivalis* – are the exception since they hate drying out and prefer to be planted 'in the green' as soon as they have finished flowering in March.)

In spring, plant pot-grown wildflowers as soon as they are available. For best results they'll need a little aftercare. There's usually enough natural rainfall to keep them watered to start with, but it's advisable to water new plants regularly once the surrounding trees start creating competition. You'll also need to remove any weeds that might try to smother them, at least for the first season. But don't do any dead-heading – leave woodland wildflowers to shed their seed naturally, then in autumn just cut down dead stems and have a light tidy-up.

A wild woodland garden isn't entirely free from work. It still needs a little management to keep it in shape. There are always opportunists such as nettles, brambles and unwanted tree seedlings which are quick to colonise any suitable spot, so take regular walks through the area in the growing season and remove any unwanted new arrivals.

Dead trees may need attention to make sure falling trunks or branches can't pose a danger to people or property, but don't rush to tidy away the odd fallen trunk or dead branch when it's safely on the ground since rotting wood provides bed and breakfast for all sorts of beetles. If you like a tidier look, stack up dead wood or turn it into a loggery or stumpery, so it becomes an attractive wildlife feature.

TREE SEEDLINGS

Sycamore trees shed huge quantities of seed every autumn, and their seedlings are notorious garden 'weeds'. Saplings can grow several feet in a single season, and before you know it you have a big tree that takes up a lot of light, water and nutrients and ruins the balance of a woodland garden, so they need taking out. If you catch them early enough the seedlings are quite easy to dig out, but within a year or so they are too well established to get out easily – in this case the best policy is often just to cut them off at ground level and keep cutting them back every time they re-grow, before the new shoots reach more than an inch or two high. In time they'll die off.

Ash tree seedlings can be a similar nuisance and for ease of removal it really does pay to catch them young at the two-leaf seedling stage when removing them is a doddle. Other tree seedlings such as oak, chestnut or hazel (which often arrive as seeds buried by squirrels or jays) may be worth leaving if you have room to allow them to develop, but you shouldn't consider having them close to your house (the golden rule is plant them no closer than their eventual height). But be aware that even as young trees they'll cast a lot more shade than many trees. When you want to grow other plants underneath, trees such as birch and rowan are best, as their canopies cast only very light shade.

WOODLAND WILDFLOWERS RECOGNITION

1 Wood anemone (*Anemone nemorosa*): a short, spreading perennial growing from creeping underground stems and forming dense carpets 5–25cm (2–10 inches) tall, flowering from March to May. Each flower stem bears a ferny frill halfway up and is topped by a single large white bloom that faces upwards when the sun shines on them, but nods and half-closes in the evenings and in shade. When the flowers are over, large foliage appears, growing directly out from the underground stems. Good for clearings and woodlands' edge as, unlike many woodland plants, they need a fair bit of direct sunlight. Humus-rich, well-drained soil is essential.

2 Wood sorrel (*Oxalis acetosella*): a short, spreading perennial growing from creeping underground stems forming carpets 5–13cm (2–5 inches) high, with shamrock-like leaves that fold shut at night, and solitary white, cup-shaped flowers, one per stalk, facing upwards by day and drooping at night. Flowers April to June. For leaf-mould-rich soil in light shade.

3 Bluebell (*Hyacinthoides non-scripta*): a spring bulb whose leaves and flowers emerge at roughly the same time, growing 20–38cm (8–15 inches) high with arched heads of nodding blue flowers held slightly above the wide, grassy foliage for roughly four weeks, sometime between April and June depending on the area and the severity of the winter. Foliage dies down in July. Grows in sun or shade. Plant native bluebells grown from cultivated stock, not wild bulbs, and avoid the Spanish bluebell (*Hyacinthoides hispanica*) as it's a different species which hybridises readily with our native bluebell and creates mongrels that quickly take over and put the native population at risk.

4 Snowdrop (*Galanthus nivalis*): a familiar early spring bulb, 8–20cm (3–8 inches) tall, flowering February–March with nodding green-and-white flowers growing slightly above grassy foliage. Spreads to form large clumps or even carpets when left undisturbed for a long time. Grows in light dappled shade or half sun.

5 Wild daffodil (*Narcissus pseudonarcissus*): the traditional yellow trumpet-style daff that's a semi-miniature 20–30cm (8–12 inches) high, flowering February to early April. Rare in the wild, but sometimes cultivated bulbs are offered for sale.

6 Ramsons or wild garlic (*Allium ursinum*): grows even in heavy shade and forms dense carpets, 30–45cm (12–18 inches) high. The plants have wide leaves with pointed tips liek those of lily of the valley, and typical allium flowers – a loose sphere of small white starry flowers on long stalks radiating out round the tip of a wiry flower stem – from April to late July. Emits a strong smell of garlic when bruised or trodden underfoot.

7 Wild strawberry (*Fragaria vesca*); a perennial plant, 5–20cm (2–8 inches) high, forming numerous small, loose-rosette-shaped plants with three-lobed leaves familiar to anyone who grows cultivated strawberries. Plants spread by runners, with a baby plant at the end of each, covering fair-sized areas. From April to July bears white flowers similar to cultivated strawberries but much smaller, followed by tiny berries about the size of the tip of your smallest finger, which are eaten by a range of woodland birds and animals.

8 Lesser periwinkle (*Vinca minor*): a spreading evergreen with pairs of oval-pointed leaves spaced along low, sprawling stems that root as they run along, forming mats 30–60cm (1–2 feet) deep, studded from March to May with purplish-blue, star-shaped flowers which have a small white ring in the centre of each. Far less invasive than its chunkier relative, the greater periwinkle.

9 Sweet violet (*Viola odorata*): a woodland species forming loose rosettes of heart-shaped leaves, 5–10cm (2–4 inches) high sprinkled with sweetly scented blue-violet to purple flowers from January to April. The seed capsules are roughly round and don't split open until some time after they have dropped to the ground, unlike the similar-looking dog violet (whose seed capsules, held in threes, burst open on the plant).

10 Lesser celandine (*Ranunculus ficaria*): a shade-lover forming low rosettes of small, heart-shaped, glossy leaves that carpet damp areas of woodland with bright yellow flowers from March to May. The leaves die down and disappear in midsummer. Spreads via underground bulbils.

11 Stinking hellebore (*Helleborus foetidus*): a rare wildflower that's more often cultivated in gardens. Finely fingered evergreen foliage grows in airy clumps to 75cm (30 inches) high, with sprays of green, cup-shaped flowers from February to April. Try as I might, I have never been able to discover a pong – even when the leaves are crushed!

12 Red campion (*Silene dioica*): a perennial, 30–90cm (1–3 feet) high with paired leaves along the flowering stems which branch slightly towards the top and bear rich pink, star-shaped flowers growing from a small 'purse' from May to June. Grows in partial sun in clearings and woodland edges.

13 Bugle (*Ajuga reptans*): low, creeping plant with a loose rosette of purplish-flushed oval leaves spreading by runners that root where they land, forming a carpet a few inches deep. The flower stems are upright, 10–20cm (4–8 inches) tall, with pairs of small, oval leaves along them and a loose spike of blue, dead-nettle-like flowers at the top from May to July.

14 Greater stitchwort (*Stellaria holostea*): an untidy light-shade-loving plant, 20–30cm (8–12 inches) tall with weak, spindly stems that largely rely on surrounding plants or grasses for support. Each stem bears long, narrow, paired leaves and is topped by a loose spray of white, star-shaped flowers from April to June.

15 Foxglove (*Digitalis purpurea*): a familiar old favourite for light dappled shade and woodland clearings. Bolt-upright plants, 60cm–1.5 metres (2–5 feet) tall, with a rosette of large, downy, pointed-oval leaves at the base from which emerges a long spike of thimble-shaped mauve-pinkish-purplish flowers with spotted throats. Much visited by bumblebees.

16 Hedge woundwort (*Stachys sylvatica*): upright plants 30–90cm (1–3 feet) high with nettle-like (but non-stinging) leaves arranged in pairs up the flower stem, which is topped by a short spike of small, deep mauve-pink, dead-nettle-like flowers in July and August.

17 Cyclamen or sowbread (*Cyclamen hederifolium*): a rare wildflower that's often grown in gardens. The squat, saucer-shaped tubers grow on, or just above, the surface of the soil with ivy-like leaves, often prettily marked with a faint Paisley pattern, and typical miniature cyclamen flowers in August and September. Self-seeds gently to form small colonies which can in time almost carpet woodland floor in light shade. Pollinated flowers are followed by round seed capsules, whose stems coil like springs, bringing them down to ground level; mice often steal the seeds for their sweet, sticky coating, which helps to spread the species.

18 Herb Robert (*Geranium robertianum*): a wild hardy cranesbill, 15–45cm (6–18 inches) high with wiry, red-tinged stems bearing deeply divided ferny foliage. From June to September the stems are scattered with loose sprays of small but typical hardy cranesbill flowers in pale mauvish-pink, followed by long, beak-like seedheads. In autumn the leaves take on fiery red tints. Grows in light shade, partial shade or sun; the red stems and leaves turn brighter in sun. Some folk love the strong odour when its foliage is bruised, others hate it. I can never make up my mind!

WILDLIFE PONDS

'What's the difference between a wildlife pond and the ordinary sort?' people often ask.

Well, the classic garden pond is specially designed to look decorative and meet the needs of fish rather than wildlife. It is often quite a formal feature with a geometric shape, steep sides and paved edges; it may also have a fountain or water gushing from an urn, a statuette or other ornaments. There'll probably be a few waterlilies and marginal plants, and though birds can usually reach in to the water to take a drink, they can't walk in and out so they can't take a bath. You might find a few frogs and tadpoles, but conditions are not ideal since young froglets can't climb out of the water once they've grown their legs, unless you make a 'bridge' especially for them.

A wildlife pond on the other hand is designed to look natural and it's constructed with wildlife in mind. It has gently sloping edges clad with turf or gravel and pebbles, which lets birds walk in to take a bath, and creatures such as hedgehogs can climb out easily if they fall in. You're far more likely to encourage amphibians such as frogs, toads or newts and a range of aquatic insects, since the facilities will support an entire aquatic food chain. There's often room for a bigger selection of waterside plants. You can still have a few fish if you like, but instead of 'fancy' fish it's best to go for wilder types such as roach or rudd that will feed on mosquito larvae. Water wildlife such as frogs don't mix all that well with fish (fish eat tadpoles, and adult male frogs sometimes 'drown' fish in the breeding season by clasping them tightly and holding their gills shut), so as a general rule it's best to go for one or the other, and cater specially for whichever you've chosen. That said, I chose frogs and newts, but roach arrived on the feet of some passing duck and I now have a busy shoal of them. But that's wildlife – it chooses you, as much as you choose it.

The good news is that a wildlife pond is a lot easier to create and maintain than any formal water feature.

HOW TO MAKE A WILDLIFE POND

•••

MARK OUT THE AREA; it can be roughly round if you like (mine is sort of kidney-shaped), but in a small space a crescent or teardrop shape will give you a larger area of 'beach' round the edges, which increases its value for wildlife. Lay a hosepipe on the ground to outline the proposed shape, then go indoors and see how it looks from an upstairs window. It's easy to 'tweak' the shape or the size at this stage, so take your time. If the hosepipe is cold, run hot water through it to make it more flexible.

STRIP OFF ANY TURF, AND DIG OUT the area for the pond, creating a saucer-shaped depression shelving gently down from the edges to the centre. If you want to keep fish, the centre of the pond needs an area at least 45–60cm (18–24 inches) deep where the water won't freeze solid in winter. But if you don't want fish, it's perfectly acceptable to make a shallower shape, more like a large sunken birdbath. Even so it needs to be at least 30cm (12 inches) deep in the centre, otherwise it'll evaporate to nothing in a dry summer.

SMOOTH THE INSIDE so it's like a shallow bowl, then line the interior, first with special pond 'underlay' to prevent the liner perforating (you can use a 5cm/ 2 inch layer of soft sand if you prefer) and then with a sheet of flexible pond liner. Black butyl – sold at aquatic centres and the pond department of normal garden centres – is best; it might be more expensive than some materials, but it lasts longer than the thick black polythene that's sometimes sold as an economical substitute. Make sure there aren't any holes or the pond will leak.

UNROLL THE LINER OVER THE UNDERLAY in the excavated depression and let it 'relax' into place on a warm sunny day. Slowly trickle water in from a hose so that the weight gently bears the liner down into place. Alternatively, leave the pond over winter so that it fills with rainfall, which is a much better water for plants and aquatic wildlife. When it's full trim the edges of the liner, leaving a good foot overhanging all round the sides. Smooth this out well, and bury the surplus shallowly into soil to hold it down.

NEXT, LANDSCAPE THE SIDES of the pond. Unroll turves so they run down from adjacent lawn and right into the edge of the water. Alternatively, spread gravel and pebbles, plus some larger cobblestones, thinly and evenly over the liner to conceal it and create 'beaches' – some of the stones will slide down into deeper water, which is why the edges need to shelve gently or the pebbles will all end up in the middle of the pond with the edges left bare. If need be, sink some planting baskets filled with stones to create barriers part-way down the slope to stop the gravel

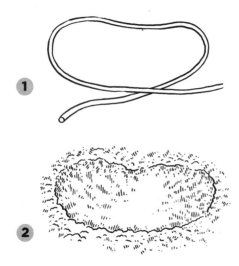

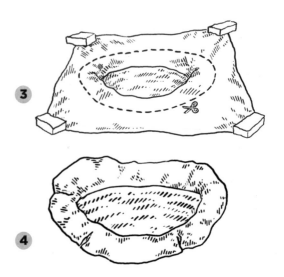

sliding down any deeper. (These can house water plants later, so the effect will look quite natural.)

FOR AN EVEN MORE NATURAL EFFECT you can have *some* turf and *some* areas of shingle 'beach' round the same pond. For decoration, add the odd rock or piece of petrified log, artistically arranged, and use architectural waterside plants such as gunnera or shrubby willows with coloured bark – these look stunning pollarded to save space.

DO THE PLANTING IN SPRING, from late March or early April onwards. Plant 'plugs' of moisture-loving wildflowers such as lady's smock, violets and primroses into the turf, and add banks of waterside perennials such as marsh marigold (*Caltha palustris*) or the much taller purple loosestrife (*Lythrum salicaria*) in the muddy shallows round the edge. Put marginal water plants (the sort that grow in shallow water) such as bog bean (*Menyanthes trifoliata*) in planting baskets filled with gravel or pond-compost. (Don't use garden soil; it contains nutrients which will make the pond water turn green.) If the centre of the pond is 60cm (2 feet) deep you can plant a water hawthorn (*Aponogeton distachyus*) or a dwarf waterlily, otherwise simply float frogbit (*Hydrocharis morsus-ranae*) which has tiny waterlily-like leaves. Unless your pond is more than 10m (30 feet) across, don't be tempted to

plant native wild white waterlily or yellow flag iris (*Iris pseudacorus*) as they are far too big and invasive – they'll quickly take over. But it's quite acceptable to grow pretty cultivated water plants such as golden club (*Orontium aquaticum*) or water irises; they look very natural in this environment and the roots do a great job by removing nutrients from the water and creating a habitat for beneficial micro-organisms.

ONCE THE POND IS ESTABLISHED and the plants have started to grow and cover some surface so there's a bit of shade, wildlife will arrive on their own. Don't try to introduce tadpoles or other creatures; they'll turn up of their own accord when conditions are right. If you want to put a few fish in, introduce some oxygenating weeds. Elodea is often recommended; it is an alien and spreads rather vigorously but it is evergreen, so it works all year round, which other water weeds don't do. If you want to stick to native species, try the water buttercup (*Ranunculus aquatilis*) and water milfoil (*Myriophyllum distichum*).

IF YOU DON'T HAVE FISH and therefore don't need year-round oxygenators, you can use prettier wild plants such as water violet (*Hottonia palustris*), which needs a well-established pond before it 'takes', so don't bother putting it into one that's less than three years old.

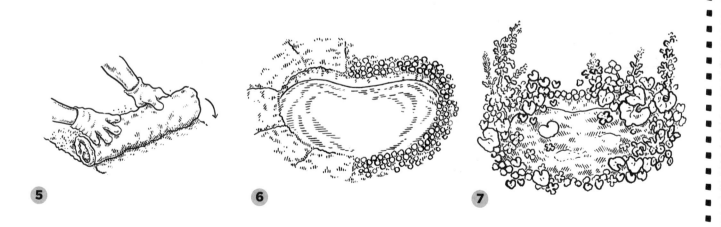

5   6   7

POND MAINTENANCE
・・・

SPRING

IF THE POND TURNS GREEN IN SPRING, as often happens at the start of the season (especially with new ponds), avoid using chemicals to clear the water. Instead, leave it alone. Once the water plants grow, the water will start to clear naturally. The roots absorb nutrients from the water that would otherwise 'feed' algae, and by cleaning and oxygenating the water, plants encourage the microscopic water wildlife to increase in number and get back to work at treating the water after their winter break. If you want to help things along, especially in the first year or two before the natural systems have got up to strength, simply sink a pad of natural untreated chemical-free barley straw into the water; it acts like a housing estate for beneficial micro-organisms.

SPRING IS ALSO THE BEST TIME to introduce new water plants; if you buy small plants cheaply in net pots, repot them into 20–25cm (8–10 inch) planting baskets filled with gravel and sink them slowly into position – on a brick or two at first until they grow and can be lowered further. The planting depth shown on the label when you buy water plants refers to the number of inches of water that the plant likes above the top of its planting basket. Don't put them down too deep or they'll 'drown'.

IF YOU HAVE TADPOLES, there's no need to feed them since a healthy pond will generate its own food. Tadpoles feed on algae at first, and as they grow larger they'll increase their diet to include small water creatures, such as daphnia (water fleas), which arrive all on their own.

LATE SPRING IS THE BEST TIME TO REMOVE, divide and replant any overgrown marginal plants, except waterlilies (which only need dividing when they are seriously overcrowded, and then do so in June) or water irises (which need dividing a few weeks after they finish flowering, or you'll miss out on the show for a season). Again, use gravel, stones or pond compost, not garden soil.

SUMMER

DEAD-HEAD WATERSIDE PLANTS when you don't want them to self-seed, but smaller and less rampant species such as primroses can safely be left to do their own thing.

IF YOU'RE CUTTING GRASS CLOSE TO THE POND, make sure clippings don't go into the water or they'll break down and use up oxygen, besides adding to the layer of silt building up in the bottom.

IF OXYGENATING WATER PLANTS become overgrown, thin them out – simply tug whole handfuls out. Rinse them out in the shallows at the edge of the pond and leave them lying at the edge for a day or two so that water creatures can escape back into the pond. When they are dry, dispose of them on the compost heap – water weeds are packed with nutrients and make a great natural 'starter'.

AUTUMN / WINTER

WHEN WATERSIDE PLANTS START DYING DOWN naturally, cut them back to within an inch or so of ground level. Cut marginal plants growing in the pond down to the water level, and tug out yellow or rotting waterlily leaves. Tidy up grass, wash pebbles if they have gone green, and renew gravel that's 'disappeared' from your beaches.

WHEN YOU DON'T KEEP FISH IN A POND there's no need to cover it with netting in winter, since herons don't have any reason to visit, and covering the water prohibits wildlife from visiting and may even lead to species such as hedgehogs becoming entangled.

SINCE THE ROACH ARE NOW SO WELL established in my pond, I'm quite happy for a heron to take a few, and my greatest delight has been the arrival of a kingfisher – nothing beats the magic moment of that turquoise flash that betrays its presence – and the fact that it did not mind me standing still and watching it from a distance of just six feet came as a wonderful surprise.

THAT SAID, IF THERE ARE BIG TREES NEARBY it's worth covering your pond with netting for a month or so every autumn to stop leaves falling in. Otherwise they'll foul the water and use up all the oxygen; this will kill off fish and aquatic wildlife and turn the water stagnant and smelly.

AFTER A FEW YEARS MOST PONDS start filling up with sediment from decomposed water plants etc., so don't wait until yours fills itself in; wait until all the plants have died down and scoop out some of the silt. Don't clear the pond out completely; leave at least an inch of silt all over the bottom since it houses the beneficial bacteria that help keep the pond clean. There's no need to empty the pond of water to do this, though it's a pretty mucky job – I'd recommend wearing your oldest and tattiest gardening clothes and throwing them away afterwards. In larger ponds a pair of waders is a must.

WILDLIFE POND INHABITANTS
. . .

1 Dragonfly: colourful flying insects that dart low over ponds looking for prey or a place to lay their eggs – they'll only choose ponds that contain some upright-stemmed plants since the larvae will need these to crawl up when they're ready to emerge as the next generation of adults. Dragonfly larvae are ugly-looking monsters that spend up to two years living in the water feeding on tadpoles, fish fry and other small water creatures.

2 Damsel fly: more slender and graceful than dragonflies, usually having an electric blue or shiny red body. They have a similar lifestyle and need similar conditions to their beefier relations. Their wings fold backwards rather than remaining at right angles to their bodies.

3 Slaters: small, grey, woodlouse-like creatures that patrol the sediment on the floor of the pond, feeding on decomposing organic debris. Ugly but useful. They are present all year round. Birds will often dip into a pond to catch them; blackbirds and crows seem especially keen.

4 Freshwater whelks: the common pond snails with pointed shells which feed on algae and decomposing plant remains. They lay eggs on waterweeds and the underside of waterlily leaves – look for one centimetre (half-inch) 'tubes' of jelly with small black dots – which are eaten by fish and other water wildlife.

5 Water fleas (daphnia); the pinhead-sized 'dots' you sometimes see in the shallow edges of mature ponds in warm weather in summer; they live in shoals suspended in the water, milling aimlessly around in short, sharp jerks. They are a popular food for fish, tadpoles and many other water creatures, and their presence is a sign of a healthy pond.

6 Frogs; amphibians which visit the pond in February/early March to breed, the small males pursuing the larger females to mate. Large, cloud-like blobs of frogspawn are left resting among water plants near the surface of the pond shortly afterwards; tadpoles soon hatch and feed on tiny pondlife. By midsummer they've developed back legs and started turning into froglets; the young frogs spend a lot of time in and around the pond for the rest of the season. In winter some frogs hibernate in the mud at the bottom of the pond, while others hide up under piles of dead leaves or rotting plant debris, or in chinks in dry stone walls or log piles; in very cold weather they'll often bury themselves nose-deep in soft mud. Adults appear quickly after a new pond has been built; it's not true that they always return to the pond where they were born, but they'll usually be found somewhere fairly close.

7 Toads: far less common than frogs, but the two can be easily told apart since toads have a warty skin and *crawl* whereas frogs are smooth-skinned and *hop*. Toads only visit water to breed and otherwise remain on land, feeding on slugs, worms, beetles, etc. Toadspawn is laid in long, jelly-like strings draped round water plants, several weeks later than frogspawn. Toadpoles look similar to tadpoles, but wartier.

8 Newts: think of water-loving lizards; adults will 'appear' once a pond has matured for several years if the facilities are suitable. Don't try to introduce them artificially. Newts lay eggs individually in dense waterweeds, the young are tadpole-like, but with prominent, feathery external gills. Adults remain in the pond for the spring then return to land, and the young leave the pond at the end of the summer; they all hibernate for the winter in chinks between stones and similar places. There are four British newt species, but the common newt is by far the most often encountered in garden ponds.

WILDLIFE PONDS **211**

BATS

Wildlife gardens, wildflower meadows and ponds are good features for attracting bats, which swoop low at dusk hunting moths and midges that are in turn attracted to the flowers or the surface of the water. But any kind of garden run on reasonably organic lines will do just as well since they both provide a good source of the bats' natural food.

You can also encourage bats to the garden by planting night-flowering plants that attract moths. One of the very best for this job is the thornapple (*Datura stramonium*) – a strange and exotic looking 50–90cm (20–36in) plant with shiny leaves and large trumpet flowers in white or light lilac that only open at night and emit a haunting fragrance. These are followed by large, round, spiky seed cases similar to those of conkers. (All parts of *datura* are extremely poisonous so it is perhaps best avoided where small children are around.) Another good bat/moth-plant is the old-fashioned tobacco flower (*Nicotiana affinis*). Avoid modern named varieties and go for the plain white species which grows about 90cm (3ft) high and whose gently scented flowers are crumpled by day but open at night.

Moths are also drawn to light, so leave the patio lights or security lights switched on, or set up a few solar lights somewhere that you'll be able to enjoy the flying display from inside the house or the conservatory. (Tip: have a light on outside in the garden, but sit in the dark indoors yourself and keep still so you don't frighten the bats away.)

If bats live in your area, it's also worth putting up bat boxes which they may use to breed, roost or hibernate in. Bat boxes are like bird nest boxes, but instead of the usual entrance hole they have a narrow letterbox-like slot near the base just above a grooved 'landing strip'. Site bat boxes 5m (16ft) up in large mature trees surrounded by plenty of leaves to keep them cool in summer. Bats may sometimes hibernate in vacant bird nest boxes in winter; leave the boxes undisturbed just in case.

It's almost impossible to identify bats by sight, but an electronic bat detector will pick up and slow down their high-pitched squeaks, which are made to echo-locate prey when hunting, and by giving the frequency of the sounds, the gadget enables you to identify the different species. Another good way to discover more about the world of bats is by joining a 'bat walk'. These are held by some nature reserves and large stately gardens on summer nights – especially National Trust estates – who supply a suitably equipped expert.

BUTTERFLIES, BEES AND MOTHS

On a sunny summer's day, there's nothing quite so relaxing as the sound of bees buzzing busily and the sight of butterflies flitting round the flowers. But both are fast becoming endangered species. Out in the countryside their numbers are falling drastically. Experts can't pinpoint exactly what's caused the crisis, though it seems likely to be a combination of factors including loss of habitat due to modern farming methods, climate change, bad summers, wet winters, disease and parasitic mites. It means that butterflies and bees are increasingly reliant on gardens. The rise of organic growing techniques and more natural gardening styles is making our gardens valuable habitats for butterflies and bees, and it's not difficult to make your plot even more insect-friendly.

In the cultivated parts of the garden you can help by increasing the range of flowering plants you grow, particularly single-flowered species and the so-called 'bee plants', which have naturally nectar-rich flowers that adult insects like to visit. Try to include some that flower at different times of year, even in 'difficult' times such as midwinter, so there's always a handy source of nectar for any insect that is out and about. (Bumblebees in particular work far longer hours and over more of the year than the domestic honeybee.) And in a wild garden, plant a range of flowering native trees, shrubs and wildflowers with flowers of different shapes, so there's something to suit as many different types of insects as possible.

Breeding facilities are more of a problem. It's difficult to provide good breeding sites for bees, but a dry grassy bank may attract bumblebees, which have often taken over old mouse holes, while a rather sparse wildflower lawn that's rarely mowed can house solitary bees, which nest in small holes they've burrowed in the ground. For butterflies and moths, the secret is to grow the particular plant (or plants) that acts as a nursery for their caterpillars, and a wild garden is full of opportunities. Grasses are great crèches for caterpillars of a lot of species that don't often appear in 'polite' gardens, although the caterpillars that live on grasses are often small, green and hard to see (and even harder to identify).

A wildflower meadow is a good way to encourage a far wider range of butterflies than usual to visit your patch. Caterpillars that feed on wildflowers and shrubby native plants are usually a lot easier to see and identify; they often bear bold patterns and bright colours – some kinds are hairy, and others display strange behaviour – to put off any lurking potential predators.

Butterflies and bees have been popular with garden wildlife lovers for years, but for people who've taken an interest in garden insect life, the fastest-rising hobby is moths. Though a lot of them are a dull brown/grey there are some more colourful species, and many moths have quaint, archaic sounding names, such as the Hebrew Character and the Coxcomb Prominent, which give them a curiosity value that they might not otherwise seem to have. Although a few moths fly by day or can be spotted resting during daylight hours, the vast majority fly at night, so the way enthusiasts observe them is by attracting them with a light. But to avoid having to sit up for much of the night, a real enthusiast will often use a moth trap and leave it out all night. Otherwise you are most likely to find moth caterpillars, which are usually far more conspicuous than the adults once you know what to look for and which host plants they live on. (For butterfly recognition, see page 270.)

HOW TO TELL BUTTERFLIES FROM MOTHS

It's rather an inexact definition; most people assume that day-flying species are butterflies and night-flying species are moths. But when you look closely, butterflies have small 'knobs' at the ends of each antennae, which are absent in moths – the biggest exception to the 'rule' are the burnet moths (several species of which, to confuse things more, can also be seen out during the day).

MOTH VARIETIES

...

1 Mullein moth: adults are small, a nondescript buff colour and active from May to June, but they're not usually seen – perching on twigs in a tent shape and looking like a bit of dead leaf. The caterpillars are far more visible: white with orange-red heads and orange stripes across the back patterned with straight rows of black dots, found on buddleia or verbascum leaves in June and July. Curiously they usually feed on verbascum leaves in the second year in my garden – when they are coming up to flower.

2 Cinnabar moth: a black, orange and red moth usually perching with folded wings by day though it flies by day and night; the black forewings are outlined with red along the leading edge, with two red blobs on the outer edge, the hindwings are orange outlined in black. The caterpillars are very conspicuous, with bold orange-and-black rings over their entire body; they are usually on ragwort but sometimes on coltsfoot or groundsel. The caterpillars are poisonous so birds and other predators won't eat them.

3 Hummingbird hawkmoth: a day-flying, dusky grey moth showing occasional flashes of pale orange underwings. A summer visitor, seen June–September, it is often mistaken for a small hummingbird as it darts between flowers with a loud humming sound, occasionally stopping to hover and dip its exceptionally long proboscis into fuchsia, honeysuckle, periwinkle, and many other garden flowers. Adults sometimes lay eggs on bedstraw but the species is not thought to succeed in breeding here.

4 Elephant hawkmoth: an easily identified pink and light-khaki night-flying moth, active in June, that quite often turns up in moth traps but is rarely seen otherwise. The light brown caterpillars have a short 'tail' at the rear and two large false eyes at the front; this end of the creature inflates when attacked, enlarging the 'eyes' to scare predators off; they are found on willowherb and bedstraw in July and August.

5 Convolvulus hawkmoth: at 13cm (5 inches), this moth has the largest wingspan of any insect found in Britain. It flies mostly at dusk from July to November, and occurs most in the south-east of England. Adults mostly visit flowers of bindweed, but also honeysuckle, clematis and flowering tobacco. The caterpillars feed on leaves of several convolvulus species including garden morning glory, but are rarely found in this country. It is a migrant, visiting annually from the continent.

6 Deathshead hawkmoth: a very large, brown, night-flying moth with dull orange markings and a scary skull pattern between its 'shoulders'; seen May to October. The large, fat, segmented caterpillars (up to 13cm/5 inches long) are pale lime-green patterned with regular, sloping, light mauve-and-green stripes and a row of dark spots on the sides; the rear segments each have stumpy 'peg legs', and at the far end there's a short 'tail'. They feed on Duke of Argyll's tea-tree (*Lycium barbarum*), but are sometimes spotted in kitchen gardens on potato or tomato foliage, and emit squeaks or clicking sounds when attacked.

7 Privet hawk-moth: a large, brown-marbled, night-flying moth with long, rather narrow and very pointed wings, the body is brown, ringed with pink. Active in June/July but rarely seen. The large, fat, segmented caterpillars are green-patterned with pink and green angled stripes down both sides, the rear segments have 'peg legs' with a short 'tail' at the far end. It's found on privet in July/August.

8 Garden tiger moth: a medium-sized, night-flying moth with brown and cream 'camouflage patterned' forewings with surprising, bright orange hindwings marked with large black blobs, which show up in flight or taking off, but in daytime it sometimes flashes its wings to scare predators from its resting places on tree bark. It is seen in July and August. Its caterpillars are the familiar 'woolly bears' covered with long brown bristles, and can be found on almost any soft-leaved garden plants at almost any time of year.

HOW TO MAKE A MOTH TRAP

. . .

A MOTH TRAP IS THE BEST WAY to find out what is flying round your garden after dark. You can buy a professional moth trap from entomological suppliers (they sometimes advertise in wildlife magazines, especially the quarterly publication sent out to members of Butterfly Conservation), but they have rather hefty price tags. Set it up outdoors on a fine evening (it needs plugging into a mains socket) and leave it on all night, then come back early in the morning before the sun gets up and 'cooks' the occupants. Tip the night's 'haul' out into large glass jars and identify them as quickly as possible, then let them go into a cool, shady bit of shrubbery where they can quickly hide themselves away for the day.

IF YOU ARE GOOD WITH YOUR HANDS you might be able to make your own copy of a bought moth trap; it's basically a box with a special type of very bright light suspended over the top that attracts moths, which then flutter down a chute into a chamber filled with bits of torn-up egg boxes into which the moths crawl away and hide. The whole thing needs to be protected from dew and rain since the light is electrical.

OTHERWISE, MAKE DO WITH a Heath Robinson version, which is quite good enough to get you started. Moths are attracted to any outdoor electric light such as porch or patio lights; some of the stronger solar lights also attract them, or you can use a powerful torch (some extremely powerful rechargeable torches are available nowadays) with a piece of soft white cotton fabric draped over the lens. Set out a large white cloth on a table or a box, 30 centimetres (1 foot) or so under the light, and scatter torn up egg boxes over the surface of the fabric. Moths will come close to the light then drop down to the white cloth and crawl into the bits of egg box. Don't handle the moths themselves or you'll damage the delicate coating on their wings; pick up the bit of egg box they are clinging to and put them carefully into a wide-necked jar while you identify them – do so as quickly as possible, then release them straight away.

HOW TO ATTRACT BIRDS

. . .

BIRDS ARE ATTRACTED to gardens that provide them with food and water, but they'll linger longest where they feel secure, so you'll see far more birds in a garden that provides them with plenty of cover, too.

BIRDS ARE NERVOUS CREATURES, and they like to withdraw to fairly mature trees and shrubs, a hedge or a climber-clad wall, where they can perch in safety between bouts of feeding. The mistake a lot of people make is to hang bird feeders or stand a bird table in the places that give the best view from the house; when they're right out in the open birds don't feel safe so they don't stay long. They'll spend more time at feeders that are closest to a safe, leafy retreat so they can hide at the first hint of a threat. Try to find a spot that fulfils their needs and gives you a good view, too.

WHEN IT COMES TO DRINKING and bathing, a wide, shallow bowl of water placed on the ground encourages birds to extend their visit, but best of all is a wildlife pond. You'll often see flocks of birds drinking and splashing about in the shallows at the same time, since there's safety in numbers. Sparrows also like to dust-bath, so it pays to have a patch of soft, fine, dry soil or silver sand under shrubs especially for them. It helps keep their feathers in good condition, it's great fun to watch and it might just encourage these twenty-first century rarities to take up residence with you. A huge dome of a bay tree outside our back door support a two-dozen-strong colony of house sparrows (when they are not nesting under our eaves) and so the area has now become known as 'Tower Hamlets'!

ANOTHER GOOD WAY TO ATTRACT more birds, and a wider range of species, is to increase the amount of wild food that a garden provides over as much of the year as possible. This can easily be done by growing a good variety of plants that yield edible fruit, berries or seeds, or those that house insects such as small caterpillars and greenfly during the spring, when birds such as blackbirds and bluetits are bringing up chicks.

PLANTS TO ATTRACT BIRDS

...

You can feed nuts and seeds all the year round in feeders, but it's helpful if you can rely on nature, too, by planting natural food sources.

1 Crab apples: small-fruited varieties are best as they are most easily swallowed; 'Golden Hornet' is a favourite in autumn with blackbirds, thrushes and redwings, who pull them straight off the trees. Some varieties drop and are pecked and eaten off the ground once they've softened slightly.

2 Windfall apples: whole eating and cooking apples are readily pecked on the ground by blackbirds, thrushes, redwings and fieldfares.

3 Amelanchier: small garden tree producing small red fruits in midsummer, which blackbirds in particular just love.

4 Sunflower: leave the dead flower heads so that seeds can form, then in late summer and autumn various finches will take them straight from the plants.

5 Redcurrants: blackbirds pinch them off the plants in summer to feed to parties of fledglings they've brought round to teach how to feed themselves; it's worth growing a few bushes especially for them in a wildlife corner to watch the fun.

6 Elder, rowan, cotoneaster, pyracantha, myrtle, hawthorn and wild ivy: all of these treats are enjoyed by blackbirds in a changing sequence through autumn and winter. It is especially worthwhile including some of the later-ripening berries (ivy in particular) in case of a hard winter. In a very bad winter, gardens with good crops of late berries sometimes attract waxwings visiting temporarily from Scandinavia.

7 Teazel: dramatic architecturally-shaped wild garden flower whose spiky seedheads attract goldfinches.

8 Thistle: wild and cultivated thistles and their relatives (which include several perennial garden flowers, also artichokes), attract goldfinches to feed acrobatically from the seedheads.

OTHER GARDEN WILDLIFE

A well-stocked wildlife garden automatically provides all the facilities to make a large range of creatures feel at home. When there are plenty of trees and shrubs for cover, long grass and wildflowers, a pond, plus a log pile, dry stone wall, pile of dead leaves or heap of rotting dried grass cut from your meadow, you really don't have to do anything more to encourage visitors except *leave it alone* as much as possible.

You can walk round the garden, of course, but it pays to keep to the paths – it's worth setting up seats or even a small 'hide' in key places that offer a good view. But resist the temptation to push your way through clumps of long grass and wildflowers, or to keep peering into nests or nest boxes, and if children use the area, encourage them to visit quietly – the less wildlife is disturbed, the more likely it is to stay around.

In a surprisingly short time a wildlife garden 'settles down' and starts to generate all sorts of natural food supplies that soon become part of a long and complex food chain that's largely self-supporting.

In the pond, beneficial bacteria get to work breaking down decaying plant matter, fish droppings and other organic materials, which feed on the plants that in turn oxygenate the water and provide shade, shelter and breeding sites for tiny creatures such as water fleas (daphnia), slaters, tadpoles and efts (baby newts). In the natural cycle, these creatures are consumed by birds and larger creatures, who in any case will be dropping in to drink and bathe.

In the grass and under shrubs, slugs, snails, beetles and worms provide food for hedgehogs, shrews, birds and even foxes. And droppings, along with fallen leaves and other plant remains, are recycled by soil bacteria and ground-living insects such as woodlice back into humus that in turn feeds worms and plants, which are all recycled endlessly.

WILD GARDEN VISITORS

...

1 Hedgehog: popular prickly creatures that roll into a ball when threatened and come out mainly at night to feed on worms, slugs, caterpillars, woodlice and beetles, though they'll also eat dead birds and other carrion. They mate (rather noisily) in April, bear young in early summer and feed heavily in autumn to put on weight to see them through winter hibernation. They'll hole up in leaf piles under hedges or sheds, etc., from late October or November until March/April, but in a mild winter may emerge briefly to hunt for food. If you want to feed them (and it's worth doing so just before, and after, hibernation, and if they come out in winter), special dried or tinned hedgehog food is available from pet shops and wildlife centres, or put out whole peanuts of the sort used to feed birds (not the salted sort), or tinned cat food – but not fishy flavours, only meat. And don't give them bread and milk; they can't digest it and it upsets their stomachs.

2 Fox: thrive in a huge range of environments due to their ability to eat an assortment of things from mice, voles and rabbits to road-kill and dead birds. They also forage from dustbins and take food put out on lawns for birds; in autumn they'll eat fruit such as blackberries and windfall apples. Coastal foxes will patrol the beach at night in search of dead seagulls and anything else edible that's been washed up. They live in family groups and raise their cubs in a den, which might be a hole in a bank or hedge-bottom, or a hollow under a large tree stump, old shed or other outbuilding. In winter you'll often hear foxes yelping and making unearthly screams as part of their courtship; the cubs are born in early spring and you may see parents out hunting by day for a while when they have cubs to feed.

3 Grass snake: potentially our largest snake, up to 1.2m (4ft) long, olive green to brown (sometimes marked with darker bars) with a conspicuous yellow or off-white 'collar' round the neck. It feeds mainly on frogs, so it's usually found in grassy places near a pond, and may be seen swimming. Grass snakes often bask in the sun on fine days, or rest in damp shady places such as under an upturned boat, or large flat piece of wood. Adult females lay eggs in June in piles of rotting vegetation including compost heaps, which provide the warmth to hatch them; the young emerge in late August/early September. Grass snakes hibernate in crevices and holes from October to April.

4 Slow worm: technically they are legless lizards rather than snakes; like lizards, they can shed their tail to escape from a predator; it eventually regrows. Slow worms have glossy bronze skin and live in wild, grassy places, often burrowing into piles of rotting vegetation (including the compost heap), feeding mainly on slugs. They mate in spring then lay eggs, from which the young slowworms emerge in August or September. They hibernate from October to March.

5 Shrew: very active, small, carnivorous rodents with long, pointed, 'bottle-shaped' noses and short tails. They have to eat every few hours so they hunt day and night for worms, slugs, snails, woodlice and insects. Shrews are extremely territorial, emitting high-pitched shrieks to deter rivals; in wild gardens you'll hear them more often than see them. The young are born in April, but predators rarely take them as they taste foul; the big exception is owls, which don't seem to mind.

6 Wood mouse: also known as long-tailed field mouse, it is probably the most common British mammal, but is not often seen as it's nocturnal. It has a sandy brown back and white undersides, with very large ears, a long tail and long back legs which it uses to leap along the ground kangaroo-like when it's in a hurry. It has up to four litters of young each year, from March onwards, which it rears in a chamber inside a network of underground burrows. It feeds mainly on seeds, insects, grubs, fruit and berries, but will also bite open snail shells to eat the occupants. It is preyed on by owls, foxes and domestic cats.

7 Bank vole: the other common rodent inhabitant of a wild garden; often seen by day – look for the chunky shape, small ears, short tail, short nose and short legs with chestnut coat (slightly grey on the underside); it

scurries along instead of leaping like a wood mouse. Bears four or five litters of young each year, between early spring and autumn. Feeds on hazelnuts, berries, seeds, fruit, fungi and some greenery. It is preyed on by owls, kestrels, foxes and cats.

8 Mole: a chunky, hamster-sized animal with a black, velvety coat that doesn't lie flat in one direction like those of dogs and cats, allowing the creature to move backwards or forwards with equal ease in tight tunnels. Moles have tiny eyes, a bare snout and large, spade-like front feet it uses for tunnelling. They are rarely seen as they live underground the majority of the time, but most people are familiar with the molehills that they push up in grassland and lawns to get rid of soil generated when they are tunnelling into a new area. (Though these make moles unpopular with lawn-lovers, molehills aren't a problem in a wild garden.) Moles feed mainly on earthworms, which they 'harvest' from the walls of special 'feeding tunnels' that are patrolled regularly; these are quite separate from the tunnels used for rearing their young; they have one litter per year, born in April or May. The only natural predators of moles are owls, since they taste too unpleasant for other potential predators.

9 Grey squirrel: aerial athletes that leap from tree to tree or scamper across short grass. They build dreys which look rather like scruffy crows' nests (except that dreys are close to the trunk, not usually out on branches), high up in large trees for rearing their young in spring. They feed on young shoots and tree bark, bulbs, flowers, and in autumn are often seen burying nuts and acorns to act as winter reserves – grey squirrels do not hibernate. Alas, these aliens have seen off our native **10 Red squirrel** in most parts of the UK – its strongholds are few and far between now, but they can be spotted on the Isle of Wight, Brownsea Island in Poole Harbour, and in parts of Scotland, Cornwall and Lancashire.

CHAPTER 5

COUNTRY ARTS AND CRAFTS

We find them inspiring now; those country crafts and skills that have a nostalgic as well as an artistic appeal. But today's arts and crafts were yesterday's essential home-maker skills. Country folk throughout history have had to make small incomes stretch a long way by making and doing as much as possible for themselves. Everything from rush lights and baskets to the walling and thatching of their homes and essential agricultural equipment were originally home-made. Today hand-made goods are a great luxury and expensive to buy – the sorts of things you might buy as gifts at a craft fair – but by learning an old country skill you can do-it-yourself, and discover a rewarding new hobby as well as having a fashionably accessorised home.

PRACTICAL CRAFTS

You don't have to be skilled with your hands to enjoy *every* practical craft; all are creative, and even if the end result is relatively simple, it's very satisfying to see something useful appear from a few basic raw materials. Most old country crafts can be done without much in the way of workshop facilities at home, just a few basic hand tools. Indeed, old countrymen used to make everything they needed for themselves, including the lathes that they used to 'turn' wood, using raw materials that grew wild in woodland. Today it's a fascinating experience to watch them demonstrating their crafts at country fairs and agricultural shows.

GROW YOUR OWN WALKING STICK

Now you might think that walking sticks are just for those who are shaky on their pins. Not a bit of it. A stout walking stick makes a great companion when you're out for a country stroll (for helping you climb hills and slash aside nettles that block your path) and while there's a good selection available in gents' outfitters, and an even bigger selection at stick-makers stands at country shows and craft fairs, it's fun to make your own.

You might be lucky enough to find a suitable stick already growing in the countryside. Ash or hazel are the favourites for walking sticks, though you can also use sturdy stems from oak, sycamore and other trees. The most suitable sticks are to be found on trees that have been previously coppiced, which encourages them to grow long, straight, strong stems. If you can find one with a bend or knotty bit that makes a natural handle, it's a simple matter just to cut it virtually ready to use. Cut just above the 'handle' at the top, then cut the stick off a bit longer than you want, and remove any leaves or small side shoots to tidy it up. You can then trim the finished stick to exactly the right length for your height. 'Instant' sticks are most easily spotted in winter, when the leaves have fallen from the trees, but if you happen to see a suitable piece in summer it's perfectly fine to cut it then.

Otherwise you can 'train' your own stick. Search for a suitably straight *young* stem that's still pliable, ideally during the growing season when the stems are at their most bendable, and tie a knot in it, or tie it over at an acute angle with string, so it forms a handle in due course. Then leave it to continue growing until it's thick enough to cut and the handle 'sets' solidly – perhaps a year or two later.

If you want to start from scratch, grow an ash or hazel tree in a stretch of your own mixed country-style hedgerow or a corner of your wild garden, and coppice it (cut it down about 15cm/6in from the ground) when it's several years old to make it produce suitable shoots. Save the straightest and strongest to make into a walking stick. Again, bend the handle into shape and secure it with strong string or tie a knot in it while it's still whippy enough to bend easily, and leave it for a year or two. Then cut the stick, ideally over the winter some time between leaf fall in autumn and well before bud-burst in spring, when there's naturally as little sap as possible in the wood.

Once you have cut your walking stick, leave it to season for a while in a cool, dry shed. Then make a metal ferrule to protect the tip from wearing down through use. Use a hacksaw to cut a 2.5cm (1in) length of copper pipe of suitable diameter (available from builders' merchants) and hammer it on over the end of the stick. Whittle the end of the stick slightly if necessary, and to make it fit tightly, heat the piece of pipe to make it expand so it slips on. It will then shrink slightly as it cools, making a tighter fit.

PROFESSIONAL STICK-MAKERS

You can sometimes see a professional stick-maker demonstrating his skills at a craft fair or countryside show. He starts out with a stack of suitable lengths of straight seasoned stem set aside, then he bends the handle of each walking stick individually, using damp heat. This comes from an old oil drum full of wet sand, which is heated over a burner, and the ends of the sticks are pushed into the hot, wet sand until they can be bent using a 'form', which might be something as simple as several strong wooden posts driven into the ground. He'll push the end of the stick between two of the posts and use the length of the stick as a lever to bend the business end round into a hooked shape to make the handle. If the wood becomes too tough to bend, he'll put it back into the hot, damp sand to soften up again while working on another stick. In this way he can be working on a dozen or more sticks at the same time.

Really skilled makers will carve elaborate handles from wood or horn into the shape of dogs', horses', pheasants' or badgers' heads. These are real works of art and the finest exponents rightly charge decent sums for their handiwork. One of the greatest stick-makers was Norman Tulip, whose little paperback 'The Art of Stick Dressing' will show you just what can be achieved.

MAKING A BESOM BROOM

Cut an armful of 1–1.2 metre (3–4 feet) long twigs from a birch tree in autumn, after leaf fall. Choose a tree whose canopy needs a little thinning, then bundle them up and leave them to season in a woodshed or similar place so they dry out slowly for several months. It's important that they remain flexible rather than turning brittle. Stand the bundle up on end and tap it down so the thickest ends of the twigs are all lined up, then roll the bundle round, pressing as you go, so the twigs are packed tightly together. Push a stout wooden broom handle that's been sharpened at the end, or a strong 90cm (3ft) length of homegrown hazel pole, into the bunch so that the twigs overlap the handle by 30–45cm (12–18in), and fix securely in two or three places with strong lengths of garden wire twisted tight with pliers so the twigs can't slip out. Lastly, snip the thin ends of the twigs so they are all roughly the same length to form the long, flexible 'bristles' of the brush; it should end up looking like the traditional witch's broom, standing roughly 1.2–1.3 metres (4 feet to four-feet-six) tall. Use it to whisk wormcasts off a lawn, or to sweep up leaves round the garden, but remember that it is most effective when held horizontally, almost parallel to the ground, rather than upright like a conventional broom.

As an alternative to birch, bundles of long heather stems can be used to make a similar sort of broom. These were once much used north of the border as indoor brooms for sweeping solid stone floors.

You can leave a stick as it is, with the natural bark – sanding off any rough stem bases – or varnish it (it doesn't need 'peeling'). That'll give you a good basic country walking stick. But if you get the 'bug', you might enjoy trying a few more elaborate versions.

To make a stick with a carved handle, select a suitable strong, straight shoot growing out at an acute angle from a thicker branch. This time, don't just cut the straight shoot – cut the branch a few inches either side of the point where the thinner shoot emerges, so your stick has a lump of thicker branch attached at the handle end. Then carefully carve that to make a curved handle with a fist-grip, or carve it more to create a figured handle.

A thumb stick is a special kind of walking stick that's a little longer than usual, with a V-shaped notch at the top instead of a conventional handle. It's designed for hikers walking over rough or hilly countryside, and as the name suggests, is used with your thumb hooked over the notch, instead of the palm of your hand grabbing a conventional knob or handle. If you want to make your own thumb stick, it's just a case of finding a suitable long, straight, strong stick with a pair of equal-sized shoots forking out from the top, and cutting it off at the top 5–7.5 cm (2 or 3in) above the place they branch out so you are left with a 'V'. The shank of the stick needs to be rather longer than for a normal walking stick; thumb sticks are usually about 1.3–1.5 metres (4 feet 6in to 5 feet) high – for maximum comfort they want to be roughly the same height as your shoulder. The idea is to give the user extra purchase over uneven or sloping ground, when a normal stick would drop down the dip and be of little use.

Shepherds' crooks are long, straight sticks with large, curving metal hooks at the end instead of handles; the hook is just the right size to catch a sheep by the hind leg. Ask a blacksmith to make you one out of metal, unless you can buy one ready-made from an artisan walking stick-maker. Pare the top of the stick roughly to fit, and heat the open end of the metal crook to make it expand so it can just be forced over the end, and as it cools and shrinks it'll make a tighter fit. Some shepherds' crooks have their hook carved from a piece of ram's horn. These can be glued onto the shaft, but they need to be really firmly secured if they are to be strong enough to use for practical purposes – many are simply decorative pieces useful for walking but less robust when it comes to catching your ewe.

Besom brooms are traditionally made from birch twigs cut for the purpose in autumn. Using a simple technique, you can produce a natural and hardwearing broom.

BASKET WEAVING

Baskets of various shapes and sizes were once used for all those jobs that today we'd use carrier bags, cardboard boxes and plastic trays for. There were special baskets for shopping, for picking crops or carrying them to market, or to fit on the front of a bike so that tradesmen could use them to make deliveries; basketry was even used to make eel traps, bird cages and crab or lobster pots, and for a long time office-workers had woven cane 'in' and 'out' trays on their desk for stashing paperwork. Basket making was still being taught in art and craft classes when I was at school, and it was regularly used in occupational therapy to help patients recovering from long-term conditions, by encouraging mental and manual dexterity, not to mention concentration.

Today, baskets are mostly used as decorative containers for fresh fruit, eggs or dried flower arrangements, as cutlery trays inside drawers, and for smart picnic hampers, while wicker chairs are popular as conservatory furniture.

Willow is the traditional material for making baskets. Basket-makers use long, thin, straight willow wands with the outer bark peeled off; when woven together these become what's know as wickerwork. Willows were once specially cultivated for basket-making in many parts of the country where the ground is naturally boggy, but those that still exist today are found on the Somerset Levels. The species that's used for the job is the common osier, *Salix viminalis*, which grows very vigorously so that crops of 'withies' – the strong, straight, slim stems – can be harvested fairly often without weakening the growth of the 'stools'.

Willow for basketry is cut during the winter; traditionally the job was done using a sickle to cut a handful at a stroke. The withies were tied into bundles and taken down river on a small boat to a collecting point where groups of workers stripped the bark from each stem individually by pulling it sharply through a forked blade in the end of a long iron bar set into the ground, but nowadays it's a bit more mechanised. The willow was then stored until needed.

Before it can be turned into baskets, dry willow must first be soaked so that it regains its flexibility; domestic basket-makers dunk it in a bath of cold water overnight so that it's ready to use the following day. It then needs to be used shortly after it's been removed from the water, otherwise it starts to dry out and become hard again, especially if you work in a heated room.

HOW TO WEAVE A BASKET

...

TO MAKE A BASKET you need a flat wooden base of the right shape and size for the type of basket you plan on making. Today they are sold at hobby shops, usually made of plywood, with ready-made holes to take the 'uprights'. (The same shops sell the willow, or 'cane' as it's often called.) You'll need two grades of cane – a slightly thicker one for the uprights, and thinner cane that's used for the actual basket-weaving.

FIRST THE UPRIGHTS ARE INSERTED into the holes in the wooden base; these, together with the base, will provide the structural strength of the basket's framework. The uprights are pushed through the base by several inches, then the base is turned over and the protruding lengths of cane are woven together to make a 'rim' on which the basket sits. More importantly it holds the uprights firmly in place so they can't be pulled out.

WITH THE BASE AND UPRIGHTS IN PLACE, the work is turned right-side up and thinner 'cane' is woven between the uprights to make the sides of the basket. The first length of cane is held in place by tucking one end behind one of the upright rods, then the other end is woven round the rods from there on, bending it

alternately behind, and in front of, each rod in turn. When you reach the end of the length of cane, make sure the very end is left *inside* the basket, where it won't show. Use a short-nosed pair of secateurs to snip the protruding end off short, so it's tidy. Start weaving with a new piece by tucking it in behind the same rod that the last piece of cane ended at, so again it is inside the basket – the join won't show on the outside of the work.

ONCE YOU'VE GOT THE HANG OF BASIC weaving, you can move on to more advanced techniques. More decorative effects can be created by weaving with three parallel rods all at once, or by weaving two behind and one in front of each upright rod. It's also possible to miss out sections and alternate basketry with open space where the uprights are crossed over to make a decorative row of diamond shapes, before the sides continue with more weaving.

WHEN YOU'VE REACHED THE TOP OF THE WORK, the rim of the basket needs finishing off neatly. To do this, the ends of the rods are bent over and woven to make a rigid border that stops the weaving unravelling and gives the finished basket a strong edge.

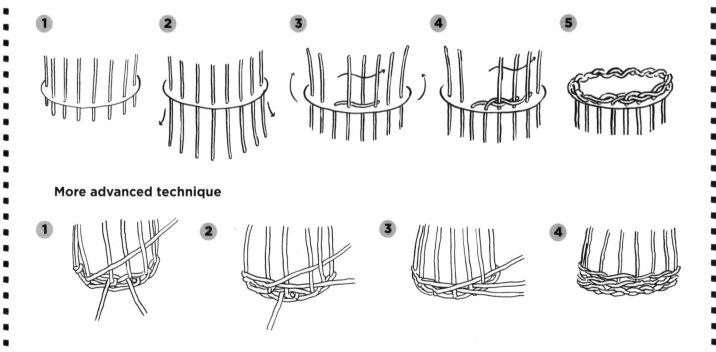

More advanced technique

ALTERNATIVE BASKET-MAKING MATERIALS

If you fancy creating naturally coloured baskets, use the stems of coloured-stemmed dogwoods or ornamental willows, which you can grow at home especially for this job. Good varieties include: *Cornus alba* 'Westonbirt' (sealing-wax red stems), *Salix alba vitellina* 'Britzensis' (orange stems), *Salix alba vitellina* (golden yellow stems) and *Salix daphnoides* (purple stems). *Salix purpurea* has variable colouring to its bark, varying from light purple to shiny green. You can use stems removed in normal pruning, but if you want any quantity, consider growing a row of plants especially – they root easily from cuttings pushed into the ground where you want them to grow, any time during the winter. Allow the young plants to establish themselves for three years before taking your first crop; from then on cut the plants down hard (to within 7.5–10cm/3 or 4 inches of the ground) every few years. This makes them produce long, straight, unbranching stems that can be harvested in much the same way as 'proper' basket willow, but without stripping the bark afterwards.

LIVING WILLOW SCULPTURES AND STRUCTURES

Nowadays willow is in demand for creating living garden decorations, arches, small rustic shelters or woven fencing. The osier used for basket-making is ideal as it produces the long, slim stems needed for this sort of job; for small 'living sculptures' any of the colourful decorative species listed above for making homegrown baskets can be used.

Fresh, live withies should be bought in late winter and pushed into prepared ground where they take root and start growing the following season. It's vital to use good-quality withies; if they have been harvested too long, they'll have dried out so they die instead of taking root.

To make living sculptures, arches or shelters, bend the withies into shape and tie them in position so they 'set'. To make living willow fencing, push a row of withies spaced a foot apart into the ground at an angle of 45 degrees, then push a second row in so the stems alternate with the first, angled in the opposite direction, and weave the two together so they form a series of diamond shapes, something like a chain-link fence.

Once willow structures or sculptures have taken root, they will start to produce side shoots along their length, so the creation will need to be clipped and pruned regularly to keep its shape and definition.

MAKING TRUGS

Trugs, or 'Sussex trugs' as they are often called, are traditional shallow 'baskets' made from thin wooden slats. Trugs are traditionally used for gathering cut flowers, vegetables, salads, fruit and other relatively fragile produce from the garden; they are also good for collecting eggs, given a handful of straw in the bottom as 'cushioning'.

The basic structure of the trug is formed from two slim ash or sweet chestnut 'wands' split in half lengthwise with a sleaving axe called a 'froe'. These are steamed to soften them so that they are pliable, then bent round a jig to create two rounded shapes; one of these, shaped into a hoop, becomes the handle of the trug and the other is shaped into a rectangle with curved corners that becomes the rim of the trug. The two are slotted together so they cross in the middle. Strips of thin, split cricket-bat willow are then nailed to one end of the rim and bent round before being nailed to the other end. (These strips are prepared in advance, steamed to shape and shaved down so they are narrower at the edges than in the middle so the pieces fit together to create a boat-shaped 'bowl'.) Wooden 'feet' are nailed to the base of smaller trugs so the finished trug stands up straight.

Stored in a dry shed, I get upwards of five or six years' use out of mine before their bottoms go, and they are wonderfully user-friendly, slung over your arm while you go about your tasks in the garden.

HURDLE-MAKING

Hurdles are one of several traditional woodland products that are still made in winter when coppice is cut. Suitable poles of various thicknesses are set aside ready to use for this job. Each hurdle is like a lightweight rustic fencing panel. There are two types of hurdles: gate hurdles and wattle hurdles, both with very different jobs.

Gate hurdles – usually made from sweet chestnut – are the original temporary sheep fencing. A gate hurdle looks a bit like a rustic five-bar farm gate made from natural poles, with a longer spiked pole at each end so it can be pushed into the ground to make it stand upright. It had all sorts of uses in the past. A gate hurdle could be forced into a weak spot in a hedge to stop the animals from wandering, but its main use was to construct temporary enclosures known as 'folds' to restrict sheep to particular areas of a field. This was commonly done when sheep were turned out onto unfenced stubble fields, or fields of turnips or kale in the autumn or winter, and at any time a shepherd needed to restrict them to a particular area of grazing instead of letting them have access to an entire pasture all at once. In country gardens, hurdles are useful as rustic boundaries for a kitchen garden or other working area, and dwarf hurdles perhaps 30–45cm (12–18in) high and 45–60cm (18–24in) long are great favourites of mine for pushing in along the edges of borders to keep flopping flower stems off the lawn, so the mower can pass alongside without chopping up the blooms.

There's a fair bit of skill in making serious sheep hurdles, but it's not too difficult to make a few small ones to use as rustic edgings for your flowerbeds at home, or to stop the dog running straight down the garden path and crashing into the veg patch beyond. Simply scale down the full-sized 'recipe'.

HOW TO MAKE A GATE HURDLE

...

USE A BILL HOOK TO TRIM A PAIR of strong sweet chestnut or ash posts, a little longer than waist-high, to shape. Strip off the bark and 'whittle' them so each has flat sides. Drill a row of seven evenly spaced holes about 2½cm (1 inch) in diameter up the side of each post, going right through the wood. These perforated posts will be the vertical ends of your hurdle.

NEXT MAKE THE RAILS FROM 'green' (i.e. unseasoned) sweet chestnut or ash – you need seven for each hurdle, about 1.2 metres (4 feet) long, from slightly slimmer lengths than you used for the upright posts. Taper the ends so they fit tightly into the holes in the posts, with 2½cm (1 inch) or so sticking out of the far side when they are in position. Slot the horizontal rails into the vertical posts and hammer a nail through the end of each rail so it can't be pulled back through the hole. Cut off the protruding ends. Then cut three more halved poles to form braces, one upright across the centre of the hurdle, and two sloping ones forming a V shape from the bottom corners to the centre top, and nail these in place to give the structure lateral strength.

TO FIX HURDLES IN PLACE, make a pair of holes in the ground a hurdle's-length apart by hammering a spike a short depth into the ground, then pulling it out. Stand the hurdle in place with the spikes at each end resting in the holes made by the spike, then use a wooden mallet to drive the pointed ends gently down into the ground. When you have several hurdles in place in a row, you can tie the tops of the end poles together to hold them more firmly in place.

THE TECHNIQUE IS EXACTLY the same for making the smaller garden hurdles.

WATTLE HURDLES ARE LIKE SECTIONS of basketry, made by weaving lengths of split hazel round a series of upright hazel poles to make large, oblong panels. Wattle panels were originally used in medieval house construction; the panels were set into a timber frame and plastered with a mixture of mud, chopped straw and manure, sometimes with chalk added, to form wattle-and-daub walls. Interior walls of humble cottages would often be made from plain unplastered wattle panels, to save effort, though in more upmarket establishments they were plastered and lime-washed (the original 'emulsion paint'). Wattle hurdles might also be used as temporary enclosures for sheep, perhaps to make a pen into which a sheepdog can gather a small flock of sheep if they need attention, and at lambing time to make a temporary enclosure for expectant ewes or a group of orphan lambs.

NOWADAYS WATTLE PANELS made from slim, but unsplit poles are often used as rustic fence panels for gardens. They make good windbreaks for exposed gardens and they're ideal for screening-off a kitchen garden, or providing temporary shelter for a young hedge while it grows up, but they have a rather limited life – usually about five years – before the wood becomes brittle and they start to break up. Spraying them with a water-based timber preservative will help to prolong their life. Hazel hurdles will last a year or two longer. Again, the real thing requires woodland craft tools and skills to make, but it's not difficult to create a small version at home for use in the garden.

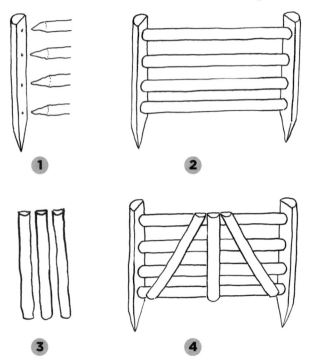

HOW TO MAKE A WATTLE OR HAZEL HURDLE

...

THE FIRST ESSENTIAL IS A THICK, heavy log split in two down the middle and stood cut-surface up (today we'd probably use a railway sleeper), with a row of holes driven into it at regular intervals every 15–20cm (6–8in); this acts as the 'mould' or 'template'. Next you need a supply of hazel poles to form the uprights of the hurdle. The uprights need to be as tall as you want your panel to be, with points at the bottom ends. At each end of the hurdle you need a slightly thicker pole that's about 15cm (6 inches) longer than the others, with a longer point at the tip. Lastly you need a supply of split (correctly known as 'riven') hazel, or else slim, straight 'green' hazel or willow stems that are capable of bending without breaking, which will be used to make the horizontal 'weave' of the wattle.

TO ASSEMBLE THE HURDLE the uprights are stood in the holes in the 'mould', with the longer, stronger poles at each end. (These will give the finished hurdle greater stability when they're pushed into the ground.) Then 'weave' the split hazel or slim 'wands'

backwards and forwards between the uprights. At the end of a row, tap the work down so it sits tight against the top of the 'mould', then bend and twist the remaining length of hazel stem you're using so that it forms a 'hinge' that easily bends round the end-post without breaking, then use it to continue 'weaving' the next row. When you reach the end of the first piece of hazel, tuck the end of a second length into the work alongside it to hold the new piece in place, and continue weaving with that; it's exactly the same as basket-weaving (see page 229). When you reach the end of the second row, again tap the work down firmly and continue 'weaving' until you reach the top of the upright posts. (Traditional hurdle makers always left a small square hole in the weave near the centre-top of each hurdle, so the end-user could put their arm through to carry a number of wattle hurdles at the same time.) The finished wattle or hazel hurdles can be stacked until you need to use them.

POST AND RAIL FENCING

Post and rail fencing is extensively used in the countryside to fence paddocks, particularly for horses and ponies, which often injure themselves by running into barbed wire, but it's also used anywhere where barbed wire is unsuitable or unattractive. It makes a cost-effective boundary for a country garden, which doubles as a support system for blackberries, Virginia creeper or large climbing roses that may be difficult to accommodate elsewhere. ('Rambling Rector' and 'Kiftsgate' both look particularly stunning grown in this way, and they flower far better when their main stems are trained out horizontally along a fence.)

Traditional post and rail fencing consists of strong (usually oak or chestnut) posts that are usually square in cross section, with a row of two

or three oval-shaped holes cut through them. The horizontal rails are usually flat-sided, or nearly so, and these have their ends chamfered to slot into the holes in the posts. The holes are usually wide enough to take the ends of two rails, which enter from each side of the post and 'wedge' each other firmly into place to form a continuous straight row running the entire length of the fence.

Nowadays a more economical version is often constructed using rustic fence posts that have been split to give them one flat face, and narrower split poles as the horizontal struts, nailed together so that the flat sides of the posts and the horizontal rails are face to face to make a strong join.

Most people nowadays employ a local firm to supply *and* erect this type of fencing since they'll have all the right equipment for driving posts in quickly and efficiently, and the experience to do a good job. But if you decide to do it yourself, the trick is to mark out a straight line along the boundary and clear it of weeds and rubbish, then put a post in at each end of the run. Dig holes for the posts and check that each is upright (with a spirit level). Hammer rubble round the base of each post to hold it firm before returning and re-firming the soil. Then fix a taut string between the first and last fence posts, along the top, to use as a guideline for keeping the fence straight. The posts need to be buried 50–60cm (20–24in) deep, with their centres 2.4m (8ft) apart. Start work at one end; put in a second post but don't fix it firmly in place; attach the pair of rails, or 'cross members', from it to your first post. This gives you the chance to check they run parallel and are lined up correctly with the line running between your two marker posts. When you have the first section of fence correctly aligned, put more rubble down the hole and use the end of a spare wooden post to ram it firmly down so the second fence post is fixed firmly in place. Work your way along the entire fence in the same way, putting in a loose post, connecting the poles, lining it up properly and then firming the post in place. Tubular post hammers can be used to knock in the posts (rather than a sledgehammer which will often split

the ends) but it is more difficult to keep the posts vertical than it is if you dig holes and adjust them as you go.

Nowadays it's quite common to find that a post and rail fence is reinforced in some way, when it's used round a field intended to house smaller livestock. Some people will fix strong wire mesh (such as 'pig netting' or 'sheep netting', which has large, strong squares about 10cm/4in wide) to post and rail fencing, which makes the resulting enclosure far more dog-proof, or suitable to hold livestock such as sheep, pigs or goats, which could push their way between the horizontal rails of plain post and rail fencing. Attach the wire to the uprights before you put the cross-members in position; this makes for additional strength. (Don't use this sort of netting if horses are kept in the paddock since they get their hooves tangled in it and it can cause injury, or at least pull off a shoe.) As belt and braces, some owners also add a single strand of electric fencing along the very top of a post and rail fence to prevent livestock such as horses or cattle leaning over the top to eat out-of-reach grass, which can damage the fence, or they'll use a single strand of electric fencing halfway up post and rail fencing with 'pig netting' or small-mesh wire netting at the base to keep smaller animals in. Check all fences regularly for repairs.

HEDGE-LAYING

A neatly laid hedge is a far more effective barrier than a normal hedge – it's the age-old way of keeping livestock *in*. It is a living, growing, self-renewing 'fence' made of hedging plants that have been bent over at an angle and 'woven' through a series of posts knocked into the hedge-line. When a hedge is properly laid there are no gaps at the base or weak spots where animals can push through. As a bonus, a well-laid hedge needs a good deal less maintenance than a regular hedge since it grows far more slowly than usual. But it does take a fair bit of work to lay a hedge in the first place. It's a winter job, traditionally carried out when there's no other work to be done on the land.

Hedge-layers start with an existing hedge which has usually been a bit neglected, so it's overgrown in places and gappy in others. The only materials you need are a billhook, a sledgehammer, a supply of ash or hazel posts roughly 5cm (2in) thick and 1.8m (6ft) long and pointed at one end, and some long, slim, straight hazel or willow poles about 3m (10ft) long, a little more than finger-thick. (All of these can be cut from your own area of coppice, if you have some on your land.) It's a good idea to wear heavy leather gloves since a lot of hedges consist largely of hawthorn, which is prickly and hard on the hands; stout gloves also offer some slight protection against cutting yourself with the billhook.

The first part of the job is to clear any brambles, nettles and other rubbish from the base of the existing hedge, and then thin out the stems of the plants that form the hedge. Chop out or saw off thick old stems at ground level, leaving the younger ones that ideally are about 2.5cm (1in) thick.

Start 'laying' at one end of the hedge. Use the billhook to cut about three-quarters of the way through the first stem, leaving a bit of wood and the bark attached to it as a 'hinge' so the stem can be bent down. You'll think that it can't possibly survive, but it will! Lay it along the line of the hedge. Do the next half dozen or so stems in the same way. (There's a 'hook' at the end of the billhook blade, which is used for snagging an individual stem and pulling it towards you if you can't reach it easily.) Then use the sledgehammer to knock a row of six posts in along the hedgeline, from your original starting point, spacing them about 76cm (2ft 6in) apart. Don't hammer too hard or the posts may split. Now weave the slanting stems between the posts, leaving the bushy tops pointing into the field.

Proceed all the way along the hedge, cutting partly through the base of about half a dozen stems at a time, then banging in the next few posts and weaving the 'laid' stems in round them. When you reach the end of a run of hedging, finish off by 'weaving' three or four of the long, springy, finger-thick poles along the top of the posts, in the same way as weaving baskets, then tap the weave down firmly with a mallet and cut the tops of the posts off level. Lastly, clip the newly laid hedge tidily so the top is all the same height and the sides are an even thickness. It's a slow, hard job but a hugely satisfying one.

The following spring, forests of young side shoots will grow upwards from the slanting main stems; these will thicken up the hedge. You'll need to trim the whole hedge once a year (again, this job is usually done in winter or very early spring, when there's little farm work to be done, and well before any birds start nesting in the hedge) but it won't grow as much as a normal hedge, which means that far less trimming than usual is involved. A laid hedge can last up to twenty years before it needs doing again.

RESTORING A BADLY NEGLECTED HEDGE

When there's an old hedge which is in very poor condition with lots of gaps, it's not essential to pull it out and replant; it can be restored. Cut it down to a few inches above ground level in late winter. Strong new shoots should appear the next spring, and they'll emerge quite thickly from the old stumps. Any serious gaps can then be filled by planting new hawthorn saplings. Within three or four years you'll have a respectable fringe of strong new hedge round the field, which can then be laid quite easily since all the stems will be about the right size. While the new hedge grows there's clearly not a good enough boundary to keep livestock in the field, but the ground can be used to produce a crop such as potatoes, mangels for stockfeed, or grass to cut for hay.

DITCHING

A lot of country hedges are accompanied by a ditch, running round the outside of the field, to allow rainwater to drain away quickly from the pasture. 'Ditching' was another traditional winter job, usually done by farmhands after trimming the hedges, and it involved clearing ditches of brambles, weeds and rubbish, then shovelling out the accumulation of silt so that when snow melted in early spring or there was a spell of torrential rain, surface water ran into the ditches. Ditching was vital to prevent country lanes from flooding, and it also avoided muddy patches forming in fields where livestock would then turn the grassland to unproductive mud. The silt removed from ditches is usually quite rich in nutrients from decomposed leaves etc., so it was often spread along the foot of the hedge. It was also traditionally used on cottage gardens, particularly for top dressing veg plots. Today, ditches along country roads are usually cleared by the council, and the silt removed along with the rubbish, but farmers still do the 'hedging and ditching' round fields within their own land.

STILES FOR CROSSING DRY STONE WALLS

Where walkers need to cross over a dry stone wall to follow a footpath, a special type of stile is called for. The conventional step-type stile used in lowland fields is not tall enough, and even if the landowner left a gap in the wall, a normal stile wouldn't prevent the notoriously agile hill sheep getting through. Ladder stiles are the answer; they consist of a tall set of stout timber steps (complete with handrail) that go up-and-over the full height of the wall. This type of stile is deliberately designed to be too steep for even the nimblest sheep, and they are not that easy for walkers who aren't as nimble-footed as they might be either.

DRY STONE WALLING

Dry stone walls started life when early farmers picked up the stones that littered their land and piled them up out of the way, round the edges of the fields. The original piles made useful markers indicating ownership of the land, and when livestock was introduced it made sense to stack the stones in rows so the animals couldn't wander. Over many generations of stone-picking, walls 'grew up'. Today if you go walking in countryside where the fields are outlined with dry stone walls, such as in Yorkshire and the Lake District, it's clear from even a casual glance that a dry stone wall involves a fair degree of craftsmanship – it's much more than just a pile of loose stones.

Seen in cross section, a dry stone wall consists of *two* walls that lean in slightly towards the centre, which is filled with a mixture of smaller stones, rubble and soil. (This is how wildflowers and even small trees are able to grow in dry stone walls. In Cornwall the walls known as 'Cornish hedges' traditionally have a row of plants – often hardy fuchsias or valerian – growing along the top.)

The two outer walls that make up a dry stone wall are linked periodically by a wider stone that runs the full thickness of the wall, right through the centre, to 'tie' the two sides together, very much like the metal ties builders use when building houses of brick with cavity walls. At the foot of the wall are the largest stones of all, which act as 'foundations', and along the top you'll usually find a row of flattish stones stood on end, or a row of larger, flat, coping stones that cover the entire top of the wall, to make a 'capping' that helps to keep water out.

A new dry stone wall takes a long time to build, but once done it will last for centuries, with only minor repairs if perhaps a small section collapses – if it's repaired quickly it should prevent further damage where livestock or walkers push through, or weather gets in and erodes the soil centre.

HOW TO MAKE A DRY STONE WALL

FIRST MARK OUT THE area for the base of the wall and excavate a trench, since the wall needs to rest on bedrock or very solid subsoil. (You can't build a heavy stone wall on soft soil as the weight will make the ground sink unevenly causing stones to fall out.)

TO MAKE THE FOUNDATIONS for the wall, lay a firm base of large, flat stones. This should extend slightly wider than the base of the wall itself. Then at each end of the section of wall you are planning to build, set up a timber frame the same shape as the cross-section of the wall. Run several taut strings between the two frames to act as guides so the stonework is constructed to the right shape and size, with edges that slope at the correct angle; this helps to keep the work uniform all the way along.

THEN START BUILDING THE WALL UP, using the biggest stones at the bottom and slightly smaller stones as the wall rises. The great art of making dry stone walls lies in choosing stones that fit together

fairly well. As the two outer walls rise, the centre is packed carefully with smaller stones and soil, again taking care that they all fit together to make the shape as strong and solid as possible. And as each new course of stones is added, the strings running between the timber frames are raised so the waller still has his guidelines to work to. Expert wallers do the job by eye!

WHEN THE WALL REACHES roughly half its eventual height, a series of large stones is placed across the centre of the wall to act as 'ties' and the work continues as usual up to the top which, due to the sloping sides, will be less than half as wide as the base of the wall. The final job is to crown the top with a row of coping stones to keep out the rain.

MAKING WHISTLES

Whistles have been used since prehistory for attracting attention, as basic one-note musical instruments, and at celebrations or special occasions for the sheer joy of making a noise and letting off steam. Nowadays, apart from policemen, referees at football matches and school teachers on playground duty, there are relatively few serious uses for whistles. But a loud, piercing whistle is a useful piece of safety equipment for hikers and ramblers in remote places as a means of making contact with companions lost in fog, or as a means of letting search and rescue services know where casualties are in case of accidents. But whether you truly need one or not, it's great fun to make your own, from the same sort of materials that our primitive ancestors used: bone or wood.

HOW TO MAKE A WHISTLE

• • •

Choose a short piece of stick from a youngish (1–2 year old) stem of a tree or bush with hollow or pithy stems; elder is a good example. Cut your stick about 10–15cm (4–6in) long, with a leaf-joint at one end since the stems are solid at the joints. Push a thin piece of wire carefully up through the centre to remove the soft pith, but don't hollow out the whole length of the stem – leave the end with the leaf-joint untouched so the end is 'blocked' naturally. Measure an inch down from the open end of the tube, and then make a small sloping cut at 45 degrees to the stem and a straight cut at 90 degrees to the stem, so the two meet to form a small notch. Whittle the open end slightly so it makes a flat mouthpiece to blow into, and wedge a flattish sliver of wood into it so there's only a small hole to blow through; this hole needs to be in line with the notch cut in the top of the whistle. Primitive people used to make something very similar out of slender animal bones with a knuckle at one end and a broken-off end at the other end which they blew down, with a small hole bored carefully into the top surface to create the sound.

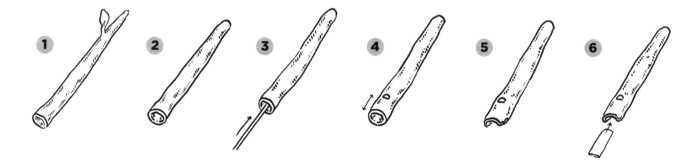

THATCHING

Thatch is the very oldest form of roofing used in this country; it's covered Iron Age huts, medieval hovels, farmhouses and barns, and Victorian farm workers' cottages. Over the last 150 years a lot of thatch has been replaced by cheaper or more low-maintenance roofing materials such as corrugated iron, slates or concrete tiles, but nowadays many picturesque thatched period country houses are listed buildings that have to have their existing appearance maintained using traditional building materials.

The type of material originally used to make thatch varied all round the country depending on what was available locally. In East Anglia and other boggy areas, reeds (common reed, *Phragmites australis*) were mostly used. In the north of Scotland and the Hebrides it was more often heather; elsewhere bracken made an economical roofing material, and in cereal-growing lowlands the straw left over from crops of oats, barley, rye or wheat was used – traditional varieties had long stems that made them suitable for the job.

Today, although Norfolk reeds give a far longer-lasting thatch (75 to 100 years), they are also expensive and in short supply, so most thatching is done with wheat straw. It's no longer possible to use left-over straw from cereal crops because modern wheat varieties have short stems, designed to prevent crops being flattened in bad weather, so instead, special varieties have to be grown deliberately for thatching. A straw thatch, however, will only last between 25 and 45 years.

Thatch makes for great-looking rustic chocolate-boxy cottages, and it provides natural insulation that keeps heat in and sound out. It's the most practical form of roofing for old cottages made of cob or wattle and daub, since they need a deeply overhanging roof to stop their earth-based building materials deteriorating and washing away in the rain, and thatch does the best job. However, it's seen as a greater fire risk than a tiled roof; owners of thatched homes tend to be nervous on bonfire night when smouldering spent rockets can shower down on them. Insurers often demand a premium for thatched roofs, and due to the risk of sparks, a policy may insist that open fires aren't used, or that wood-burning stoves meet specific requirements. (The Thatched Owners Group offers advice and insurance: www.thatched-group.com.)

The sight of a charming, old-world cottage being re-thatched, looks the very picture of an idyllic rural scene. But there's a heck of a lot more to it than meets the eye; even today a trainee thatcher has to serve a seven-year apprenticeship.

First, the straw has to be prepared – usually by the apprentice. After the wheat is harvested, the loose stems are collected and forked into layers which are damped with water to make the stems more pliable. Then, handfuls of straw are pulled out individually and laid out in the same direction so that, gradually, a higgledy-piggledy heap of straw is turned into straight bundles. Six bundles at a time are gathered up into the 'mouth' of a long, forked stick; the 'mouth' is closed with a string to hold the bundles in place, and the stick is used to carry the material up the ladder onto the roof to the master thatcher.

Most thatching today consists of re-thatching a roof that's reached the end of its working life. The old rotted thatch will be stripped off, leaving a layer of sound thatch underneath to act as the base for a fresh new top layer. The thatchers work on one strip of the roof at a time, while the rest is covered with tarpaulins. With long-straw thatching, the thatcher starts at the eaves by spreading a 10cm (4in) thick layer of straight straw placed at 90 degrees to the ground. This is combed flat with a special tool known as a side rake, then fastened in place with a long hazel stick which is held down by a row of bent hazel 'hairpins' with sharp points at each end, which are hammered into the older thatch below. He then moves up the roof, laying a second row of thatch so that it overlaps the first slightly (and covers the hazel stick securing it). He keeps working in this way until he reaches the ridge of the roof, then works across the entire roof in the same way, one strip at a time. Thatching with short straw or reeds uses slightly different methods, but all thatchers finish the roof-ridge off decoratively – often with a scalloped finish – and may include an ornamental feature such as a peacock, pheasant or squirrel somewhere on the roof as their 'signature'.

TYING KNOTS

Knots have 101 practical uses in the countryside, for anything from tying up your trousers to making your own rope-mesh hay-net for feeding a pony, and the ability to tie the right knots for particular purposes is essential for all sorts of people including farmers, fishermen and sailors, and climbers, whose lives may depend on it.

Knots are also used decoratively; they inspire jewellery designs (lover's knots and Celtic knots feature regularly in brooches, etc.) and knots are used for spacing pearls and semi-precious stones such as amber to make necklaces. A collection of tidily tied knots mounted on a board and framed is often used as a rustic display in beach-hut style summer houses in seaside gardens, in country lobbies just above the row of family Wellington boots or on boats.

The great art to tying *useful* knots is twofold. First you need to know which knot to use for which job, and then practise, practise, practise until you can almost do them instinctively – when you really need a knot, there won't be time to look up the instructions in a book.

THE REEF KNOT

For tying string round parcels, for tying up trousers when your belt breaks, or on a sailing boat to reef sails and for tying up sail covers.

Use with string that has two working ends; cross one end over the other and tie a simple half-knot, then cross the opposite working end over the other and make a second half-knot; pull both ends tight – the knot should lie flat and form a rough figure-of-eight shape.

Remember the old rhyme, 'left over right, and right over left' and you'll always tie a reef knot and never a granny knot; a granny will slip, and a real reef knot will not.

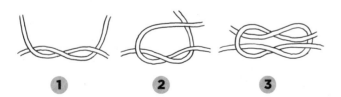

THE BOWLINE

For making a loop at the end of a length of rope that stays securely put without slipping or tightening. Used for making a loop at the end of a mooring rope to throw over a bollard to secure a boat.

It's easier to do than it is to describe. Start with the short end of the rope pointing towards you and the long end away from you. Take hold of the rope with the fingers of both hands, spacing your hands about six inches apart, 30cm (1ft) from the end of the rope. Make a loop by crossing the rope in your right-hand fingers over the rope in your left-hand fingers. Holding the loop in position with the fingers of your left hand, take the end of the rope with your right and pass it behind the lower curve of the loop and up through the centre, then pass it round the back of the long end of the rope, and back through the loop again. Tighten the knot you've created round the neck of the loop and it'll hold firmly without slipping or turning the loop into a noose.

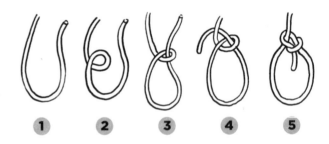

THE SHEET BEND

Used in making nets, or to join two pieces of rope together when they are of slightly different thicknesses, though it can also be used to join two ropes of the same thickness.

Make a loop in the end of one rope, then pass the tip of the second rope through it from back to front, then around behind the first rope and back under itself at the front, so you end up with two loops looped through each other. Pull it tight.

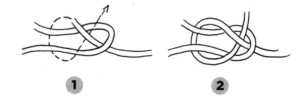

THE CLOVE HITCH

This looks like two turns of rope placed one on top of the other, and is very easy to tie. It's used in net-making, for securing fenders on a boat and for tethering a horse to a rail in a hurry, with a rope attached to its halter. The clove hitch at its best is used to secure something that pulls steadily against the knot from the same direction. Otherwise it can easily loosen and come undone, so it's not something to leave for long.

Pass the rope over and round the rail from front to back, then cross the rope over itself in front of the rail and pass the rope over the rail again, also front to back. Tuck the spare end under the diagonal crossing the centre of the knot and pull it tight from the 'long' end. To release the knot quickly, give a sharp tug on the short end; the knot immediately loosens.

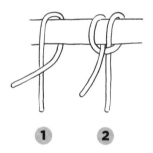

THE ROUND TURN AND TWO HALF-HITCHES

Used for securing a rope to a post, ring or rail, for mooring a boat or tethering a horse.

Pass the rope twice round the post or ring, then cross the working (short) end over the other (long) end so it makes a loop and pass the working end through this. Pull it tight so it slips up to the post or ring. Make a second loop in the same way, passing the working end through again, making sure it's in the same direction as last time, and again pull it tight so the pair of tight loops slip up to the 'long' end of the rope, jamming them tight.

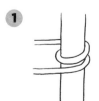
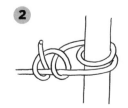

THE SHEEPSHANK

Not so much a knot as a hank! It's used to shorten a length of rope when you don't want to cut it (perhaps to take up some temporary slack), or to double up a weak section of rope to strengthen it, but it's mostly for tidying a rope up so it can be hung up without fear of tangling or uncoiling and getting itself in a terrible mess.

Gather the part of the rope to be tied up into a 'hank' so it's bunched together in a series of parallel lines with U-shaped bends at each end. Make a loop in the rope coming from the bottom of the hank and twist it 90 degrees so it crosses on itself, then slide it over the U-shaped lower end of the hank of rope. Do the same with the rope coming from the top of the hank, and slide the loop over the U-shaped upper part of the hank of rope; tighten the loops at both ends of the hank.

MAKING A CRICKET BAT

There are still quite a few villages with their own cricket teams, and for much of the summer, Saturday afternoons are enriched by the traditional sound of leather on willow from the village green as the local lads take on a team from a nearby village. The cricket pitch is cut especially for the occasion: in the very centre a square of grass is shaved short for the wicket, where the main action takes place, surrounded by the outfield where the grass is cut roughly to lawn-length – this is where the fielders take up their places, waiting to make catches. Larger villages and small market towns often have a cricket pavilion, with screens and scoreboards and folding seats for onlookers. There is a strong social side to village cricket; a lot of the after-match action being centred round the village pub, and the cricket club often organises dances or end-of-season suppers.

Nowadays most of the cricket bats are bought from the local sports' shop. It's been a long time since players made their own bats, and it's not particularly easy to do but, especially when you see an old bat on display on a pub wall, it's fun to know how it was done.

PRODUCTION OF CRICKET BATS

Cricket bats are made from a special variety of white willow, *Salix alba* var. *caerulea*. They were traditionally made by hand. Pieces of willow wood were cut roughly to size then treated with wax at both ends and left to season slowly to make sure that the finished wood wouldn't crack or warp. A piece of timber was then cut with a saw to roughly the size of a blade – the maximum length allowed is 96.5cm (38in) and the maximum width is 12cm (4.75in) – and shaped so that one side of the blade was flat and the other had a raised ridge up part of the centre. The bat was next pressure-treated to strengthen the fibres, using a pressure of 900kg (2000lb) per 6.5sq cm (1 sq in); on a small scale bats were pressed between pieces of flat iron using clamps. A splice was then cut in one end of the blade to fit the handle, which was made of cane

interspersed with strips of rubber. The base of the handle was cut into a wedge shape which was fitted tightly into the splice in the blade and fixed with wood glue. A draw-knife, or planer, was then used to pare the blade to shape. It was then finished with sandpaper; a cricket bat took a great deal of sanding in several sessions over a number of weeks to produce the required fine finish. The handle would then be brushed over with glue and tightly bound with twine for strength before a grip was pulled over it, then the blade was waxed.

The eventual owner would rub linseed oil into the wood regularly to stop it drying out and splitting, and to maintain the suppleness; in time, an old bat would turn a rich yellowy-brown colour, almost as if it had been varnished. Nowadays bats are factory-made and the handles given a more sophisticated, rubbery-type hand grip.

DECORATIVE CRAFTS

All sorts of arts and crafts that, today, are undertaken for fun and to decorate the home, once had serious purposes. They would have been carried out in the evenings, after the day's 'serious' work had been done, usually around the kitchen table after supper, or in an armchair by the fire, originally by candlelight, and they'd have provided a few much-needed home comforts for people living in the countryside.

POTPOURRI

Potpourri is a natural air freshener made from dried flowers and herbs plus other fragrant ingredients which could include citrus peel, fir cones, pine needles and shavings of scented bark such as cedar. In grand old houses it used to be placed in a decorative china potpourri jar which was often shaped like a dovecote or something similar, with plenty of holes for air to percolate through, but nowadays it's usually just piled into a shallow bowl out in the open, so it looks attractive as well as smelling great.

We're told that it is out of fashion now that plug-in air fresheners and scented candles are so popular, but it still has a kind of rustic charm and it's very easy to make your own using homegrown ingredients from the flower garden. Collect and dry them during the summer as the different kinds of flowers become available, then store them to blend and put on display in the winter, which is when you really need a bit of fragrance in the home – when you keep the windows shut, a house can soon start to smell a tad stale. Potpourri is designed to bring back the fresh scents of the summer country garden.

To make potpourri, pick fresh flowers when they are just approaching their best. Ideally, pick them first thing in the morning, when the dew has dried but before the sun has heated them up too much. Scented flowers are best, but others can be added for their colour. Some flowers are dried whole, while with others it's only the petals that are used.

Roses are classic potpourri flowers; red varieties keep their colour best but they are not always the strongest scented – apart from 'Alec's Red' or 'Deep Secret' – so mix them with more fragrant kinds. Pluck the petals off individually. If you grow miniature roses, whole tiny rosebuds can be snipped from their stems and dried while they are still tightly closed – red and pink ones look best. They look so dainty that they are very pretty in a dish of their own in a bedroom.

Lavender is the other classic potpourri flower. Snip whole heads off when they've expanded fully, but before they start drying out naturally, and avoid any that have turned a tad 'soggy' if it's a damp summer. You can also dry whole stems of lavender complete with the flower heads, then cut them all the same length and tie them with ribbon like sheaves of lavender 'straw'.

The petals of pinks, calendula marigolds, delphiniums and citrus blossom are also good for making potpourri, as are whole chamomile flowers.

Fragrant herbs help to give finished potpourri 'body', so pick individual leaves of bay, myrtle, lemon verbena and rosemary needles, using only those that look perfect – avoid torn, tattered or blackened ones. You might also like to use leaves of purple sage, pineapple sage, mint (especially unusual kinds such as eau de cologne mint, which smells just as the name suggests) and many of the various scented-leaved pelargoniums, which are available in apple, citrus, spice, mint and pine fragrances; they all dry out quite attractively. Lavender leaves can also be used; they retain all the scent of the flowers and tend to keep it a little longer.

Dry the potpourri ingredients in a dark, dry, airy place that's not too hot. The airing cupboard is fine if the door is left ajar so there's some air circulation, otherwise use a corner of a spare bedroom or utility room that's well away from a window. Spread the petals and flowers out thinly, ideally only one layer deep so they dry quickly, and stir them gently every few days to help them dry evenly. 'Found' ingredients such as fir cones, pine needles and acorns should also be well dried; they'll often take a bit longer to dry thoroughly than flowers and herbs, so treat them separately. It's also worth drying out some twists of citrus peel: lemon, orange, tangerine or mandarin, or thin slices of fresh kumquat. These dry best in a baking tray left in a very cool oven for several hours; in the airing cupboard they tend to go mouldy. They keep only a faint fragrance, but they give the finished potpourri mixture more colour, texture and variety.

When completely dry, store the flowers, herbs and peels etc., in cardboard boxes lined with tissue paper in a warm, dry cupboard till you are ready to make up your potpourri. (Avoid using screw-top jars since flowers may turn musty or go mouldy in a totally sealed container.) It's essential to keep the dried flowers and herbs in the dark, as their colours soon fade when they are exposed to sunlight.

ORRIS ROOT

Traditionally, orris was used to preserve the scent of potpourri. Orris is the root of a particular species of iris. When dried and powdered, orris root has its own perfume, rather like violets. It's not that easy to buy nowadays, but it's fairly easy to grow and make your own. Grow *Iris florentina* in a sunny part of the garden, and after a couple of years dig it up in the same way as you would to divide a bearded iris growing in your herbaceous border; remove a tuber or two, grate them finely and leave the 'shavings' in a warm place to dry, then use an old coffee grinder or a pestle and mortar to turn them to powder. Store in a dry screw-top jar and stir into potpourri as needed. In medieval homes, before people owned chests of drawers, orris dust was sprinkled between layers of linen sheets stored in chests to keep them smelling fresh instead of turning musty in winter.

To turn the various ingredients into potpourri, lay them out on a table along with any others you have bought – perhaps whole spices such as cloves, nutmeg or cinnamon sticks or whole nuts – ready to start assembling your potpourri. But don't just tumble everything randomly together; as a general rule it looks best to 'mix and match' ingredients that team up naturally, so make separate potpourri mixtures of herbs, spices and country garden flowers. Pile them into suitable containers such as baskets or pretty china bowls to suit the place you'll be displaying them.

The big mistake most people make is to try to keep potpourri for far too long; it's at its best for the first three months or so, but after that it tends to lose its scent. You can 'freshen it up' by sprinkling a few drops of floral oil (the sort sold for aroma-therapy at chemists' shops); lavender or rose are best for the job but you might like citrus or one of the herbal varieties. You can keep 'refreshing' a bowl of potpourri for another three to six months, or as long as the petals and leaves still look fresh and colourful. But after a year the colours of potpourri fade and it starts to look very sad, so it's best binned and replaced with a fresh new season's batch.

DRYING FLOWERS

When you enjoy having cut flowers in the house, it's very easy to continue out-of-season by using flowers that you've dried during the summer.

Only certain kinds are suitable, but enthusiasts often grow a few rows in a special 'cutting garden' or in the veg patch, so they can be 'cropped' without making gaping holes in the best borders.

Some of the most suitable flowers for drying are annuals, including helichrysum (straw flower), statice, cornflower, larkspur and safflower, also seedheads of poppies, love-in-a-mist and decorative grasses. Quite a few perennials also dry well, particularly achillea, acanthus, santolina, liatris, echinops and eryngium. Some seedheads are also good for drying: physalis is brilliant for the rows of orange, ping-pong ball-sized 'Chinese lanterns' that hang from the stems in autumn, and ornamental grasses and honesty are fun. You can also dry heads of teasel from the wild garden; they look good lightly sprayed with white or silver to create a frosted effect, especially for Christmas decorations.

Pick flowers and seedheads for drying very slightly *before* they are at their best, since they'll continue to develop for a short time while they are drying. (If you pick them at their best they'll often 'go over' and fall apart when they are fully dried. This is particularly true in the case of seedheads of ornamental grasses.)

All the above can be tied up in small bunches and dried hanging upside down in an airy place out of direct sunlight; a utility room or shed is ideal. If you want to dry hydrangea heads, gypsophila, love-lies-bleeding (amaranthus), then they do best stood in empty jars to dry out right-way-up. Some arrangers stand hydrangeas in a solution of glycerine (from chemists) and water, which makes them take on fascinating tints and shades as they dry out, besides preventing them from turning too papery. And although you can dry grass seedheads and honesty upright, the very best results come from lying them flat on a clean cloth on a slatted shelf or a wire-netting framework. This is also the best way to dry any flowers that droop, bend or try to turn up to the light if you dry them any other way.

Once they are completely dry, you can arrange dried flowers, grasses and seedheads in much the same way you'd use fresh flowers in a vase – but of course without any water. If they need support, use brown flower arrangers' foam to hold them in place, not the green sort that's meant to absorb water and support fresh flowers. They can also be used for making potpourri and for crafts such as collage.

If the flowers aren't needed straight away, store them carefully in a cupboard in cardboard boxes with lids (old shoeboxes are perfect if the flowers fit inside, or in small bunches loosely wrapped in tissue paper to avoid the blooms getting dusty).

Helichrysums have heads that droop after they've dried, so they are usually snipped from their stems and used as loose flowers – perhaps added to potpourri to beef it up – or they are given 'fake' stems made from florists' wires. These have to be pushed through the flower head, then the top end is hooked over so it holds. The wire is then pulled back down so the hooked end is hidden in the bloom where it won't show. Leave the long bottom end of the wire to act as a 'stem' which can be wrapped in green tape if it's going to show and you want a more realistic-looking finish.

Delicate seedheads such as grasses tend to hang on to their seeds best if sprayed with a kind of fixative; look for suitable products in craft shops. Traditionally hairspray was used, but it needs treating with caution as it makes the finished heads very inflammable.

Dried flowers don't keep in pristine condition for as long as some people think. When they are on show in an arrangement in a room they gather dust which is difficult to dislodge – a gentle shake or a light waft with a hairdryer on a cool setting can help. They also fade when exposed to sunlight and can turn quite brittle in a warm, dry room so they crumble or break if touched. Old arrangements can look quite 'tired', so it's best to use them for no more than one year and then replace them with a freshly dried batch, and do a new batch each summer.

GROW YOUR OWN GOURDS

Ornamental gourds make great natural decorations. They grow on long, scrambling, annual vines that look good trailing over an arch or on a fence or trellis; they can also be grown in a tub on the patio, given suitable support. (Three plants grown this way up a tripod of rustic poles makes a great project for children.)

Raise your own gourd plants from seed; a packet usually contains a mixture of several different varieties. Sow two per 9cm (three-and-a-half inch) pot on a warm windowsill indoors in April, and don't plant the young plants outside until the last frost is safely past, which won't usually be until mid to late May. Grow them in rich soil or a tub of potting compost in a sheltered, sunny spot and allow the vines to climb using their tendrils. In summer it's fun to watch the baby gourds appear, swell up to roughly fist-size and change colour.

The decorative fruits start to dry out naturally on the plants in autumn. Cut them in late September or early October, before the first frost, clean the skins with a damp cloth and bring them into a warm room to finish drying slowly. A lot of people like to varnish their gourds to make them shiny, but this can make them rot faster since the skin can't 'breathe'. This won't matter if you only plan on keeping them over the winter, but a better alternative is to buff them up with a soft cloth and a spot of spray-on furniture polish.

FLOWER CONFETTI

If you're planning a country wedding in summer, real flower petals make a fashionable and 'green' alternative to paper confetti or rice. Petals are often acceptable at venues that don't allow conventional confetti or rice due to the mess left behind afterwards (but always check in advance). If you have a well-stocked garden or have a local supplier, you can use *fresh* flower petals, but there's always a risk that the 'juice' will stain clothes; white and very pale pastel petals are safest in this respect, but even so, dried petals are usually preferred. They are also far easier to prepare in advance and store, and can be ordered from specialist suppliers, usually flower farms who prepare their own mixtures. Find them by searching the Internet.

CUTTING GARDENS

WHEN YOU WANT TO CUT FLOWERS in reasonable quantities to bring indoors without spoiling the look of your borders, the solution is to keep a 'cutting garden'. This can be located somewhere that's not on view from the house, and which is kept especially for cut flowers. Some people like to create a separate bed, and others will use one end of the veg patch or allotment. To be cost-effective, raise your own annuals from seed, and be sure to include some of the many bulbs, perennials, shrubs and roses that provide good cut flowers, too.

Hardy annuals: grow from seed sown in rows where they are to flower, from mid March to the end of April. Good kinds include calendula, *Ammi majus* (Queen Anne's lace), candytuft, cornflower, marigolds, larkspur and sunflowers; also several small ornamental grasses such as quaking grass.

Sweet peas are hardy annuals, but are usually sown in late October/early November in a cold frame or unheated greenhouse (for the earliest flowers) or February/early March under cover in small individual pots and planted out in late March or April when 5–7.5cm (2–3in) tall. To produce flowers with long, straight stems, train each plant up its own string and remove all the tendrils. You will, though, be able to pick perfectly usable flowers from plants allowed to scramble up netting or trellis, which take less work.

Half-hardy annuals: grow from seed sown in a heated propagator in a greenhouse or on windowsills indoors in March. Prick the seedlings out when they are big enough to handle and don't plant them outside until after the last frost, around mid to late May – at the same time as young plants you may have bought from a nursery or garden centre. Good varieties include antirrhinum, aster, amaranthus, cosmos, eustoma, salpiglossis, phlox, stocks, zinnia and annual rudbeckia.

Perennials: usually bought as reasonable-sized plants for planting in spring, but many kinds can be grown from seed, treated as either half-hardy annuals sown in February, when many kinds should flower the same year, or as hardy annuals sown outside in May/June, in which case the young plants need transplanting to flowering places in autumn; they'll start flowering the following year. Good kinds include: achillea, astilbe, astrantia, delphinium, echinacea, eryngium, rudbeckia, scabious, gypsophila, pinks and *Sedum spectabile* (ice plant) which some arrangers pick as flat green heads of buds instead of waiting for the pink flowers to open.

Bulbs, corms and tubers: start frost-tender kinds in pots under cover and plant them outside after the last frost – dahlias are particular favourites with arrangers. Plant hardy kinds such as liatris, ornamental alliums, lilies, dutch iris and spring bulbs, including daffodils, as soon as the bulbs or roots become available in the shops, or order from bulb catalogues.

Roses: any roses can be used as cut flowers, but the most popular varieties for cutting are the heavily scented red varieties such as 'Alec's Red', 'Deep Secret' and 'Fragrant Cloud'; orange-red 'Superstar' is an old favourite with fragrance and good long stems. Keen flower arrangers often like unusual colours; they'll often grow stripy roses such as 'Harry Wheatcroft', 'painted' roses (such as 'Sue Lawley'), green roses (such as 'Greensleeves') or caramel-brown roses (such as 'Julia Clements').

PRESSED FLOWERS

Pressing flowers was a great hobby when I was at school – sandwiching common wildflowers between sheets of newspaper and flattening them under a rug in the front room. It was a great summer holiday project and I still treasure the scrapbook of buttercups and cow parsley, coltsfoot and vetches that won me first prize at junior school aged eight!

Nowadays picking wildflowers from the countryside is frowned on. It's a great shame. There's a danger that children are becoming more and more divorced from nature, and collecting *common* wildflowers, that are available in abundance, should be encouraged. They don't need to take armfuls; just single specimens without roots that will encourage them to develop a knowledge and love of the countryside that might otherwise seem distant and puzzling. Garden flowers, too, are quite acceptable for pressing, and some – such as pansies – are particularly successful. They can be used to make home-made greetings cards, bookmarks and pictures. Pressing flowers is a great way to get children interested in flowers and crafts, as they can use the end result to make small gifts for grandparents. Sheets of plain or coloured card, and also blank greetings cards sold especially for this job, are available from craft shops.

You can still use the newspaper and rug – or the large-book-and-blotting paper method – but nowadays proper flower presses are available, again from craft shops. The best flowers for pressing are those with naturally fairly flat faces since they don't change shape; pansies and violas are great favourites. With more three-dimensional flowers, it pays to 'arrange' the petals nicely before applying pressure so that they press in a reasonably natural-looking position. If you want to press the sort of flowers that have a hard, chunky centre (like the yellow bit in the centre of daisies, or the green calyx at the base of a rose bloom), remove the petals carefully, press them individually and then re-assemble the flower complete with authentic stalk as you stick it onto backing paper. If in doubt as to how a particular flower will turn out, try one or two first to see what happens – you've nothing to lose.

Most flowers and leaves are completely dry after two weeks in the flower press. Arrange them carefully on your chosen card and glue them in place with a suitable craft glue.

It's not only flowers that you can press; when you want to make a posy-effect for a picture it's handy to have some pressed foliage as well – and it doesn't have to be the foliage from the flower you are pressing. You can cheat and use any leaves that press well and create a suitably decorative effect. Flat grass blades are easy to press, and ornamental varieties with red, gold or stripy leaves look stunning. Anything with striking shapes, such as horse chestnut leaves, also look good. You can press autumn leaves, too; those of Japanese maples are especially stunning and will keep most of their colour – pick them when they show superb colours but before they start to dry out naturally, and press them flat straight away before they start to curl up at the edges. Leaves that won't press well, are thick, juicy or succulent ones, so avoid cyclamen and sedums.

But if you are pressing flowers for a school botany project, or making a picture in the style of a botanical illustration, then you'll need to be strictly accurate. Aim to show an open flower, a bud, stems and foliage, and possibly even roots of common types. Lay them out attractively and identify them either with typed labels or your best handwriting. You'll have a souvenir that lasts longer than your lifetime.

HOW TO MAKE A POMANDER

A pomander was originally carried by the upper classes when they had to travel through the streets in medieval Europe, since it was thought that something nicely scented could ward off plague and pestilence. Judges at the time would take a pomander with them into their courtroom as an antidote to the 'noxious airs' rising from the jails below, and today judges still carry 'nosegays' – small bunches of flowers – on official occasions.

Today pomanders make lovely, natural, fragrant Christmas decorations redolent of citrus and spice; try lining a row of them up along a mantelpiece or hall windowsill at Christmas.

For each pomander you'll need a citrus fruit (an orange was the traditional choice but you can use lime, lemon, grapefruit or tangerine), enough whole cloves to cover or decorate your citrus fruit, and a length of narrow ribbon about 30cm (12in) long.

Use a sharp-pointed cocktail stick to make a series of evenly spaced holes all over the surface of the skin of the fruit, then press a whole clove into each hole, pointed end first, leaving the knobbly end flush with the skin. You can make patterns with the cloves but for the longest-lasting pomanders, cover the entire surface of the fruit with cloves – but remember to leave a bare narrow strip all round it where the ribbon will go. (If you fancy a more heavily spiced pomander, dust the clove-studded fruit in powdered nutmeg, allspice or cinnamon immediately after pushing the cloves in; enough of the powdered spice will stick to the dampness on the skin.)

Lastly, tie the ribbon round the fruit so that it crosses over top and bottom and is held firmly, then tie the loose ends of ribbons into a bow on top of the fruit or use it to make a loop to hang it up.

CANDLE-MAKING

In bygone times, impoverished country families made their own candles using tallow from clarified beef, bacon or pork fat (often left over from the Sunday joint), with plant material as wicks – they'd use the pith from the centre of dried rushes, or the furry stems of dried mullein plants. The resulting candles were a bit smelly and smoky; they also spluttered badly, and didn't give off much light.

Wealthy households always used the far superior beeswax candles. These were made by dipping weighted wicks into melted beeswax, and as fast as each coat of wax started to set, it was dipped again to gain an extra layer, so the candles grew fatter. Artisan candle-makers would make a dozen or more candles at a time by draping a row of long wicks over a stout pole, then dangling these down into a vat of melted wax. By lifting each end of the pole up and down, pairs of candles formed. When they were cold and the wax was thoroughly set,

each pair of candles was separated by cutting through the length of wick that joined them.

Now candle-making is a flourishing hobby, and craft centres and hobby shops sell kits containing everything you need. But when you have a home-grown supply of beeswax, you can do it yourself from scratch.

ECONOMY TIP

Whether you burn home-made candles or ones you've bought from a shop, save up any drips of spilt candle wax along with your old candle stubs. When you have enough, melt them down in a tin can in a bath of hot water, using the method opposite and you can reuse them to make a new candle, which only needs a new piece of string for the wick.

HOW TO MAKE A CANDLE

FOR YOUR CANDLE WICKS, use good-quality cotton string. You next need a mould. Use a strong plastic tube of suitable diameter (perhaps cut the bottom half off an empty washing-up liquid bottle, for a large, fat, church-type candle). Lubricate the inside with a little vegetable oil so that the candle can slide out easily afterwards. Cut a length of string a few inches longer than the length of your mould. Drip a blob of molten beeswax into the base of the mould and press one end of the string down into it, then give it a few moments to set firmly so that it is fixed securely. Then tie the other end of the string to the middle of a short, straight piece of stick rested on the rim of the mould; wind the string round it just enough to tighten the wick until it hangs straight down the centre of the tube. Stand the mould upright on a tin plate or similar heatproof surface that can catch any spilt wax safely.

NOW MELT THE BEESWAX BY heating it gently inside an old, but clean, tin can standing inside a saucepan of hot water. (Don't put it directly into the pan or you'll have a dreadful job cleaning it afterwards.) When the wax has melted you can add other ingredients to colour, scent or decorate the finished candle. You can use food colouring or special dye for candles bought from a craft shop, some scented oil (the aromatherapy type, in whatever fragrance you fancy – lavender is always popular) or some pieces of dried herbs, spices, dried lavender flowers or pieces of dried petals or small fragments of mixed potpourri. Mix these in well so that they are evenly distributed. Alternatively, leave the wax completely natural with nothing added; pure beeswax will produce a pale, creamy-coloured candle.

POUR A LITTLE OF THE MELTED WAX carefully into the bottom of the mould. As soon as the base starts to set, stand the mould in a container of cold water before filling the rest of the mould with melted wax. When the entire tube is firmly set and cold, cut the wick off about a centimetre (a quarter of an inch) above the top of the wax and slide the candle out of its mould. (If it sticks, plunge it briefly in hot water, or as a last resort cut the base carefully off the mould and push it out from there.) For a fancier finish, perhaps to make decorative candles for Christmas, buff the exterior of the candle gently with a piece of kitchen paper that's been moistened with a few drops of vegetable oil, then sprinkle it very sparingly with glitter or a few dried herbs or spices, but don't overdo it – a very light 'gilding' is quite enough.

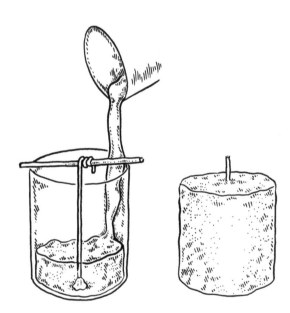

PATCHWORK AND QUILTING

Originally, patchwork and quilting were two different crafts, but today they tend to be thought of as one and the same thing and are mostly used to make patchwork quilts, which act as decorative bedspreads or can be hung on a wall just as you might hang up an expensive handmade or antique rug.

PATCHWORK

In my youth, patchwork was one of the many handicrafts children learnt at junior school. While we lads did manly things like woodwork, the girls would be doing needlecraft of various sorts, and patchwork was a regular favourite. Girls would be asked to bring small scraps of leftover material from home, and shown how to stitch them together to make tea cosies or cushion covers. They'd cut stacks of identical-sized octagonal shapes out of cardboard, then lay each one onto a piece of fabric only slightly larger. Next, they'd fold the edges of the fabric over the cardboard templates and stitch them loosely into position with long, loose stitches over the back of the shape. When they had a goodish pile of fabric-clad octagons, they'd over-sew the edges neatly together so that they formed a honeycomb-like piece of patchwork. Once they'd stitched enough together to make the shape and size required for their finished item, they'd snip the stitching that held the cardboard shapes in place, remove them from the octagons of cloth, and then sew the whole piece of patchwork onto a 'backing cloth' to make the finished article. Oh, it took ages to do but the sense of achievement was worth the slog!

Patchwork was – and is – cheap to do, yet it produces very attractive items from 'leftovers'. In days gone by thrifty housewives always saved up all their remnants of fabric and off-cuts from other jobs, so they didn't need to buy anything. Half the skill lay in choosing, from amongst the various odds and ends, pieces that would go well together in the finished work. Most people chose a mixture of patterns in several shades of one colour, so the result looked stylish rather than garish. And back in the days when country folk did patchwork to make larger items like throws, bedspreads, or even curtains out of oddments, they'd usually use squares or diamonds instead of octagonal shapes, since they were faster to sew and made better use of the material, so there was less waste. But the end result was still very homely.

QUILTING

Think of a quilted jacket and you'll see the difference between patchwork and quilting straight away. A quilt is two layers of fabric with a thicker, fluffier, insulated layer between them, held in place by decorative stitchwork. A patchwork quilt is pretty and practical; it might consist of fabric shapes sewn on to a plain-coloured cover with a thicker, insulated layer inside, or it could be a patchwork cover that sandwiches a thicker insulated layer in between, with stitching outlining the patterns made by the patchwork.

Quilting is often done by a group of enthusiasts, and the work is usually stretched on a frame that holds the underlying fabric taut while the decorative pieces are being stitched on. A few country villages still have quilting clubs today. In the USA, handmade quilts are heirlooms passed down through country families, and the style – recreated in ready-printed fabric – is still much in use for traditional bed coverings there today.

SPINNING

Natural sheep's fleece is thick and fluffy, far removed from the woollen yarn used for knitting or weaving into fabrics. It takes a complicated process to turn the raw fleece into a useable product.

As it comes straight off the sheep, a fleece is dirty, so it's first washed well to remove grease and dirt, then allowed to dry. Next it needs to be carded. This is done a small handful at a time, and involves 'combing' the rough wool between two 'carders', which look like long-handled dog-brushes, with a mass of short, hooked wire bristles. By brushing the two repeatedly together with a blob of wool between them, the fibres are 'combed' out so that they give you a much fluffier bundle of wool that's far easier to spin. (The job was originally done using teasel heads, which are hard, fat, tubular seedheads covered with short, bristly hooks.) The carded 'fluff' is then roughly rolled by hand into a fat cylinder, ready to spin.

The earliest yarns would have been made by simply twisting and stretching the 'raw' wool by hand; it took ages. The invention of the drop spindle speeded the job up quite a bit. A drop spindle is little more than a short length of wooden pole with a hook at the top, and a heavy weight at the bottom that incorporates a reel for the finished thread to be wound round. A bundle of clean, carded wool is attached to the hook at the top and the pole is turned, which starts the device spinning. As it spins, the fibres in the wool are automatically teased out straight and twisted into a similar sort of yarn that you'd have if you bought a ball of knitting wool. As the spindle keeps turning the yarn gets steadily longer, then when the bottom of the weight reaches the ground, the yarn that's been made is wound round the reel and the spinner continues, adding more loose, fluffy wool to the original bundle at the top of the spindle. The result is a bit rustic – uneven and very obviously handmade – and it takes a long time to produce a useful quantity of useable yarn, but cottagers didn't have a lot else to do during the long winter evenings, and you could spin wool this way even in weak candlelight.

Today you can still use a drop spindle if you only have a small amount of fleece to turn into yarn, but most modern spinners use a spinning wheel. Here a bundle of raw loose wool is slowly fed from a 'storage cylinder' through a rotating 'flyer' that twists and pulls it into yarn, which is wound onto a reel, the whole thing being powered by a foot-operated treadle that turns the large wheel. Using this ingenious contraption it's possible to convert a much larger volume of fleece into yarn of a more even thickness and uniform quality, since it maintains an even tension throughout (as against the drop spindle where the tension is constantly varying). It's a satisfying craft; according to keen spinners, a spinning wheel is therapeutic to use.

Natural homespun wool can be used for knitting, both by hand or using a knitting machine, and a lot of sheep-owners like to turn their fleeces into sweaters, knitted woollen jackets, coats and cardigans, throws or shawls for members of their family or for items to sell at craft fairs. It's not just sheep fleeces that can be spun into yarn; llama and alpaca fleeces can be used (alpaca is wonderfully soft and silky), and some people will even spin the fluff clipped from their poodle, or combed from their Persian cat, to knit into highly personalised sweaters.

WEAVING

Some craftspeople like to weave yarn to make into more specialised fabrics, particularly tweed to make clothing, and for wall hangings, throws and rugs. You sometimes meet spinners and weavers at craft fairs selling a wide range of fascinating home-made items, and demonstrating how they make them.

Weaving involves criss-crossing vertical and horizontal threads tightly together to make cloth. The original method of weaving was exceptionally slow and tedious, since a row of horizontal threads tied to a wooden frame had to be separated individually and a vertical thread woven backwards and forwards between each one, then at the end of the row the vertical thread turned round the last thread and worked back along the row of vertical threads in the opposite direction.

The invention of the loom changed all that. This large weaving frame is arranged something like a tabletop, with very long threads that are unwound at one end as the work progresses, and a shuttle that passes between them adding the cross-threads, with the finished cloth being wound onto a roll at the other end. Work progresses much faster, since the long end-to-end threads (the warp) are fed through a metal plate containing alternate slots and holes, so that by raising and lowering the plate the two sets of threads are automatically separated, allowing the shuttle that bears the side-to-side threads (the weft) to pass between them. The slotted plate is operated by a foot pedal, so the operator can get quite a speed up. Between every run of the shuttle, a stick-like device is used to press the last row of work down firmly against the last, so the finished cloth is dense and evenly textured. If you see a large loom in action, it has rather a Heath Robinson air about it, with beams going up and down, threads moving, and shuttle flying, with the operator working in such harmony that he or she seems to be part of the machinery. Although a loom looks easy to use, it needs a fair degree of coordination, and a lot of the skill lies in setting up the loom and preparing the warp threads just right at the outset.

KNITTING WOOL

For people who don't want the bother of turning home-produced fleeces into useable yarns and knitting wool, it's possible to send them off to a factory and get them back ready-processed. Firms advertise in smallholders' magazines.

Single-strand yarn is mostly used for weaving; for knitting, three-ply wool is used. This is made by twisting together three thin strands of yarn in the opposite direction to the natural twist of the original yarn, in much the same way as thin rope, so the two opposing twists give the finished knitting wool a springy effect – this is what gives sweaters etc., their 'bounce' and 'stretch', as against woven fabric where the yarns are stretched taut during weaving.

Used knitting wool can be recycled. Years ago it was very common for thrifty country housewives to unpick old, worn-out pullovers by hand, wash and rewind the best of the wool (making their husbands or children sit with hands held outstretched to loop it round, forming it into hanks) and then re-knit it to make something new. Even small oddments of knitting wool weren't left to go to waste: they were knitted into squares that were sewn together to make patchwork blankets or cushion covers, or used to knit useful small items such as tea cosies or kettle holders, and I can still remember the aching arms as I held the hanks of wool for my mum!

NATURAL DYES ❋❋

A good many craftspeople enjoy using natural-coloured wool from the different breeds of sheep to make garments or rugs in a range of cream, white, grey, beige, brown and black shades, but when a larger range of colours are required the wool has to be dyed. (When tweed is made, for instance, the colours that form the characteristic speckled patterns are created by using different coloured warp threads, and changing the colour of wool in the shuttle so they create a contrasting effect where the different colours cross.)

Synthetic dyes allow any colour or shade to be used, but many craft enthusiasts enjoy dying their wool using natural fabric colourings they've made themselves from plants. Plants provided the original dyes used hundreds of years ago; even today, enthusiasts say that plant dyes have a character and vibrancy that you don't find in modern synthetic ones. The dye obtained from particular plants often bears little relation to the colour of the plant itself. The final colour it produces will also vary in shade according to the colour of the original wool and the mordant (the chemical added to dye to 'fix' it to the fabric) used, so it's interesting to see how each batch turns out.

Onion skins produce rich yellow, brown or orange shades. Marigold (*Calendula officinalis*) makes shades of yellow. Bloodroot (*Sanguinaria canadensis*) lives up to its name by producing reddish orange shades. Horsetail gives light yellow and greeny yellow shades. (Any gardener will be glad to find a good use for this notorious weed!) Dyer's chamomile (*Anthemis tinctoria*) makes amber or khaki-ish shades, weld (*Reseda luteola*) produces beautiful yellow shades, and madder (*Rubia tinctorum*, which was cultivated by dyers from the Anglo-Saxons onwards specially for use as a dye-plant) produces orangey shades of red-brown or pink. It has to be said that there are plenty of plants that yield dyes in rather earthy shades of yellows, tans and browns, but some colours are very under-represented. Blues can be produced using indigo or woad, but they are some of the most difficult and complicated dyes to make.

To create natural dyes you need suitable plant material. The best natural plant dyes are made using fresh materials, but don't pick them from the countryside – the dyes are just as good when the plants are grown in controlled conditions in the garden. A lot of suitable plants are quite common; parsley and nettles for instance. When fresh ingredients aren't available, dried leaves, petals or roots can be used (these can be homegrown or bought from craft suppliers specially for dying) and you can freeze berries to use.

You also need a mordant. A mordant is a chemical added to the plant material which makes the colour soak into the wool better, and makes the end fabric more colour-fast, though it also contributes something to the colour itself. All sorts of strange substances have been used as mordants throughout history: vinegar, salt and wood ashes to name a few. (The weirdest by far has got to be urine, which was once collected in buckets overnight by Hebridean islanders to use for 'fixing' the colours of Harris tweed.) But the most used ones are metallic: alum (an aluminium salt), chrome, tin or iron.

The exact recipe differs for each particular plant and mordant combination, but roughly the same sort of process is followed for each. You need a large stainless steel pan, something like a large preserving pan, which is kept especially for dyeing.

The natural woollen yarn (which has already been spun) is first tied into loose hanks, then soaked in a sinkful of hot water, ammonia and soft soap for an hour, followed by another hour's soaking in a fresh sinkful of the same solution at a slightly lower temperature. This part of the treatment is to get rid of oil or grease from the wool, which prevents the dye being properly absorbed. The wool is then rinsed well and dried, then kept – still in hanks – until you're ready to dye it.

It's then pre-soaked to ensure that the wool (which is naturally rather water-resistant) is thoroughly wet right through, before being treated with the mordant and the plant dye, which has been previously prepared.

Dye plants that have tough woody stems are chopped and then soaked overnight in enough soft water to just about cover them (a lot of enthusiasts save rainwater especially for this job). Soft or softer plant material, including berries, petals and the like, can be used straight away; they only need to be covered with water. Use your stainless-steel dye pan for this or you'll ruin your saucepans.

Heat the pan of water and plant material gently, but don't quite let it boil, then simmer for several hours before letting it cool. Strain it and pour it back into the (empty) dye pan. Add the wet, mordanted wool, and bring the mixture very slowly back to simmering point; simmer gently for another hour. When it's 'done', the wool is lifted out and rinsed, first in hot water, then again in progressively cooler water and finally cold water, then the hanks of wool are hung up tidily to dry.

It's worth pointing out that natural dyes will tend to fade in sunlight, and though the effect can be charming, you may want to preserve the colours by keeping throws and clothing somewhere out of direct sunlight when you aren't actually using them, to keep the colours looking fresh and vibrant for longer.

WOODTURNING

If you visit a country fair today, you may well see a woodturner selling his work, and he'll almost certainly be a retired gent who does it as a paying hobby. This is because although ordinary people once relied on wooden bowls, plates and dishes instead of expensive china, nowadays 'turned' wood items are mainly used decoratively by folk who appreciate the beauty of the natural grain of the wood, and the skill that's gone into making these items.

Since suitable wood for turning is in rather short supply, woodturners will often keep an eye out for gardeners felling ornamental trees such as cherry, walnut, pear or apple, since those have particularly attractive grains when the wood is cut across, turned and polished. But yew, maple and elm are also suitable; they are some of the many sorts of wood that were once used for making fine furniture.

A whole tree trunk has to be sawn into suitable-sized pieces and stored for some time to season, otherwise the finished items may split or buckle out of shape after they've been inside a warm house for a while. When the timber is seasoned and ready to use, the turner fits it to a lathe, which these days is electrically operated. He then uses a series of small tools to gouge the spinning section of wood into the right shape for a plate, bowl or whatever it may be. These days, pieces of polished wooden fruit are also popular; they can be used as ornaments in their own right, but they are often piled up in a turned wooden fruit bowl. Once the piece has been shaped, inside and out, it is sandpapered, finished with beeswax polish and buffed up, again all on the lathe. Individual items take hours of work to complete fully, but there's a huge satisfaction to be had from the process for anyone who loves wood.

Turning wood in a lathe is a real art form, producing beautifully crafted, ornamental pieces.

CANAL-BOAT PAINTING

The canal system was created in the late eighteenth and early nineteenth centuries as a means of linking places where raw materials were produced or imported with the factories that processed them and the cities that consumed them. At the time, canal barges were the only means of hauling heavy loads of goods such as cast iron, coal, sand, china clay and metal ore over long distances to fuel the growing Industrial Revolution.

Rising costs and competition meant that the men who worked on canal barges were eventually forced to move their families on board, so barges became portable homes as well as work-boats. A complete lifestyle revolved round canal boats, which came to be decorated in a characteristic folksy style, not unlike that of traditional gypsy caravans. Entire boats were covered with a cheery mixture of flowers (especially roses) and scenery (particularly churches, great houses or castles) against a coloured background divided into squares or ovals garnished with stars and scrolls. Even the metal buckets, milk cans and water jugs used on board were decorated in the same style. Some of the decoration was personalised, but much of it was done in the livery of the various companies that owned working canal boats.

The art of traditional canal boat painting persisted even when canals were superseded by railways and trunk roads, and narrowboats were reinvented as leisure craft for folk who enjoyed cruising the canals, enjoying the peace, quiet and wildlife.

HOW TO PAINT TRADITIONAL CANAL-STYLE ART

First divide up the area to be painted into a series of rectangles with narrow strips in between them; if you're painting containers, outline spouts and handles, paint the strips, spouts and handles bright red and the rectangles, black. Later paint your scenes, roses, castles, etc. – into panels in the black areas, and add white stars and scrolls anywhere there doesn't seem to be enough decoration; you can also outline some of the red stripes in white to further brighten up the effect.

Some enthusiasts prefer to use dark blue or a deep green in place of the red background colour, so feel free to use a little artistic licence.

The same style looks very good used for metal tubs and troughs on a patio, and it's especially stunning used for a herb garden outside the back door, since herbs tend to be very 'green', so their looks are improved by colourful containers.

GO WILD IN THE COUNTRY

CHAPTER 6

Once upon a time, hunting, shooting and fishing were *the* traditional country pursuits; they had their roots in aristocratic field sports, as well as the efforts of country people to supplement their homegrown produce with a little foraging and poaching. But the Industrial Revolution turned cities into the places where people found fun and entertainment, and country pursuits were largely left to the rural poor – eccentric parsons who watched birds or collected butterflies and those who found an outlet for their energies in that trio of traditional country sports.

Today, changing attitudes, plus more leisure time – and money – have made the countryside a place of escape for people who live and work in towns. Outdoor enthusiasts have discovered the delights of natural history, rambling, mountain-biking and catch-and-throw-back angling, to name but a few. Now, people are concerned about their environment; they are going 'greener' and rediscovering old skills, besides getting closer to their roots, even if most of it has to be crammed into weekends and holidays.

NATURAL HISTORY

One of the great joys of a country walk is being able to put names to at least a few of the birds, wildflowers and butterflies that you see. Most country lanes and public footpaths through meadows and woods will yield a few interesting sightings, but when you are keen to spot a lot of wildlife it's worth making special trips to nature reserves, the coast, Forestry Commission land or parklands owned by the National Trust or similar conservation organisations. And if you enjoy walking in groups, consider joining Ramblers, who plan organised walks for members; information on the website of local groups tells you the approximate length of the walks so you don't take on anything you can't handle, but it's amazing how quickly your ability to walk longer distances builds up when you keep at it.

IDENTIFYING BIRDS

Roughly 280 species of birds are regularly seen in the British Isles; they include full-time residents and migrants who visit temporarily – either to breed in summer or to escape harsh winters in the places they do breed. Others 'pass through' very briefly on their migration routes, stopping over to rest or refuel before moving on again. Very occasionally, we'll also get rare foreign birds that have been blown way off course. These attract a lot of excitement from 'twitchers', who travel huge distances to get a brief sighting of a rarity that's new to them, so they can add another 'tick' to their spotter's list.

The art of identifying birds lies in practice, plus a spot of study. The best way to start is by learning the easy ones first – the birds that you regularly see in your garden and in the countryside round your home. The commoner species such as house sparrows (though rarer than they once were), starlings, blackbirds, wrens, blue tits and great tits can turn up almost anywhere in towns or countryside throughout the country, and you'll probably also see thrushes, kestrels and sparrowhawks. Once you are familiar with those, start looking further afield. Certain birds are found in particular types of habitat; some are only seen at the coast, or in mountains, woods or moorland country. (You won't, for instance, find a grouse on your bird table in leafy Surrey, though you may

see a woodpecker on your peanut-feeder.) It's worth carrying a small pocket guide to the birds of Britain, for ready reference – keep it handy in the car, or your backpack when you're out walking. I wouldn't advise getting a great thick book that includes birds of Europe as it'll be packed full of species you'll never see in this country, which just makes it more difficult to identify what you *will* see. A small pair of binoculars is also a big help; choose the lightweight sort that will fit in a pocket or which you can hang round your neck on a long walk without throttling yourself; 7 x 26cm or 8 x 28cm is ideal.

When you see a bird you don't recognise, try to compare it to something you *do* know, as a rough guide to size (e.g blackbird-sized, sparrow-sized, pigeon-sized) and make a note of colour, markings or other distinguishing features as it all helps when you look it up. Behaviour can also be helpful; a medium-sized bird hovering over a roadside verge is almost certainly a kestrel. A good bird identification book will tell you the time of year, distribution and habitats for each species in its pages, which helps you eliminate a lot of possibilities and home in on the right one.

If you visit an RSPB reserve, look for the 'sightings board' that they keep at the visitor centre listing all the birds that have been seen recently on the reserve, so you know what you might expect to see during your visit. You'll often find volunteers on duty in hides or in the visitor centre who can point out birds of interest and help you to identify them, but all members are usually very helpful when you make it obvious that you're an interested beginner. You'll know there's a real rarity around if you see groups of enthusiasts dressed in khaki-green birdwatching gear, all bringing high-powered telescopes to bear on the same distant point; ask what they're looking at. (Serious twitchers subscribe to a pager service that alerts them to the location of rarities, which is how they manage to arrive at the scene of an interesting sighting in large numbers, and they're also in touch with fellow twitchers via mobile phones.)

If you become more interested, it's handy to have a DVD bird identification guide at home; besides showing you good close up shots of each bird in turn, the presenter will point out key identification features. It's a great way to learn a lot of species quickly. A good way to develop your interest further is to go on a course or a bird-watching holiday. Some bird reserves hold special walks accompanied by experts to help newcomers identify birds that turn up on their patch, and several organisations, such as the Field Studies Council, and specialist bird holiday firms, run courses or organised excursions to places of bird-watching interest with experts in attendance. (Find them through adverts in bird-watching magazines.)

THE RSPB

The RSPB (Royal Society for the Protection of Birds) owns and manages over 200 bird reserves all over the country; access is free to members and for a small admission fee to non-members. Reserves include woodland, wetlands, coastal and cliff-top habitats. Full details of the reserves, which birds you can expect to see on them at different times of year, and opening times etc., can be found on their website, which also contains photos and recognition details of British birds, details of events at reserves, local groups and activities, besides other useful information. www.rspb.org.uk

BIRD RECOGNITION – THE BARE ESSENTIALS

Smaller than a sparrow

1 Wren: a little brown bird with a slightly barred pattern and conspicuously cocked tail, found all year round in woods, parkland, gardens and hedgerows. Solitary and with a wonderfully elaborate song.

2 Long-tailed tit: a small, dumpy-bodied, pinky-brown, white and black bird with a tail three times the length of its body, found in family groups all year round in edges of woodlands, hedgerows and gardens.

3 Firecrest: along with the goldcrest, our smallest bird and relatively rare. Pale brown with a red and yellow 'stripe' on the top of its head. Often nips about in conifers.

Sparrow-sized

4 House sparrow: a cheeky bird with black-and-chestnut-dappled back and wings with grey underparts, and a rather blunt head and dumpy body, usually found in flocks; present all year round, once common in built-up areas as well as in countryside, but now becoming unaccountably scarce in some areas. Very 'chatty' in groups at roosting time.

5 Hedge sparrow (dunnock): a streaky brown bird with grey head and neck and a more streamlined shape than the house sparrow. Usually found in flocks, common and widespread in gardens, hedgerows, parkland and countryside all year round.

6 Bluetit: a lively, active, rounded blue and yellow bird common in gardens, hedgerows and parks, often hanging upside down to feed on insects under leaves. Solitary or seen in small family groups in summer. Present all year round.

7 Great tit: a size larger than the bluetit, but just as common, with strong black and yellow markings with a greenish back, found in all the same places, all year round. Solitary, or in small family groups in summer. Resident all year.

8 Pied wagtail: striking grey-and-white bird with black 'trim' and a black eye in a white face, which bobs its tail constantly. Fairly common in towns, gardens and countryside all year round. Usually solitary or found in pairs in summer, but in winter they can gather in fair-sized flocks to roost. Resident.

9 Chaffinch: the male has a conspicuous pinkish chest and underparts with blackish wings clearly

marked with two white flashes, easily seen when perching and in flight. The female is duller brown but also with black-and-white-striped wings. Seen in gardens, hedgerows and parkland, mostly individually or in pairs, year-round.

10 Greenfinch: yellowy-green birds with a yellowish streak down the front edge of each wing; the colours are brightest in spring. Commonly found in small flocks in gardens, hedgerows and parkland, all year round.

11 Goldfinch: showy beige, black and gold bird with a red-and-white face, the black, red and gold colours showing up clearly both in flight and when perched. Sometimes seen in fair-sized flocks in countryside and wasteland, especially where thistles or teazel seedheads are present, as the birds feed on the seeds. Resident.

12 Robin: the most instantly recognisable of any resident bird, dumpy with an orange-red breast and rather upright stance, often bobbing slightly; very common in gardens, hedgerows and parkland.

Blackbird-sized

13 Blackbird: male is all-black with a bright yellow beak and yellow ring round the eye; female and juveniles are all-brown. Common in gardens, hedgerows and parkland, mostly solitary but in spring parents often seen feed youngsters on the ground. Resident.

14 Starling: rather slender shape compared to the blackbird and slightly smaller, with glossy, iridescent black feathers regularly spotted with silvery white, especially in spring. Youngsters are the same shape and size but a dull grey-brown shade. Commonly seen in small flocks in the countryside, and in winter large flocks swoop and wheel towards dusk as they gather to roost communally in large trees or reedbeds. Resident, though some migrate.

15 Song thrush: brown-backed bird with cream face, breast and underparts heavily speckled with brown, almost chevron-shaped 'dots'. Mostly solitary; less common than some years ago; in gardens, hedgerows and parkland. Resident.

16 Redwing: very similar to song thrush but with bright orange-red 'armpits' and a distinct cream eye-stripe, seen in small flocks; a winter visitor to hedgerows, parkland and sometimes gardens in search of berries.

17 Great spotted woodpecker: a showy, piebald-effect black-and-white bird with bright red undertail; male also has a red cap on his head. Hammers its beak on dead branches in spring to warn off rivals. Seen perching on upright tree branches, pressing its tail flat against the branch for support; often visits peanut feeders, also seen in countryside trees and parklands. Resident.

Pigeon-sized

18 Wood pigeon: a very common plump, pinkish-grey bird with a white collar, faintly surprised facial expression and yellow eye, making loud five-note cooing calls when perched. Often seen in flocks in fields and tall trees in parkland and countryside, especially in winter. Individuals or small groups often visit gardens. Resident.

19 Collared dove: very common, less plump and slightly smaller than the wood pigeon; all-over beige-grey with a black collar, eye and beak. Sometimes solitary or found in small groups in gardens, farmland trees and parkland. Cooing call similar to wood pigeon's, but only three coos per phrase instead of five. Resident.

20 Jackdaw: dark grey-black body and greyish neck. Bright eye with a white iris. Common in gardens, woodland and clifftops and a great nester in chimneys. Resident.

21 Sparrowhawk: common bird of prey which flies rapidly through gardens or trees in the countryside from a safe perching place to catch other small birds; never hovers like a kestrel. Male has blue-grey upperparts and pale, faintly barred underparts; female is larger with brown upperparts and paler underneath. Resident.

22 Kestrel: common small bird of prey, with chestnut-brown upperparts patterned with darker bars or spots, and lighter underparts which are also spotted or streaked, usually seen hovering over roadside verges and fields hunting for mice and other small prey, or perched at the top of telegraph poles. Resident.

23 Green woodpecker: striking, bright green bird with bright red cap and yellow rump, best seen on the ground probing for ants and other grubs, or perched in trees. In flight it flaps and glides alternately. The loud, harsh yelping call gives rise to a common country name – 'yaffle'. Resident.

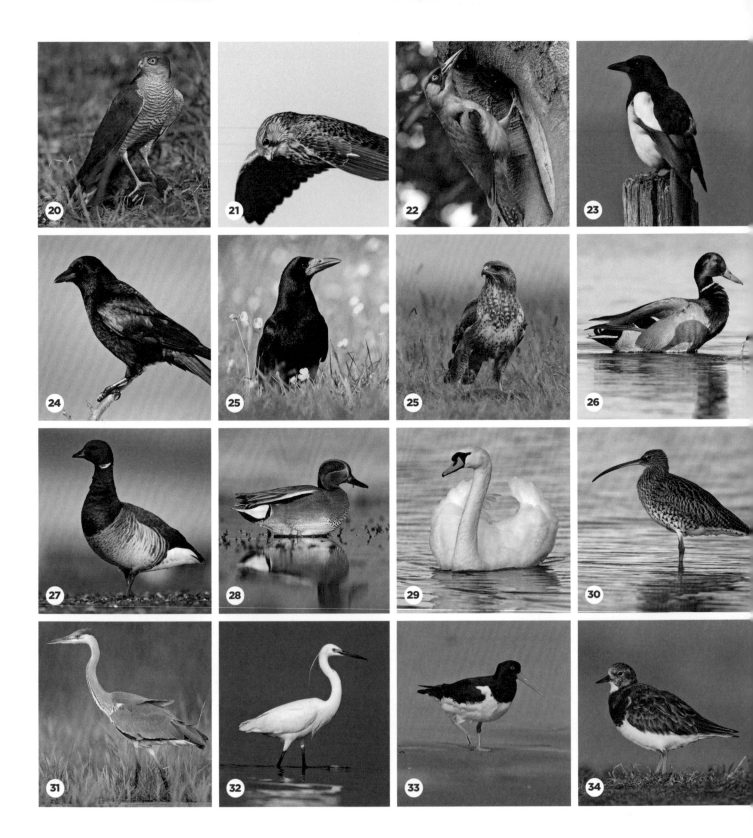

Larger than a pigeon

24 Magpie: easily identified black, blue and white 'crow' with a very long tail which is approximately 1½ times the length of the body. Usually spotted on its own or in small groups, especially in summer when the young birds tend to stay together, in gardens, farmland, parkland and countryside. Resident.

25 Carrion crow: strong-looking all-black bird with glossy feathers, a slightly down-curved beak and bare, black legs. Solitary or found in small groups, in gardens, farmland, parkland and wild countryside. Resident.

26 Rook: crow-like and similar size, but more tatty-looking, with shaggy feathers, a bald face and straight, dagger-like beak. Legs have long, loose, shaggy feathers hanging down round them so it looks as if it is wearing short, baggy trousers. Nests in large groups at the tops of clumps of tall trees, and flies or feeds on the ground in flocks. Resident.

27 Buzzard: a large bird of prey, bigger than a rook or a crow; dirty brown colour from a distance, at closer range you can see a barred pattern under the wings with a black outline round all but the leading edges, and white area inside, which darkens and develops the barred pattern closer to the body. Tail is barred. Resident.

Waterfowl

28 Mallard: the commonest duck on inland ponds, lakes and rivers, as well as coastal estuaries and inlets. The drake is mostly grey and brown with a bottle-green head, a white-outlined blue panel in each wing, with black tail and orange legs. Female is dappled brown all over with a white-outlined blue panel in each wing, and orange legs. Resident.

29 Brent goose: small, mallard-sized goose, with black head, neck and breast with a white ring round the neck, grey bars on its belly, and a black and white tail. A winter visitor, seen in flocks feeding on muddy estuaries and saltmarshes at low tide, and in nearby fields at high tide, along the south and east coasts. A white-bellied form is sometimes seen on the west coast.

30 Teal: our smallest duck, seen in largest numbers in winter though some present year-round. The drake is grey-brown with a chestnut-and-bottle-green head, bright green panel on each wing, and a conspicuous fawn, almost-triangular patch near the tail, most visible when the bird is swimming or standing. The female is similar to the female mallard, but slightly smaller and with a green, not blue, panel in each wing. Found in flocks in lakes, reservoirs, wetlands and along the coast at estuaries and saltmarshes; mostly seen in winter.

31 Mute swan: the common swan that is seen on lakes, rivers, and coastal estuaries and inlets. It is a large white bird with a long neck carried upright, a bright orange beak and a black 'bump' at the base of the beak, which is larger in the male. Mostly seen in pairs or small flocks. Resident.

32 Curlew: a large dappled-brown wading bird with long legs, a very long, down-curving beak, and a mournful 'cur-*lee*' cry, which is found in wetlands, moorlands, coastal estuaries and saltmarshes, and also boggy fields. It is usually seen solitary or in small flocks, but in winter it can be seen in quite large groups.

33 Heron: a large, upright grey bird with a long black and white neck and dagger-shaped head with black cap, a long yellow beak and a rather determined look. Found at the waterside round coastal estuaries and inlets, also inland lakes, rivers and ponds – it can make a nuisance of itself in domestic fishponds. It flies with its neck bent back and feet trailing, which creates a distinctive shape, and flaps its large wings rather slowly. Usually solitary, though it does breed in colonies, with the nests grouped at the tops of tall trees. Resident.

34 Egret: unmistakable large, white, upright, heron-like bird, but a size or two smaller, usually seen wading in shallow water or poised on the banks, at coastal estuaries, inlets and saltmarshes, also inland rivers and lakes. Usually solitary, or you see several well spaced out along the same bit of bank. Resident except in long, cold winters.

35 Oystercatcher: a distinctive black-and-white bird with long, bright orange beak, an orange ring round the eye and bright pink legs, found in small flocks feeding by probing the mud along rocky or stony coastlines, estuaries and inlets. Resident.

36 Turnstone: a very 'busy' little short-legged bird with dappled brown upperparts and white underneath with orange legs and a short beak. Usually seen scurrying around in small flocks along rocky or stony coasts, actively turning over pebbles and bits of seaweed looking for food. Not as shy as most seabirds, allowing you quite a close look. Resident.

IDENTIFYING BUTTERFLIES

Of the sixty or so butterflies that can usually be found in the British Isles, only roughly a dozen are very well known; they are the ones that fairly commonly turn up in gardens as well as countryside hedgerows and meadows. Butterflies are the good-looking, day-flying end of the lepidoptera clan, which also includes a far greater number of moths (see pages 214–15), which (with a few exceptions) are usually duller-coloured night-flying creatures. All British butterflies and moths are rapidly declining in numbers, largely due to loss of natural wild habitat, so it's worth making special trips to visit good butterfly territory in summer if you want to see a good selection. Good places include wildflower meadows and long grassy areas in parkland around stately homes, chalky hillsides, nature reserves or our few butterfly reserves. In your own garden it's well worthwhile doing anything you can to increase the availability of nectar-rich flowers and suitable caterpillar food plants to help halt the decline.

It's best to start by learning the easy butterflies first – the colourful ones that visit your garden and the countryside in your immediate area. Once you know those, anything new that turns up automatically stands out, and by looking it up in a book you can soon add to your knowledge. (Again, a small pocket guide that only lists the ones you are most likely to see is the best way to start.) Things to look for when identifying butterflies are colour, size and any obvious markings, but also take note of the habitat (fields, woods, roadside verges), the flowers they are feeding on, and time of year. Take your butterfly book with you on countryside outings. It also helps to take photos to compare with pictures in a book later; try to snap a butterfly that's keeping still with its wings held wide open, sunbathing or sipping nectar from a flower, so all the markings show up well. Store your photos in a special file on your computer; it's a good way to build up a collection without harming the wild population – unlike Victorian naturalists who used to catch butterflies, chloroform them and pin them down in glass cases.

The best times for spotting butterflies are summer days when the weather is warm, still and sunny, though a few species aren't fussy. Caterpillars are more difficult to identify since a good many of them are a nondescript green, which

acts as brilliant camouflage when they live in grass or foliage, but a few 'regulars' can be identified by a combination of coloration and markings, not to mention the host plant they are living on.

BUTTERFLY RECOGNITION – THE BASICS

1 Small tortoiseshell: a very familiar, medium-sized orange-and-brown butterfly with a row of alternate brown and cream 'squares' along the front edge of its forewings, and a row of tiny blue half-moon shapes along the other edges of the wings, seen June/July and August/September in flowery countryside, allotments and gardens. Caterpillar: hairy black-and-yellow-striped, seen in groups on nettles, May/June and July/August.

2 Peacock: an easily identified dull red butterfly with brown-edged wings and a conspicuous 'false eye' (a buff patch with a dark circle in the centre) on each wing-tip. Caterpillar: spiky and black, June/July, seen on nettles.

3 Painted lady: a fairly large, soft orange-brown butterfly, strongly patterned with black spots with black-and-white-spotted triangles at the tips of the forewings; they are migrants, reaching us from the continent May/June to spend the summer here.

Found in flowery countryside, allotments and gardens. Caterpillar: spiky, on nettles and thistles, August/September.

4 Red admiral: a familiar, medium-large butterfly mostly black with orange bands outlining the hind wings and several large white spots at the tips of the forewings; seen May to October feeding on all the popular bee plants in gardens, also teazel, clover and ivy, and drinks juice of rotting windfall apples. Caterpillar: solitary, spiky, black and white, seen on nettles or wild hops.

5 Comma: a very distinctive orange butterfly with scattered brown spots and ragged edges to the wings; white 'commas' on the undersides; seen July, and September/October feeding from flowers of brambles, hemp agrimony, knapweed and thistles in countryside hedgerows and wasteland. Caterpillar: solitary and buff-coloured, disguised as bird droppings, mainly found on wild hops, also sometimes nettles.

6 Gatekeeper: a smallish, orange butterfly with brown 'trimmings' and a double 'false eye' on the wings, mostly seen in the south of Britain in July and August. It often follows people through gates and gaps in footpaths (hence the name) in the countryside or along grassy meadows; the adult

feeds on nectar of brambles and other hedgerow flowers. Caterpillar: dull greyish 'grubs' living on grasses most of the year.

Blue butterflies

7 Holly blue: a small blue butterfly, a deeper blue above and paler below the undersides, also faintly speckled with tiny black dots; females also have a darker navy/slate band round the edges of the forewings; seen March to October, fluttering around but rarely settling in hedgerows and gardens. Caterpillar: small, short, fat green caterpillars with hooked, dull reddish spikes; found on holly buds in spring and ivy buds in autumn, though they can also feed on buds of bramble, spindle and dogwood.

Yellow butterflies

8 Brimstone: a pale yellow butterfly with a small, dull orange spot in the centre of each of its four wings. Seen from February to November visiting wildflowers, especially primroses, for nectar, in countryside hedgerows. Caterpillar: all-green, exactly the same shade as the plant it is eating, which is either buckthorn (*Rhamnus cathartica*) or alder buckthorn (*Frangula alnus*) – both rather unexciting scrub shrubs, but worth growing as butterfly crèches.

White butterflies

9 Orange tip: the female looks suspiciously like a cabbage white; male is similar but with conspicuous orange tips to the forewings. Seen in May and June in countryside hedgerows, wasteland, allotments and gardens. Caterpillar: green, well camouflaged as they are the same shape and colour as the seedpods of their food plants; found on lady's smock (*Cardamine pratensis*), garlic mustard (*Alliaria petiolata*) and run-to-seed brassica plants in kitchen gardens – the adult lays its eggs in the flowerheads.

10 Marbled white: a large, showy, black-and-white butterfly which flies slowly and feeds with wings held open, especially on knapweed and scabious in July/August. Caterpillar: grassy-green, found on long grasses, especially fescues, over most of the year.

11 Large white: a very common large, white, butterfly with black tips to the forewings; the female also has two black spots on each forewing. Seen April to September in hedgerows, flowery countryside, wasteland, allotments and gardens where it is a notorious pest of brassica plants. Adults feed on the nectar of a wide range of wildflowers. Caterpillar: black-and-yellow striped, found in colonies on brassica plants and nasturtiums in gardens, and also on many wild members of the cabbage family.

12 Small white: another very common butterfly, two-thirds the size of the large white, with dark tips of the forewings; males also have one black spot and females two. Seen March to September in the same places as the large white. Caterpillar: solitary, small and green, found on both wild and cultivated members of the brassica family.

Brown butterflies

13 Meadow brown: a large, dull brown butterfly with one 'false eye' on each front wing, seen in any weather from June to August in meadows. Caterpillar: solitary, striped in two shades of green, usually living on cocksfoot grass; can be found most of the year.

14 Ringlet: a dark brown, medium-sized butterfly with white-ringed darker spots found in any grassy areas; flying in all weather from June to late August. Caterpillar: a dull beige 'grub' with a slightly darker central stripe, feeding on bramble; found most of the year.

15 Large skipper: a small, brownish butterfly with short wings that flits quickly from flower to flower in June and July. Caterpillar: grass-green, found on false brome grass and cocksfoot living inside a tube made by rolling the edges of a blade of grass and gluing them together.

16 Speckled wood: a fairly dark brown, medium-sized butterflies whose wings are edged with a row of small irregular-shaped buff patches, with one 'false eye' on each forewing and three on each hind wing. Adults found flitting about in shady places under trees and shrubs from late spring to late summer. Caterpillar; green, tubular and grass-like, found on several kinds of grass.

IDENTIFYING WILDFLOWERS

The great thing about identifying wildflowers is that, unlike birds and butterflies, they *stay still*, so you can get a good long look at them, which makes it easy to compare what you see with pictures in field guides. Again, a pocket flower identification book is ideal to take with you when out walking, but it's handy to have a larger, more detailed book back home for further information. Again, whenever possible, take a photo to help with identification later or to add to the collection on your computer.

Things to look for when trying to identify flowers are the colour, shape and size of the flower, the height and shape of the plant (tall/upright, climber, or low/spreading), the habitat and time of year. It's also handy to have a good look at the shape of the foliage. Don't try to tackle the entire flora of Great Britain in one go; there are about 2,500 different species, a lot of which have only minor differences. Get to know the commonest flowers first, especially those that grow in your local area, and then look around for anything that's new to you. As with birds and butterflies, the showier flowers are always easiest. A good place to start when identifying something new to you is to see what its flowers look similar to – cow parsley-like, buttercup-like, daisy-like, dandelion-like – since that's a good clue as to the family to which it belongs.

WILDFLOWER RECOGNITION – THE EASY-TO-SPOT, COMMONER ONES

White flowers

1 Large white waterlily (*Nymphaea alba*): large, flat, floating leaves present from late spring to autumn, and the biggest flowers of any British native plant, 15cm (6in) across, from June to August, opening only for a short time around midday. Grows in deep water in ponds, lakes, canals and slow-moving sections of rivers.

2 Goosegrass, or cleavers (*Galium aparine*); a familiar 'weed' with long, straggly stems growing to 1.7m (6ft) and bearing whorls of five narrow leaves, all having tiny hooks that enable the plants to scramble up into hedgerows, fences and other plants, creating dense mats. Towards the tips of the stems, tiny white flowers are followed by small round seedheads that come off on clothing.

3 Yarrow (*Achillea millefolium*): a familiar wildflower with feathery foliage and upright stems 15–60cm (6–24in) tall topped with flattish-topped sprays of white (sometimes pale pink) flowers all summer, which act as favourite mating grounds for several insects. Found on roadside verges and other, undisturbed grassy areas. Also occurs as a common weed in lawns, though regular mowing prevents it from flowering.

4 Mayweed (*Matricaria maritima*): dome-shaped clumps 25–60cm (10–24in) high and much the same across of feathery foliage on green stems, topped by white daisies with yellow centres, flowering July to September. Looks a lot like garden chamomile, but lacks any scent. Grows round the edges of fields, on neglected allotments and wasteland.

5 White dead-nettle (*Lamium album*): short, clump-forming plants growing to 45cm (18in) tall with pairs of non-stinging nettle-like leaves and whorls of white hooded flowers clustered in the leaf axils from May to October. Commonly occurs as a weed in allotments and gardens, also on roadside verges, hedge bottoms and wasteland.

6 Hogweed (*Heracleum sphondylium*): a cow parsley-like plant, but more solid and chunky looking, usually 90cm–1.5m (3–5ft), flowering in all the same places as cow parsley – roadside verges, hedgerows and woodland edges – but several weeks after cow parsley flowers are over, from June to September. (Not to be confused with the rare giant hogweed, which is 2.5m (8ft) with enormous flowers and leaves, and thick stems; to be left well alone since the whole plant has irritant sap.)

Greenish flowers

7 Cuckoo pint, lords and ladies (*Arum maculatum*): a striking and unmistakable plant 15–30cm (6–12in) tall, with large, 15–20cm (6–8in) arrowhead-shaped leaves, sometimes heavily spotted with purplish black, and creamy or pale green hooded spathes 15–20cm (6–8in) tall, housing a brown spadix, in April and May. When the flowers are over, a cluster of orange berries forms at the end of the old stem. Grows in damp, shady places, usually woodland, hedge bottoms and ditches.

8 Stinging nettle (*Urtica dioica*): a very well known tall, clump-forming plant with upright stems to 1.5m (5ft) tall, bearing paired, jagged-edged leaves with powerful stings; from May to September short dangling stems of tiny greenish flowers grow towards the tops of the stems. Although generally disliked, the nettle is a valuable plant, being the well-defended home to five different kinds of butterfly caterpillar.

9 Jack-by-the-hedge (*Alliaria petiolata*): a common wildflower of semi-shady places round woods and along hedgerows; a narrow, upright plant 30cm–1.2m (1–4ft) tall, with frilly-edged, heart-shaped leaves growing alternately all the way up a single straight stem which is topped by a cluster of small white flowers from April to June.

10 Dog's mercury (*Mercurialis perennis*): upright stems 30–45cm (12–18in) high, bearing paired leaves, topped with short, airy spikes of tiny green flowers that are barely noticeable, except that the plant grows in large, dense carpets so the flowers look like a faint 'haze'. Found in deep shade in woodland, flowering February to April.

Yellow flowers

11 Marsh marigold, kingcup (*Caltha palustris*): like a giant buttercup, with large, golden, chalice-shaped flowers from March/April to July and glossy heart-shaped leaves, growing in mud and shallow water at the edges of ponds or streams, also in ditches and boggy areas that stay damp even in summer. 30–45cm (1–2ft) tall.

12 Yellow water lily, brandy bottle (*Nuphar lutea*): large, flat, round floating leaves the size of dinner-plates. Present late spring to autumn; in summer bears yellow flowers resembling large, waxy buttercups which stand several inches out of the water, followed by green, flask-shaped seedpods, earning the plant its alternative common name. Grows in still water of ponds, lakes and canals.

13 Hedge mustard (*Sisymbrium officinale*): a strangely wiry-looking plant, with a shaggy rosette of leaves near the base of smaller ones on the lower stems, but mostly made up of a main, stiff upright stem supporting stiff side branches that stand out from it horizontally. The tips of the shoots bear tufts of tiny yellow flowers from May to September. Found on roadsides, along hedgerows and on wasteland and round the edges of fields, height 30–90cm (1–3ft).

14 Fleabane (*Pulicaria dysenterica*): a common wildflower that was used in medieval times as a strewing herb to repel insects, and also dried and burnt to repel fleas. It forms large colonies of upright stems, 30–60cm (1–2ft) high, with narrow, lance-shaped leaves arranged alternately along them, topped with loose clusters of yellow daisy flowers in late summer.

15 Coltsfoot (*Tussilago farfara*): a common wildflower with scalloped-edged leaves, white on

the undersides with mauve-pink leafstalks and ribs growing straight out of the ground, as do the flower stems which are brownish-buff and very scaly-stemmed, topped by bright yellow 'daisies' in March and April. Spreads by underground stems to form large, dense colonies approximately 20cm (8in) high on cultivated ground, allotments and wasteland, especially on heavy and damp soil.

16 Ragwort (*Senecio jacobaea*): a common 'weed' of meadows, grassland and pasture, with tall upright stems and coarsely toothed leaves (which smell unpleasant if crushed) topped by loose sprays of yellow daisy flowers. Poisonous to livestock, but home to the stripy cinnabar moth caterpillars.

17 Yellow flag (*Iris pseudacorus*): a strong, clump-forming plant with long, spear-shaped leaves and tall stems up to 90cm (3ft) high, topped by yellow, three-petalled typically iris-shaped flowers in June and July. Grows in shallow water at the edges of ponds and lakes, also in marshy ground and ditches that stay wet even in summer.

18 Meadowsweet (*Filipendula ulmaria*): straight, upright stems, 60cm (2ft) high, bear alternate compound leaves made up of five pairs of leaflets with a larger one at the tip, topped with sprays of aromatic flowers from June to August. Found in damp meadows, marshland and woodland edges.

19 Rayless chamomile, pineapple weed (*Chamomilla suaveolens*): resembles mayweed, but with no petals on the daisy flowers, just greenish-yellow centres. The foliage smells strongly of something similar to pineapple. Plants are small and bushy rather than dome-shaped, 10–30cm (4–12in) tall and as wide, flowering June and July. Grows on wasteland, roadsides and field edges.

Blue/purple/lilac flowers

20 Tufted vetch (*Vicia cracca*): a scrambling plant, 60cm–1.5m (2–5ft) high, with ladder-like leaves ending in a short curly tendril, bearing short stems topped by showy spikes of tiny, lavender-blue flowers from June to August. Grows along hedgerows and field edges.

21 Sea holly (*Eryngium maritimum*): a rather 'artificial'-looking seaside plant growing on pebbly or sandy shores, with prickly, silvery-green leaves and stems to 90cm (3ft) tall, topped with shaggy,

metallic-silvery rosettes that surround a small cluster of bluish flowers, from July to August.

22 Spear thistle (*Cirsium vulgare*): tall striking thistle with strong upright spiny stems growing to over 1m (3ft) high; bold, jagged foliage whose every jag is tipped with vicious spikes; the large, knobbly flowerheads have tufts of stiff, narrow, pale purple petals protruding from the tops of what look like very prickly, green 'pineapples' an inch or two high and almost as wide. Grows in grassland, roadside verges and meadows, and though less plentiful than many thistles such as creeping thistle, this is one of the most easily identified.

23 Purple loosestrife (*Lythrum salicaria*): tall plants, 90cm–2m (3–6ft) tall, with leaves arranged in whorls of three along the upright main stems, topped by long, often quite showy spikes of mauve-pink flowers from June to August. Grows in damp areas, especially watersides and marshy places.

24 Woody nightshade (*Solanum dulcamara*): a bushy-looking wildflower with small, glossy leaves on semi-woody stems, bears clusters of purple, potato-like flowers with a yellow 'beak' on short stems towards the tips from June to September; followed by small oval berries that ripen from green through yellow to orange-red. Found scrambling into hedgerows or as a bushy plant on wasteland.

Red/pink/mauve flowers

25 Lady's smock (*Cardamine pratensis*): a petite plant, 15–38cm (6–15in) high, with a cluster of rather watercress-like leaves around the base and weak stems bearing ladder-like leaves, leading up to short heads of smallish, pale lilac-pink flowers in late spring and early summer. Grows in damp grassy places, such as meadows and waterside turf.

26 Ragged robin (*Lychnis flos-cuculi*): airy stems with pairs of long, narrow leaves, 30–75cm (12–30in) high, topped by loose sprays of shaggy pink flowers with branching, spidery petals in May and June. Grows in damp meadows, marshes and fens.

27 Great willowherb (*Epilobium hirsutum*): very tall plants 1.2–2m (4–6ft) high, growing in large clumps often spreading to cover entire banks. The tall, upright stems are clad from top to bottom in evenly spaced pairs of narrow, lance-shaped leaves with very faintly toothed edges, and towards the top individual mauve-pink flowers grow from the leaf axils on short stalks in July and August; these are followed by thistledown-like seedheads. Grows in wet places, marshland, fens and riverbanks.

28 Hemp agrimony (*Eupatorium cannabinum*): tall, striking plants 90cm–1.5m (3–5ft) high, with straight, upright stems bearing pairs of compound leaves that open out all round the stem like many tiers of frills. Stems are topped by roughly domed heads made up of many small, mauve-pink flowers in August and September, which are popular with several kinds of butterflies.

29 Scarlet pimpernel (*Anagallis arvensis*): a small, prostrate plant up to 30cm (12in) across with sprawling stems that radiate out from a central point, bearing pairs of small, heart-shaped leaves. Towards the tips of the short, slender stems are small five-petalled flowers in coral red from May to August. They close up at night and in bad weather, hence the common name of 'Poor Man's Weather Glass'. Grows on any cultivated ground such as allotments, wasteland and at the edges of fields.

30 Butterbur (*Petasites hybridus*): a solid, chunky-looking plant that spreads by underground stems, producing colonies of leaves and flowers that each grow on their own short stalks straight out of the ground. The rounded leaves have mauve-pink-tinged veins and leaf stalks, and strange flowers with short, thick, scaly, buff-coloured stalks topped by clusters of short, fluffy, pale pink florets, followed by white fluffy seedheads. The leaves, which are small and underdeveloped when the flowers appear in March to May, continue to expand during the summer and can end up very large

indeed, up to 60cm (2ft) or more in diameter. Grows in damp areas, along roadside verges, ditches and streams.

31 Common mallow (*Malva sylvestris*): a large, bushy-looking plant with stiff, horizontal stems bearing typical mallow leaves and mauve-pink flowers with five slightly spidery petals that'll be familiar to anyone who grows cultivated mallows in the garden. 30cm–1.2m (1–4ft) high and the same across, flowering June to September. Grows on wasteland, roadsides and near seashores.

32 Himalayan balsam or touch-me-not (*Impatiens glandulifera*): a giant distant relative of busy lizzie, the plant is a dirty word with environmentalists since it's a foreign invader that spreads rapidly along inland waterways, smothering out our native flora. Tall, thick, succulent stems grow to 2.2m (7ft) high, with spear-shaped busy lizzie leaves, topped by airy sprays of pinkish-lilac, helmet-shaped flowers on thin, wiry stems, from July to October. The seedheads 'pop' explosively, sending showers of seeds some distance, which helps the plant spread.

WILDFLOWERS BY HABITAT

Damp meadow, spring: lady's smock **summer:** meadowsweet.

Hedgerow, summer: honeysuckle, wild hop, bramble, dog rose, cleavers, bindweed.

Meadow, spring: primrose, cowslip, lady's smock **summer:** ox-eye daisy, meadow and creeping buttercup, ragwort.

Pebbly coast: sea holly, horned poppy, thrift, sea kale.

Pond and pondside: yellow flag, bulrush, reed, great white waterlily, yellow waterlily, great willowherb, purple loosestrife, Himalayan balsam.

Roadside verge, spring: cow parsley **early summer;** hogweed.

Wasteland, neglected cultivated ground including allotments, strips round the edges of fields: scarlet pimpernel, field poppy, field bindweed, groundsel, sow thistle.

Woodland, spring: bluebell, wood sorrel, wood anemone, dog's mercury, violet, wild strawberry.

IDENTIFYING TREES

The main things to look for when trying to put names to countryside trees are leaves, bark and flowers, fruits, berries or nuts, depending on the season. It's also worth considering what sort of habitat you are in; certain trees are common in hedgerows, others in woods, while in parklands around stately homes you may encounter a mixture of native trees and large ornamental species that have been introduced from abroad. Normally you'll find several different kinds of trees growing in close proximity to each other, but forestry plantations and certain managed woods (especially ones that were once coppiced for sweet chestnut or hazel poles) may contain almost entirely the same species, as they are cultivated as a crop.

TREE RECOGNITION – THE MOST FREQUENTLY SEEN SPECIES

1 Common alder (*Alnus glutinosa*): mostly seen on wet, damp or marshy ground and on banks of rivers and streams. Look for regularly spaced tiers of branches and a neat, almost conical shape, and clusters of tiny woody 'cones' which are the remains of female catkins. In spring, long, yellowy tails of male catkins can be seen on the same trees as round, greenish female catkins.

2 Goat willow (pussy willow) (*Salix caprea*): common shrubby tree or larger, multi-stemmed tree of damp or marshy places, ditch-edges, and banks of rivers or streams, with oval, grey-green leaves and rather straight stems; in early spring the silky grey male catkins (which later develop a 'fluff' of yellow anthers) are often picked as pussy willow.

3 Beech (*Fagus sylvatica*): a classic large parkland tree which also grows in shady woodlands on chalk downland. Spreading and stately, with a thick trunk of smooth grey bark and semi-shiny, oval leaves marked with a strong herringbone pattern of ribs. Instead of dropping their leaves, mature trees retain them until late into the following spring (a characteristic known as 'marcescence').

4 Sweet chestnut (*Castanea sativa*): another classic large parkland tree, with thick trunks of characteristic, deeply ribbed bark that spirals slightly up the trunk. Leaves are long, narrow, pointed at the tip and outlined with serrated edges, and bearing a very pronounced, regular herringbone pattern of ribs. In autumn large spiky cases house the nuts.

5 Sycamore (*Acer pseudoplatanus*): our largest member of the maple family, with rough-textured grey bark and fairly large, three-lobed leaves, dark green above and pale green below, often showing blackish 'tar spots' (caused by a common fungus disease). From late summer onwards, clusters of winged 'keys' can be seen hanging down from near the tips of branches, and in autumn these ripen to brown and spiral down to earth, giving rise to colonies of fast-growing saplings.

6 Oak: perhaps the most traditional of British trees, with some very elderly examples to be found in Sherwood Forest and the New Forest. The oak is actually two different species. Both look very similar, growing to a good size with neatly and evenly fissured bark and the classic oak leaves and acorns, and both can occur anywhere in Britain. But English oak (*Quercus robur*) is the commoner in the south of England and has acorns *with* stalks, while Sessile oak (*Quercus petraea*) occurs mostly in northern Britain and has acorns *without* stalks, which grow straight from the twig. Some of the ancient oaks (*Q. robur*) in Windsor Great Park are more than a thousand years old.

7 Horse chestnut (*Aesculus hippocastanum*): another popular parkland tree that's also much planted as avenues leading up to grand country houses and along smart old residential streets in towns. Bark is scaly textured and reddish to ash-brown; leaves are unmistakable 'fans' of eight long, spatula-shaped leaflets arranged in a circle at the end of each stalk; flowers are fat 'candles' made up of many smallish white or deep pink florets arranged in short, squat, upward-facing spikes that are dotted all over the outer canopy of the tree in late spring/early summer. Shortly before the leaves turn brown and fall in autumn the prickly cases fall, splitting open to reveal the shiny conkers.

8 Ash (*Fraxinus excelsior*): an elegant tree with compound leaves made up of several small leaflets arranged in pairs along a stem, with one sticking out at the far end; buds at the tips of the stems are matt black (a good identification point, especially in winter). In spring, clusters of long, narrow green 'keys' can be seen near the tips of the stems. More common in countryside with limestone or chalk.

9 Scots pine (*Pinus sylvestris*): one of the original native species that colonised the country after the ice age, today most common in Scotland. Tall, straight, upright, reddish-brown trunk whose bark has a platelet-like pattern. Conical green cones, pointed at the tips, develop near the ends of the shoots and turn brown in their second year, but it's not until their third year that they mature, open and release their seeds. The long, slender needles grow in pairs, joined by a brownish scale at the top.

HOW TO TELL THE AGE OF A TREE

If the tree has been cut down and you can see a cross-section of the trunk, count the growth rings. Trees 'lay down' one growth ring each year, and besides revealing the age, you can tell by the width of each ring how good the growing season has been – the annual growth ring is wider in a year in which there was plenty of rain and temperatures were mild.

You can estimate the approximate age of a large old tree by measuring its girth at 1.5 metres (5 feet) above the ground. This is only reasonably accurate for a deciduous tree with a full crown of branches and which is growing on its own. On average a tree grows 2.5cm (1 inch) 'fatter' every year. So a tree measuring 3 metres (10 feet) round the trunk will be roughly 120 years old.

To tell the age of coniferous trees, count the whorls of branches from ground level all the way up the trunk; the number is approximately the age of the tree, since a conifer grows a new 'ring' of branches from the top of its trunk each season.

TRACKING ANIMALS

Large animals are very easy to identify when you can get a good view of them, but since they are usually nervous of humans, the best clue you will often have of their presence is their tracks in mud, soft earth or snow. But tracks can tell you much more than which animal has been there; they show you which direction it was travelling in. The depth of the footprint plus any smudged skid marks also give a clue to how much of a hurry the animal was in – and a set of predator prints running through the first sometimes shows what might have been chasing it. Look out too for smaller prints of the same sort, suggesting a mother animal with young. Besides tracks, look for tufts of fur trapped on barbed wire fences – it's easy to spot the reddish fur of fox or the long, bristly hair of badger – and look out for characteristic droppings. When animals regularly use the same route, you may also see a distinct 'tunnel' through undergrowth where they push through the same place regularly, and at the waterside you can sometimes see 'slides' where ducks slither down a steep muddy bit of bank into the water. With practice you can become quite a good countryside detective.

FOX

1 A fox leaves paw prints similar to those of dogs and cats, with four toes round a larger 'pad'. Look for claw marks at the end of each 'toe print'– cats don't leave claw marks. Dogs and foxes both do: dogs have rounder and often larger paw prints, those of foxes are narrower. Fox tracks can be found almost anywhere in town or country and also (perhaps rather surprisingly) along the seashore. You may sometimes spot the remains of prey or perhaps just scraps of fur or feathers showing where a fox has had a successful hunt.

RABBITS AND HARES

2 These leave very distinctive paw prints consisting of a pair of long outer prints with two smaller ovalish prints between them, as the animal moves by hopping from both back feet to the smaller front feet which it 'runs' with, placing one down after the other. It's not easy to tell rabbit from hare prints; rabbits are usually smaller, and the animals occur in groups, while hares are mostly solitary, though in spring two or three will chase each other. But both animals are reasonably easy to see out in daylight. In a large rabbit colony you'll find piles of droppings in a conspicuous spot, used as territory markers, and you'll almost certainly see rabbit holes and tufts of soft grey fur caught on brambles.

DEER

3 Deer leave cloven hoof prints (i.e. a pair of roughly teardrop-shaped indentations per footprint with a gap up the middle). Deer hoof prints have pointed tips at the front and are slightly wider at the back. You can tell them from cloven-hoofed farm livestock because sheep, pigs and goats all have rounded tips to their prints, and those of cows are very much bigger and deeper. (When prints are left by livestock you can usually see the animals in the fields, or at least their characteristic droppings, though in places where livestock roam freely in the countryside, such as the New Forest, it can be harder to tell straightaway.)

RODENTS

Rodents leave tiny tracks close together in rows; look for a good set of prints and count the toes – rodents always have five toes on the back feet and four on the front feet. Rat tracks look like a staggered row of small starbursts; mouse tracks have occasional narrow lines between the footprints, since a mouse drags its tail along the ground. Squirrel tracks (**4**) show pronounced claw marks at the ends of the toes.

BADGERS, WEASELS AND STOATS

All the members of this family, which includes mink and otters, have five toes on each foot, so look for some clear prints and count all the toes. Size is a bit of a clue. (**5** shows a badger's prints.)

BIRDS

6 Birds have three-pronged footprints, sometimes with a long toe print sticking out of the back as well. It's fascinating to observe the winding tracks of wading birds in soft mud left on seashores as the tide retreats, and you can sometimes see the bird responsible at the far end of a line of footprints, probing for marine worms and crustaceans. But in practice it's almost impossible to tell more than roughly the size of the bird concerned, and see if it has webbed feet (indicating ducks, geese and swans) or not (indicating a wader).

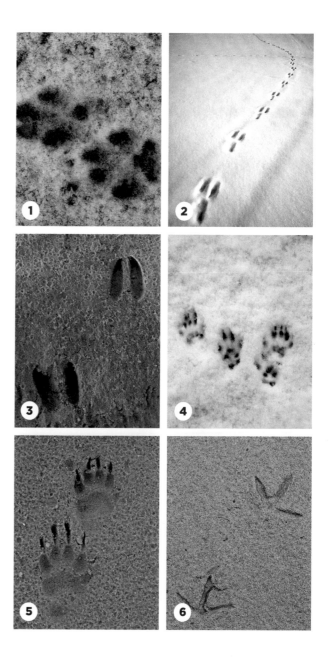

COUNTRYSIDE SKILLS

'Townies' might be dab hands at shopping, but country folk have always known where to find the things they need for basic everyday existence for free, from the land. And even today, when you'd think there's no need, a lot of people are enjoying re-learning country skills and bringing the results to the dinner table.

FORAGING

Foraging for wild food goes right back to our hunter-gatherer roots, and the instinct is still present in modern man. Holidaymakers often indulge in a pleasant afternoon's crabbing from the quay or cockling on the beach, and nowadays wild greenery, hedgerow fruit and edible fungi are becoming of interest to fashionable chefs, TV cookery presenters and food lovers. There's lots to be found for free. You may already have a few wild salads and 'greens' growing as weeds in your own garden, and the seashore and hedgerows alongside country lanes can be very productive. While there is a lot you *could* eat if forced to live off the land, the things I've listed are some of the best for eating – besides being easy to identify. But at the risk of

sounding like your granny, it pays to pick wild foods with care. Avoid polluted or litter-strewn places, anywhere close to busy main roads due to traffic fumes, or anywhere that weedkillers or other chemicals may have been used, and do ask the landowners' permission before gathering any goodies from private land. Pick with due consideration for the countryside, so don't strip an area bare, and only take perfect material that you'll be able to use without waste, back home. It's also advisable to be very certain of your identification, especially when dealing with potentially tricky customers like fungi. Look out for foraging courses and, particularly, fungus-hunting walks organised by experts.

EDIBLE PLANTS RECOGNITION

SALADS

1 Hairy bittercress commonly grows as a weed in patio containers, veg and flower gardens. The plants are small and rosette-shaped; the tiny leaves take a long time to pick but have a pleasant, watercress-like tang when used raw in salads.

2 Jack-by-the-hedge, also known as hedge garlic, has a light, leafy taste with a faint hint of garlic; the young leaves are good chopped in sauces or raw in salads in spring.

3 Dandelion is a tasty salad leaf full of minerals and vitamins, available from early spring. Pick a few of the youngest leaves from the centre of a rosette, or better still blanch the whole plant under an upturned bucket or large flowerpot for a week first, taking care to evict snails that gather underneath, then pick the young leaves when they are pale green to yellow in colour, which makes them less bitter. If you prefer to grow your own in rows in the veg garden, seeds of a French culinary dandelion are available from specialist seed firms.

4 Miner's lettuce, *Claytonia perfoliata*: an unusual but easily identifiable plant with circular leaves whose stems are joined to them in their centres, like tiny saucers on sticks, which is very tender and tasty in early spring. Sometimes cultivated as a winter salad; good for growing in tubs or window boxes.

LEAFY VEG

5 Fat hen is a common annual weed that quickly appears in gardens when rich, fertile ground has been turned over and left uncultivated. Pick healthy, intact young leaves, ideally before the plant starts to flower, and cook like spinach. Its perennial close relative, **Good King Henry (6)**, was a popular vegetable in Elizabethan times, but was superseded by the introduction of spinach.

7 Ground elder was introduced by the Romans as a culinary crop but is now a nuisance weed to gardeners, so if you have an infestation you'll be pleased to know it can be put to good use. Harvest young leaves in summer and cook like spinach.

8 Chickweed is one of the first weeds to infest newly dug ground and is very prolific. The young shoot-tips make a good green vegetable, cooked quickly in melted butter. Don't be tempted to stew great handfuls pulled up when you're weeding; the older stems are tough, stringy and tasteless. Just snip off the best young bits.

9 Sorrel is a wayside weed also cultivated as a fresh, zingy, lemon-flavoured herb and can be cooked like spinach or with lots of butter and made into sorrel sauce to eat with white fish. It also makes a wonderful soup.

10 Stinging nettle tips of young leaves picked (with rubber gloves) in spring are perhaps even better than spinach, chopped and cooked in butter. Don't bother with

them in summer when they are tough and woody.

11 Alexanders is a relative of cow parsley, found along roadsides and in the bottom of hedgerows in spring, particularly along the south coast of England. It emerges from the ground in early spring and flowers several weeks earlier than cow parsley, with slightly thicker and more robust stems topped by pale yellow flowers. It was grown as a vegetable in medieval Britain, having been introduced by the Romans for culinary purposes. Use the small flower buds raw in salads, cook young leaves like spinach, and boil the stems like asparagus and eat them with lots of butter.

12 Burdock is a large, striking plant with a rosette of huge, rhubarb-like leaves; as kids we used to throw the prickly burrs at girls on our way home from school, so the hooks caught in their hair or cardies – happy days! The young leaf stems, cut in early summer and peeled, can be eaten raw rather like cucumber, sliced in salads, or steamed and eaten with butter in the same way as asparagus.

ROOTS

13 Horseradish often grows wild on rough waste ground, and is easily recognised by its large, loose rosette of long, slightly crinkly, green dock-like leaves. In the garden – even in wild areas – it can be quite invasive since the clumps spread vigorously so you are doing yourself a favour by digging it up to make horseradish sauce. Dig some roots – you don't have to dig up the whole plant – any time from early September to early December, peel, grate (be warned, it's worse than peeling onions) and mix with double cream, a little mayonnaise and some French mustard. It's far better than anything you can buy in a jar.

14 Dandelion roots were once dug up, scrubbed, and roasted lightly in the oven for a longish time till they were hard, then ground in a coffee grinder to make an economical and caffeine-free substitute for coffee. If you want to, do so when the roots are at their plumpest, in autumn (see page 145).

FRUIT

15 Wild strawberries are tiny fruits which often lack flavour, but are fun to munch on during a walk in the woods if you spot some in early summer. Cultivated wild strawberries, grown from seed, produce larger, tastier crops if grown in the garden.

16 Blackberries ripen in country hedgerows from mid-August and may continue until the first hard frost, though fruit produced late in the season isn't of very good quality. Locals usually know the best blackberry patches and go out walking prepared with bags or baskets, plus crooked sticks for pulling down high branches to get at the best fruit, which usually grows out of reach.

17 Rosehips, the ripe, flask-shaped fruits of dog-rose, were heavily picked during the last war, when country families gathered them to make rosehip syrup, which was taken, a spoonful each day, as a rich source of vitamin C since oranges weren't available. Make your own today to pour over ice cream; it's also very good drizzled on to a baked apple or rice pudding instead of honey or jam.

HOW TO MAKE ROSEHIP SYRUP

Put 450 grams (1 pound) of clean whole rosehips through a mincer to break them into small bits, but don't liquidise them. Add the minced fruit to half a litre (1 pint) of boiling water and simmer very gently for a quarter of an hour, then strain through several thicknesses of clean cotton material – it's essential to get out all the seeds and the tiny hairs that are attached to them, which are highly irritant. (They were once used by small boys as itching powder!) Strain twice to be on the safe side, using a fresh piece of cloth for the second straining. When you have obtained all the juice (don't squeeze the fabric to try and get more out of the residue), measure the quantity and to each 300ml (½ pint) of juice, add 140 grams (5 ounces) of sugar and boil for five minutes, stirring until the sugar dissolves. The thick liquid can be kept in the fridge for up to a week in a screw-top jar.

NUTS

18 Beechnuts, commonly known as beech mast, are small, three-sided nuts inside a husk with an outer covering rather like coconut fibre door-matting, in miniature. They ripen and fall in September and October and, though small, are quite tasty when peeled and eaten straight from your hand during a country walk, or taken home, warmed lightly in butter or olive oil and sprinkled sparingly with salt. Gather beech nuts up from the ground as soon as possible, before squirrels or other rodents find them. However, the trees produce empty husks for three out of four years, so the crop is unreliable.

19 Sweet chestnuts, traditionally roasted in their shells over an open fire in winter, are also favourite ingredients to use in stuffing for Christmas turkey. The plump nuts we buy in the shops mostly come from specially cultivated plantations in California and southern Europe, but you can sometimes gather homegrown chestnuts on a country walk around the end of October. (They are smaller than 'bought' chestnuts and some years the crop is very disappointing.) Pick up whole nuts, still inside their prickly casings, off the ground; the usual way to remove the nuts from the protective exterior is by stamping on them with a heavy boot. Roast them over the hot embers of a fire, or use a proper chestnut roaster which looks like a very long-handled, lidded skillet with holes in the lid – sit this over the fire until the first nuts explode, then the rest will be ready. They are easiest to shell while still hot.

20 Hazelnuts are often grown on cultivated hazelnut bushes and filberts (a closely related variety), which are carefully pruned and cared for in nut orchards. Hedgerows containing hazel trees rarely yield much of a crop, but it's worth searching for green nuts towards the end of September to crack and eat fresh. Nut shells lying on the ground are invariably empty.

FUNGI

Make absolutely certain you know what you are identifying here before you pick them, since many poisonous mushrooms and toadstools look similar to those that are edible. Correctly identified, you will find that wild fungi are delicious.

1 Chanterelle is a very superior wild mushroom, popular with wild mushroom enthusiasts, found in late summer and autumn in colonies, mostly in beech woods. It is bright yellow and shaped rather like a funnel 2.5cm (1in) or so high and almost as wide, with long gills running up the stalk and branching up the outsides of the funnel. To check its identity, sniff for a faint scent of apricots. Good in omelettes or scrambled egg.

2 Parasol mushroom has a large, distinctive, wide-open, buff-coloured, umbrella-like caps up to 15cm (6in) across, with scaly surface and a faint boss in the centre; white gills underneath. Find it growing in grassland and roadside verges from late summer to late autumn. Individual mushrooms grow far apart in loose colonies. Pick younger specimens and avoid older ones whose gills or cap are turning brown. Superb flavour, best fried with bacon or added to casseroles.

3 Shaggy inkcap is also known as lawyers wig because the young mushroom has a tall, narrow cap up to 15cm (6in) high with thin slivers of skin curling back all the way up it, like a judge's wig. It is best picked at this stage – don't wait till the cap starts to open out and the gills underneath go black and inky. Good lightly fried or used in mushroom sauces or soup. Don't drink alcohol with inkcaps, as the combination reacts with some people and makes their faces turn red.

4 Field mushroom looks just like the cultivated mushroom bought in greengrocers' shops, with a white cap that starts as a 'button' with pink or white gills inside and slowly opens out to a flattish cap with buff-coloured gills underneath. Mostly found on fields where horses are grazed, but sometimes on lawns – or even on vegetable gardens where spent mushroom compost has been used as a soil improver.

5 Giant puffball is an enormous, white, football-like fungus that can be found growing in fields, hedgerows or woods. Whilst not considered the absolute best for flavour by mushroom fanciers, it's very acceptable sliced and fried in bacon fat like a mushroom steak. Regrettably rather rare now. Only pick a young specimen that's still firm and pure white; leave an older, softer or darker one to 'puff' and send its spores out to make more giant puffballs.

SEASIDE HARVEST

It's not just on dry land that you can find food for free; some seashore plants are surprisingly good, and are traditionally gathered for use in island communities. But the seaside has more to offer to keen wild-harvesters.

SEA VEG

Gather sea veg from saltmarshes, rocks etc., where the water is clear and clean, and where there's a good tidal range to keep crops 'washed'. Keep well away from sewage outlets and avoid areas where there is litter and rubbish strewn along the shoreline, as there may be pollution or dangerous waste such as broken glass or worse hidden among the plants. And avoid overpicking, so that colonies can recover quickly and you don't destroy the looks of coastal beauty spots. Anticipate sea veg being quite sandy or gritty, so wash them very well in several changes of water before using them.

SEA VEG RECOGNITION

1 Sea beet are 60–90cm (2–3ft) mounds of thick shiny leaves, growing on saltmarshes. Pick young, healthy-looking, intact triangular leaves that are roughly the same size as baby spinach leaves from the tops of the plants any time from late spring to the end of summer. Cook like spinach – steam or stir fry, and eat with plenty of butter.

2 Samphire bears strange thin, green, segmented cylindrical shoots, faintly asparagus-like but without the tips, sold by posh fishmongers in early summer, and in smart restaurants as an accompaniment to pricy fish dishes. But if you can find a site where it grows, in saltmarshes and mudflats on estuaries and parts of the coastline, you can pick your own. Traditionally its peak season is for the few weeks either side of the longest day, though you *can* cut it from late spring onwards. Pick the shoots when they are about 7.5cm (3in) long. Wash the shoots thoroughly and use short

young stems raw in salads, or you can steam, boil in water or cook them in butter for a few minutes; don't add any seasoning, since their flavour is naturally salty.

3 Laver grows round rocky and stony shores all round the west coast of Britain and is traditionally used in Wales to make laver bread (which is basically a purée of the well-boiled seaweed mixed with oatmeal and fried for breakfast, eaten with bacon). The fronds are purplish-coloured, slender, and unevenly shaped; they need washing very well as they trap lots of sand and tend to be gritty.

4 Dulse is a robust seaweed that clings to stones quite well, down on the shore; the tough stems are chewed raw in the Hebrides in much the same way that we'd use chewing gum, or stewed for hours until tender.

5 Carragheen (Irish moss) is an edible seaweed traditionally used for thickening jellies, blancmange and ice cream. The purplish-brown fronds can be found on rocky Atlantic shores of Britain; it's best collected in April and May, then washed well and either dried to use out of season or used fresh straight away. Simmer fresh carragheen slowly in three times its volume of water or milk until the seaweed dissolves completely, then add flavouring and use as usual to make fruit jelly or blancmange.

6 Kelp is a strong-growing, broad, thick, ribbon-like seaweed growing at and below the low water mark, also sometimes in quite dense beds in deeper water offshore. It can be sliced raw in salads, but is often dried and cut up to use later (on its own or with other dried seaweeds) as a sea vegetable; small crumbled pieces are good sprinkled into salads or cooked rice, to be eaten with shellfish or other seafood.

7 Sea lettuce is a delicate, soft, pale green seaweed which, in the sea, looks almost like floating green tissue-paper; it's found on most shores sticking to stones or rocks. This is the seaweed sold in health food shops and oriental stores as nori, the thin, dry, green sheets used for wrapping round a mixture of raw fish and sticky rice to make sushi. It's also good dried and crumbled to sprinkle over rice or into salads, or mixed with other dried seaweed as mixed sea vegetables.

SHELLFISH

Shellfish are often considered to be out of season in high summer, but they don't become poisonous as people often believe. The myth probably began in the days before proper refrigeration was available, when seafood quickly went 'off' in warm weather, and eating dodgy mussels or winkles would have been the cause of many a gyppy tummy.

But there's a good practical reason for not collecting shellfish during the summer holidays: it is the season when shellfish spawn, so they are best left alone to produce the next generation and maintain stocks. And from a gourmet's point of view, it's fair to say that shellfish are not such high quality as usual in the breeding season because they lose weight when they are busy producing eggs, so the shells aren't so well filled.

If you're going to collect your own shellfish, avoid parts of the coast close to sewage outfall pipes (often marked on large-scale local maps, or ask in fishing tackle shops as the people in there will know), and clean the shells well before cooking. Remove the 'beard' from mussels and reject any shellfish with broken shells. Leave those that are selected for eating sitting in a bucket of clean water for 12 hours or overnight before cooking so they can flush themselves through and get rid of a lot of grit and 'bits'. Change the water several times if lots of muck comes out, or if the water looks dirty.

When dealing with bivalves (mussels, cockles, oysters), reject any which don't close themselves after they've been in their bucket of water for a while, also any which stay tightly shut and don't put up a fight when you squeeze the shell between forefinger and thumb and try to slide the two halves slightly past each other, since they'll be dead and already starting to build up bacteria inside. After cooking, reject any that haven't opened as they can't be trusted either.

SHELLFISH RECOGNITION

1 Winkles are smallish, dark grey and very pointed 'snail shells' found on rocks and seaweedy sections of breakwater that are covered by water at high tide. To cook the cleaned winkles, plunge them into a large pan of boiling water and simmer for ten minutes. The shells don't contain very much meat, but half the fun of winkles is 'winkling' them out of their shells with a pin after removing the thin film that seals the hole at the entrance to the shell. The content is all edible.

2 Cockles are familiar bivalves about 2.5cm (1in) across with pairs of pale, ribbed shells joined by a hinge at the back. They are found about halfway between the high and low water mark on wide sandy or muddy-sand shores and silty-looking saltmarshes round most of the UK. They tend to congregate in particularly favourable areas known as cockle beds, where it's easy to collect a good crop. Find them several inches under the surface; cocklers feel around for them with their feet or fingers, or use a strong garden rake. Leave small specimens behind to grow and take only the full-sized ones. After cleaning and sorting, plunge cockles into boiling water and remove as soon as they open fully, which only takes a few minutes.

3 Mussels are very common all round the coast, but be very careful only to collect them from places with clean, unpolluted water and avoid collecting mussels in summer, especially when there's an algal 'bloom' in the water (local fishermen and tackle shops will know all about these), and be sure to give them several changes of water while they are undergoing the cleaning process. Collect them from rocks well down on the shoreline at low tide; they live in decent colonies so it's easy to gather enough for a meal. To cook, plunge them into boiling water and boil for ten minutes, or follow your favourite *moules marinière* recipe.

4 Razor shells are scarcer shellfish, with long, narrow shells having square-ish corners, found several inches under the surface of very clean sandy beaches, along the low tide line. (Look up a tide table and hunt for them during the very lowest tides of the year, and take care you leave enough time to get back up the beach before you're cut off.) You may be able to tell a good razor shell site by plentiful empty shells higher up the beach; locals usually keep quiet about good sites. As you walk the sands, look out for a hole or slight disturbance, then dig fast to grab the creature, which can move surprisingly fast. After cleaning the shells well, drop them into boiling water for five to ten minutes, then extract the meat and reheat in some oil in which you've fried finely chopped shallots and a little fresh stem ginger.

SHRIMPING

Shoals of tiny common or brown shrimps can often be found in the warm shallow water of bays and sandy beaches, and small numbers can also often be seen in rock pools at low tide. In their live state they are light grey or pale buff, but being almost transparent they are quite difficult to see. They rarely swim around by day, and instead usually walk along the bottom of the sea, so you need to watch for signs of movement and then you may spot them.

To catch shrimps you need an old-fashioned shrimping net, which has a catch net (the bigger the better) with a flat edge along the bottom and a curved top which is attached to a long handle. The way to use it most effectively is to wade out into the sea and push the net along in front of you so that the flat edge 'trawls' along the seabed, disturbing the sand as it goes and sending any shrimps up and into the net. Every few yards you should stop and see what you've caught. If you've been lucky, tip your shrimps into a bucket of seawater to keep them alive until you've caught enough, and use it to carry them home in.

Boil them straight away – there's no need to leave them in clean water first – a few minutes is all it takes. When they're cooked, pinch the heads and tails off with your fingernails; don't bother trying to peel them – unlike the larger prawns you simply eat shrimps shell-and-all. They are good eaten as they are with bread and butter, but if you want to make them into something more 'special' make potted shrimps. To do this, head-and-tail your cooked shrimps, mix them with melted butter flavoured with a pinch or two of mace, then decant them into pots and leave in the fridge overnight to solidify. Eat them with wafer-thin triangles of toast.

Prawns – the larger relative of shrimps – may sometimes be found on sandy southern and western shores and in rockpools round the British coastline. Catch them in the same way as shrimps and cook them the same way, but for slightly longer; they only turn the familiar pink when they're cooked. A pint of prawns makes a good 'finger' lunch, with brown crusty bread and a glass of white wine.

CRABBING

The brown crab is the familiar species in fishmongers' shops, with a wide, smooth, flat, pinkish-brown carapace and large, black-tipped claws. It lives mostly on rocky coasts, and is caught commercially using crab pots baited with fish-heads or bits of mackerel, lowered by line from small fishing boats, tethered to buoys, and hauled in daily to collect the catch. But crabs can also be found under jetties or small quaysides that accommodate only small hobby boats and light local traffic.

In some areas there's quite a strong custom for holidaymakers – and particularly their children – to go crabbing from these sorts of places, and occasionally you may find a crabbing competition – they are regular events in some Norfolk fishing villages. The crabs are caught using a piece of fish (usually heads or other uneatable bits) as bait, tied to a fishing line – hooks aren't required, and in any case aren't allowed in competitions. The crabber sits up on the quay, lowers the baited end of the line into the water and waits till they feel a 'bite', then the line is carefully hauled back in, hopefully with the crab still hanging on to the bait. Though a lot of the crabs caught in this way are too small to eat and they should be thrown back, you can sometimes catch one that's a good size.

SPIDER CRABS

Well known to continental crab-lovers, spider crabs are now fairly commonly found off the south coast of England. They are easily identified: they have smallish, rather rounded bodies that are very spiny, with long, thin, spiny legs and narrow claws. They are good eating, but there's a lot less flesh in them than the traditional brown crab, and most of it is inside the body, there's hardly anything inside the claws. Still, the contents will make a hugely enjoyable sandwich, even if crab is considered to be the poor man's lobster!

SEA-FISHING

You can fish from the beach or from small boats off the coast without a fishing license (which you'd need for freshwater fishing, or for commercial sea fishing). Fishing from the beach is convenient since you can just wander down and get started straight away. You'll need a long (2.5–2.7m/8–9ft) fishing rod; the sort known as a spinning rod is fine, and a good, basic, beginners one along with line and reel, hooks and all the other bits and pieces that you need can be bought (often as a complete package deal for under £50) from any fishing tackle shop near the seaside – the staff will be happy to advise.

You'll need to buy live bait from the tackle shop (it doesn't keep long so buy it the day you want to use it) or dig your own lugworms or ragworms from the beach before making a start. (Look for small, slightly bubbling holes, and use a garden spade or fork to dig down quickly and catch the worm before it escapes.)

Local sea-fisherman and local tackle shops will know the best places to go beach-fishing, but the area either side of a breakwater is usually quite good. The best times are a couple of hours either side of low tide, and night-time is especially fruitful. The fish you are likely to catch will vary at different times of the year. The best way to find out what is

likely to be around on your particular stretch of coast all year is to buy a set of tide tables that come complete with a fisherman's calendar and other information from a local tackle shop. Most beach fishermen fish from about April to October; there's not much around in winter, when the fish stay further offshore.

You'll catch a wider range of species and in larger quantities from a boat. In seaside areas you'll sometimes find adverts for fishing trips on boats at so-much per head, with fishing tackle and bait provided in the price, and these are a good way to have a go since the skipper will know all the best places to find decent catches. (If it's your first time, be forewarned – a boat anchored in 'good' fishing places experiences a lot of sideways rolling motion which can cause queasy stomachs.) If you own a small boat, you can take yourself out fishing. The sort of small boat you might keep for 'messing about in' on the sea is fine for waters inshore, but be wary of venturing too far, especially in fast ebb currents. The best places to fish are usually round wrecks or over seaweed beds. Keen sea fishermen will sometimes invest in a proper little sea-fishing boat with a large area of clear deck, lockers for storing kit and a small cabin to shelter the helmsman. You can use a spinning rod (the same one you use for fishing from the beach) from a boat, or buy a special rod for the job, or simply use a fishing line with several hooks and a weight at the end.

SEA FISH RECOGNITION

1 Mackerel are familiar long, lean fish with blue-green and black striped backs and silvery undersides, often caught from boats offshore during the summer. Fresh-caught fish don't keep long, so cook and eat them or freeze them straight away.

2 Herring are long, narrow, grey-green fish with silvery scales; small herrings, which are more often found in coastal waters than adults, are also known as sprats (when very small) or (a few sizes larger) sardines or – especially in Cornwall – pilchards.

3 Grey mullet are steely silver-grey fish with large scales and thick lips, common in estuaries, natural harbours and also marinas. They are rarely seen in fishmongers' shops but are a great favourite with sea fishermen, though reputed by some to have rather a muddy flavour due to their feeding habits.

4 Sea bass is a slim, silvery grey fish, one of the most popular for eating, and also often caught by people fishing from the shore round the south of England in summer. Easily recognised by its two dorsal fins, the one nearest the head is spiny and half circular in shape when extended, the one nearer the tail is a softer, almost elongated triangular fin. Look also for a dark patch over each gill cover.

5 Pollack is a slender fish with large eyes and a lower jaw that projects further than the upper one; found close inshore during the summer and often caught by sport fishermen. This is one of the fish we are being encouraged to eat instead of traditional favourites like cod and haddock as it's a more sustainable resource.

6 Dab is a common flatfish of coastal waters, with a light brown skin faintly patterned with indistinct darker brown blotches. Rarely seen in fishmongers', but good eating, and often caught by beginners on organised fishing boat excursions.

7 Plaice is a popular flat fish whose upper surface is brown dotted with bright orange spots.

8 Cod, the familiar large, mottled, light brown-to-greyish fish with three dorsal fins and a pronounced 'barb' projecting down from the lower jaw, can be caught from many British beaches in the autumn; larger fish are caught by boat further out.

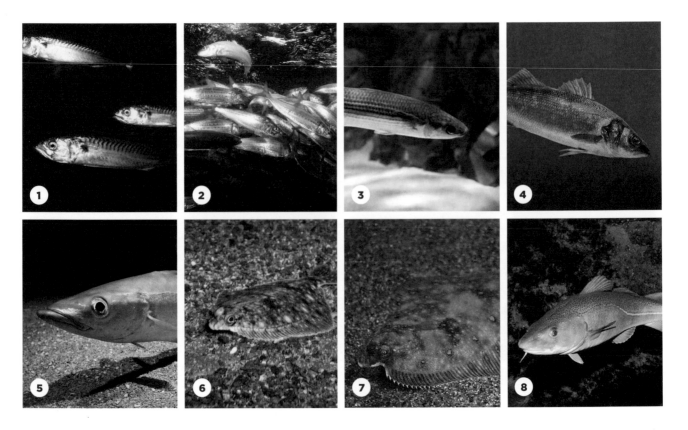

FRESHWATER FISHING

There's a huge difference between sea fishing and freshwater fishing. Freshwater fishing, or angling, is done for sport, and the fish have to be put back – the challenge is to use your skills to catch and land them. You need an annual fishing licence, which you can buy online or from a post office, and you can fish at streams, canals and rivers (depending on local bylaws), or at specially stocked and managed lakes or fisheries which are either privately owned or run by a club, where you'll need to buy a day ticket or become a member.

There's a lot of skill involved in knowing the right sort of rod, equipment and bait to get good results or to target particular species of fish, as well as the best part of the bank to stand on. Anglers will take a boxful of kit with them, including ground bait such as sweetcorn or special flavoured pellets, plus a folding seat, sandwiches and thermos of tea to set in for a long session, but it's very relaxing – enthusiasts often admit it's a great excuse for sitting around in the countryside.

Fisheries and angling societies sometimes organise special days for beginners, which is a good way to start if you don't have a 'fishing friend' to show you the ropes. You can go out for a few hours or a day on your own, and serious enthusiasts sometimes take part in matches, where the biggest weight of fish caught by the end of the day and stored in a keep net in the water, wins. (You'll sometimes see anglers taking part in a competition ranged out along the banks if you are out for a waterside walk; their concentration is immense.) Keen anglers often aim to catch the biggest-possible fish and keep note of their personal best for each species; they will often invest in special equipment for targeting particular types of fish – carp are a big current favourite. Keen anglers may even stay out overnight in all weathers, even in winter, sleeping in a bivvy tent and a down suit (which is like a fitted sleeping bag), using a 'bite alarm' to alert them that they've caught a fish.

Fly fishing (as opposed to 'coarse fishing', which uses a float and weighted line) takes place on stretches of carefully managed salmon rivers or trout streams while standing in the water wearing thigh-length waders. Instead of the usual sort of bait, fly fishermen use an artificial fly, and many different types are available to

duplicate *real* flies that fish are taking from the water surface at different times of year and in different conditions. Part of the skill of fly fishing lies in knowing which particular sort of fly to use and when. (Many serious fly fishermen like to tie their own flies, which is an art in itself.) There's a great art to casting – sending the line out over the water to the right place to find a fish, and make the fly mimic the movements of a real live fly. The trick is all in the arm movement; it's a bit like cracking a whip in slow motion. This is an art where you really do need a few lessons; you'll then need to buy 'days' or take out a membership, or rent the fishing rights to a short stretch of water. It doesn't come cheap, and while you can take a limited number of fish, you have to put anything above your allotted quota back in the water.

MAKE YOUR OWN FISHING ROD

As small boys we made our fishing rods from a long, straight, slightly flexible pole (hazel is ideal, though many lads used bamboo canes), and some button thread pinched from Mum's sewing box (it's thicker and stronger than cotton thread), which was tied to the thin end of the pole. We'd use a bent pin tied to the cotton as a hook, and as bait we'd dig up a fat red worm from the compost heap. To be honest, I don't remember ever catching anything, but it was fun hoping! This is almost exactly the way early fishermen caught fish in the days before rods as we know them today. Early fishermen even braided horsehair to make fishing line. If you want to do-it-yourself now, use proper nylon fishing line and a barbed hook from a tackle shop, though a pole 'handle' and a worm bait will still do the job.

MAKING FISHING NETS

TRADITIONALLY FISHING NETS were made by fishermen themselves using hemp twine, during the winter when bad weather meant they couldn't take their boats out fishing. They'd also mend their own nets when they got torn or damaged, and very picturesque the process looked on the quayside.

TODAY NETS ARE MADE from synthetic twine and bought factory-made, but fishermen still repair their own. To make or mend nets you need a flat piece of wood cut to the same width as you want the finished mesh to be, to act as a guide, and a netting needle – which looks like a shuttle with a bite out of one end – which the twine is wound on to. The twine is knotted together to make diamond mesh. (Square mesh is also used, but more difficult to make; both benefit from a practical demonstration, so try to watch a fisherman at work on the quay.)

TO MAKE THE TOP LINE OF THE NET, stretch a piece of lightweight rope taut between two uprights. Now, using the netting needle, tie the twine to the left-hand end of the rope with a clove hitch. Place your wooden spacer guide below this knot, loop the twine round the front, under and back up to the horizontal rope, using the spacer to show the correct width, then tie another clove hitch. Work from left to right along the rope until you have a row of half-meshes hanging evenly along the rope. To make the second row, go to the other side of the rope and work from there. Pass the needle and twine round the end of the last loop (now the first one of the next row), then pass it through the back of the loop above and tie a sheet bend. Work along the row, from left to right, tying a sheet bend in each loop. At the end of the row, go to the other side and continue until you've made your net.

YES, YOU'LL PROBABLY WANT TO BUY one now, but it's worth pointing out that these days you aren't allowed to use nets for fishing – even at sea – without a commercial fishing licence.

BOAT-BUILDING ▯▷

At one time there were boat yards all round the coast making different types of wooden boat to cater for particular jobs and various types of coastline. You can sometimes still see Thames barges and Norfolk wherries – both large, rather flat-bottomed boats with huge areas of sail, which were once used for local deliveries of goods such as coal, before the days of rail. Nobbys were fast sailing boats used for trawling fishing nets, especially for prawns, and then getting the catch back to harbour quickly so that it stayed fresh before the days of refrigeration made it possible to keep a catch on ice.

There are two basic types of construction used for wooden boats. Clinker-built boats look as if they are made from lots of narrow planks that overlap slightly along the edges. It's a technique that's thought to have been used first by the Vikings. It was mostly used for fairly small boats, such as rowing boats, sailing dinghies and tenders to larger boats. Carvel construction uses planks that are fitted together flush; such boats are stronger, but more time-consuming and difficult to make since each plank has to be carefully chosen so that it makes a perfect fit against its neighbour. The technique is mostly used for larger boats.

TRADITIONAL BOAT-BUILDING

Traditional boat-building is a rare craft these days since wooden boats take much time and considerable skill to construct, and they also need regular and expensive maintenance afterwards. A few old traditional sailing boats have been restored by enthusiasts or converted for leisure use, but nowadays new boats are mostly made of glass fibre or steel.

For inland use, it was traditional to use coracles in some parts of the country, especially in Wales. A coracle was originally made by stretching an animal hide over a semi-circular basketwork framework made from flexible willow stems, with a woven willow floor something like a hurdle, and a plank fitted across the centre to sit on. The boat was propelled using a single paddle – there's quite an art in making a round boat go forwards instead of spinning round and round. The coracle was deliberately made lightweight so that the occupant could pick it up and carry it when need be; the plank seat had a carrying handle attached, so the craft could be slung over the boatman's back.

Today coracles are still made in much the same way, but using tarred or bituminised canvas or similar materials, and even if they aren't used in earnest, a lot of coracles are bought by people who appreciate the craftsmanship involved, parking them alongside their garden pond for decoration. I had one myself, though ten years on, it has now disintegrated! It's still possible to go on a course to learn how to build a traditional coracle, at the Green Wood Centre www.greenwoodcentre.org.uk near Ironbridge in Shropshire.

OUTDOOR SURVIVAL SKILLS

When you're out in the countryside, on foot, bike, horse or in the car, and even on camping holidays, it's useful to know a few basic skills – and it's far more vital if you're making long-distance trips.

MAP-READING

Put aside the GPS for once: a good current road atlas is ideal for car trips where you're keeping to A or B roads and covering long distances. But when you're walking, horse-riding or cycling, using little back lanes and public rights of way, then a much larger-scale map covering a smaller area is far more useful. (It's also easier to carry as it can be folded open at the right part and put in a rainproof plastic map carrier, for quick reference in any weather.) The standard Ordnance Survey (OS) Landranger Series 1:50,000 scale (2cm to a kilometre/1¼ inches to the mile) is useful when you're touring by car, but large-scale maps made especially for walkers – the OS Explorer Maps 1:25,000 scale (4cm to the kilometre, 2½ inches to the mile) show all sorts of landscape features that help you to keep tabs on exactly where you are, even when you go off-road. It's far easier to follow your progress along public footpaths and other rights of way when every landmark and turn in the track is shown in detail. Even if you don't go in for serious hiking, it's worth having one or two maps of this sort that cover the immediate area round your house or somewhere you're staying on holiday, as they show up a wealth of landscape features and places of interest that may be fun to investigate.

To really make full use of any map, it's worth spending time learning the symbols shown on the legend – the 'key', which you'll find running up one side of the map. From this you can see at a glance which part of the terrain is covered by coniferous woods, mixed woodland or parkland, and you can tell the steepness of gradients in the land by how closely spaced the contour lines are. You can see the location of electricity pylons, church steeples and radio or TV masts, identify ancient burial mounds (tumuli), find public houses, a post office, camp or caravan sites, parking places, public loos or tourist information centres – any of which may be handy on a day out in the countryside.

When you know the scale of the map, you can also tell very easily how far it is between two points, just by measuring the distance on the map. As a rough and ready guide, if your thumb measures 6cm (2½in) long, you can quickly hold it against the Explorer map to measure distance – each thumbs-length being a mile (1.6km), so you can tell in advance how long a walk will be, or how much further you have to go when you're already out.

When you need to identify a precise place on the land, this is easily done by giving a map reference, also known as a grid reference. (Local branches of the Ramblers, for instance, supply a map reference for car parks where members are to meet to go for a walk, but it's also handy if you want to pass on details of a location to friends.) A map reference is made up of two letters and two sets of three numbers, e.g. TQ 235 678. The two letters are to enable you to quickly find the square in which the point lies – you'll find the letters printed in the corners of large squares on the OS map. The first three numbers are the eastings – the horizontal lines running across the map; the first two numbers of the group of three are printed in the margin up each side of the map. The second group of three numbers are the northings, the vertical lines running up and down the map; the first two numbers of the group of three refer to the numbers printed along the top and bottom margins of the map. Find the right horizontal line and the right vertical line, then follow them to the point where they cross, and you'll be very close to the spot you are looking for. The third figure in each group of three helps you home in on the exact spot, if you haven't already found it, as it indicates tenths of the distance between grid lines. (SO 235 will be found halfway between the 23 and the 24 lines.) It's worth thoroughly familiarising yourself with maps and how to use them properly if you intend doing any serious outdoor activity such as fell-walking, where getting lost can cause real problems.

If you're going walking, learn how to use a compass. Besides making sure you are heading in the right direction, a compass can help to pinpoint where you are since you can tell the direction of conspicuous landmarks.

To use a compass, hold it steady, well away from any ferrous metal (e.g. iron) or anything else that's magnetic, and place it on top of a wooden fence post or similar flat surface, making sure it is as level as possible. The needle will point to magnetic north. Rotate the compass slowly until the north marked on the face lines up exactly with the needle. It's then easy to see which direction a feature such as a railway line road or path runs (perhaps east–west) which is helpful for pinpointing it on a map. You can also take a bearing on a distant landmark such as a tower, which tells you the direction it is from where you are now. If you can find a second very visible landmark, well away from the first, and take a bearing on that, you can pinpoint your position on the map fairly accurately by plotting the point where the two bearings cross. Some superior compasses have a sight that you can rotate over the face to enable you to take more accurate bearings. But for most general walking, all you really need is a small, lightweight compass that you can carry in your pocket.

Nowadays some sophisticated walkers use a hand-held GPS (Global Positioning System), which tells you where you are within a few feet, but maps... oh, I love maps!

MAKING A CAMP FIRE

A camp fire is really just a wild barbecue you make from scratch; its main use is for cooking food or heating water to make tea, but it's handy for keeping you warm for drying wet clothes or even signalling for help in emergencies.

The main concern, any time you think about lighting a fire in the countryside, is to ensure it can't spread, so first clear the site of anything inflammable – dead leaves, dry grass etc. It often helps to make a circle of large stones or to excavate a shallow, saucer-shaped depression, since the raised sides give the flames a bit of shelter. This makes the fire easier to light as well as keeping it contained. Have a pile of loose sand or soil nearby that you can use for dousing stray flames if needed.

While one person prepares the site for the fire, send someone else off to collect suitable materials to burn. You'll need a fair stack of dry wood; look for dead branches on the ground under trees – don't break off living branches because besides damaging the trees, living wood won't burn well as it's full of sap. Have firewood in a mixture of thicknesses; thinner branches are good to get the fire going, but you need thicker bits once it's going well, as they'll burn longer. You'll also need a selection of small, very dry material to light the fire with. Dry fir cones, dry pine needles, dry twigs, dead gorse and dry leaves are good, bone-dry lichen or even moss can be good if they are the loose, fluffy sort. If you are using paper to start the fire, fold it lengthwise several times and then roll it onto a coil; this burns longer and slower than a flat piece of paper.

Make a small 'nest' of kindling, light the paper spill with a lighter or matches, and touch it to the dry material. As the fire 'catches', lay twigs into the centre of the blaze, making a pattern like the spokes of a wheel, and slowly add larger branches as the centre becomes hot. When the fire is going well, push a long, stout stick into the ground to one side of the fire, clear of the flames, positioning it at an angle so that the top of the stick is above the flames. Cut a notch near the top of the stick and hang your billy can from it. Alternatively, wait for the fire to die down to embers and balance a flat mess-tin on hot stones round the edge of the fire.

MAKING FIRE WITHOUT MATCHES

Various techniques are used by survival experts, but they are trickier than they look and can take time to perfect – you need a bit of practice at home first, when you aren't freezing cold, wet and hungry or desperate for a hot drink. The best method is to carry a small tin containing a flint and a metal bar for creating a spark, and some dry tinder (which can be wood shavings, hay-like dry grass stems or similar) to ignite. Strike the flint and metal together to make a spark an inch or two above a small, fist-sized 'nest' of your highly inflammable bone-dry tinder; when the tinder starts to smoulder, pick it up and hold it in your cupped hands whilst blowing across it very gently. When a small flame erupts, put it down on the ground in your prepared fireplace and start adding small twigs – just like you've seen Ray Mears doing on TV.

HOW TO PREDICT THE WEATHER

Clearly it makes sense to get a good local weather forecast (from the local radio and TV stations, or from Internet sites) before going off sailing, hill-walking or even just setting out for a weekend at a campsite.

A long-range forecast, available for the next seven days, is worth having when you're going to be away for several days, or when you are deciding the best day to take a trip. While you're away it's sensible to get regular updates several times a day. But if you're out of contact – or simply curious about atmospheric events unfolding in the cosmos above you – you can do-it-yourself if you know what to watch for.

Weather is famously unpredictable, so be prepared for the unexpected – even when you've taken sensible precautions. Even the old saying about 'red sky at night, shepherds delight, red sky in the morning, shepherd's warning' can't always be relied upon.

HOW TO STAY SAFE IN A THUNDERSTORM

People are very rarely struck by lightning but it does happen occasionally, and being outside in a storm can be quite frightening, especially if you are stranded in the open with no shelter.

Keep well clear of tall, and especially metal objects, since they are the likeliest places for lightning to strike. Golf courses are surprisingly dangerous since they are wide open, and golfers carrying bags of metal clubs are likely to prove the tallest conductors in the area. Tall trees may also sometimes be struck, so don't shelter underneath – you are better behind a hedge, on the side that's sheltered from the wind, or down a natural depression in the land. If there's no better alternative, lay flat on the ground so you're as level as possible with your surroundings.

Rubber boots or rubber-soled walking boots or shoes provide some insulation, but perhaps the safest place to be in a thunderstorm is in a car, since the tyres stop the charge reaching earth. Church steeples are usually protected by lightning conductors which prevents them coming to harm, and you should be safe inside any kind of building or field shelter. Head for the pub is my advice.

USEFUL RULES OF THUMB

Areas of low barometric pressure (known as 'depressions') usually bring weather that changes for the worse; areas of high pressure in summer usually bring fine weather and sometimes can mean long, hot spells, though in winter they can bring snow.

If you stand with your back to the wind, the area of low pressure will be on your left – if clouds are moving towards you from the left, expect the weather to worsen. If the clouds are coming from your right, the weather can be expected to improve. If the clouds are passing straight towards or away from you then expect the weather to stay much the same for a while.

CLOUD RECOGNITION

1 Fair weather cumulus: big, white, fluffy clouds, rather like heads of cauliflower in an otherwise clear blue sky are a good indicator of fine summer weather, which should continue for most or all of the day, with perhaps just the odd temporary cloud passing overhead to block out the sun.

2 High cirrus: long 'streamers' of wispy white cloud all running in roughly the same direction across a clear blue sky, sometimes with a few lower, fluffier clouds also present. These are usually followed within 8–12 hours by stronger winds or gales.

3 Thunderclouds: large, fluffy clouds that grow quickly and billow upwards, forming vertical 'chimneys', though it can be hard to see as these are sometimes hidden by a lowering ceiling of grey, almost smoke-like, cloud. Be warned by thickening and lowering cloud and a darkening sky on a day that started out fine and sunny. You'll sometimes see sheets of rain falling from advancing low cloud, or hear distant thunder before any lightning starts.

4 Rain clouds: sheets of grey, lowering, dark cloud and a darkening sky generally predict rain. You might see curtains of rain from the advancing edge of lowering cloud cover. On a very still day in winter, the sky often turns a strange pewter colour shortly before it snows.

5 Sea fog: dense, white mist for several miles inland along stretches of the coast, often when conditions are quite clear and it's a fine day further inland. When it's present first thing in the morning, sea fog usually clears within a few hours as the sun 'burns it off', but when it rolls in from the sea later in the day it can last quite a while. When conditions are right, sea fog can persist or reappear for many days. In coastal areas you can often predict a sea fog is on its way by the eerie sound of distant foghorns – they carry a long way in foggy conditions.

6 Fronts: a passing front can be seen when the sky is covered by low, dark cloud that has a pronounced edge running right across the sky, with a strip of clear sky visible beyond it before distant, higher cloud. This can bring a sharp change of weather, with sudden strong gusts of wind and changing wind direction, rain squalls, or even a clap or two of thunder. At sea, it's a good idea to secure loose items and shorten sail. Elsewhere, put your mac on and take shelter.

THE BEAUFORT SCALE
...

The Beaufort scale is an imperial measure and a means of enabling an observer to identify wind strength without any instruments. It is familiar to sailors and fishermen and indeed anyone who listens to the shipping forecast, but it's also applicable inland, and helps to flesh out the full impact of what you hear on radio and TV weather forecasts. Wind speed is given in knots, which are nautical miles per hour. (A nautical mile is 2,200 yards, as against a statute mile which is 1,760 yards.) One knot is roughly equivalent to 1.1 land miles per hour.

BEAUFORT SCALE

Force 0: condition – calm; sea glassy; on land, smoke rises vertically. Wind speed less than 1 knot (under 1mph).

Force 1: condition – light air; sea ripples slightly: on land, smoke drifts slightly. Wind speed 1–3 knots (1–3mph).

Force 2: condition – light breeze; sea has small wavelets but the crests do not break: on land, leaves rustle, flags flutter weakly and you can feel a faint breeze on your face. Wind speed 4–6 knots. (4–7 mph).

Force 3: condition – gentle breeze; sea has large wavelets with breaking crests; on land, flags open out, and both leaves and small twigs at the extremities of trees and bushes move. Wind speed 7–10 knots (8 –12mph).

Force 4: condition – moderate breeze; sea has some 'white horses'; on land litter starts being blown about and larger branches start swaying on trees and bushes. Wind speed 11–16 knots (13–18mph).

Force 5: condition – fresh breeze; sea has lots of white horses, with a little occasional light spray; on land, whole young trees start swaying and inland water has wavelets with slight crests. Wind speed 17–21 knots (19–24mph).

Force 6: condition – strong breeze; sea has large waves with foaming crests producing more spray; on land trees are moving more, people have difficulty using umbrellas, and telegraph wires 'sing'. Wind speed 22–27 knots (25–31mph).

Force 7: condition – near-gale; sea has large waves breaking at the top with lots of foam, producing streaks of spray; on land, whole trees wave, and people have difficulty walking into the wind. Wind speed 28–33 knots (32–38mph).

Force 8: condition – gale; sea has long, large waves whose crests produce strong streaks of fairly solid-looking spray; on land, twigs break off trees and it's hard to stand upright against the wind. Wind speed 34–40 knots (39–46mph).

Force 9: condition – strong gale; sea has tall waves whose crests tumble and roll down the waves, with large sheets of spray; on land, slight structural damage starts to occur, a few slates are blown off roofs, some tree branches break or fall. Wind speed 41–47 knots (47–54mph).

Force 10: condition – storm; sea has precipitous waves with overhanging crests, and may appear confused or 'boiling', air is filled with heavy spray which seriously reduces visibility; on land a storm of this strength is rare, but when it occurs expect some trees to blow down and considerable structural damage to roofs and buildings. Wind speed 48–55 knots (55–63 mph).

A full hurricane, force 12, has wind speeds of over 73mph.

WALKING 🥾

Perhaps the very best way to explore the countryside is on foot. Britain is full of great places to walk, and even if you are taking it easy without trying to get anywhere fast there are other interesting activities you can combine with a pleasant stroll, from fossil hunting to beachcombing.

BEACHCOMBING

One of the many delights of a seaside holiday – or a day trip – is beachcombing. You can hunt for anything that's been washed up by the tide, below the high-water mark. You may find bits of gnarled driftwood, pieces from a fisherman's net, strands of seaweed, interesting stones with holes worn through them, or the remains of glass bottles that the waves have buffeted smoothly into frosted 'pebbles'.

Then there's what's picturesquely known as flotsam and jetsam. Flotsam is the correct name given to pieces from wrecked ships or their cargoes, while jetsam is unwanted material that's been thrown overboard from boats – in days of old it was fairly common for mariners to chuck surplus cargo overboard to lighten the boat in heavy seas.

Nowadays finders don't have the automatic right to keep valuable cargoes that they've found (as

people discovered a few years ago when a timber ship shed its cargo of planks, which washed up on the Sussex coast, and another ship off Cornwall deposited all sorts of cargo, including motorbikes, onto a beach). The correct procedure is to notify the coastguard so the rightful owner can come and collect their goods.

But the popular things to collect at the seaside, at least when I was a lad, were seashells. To landlubbers enjoying their annual two weeks at the beach, it was quite fascinating to see the 'homes' of strange sea creatures, and fun to identify them. Most sandy beaches would turn up shells of mussels, cockles, whelk, top shell, slipper limpet and the occasional oyster, scallop or razor shell. The idea was to collect as many as you could, of as many different types as possible, and take them home as a memento of your visit. There you'd sort out the best to keep in a drawer as a 'collection', or perhaps to glue onto a box and varnish, to give as a gift to your mum, aunt or granny, or to keep for yourself to put useful things in. (The 'useful things' usually turned out to be next year's collection of seashells, while you wondered what to do with them.)

LITTER PARTIES

A heck of a lot of what's washed up on beaches today, alas, is litter – especially plastic bags and soft drinks bottles that float but don't decompose naturally. Some seaside Chambers of Commerce and conservation organisations organise periodic beach litter-picking sessions with volunteers helping out. Besides making beaches look untidy and unwelcoming to summer visitors, floating plastic bags in particular are a hazard to marine life. Creatures such as turtles, which feed on squid and suchlike, are often fooled into swallowing plastic bags (which DO look rather similar in murky water) and die as a result.

HUNTING FOR FOSSILS AND SEMI-PRECIOUS STONES

Fossils are the remains of prehistoric creatures that roamed the earth and seas millions of years ago, whose teeth, bones, shells or other remains – even footprints – have turned to stone over time. They are mostly found on certain stretches of coast where exceptionally low tides reveal fossil-bearing shale deposits (as happens on part of the beach at Bracklesham Bay, just outside Chichester) or after rockfalls at the base of chalky or limestone cliffs – the Jurassic coast in Dorset and parts of the Isle of Wight are well known to fossil hunters for 'finds'.

Ancient sharks' teeth sometimes wash up on the beach, and rockfalls may reveal fossilised dinosaur bones, but some fossils, such as the spiral-shelled ammonites, are often hidden inside large stones. Enthusiasts know how to recognise a likely one, and a sharp tap with a geologist's hammer splits it open, revealing the fossil inside.

Other parts of the coast turn up different ancient 'treasures'. In East Anglia the beach at Titchwell has a sunken forest not far offshore, with pieces of fossilised stumps visible at very low tides. Some East Anglian beaches produce lumps of amber – fossilised tree sap – which may occasionally contain trapped (and equally old and fossilised) insects, and at Happisburgh archeologists are finding very ancient stone tools. In Yorkshire, seams of jet (a black shiny mineral – a kind of fossilised wood – much favoured for jewellery by the Victorians) can be found in some rocks, usually after a rockfall, while semi-precious stones can sometimes be found on the beach at Robin Hood's Bay, turned up by the action of waves. They aren't as easy to find as you might think, since clearly they have not been 'cut' to give them the sparkle and polish of the finished stones you see in a jeweller's; they look more like rounded pebbles. But enthusiasts soon learn to spot them.

The great thing about this sort of beachcombing is that you are allowed to keep what you find. In no time at all a child can build up a sizeable collection of specimens and begin a lifelong interest in fossils and stones as a result.

COUNTRYSIDE AND COASTAL WALKS

The countryside and the coast are our favourite places to go out walking. Walking, rambling, hiking, fell-walking and all its variants are a fast-growing pastime – invigorating, full of great views and wildlife-spotting opportunities, free (once you get there) and good for you. Just think of all that fresh air and exercise.

Unlike many outdoor activities you don't need much in the way of equipment, just sensible, weather-proof outdoor clothes and stout walking shoes or hiking boots, plus perhaps a good walking stick or hiking pole and a small backpack for a folding mac, spare socks, snack and water to drink.

There are lots of different places to walk. An OS map (the large-scale Explorer Series is best for walkers) will show you the location of public footpaths, long-distance recreational routes and other rights of way including coastal footpaths – the Cornish Coastal Footpath is a famous walk, known for its scenic views, as is the South Downs Way. Some public rights of way go through woods, forests, fields, moorland, hills, dales and downland, so you can pick your preferred scenery. You can walk on beaches below the high-tide mark, on national nature reserves and nature reserves owned by the Wildlife Trusts (these are open to the public with no charge), also stretches of land owned by the National Trust (where entrance is allowed usually without charge – even if you aren't a member). You can walk in the New Forest, Ashdown Forest, Dartmoor and similar local beauty spots; National Parks are full of great scenic walks as is Forestry Commission land. Some places to walk are free of entry fees, but there's a small charge for parking or access through private roads, or for special events. These should be well signposted.

Members can walk in RSPB reserves, National Trust and English Heritage sites, or visit the gardens of the RHS for free, but non-members need to buy an admission ticket. It's also possible to buy annual tickets that allow you and your family to visit particular stately homes and their grounds as often as you like over the year for free, and these often include admission to special events like garden or countryside shows held in their grounds, so they can represent a huge saving if you like revisiting favourite local places fairly frequently. And all sorts of ancient sites are fun to explore on foot, from Stonehenge to the standing stones and burial chambers you'll find marked on maps.

Other brilliant sources of walks in your area are the various pocket-sized guide books of good local walks. These detail outings of varying lengths, often starting and ending at pub car parks or tea rooms, where it's hoped you'll stop to spend a few pounds on refreshments instead of just availing yourself of free parking. These are sold in local stationers, newsagents and bookshops – even garden centres. You'll also find larger books of walks covering the whole country, which are the sort to keep in the car or at home, when planning a more distant day out or a walking holiday. If you are majoring on a particular area, look for more specialist information. *Wainright's Walks* is a series of books detailing walks in the Lake District, written and illustrated by enthusiast Alfred Wainwright roughly half a century ago. They've enjoyed a return to popularity today, but the original walks he mentions sometimes pass through what is now private land, so if you want to use the books in earnest, it's worth buying the modern revised versions which include slightly altered routes which will keep you legal.

If you enjoy walking fairly seriously, and like to do so in company, it might be a good idea to join the Ramblers. Local groups meet for walks regularly, joining up at a suitable car park, and the usual length of these rambles is between 8 and 15 miles (13 and 24km). (A lot of people join because they want to get fit and lose weight, but it's also reckoned to be one of the best ways to meet a new partner, for single, widowed, or divorced middle-aged people!) Various hotels and guest houses all round the country also arrange walking holidays for guests, which will offer a leader to accompany them round scenic local paths. You can find such trips advertised in magazines devoted to the countryside or the coast.

Wherever you walk, there are some 'rules' to follow. First of all, stick to the paths. Many walks go through farmland so by wandering about at will you may be damaging crops or disturbing livestock which are, after all, somebody else's livelihood. In

HIKING POLES

Hiking poles are the latest advance on the walking stick. They look like ski poles, and came about when cross-country skiers wanted to find a way of keeping themselves fit even when there wasn't any snow on the ground, so they started walking briskly with ski poles across undulating countryside in the summer.

You can use a single hiking pole in the same way as a normal walking stick, but if you're doing it seriously you need a pair, which are used alternately – just like cross-country ski poles – using the right-hand pole simultaneously with your left leg, and vice versa, for maximum stability. Since you use your arms and shoulders more than when walking normally, hiking poles give you an upper-body workout and save your legs some of the strain at the same time as helping you along faster.

open areas, remember to keep a look out for ground-nesting birds, and avoid damage to delicate or rare vegetation (which can cause soil erosion as well as loss of habitat). Dogs should be kept on a lead, due to the risk that they'll chase livestock or disturb wildlife, and even though you are out in the countryside where you'd think it wouldn't do any harm, 'pick up' after your dog. (Don't imagine it acts as 'manure'; the nutrients in carnivore droppings can affect the spectrum of plants that grows in the ground, and eventually alter the natural flora and the wildlife – especially butterflies and insects – that live on it.) It goes without saying, take your litter home with you – as they say in countryside circles, leave nothing behind but your footprints, and take nothing away except memories, though these days you could safely add photos.

Wherever you go and whatever you do, enjoy and cherish our countryside; it is a pearl beyond price and the stuff dreams are made of. My dreams, at any rate…

FURTHER INFORMATION

For further information, look for magazines devoted to the countryside, smallholdings, and specialist crafts and hobbies, which you'll find in large stationers' shops such as WHSmith. The small ads are a good way to find products, livestock, courses and books on specialist subjects. The websites of this type of magazine are often packed with more information and make a good way of keeping up to date with issues of interest.

Countryside shows, smallholders' shows and county agricultural shows are a great way to find information, suppliers and specialist products, as well as have a fascinating day out. A list of shows appears regularly in the various smallholders' magazines; serious exhibitors may like to invest in a copy of the *Showman's Directory* (www.showmansdirectory.co.uk). Some shows also feature talks or demonstrations on specialist subjects, which often need booking in advance. Shows are also good places to make contact with local livestock-keeping groups, which provide invaluable advice for beginners getting started, or anyone looking to purchase livestock. Where possible it's worth buying tickets for shows in advance, since visitors with tickets can usually walk straight in without having to join a long queue at the pay kiosk. You'll also be doing your bit to support local folk who cherish rare breeds and the countryside as a whole.

The following books also make useful further reading. Some are new, or relatively new, titles (just lately several publishers have brought out series' of inexpensive small books on specific countryside and craft topics). Others may be out of print and best found in public libraries (which can order specific titles for you, for a small fee) or second-hand bookshops (visit www.abebooks.com to find bookshops who stock second-hand, old or out-of-print titles you are looking for).

For new natural history books (including the invaluable Collins *New Naturalist* series), go to www.nhbs.com.

FURTHER READING

Ch 1: Country Ways
Gardener's Magic, Bridget Boland
Old Wives' Lore for Gardeners, Maureen and Bridget Boland
Black Cats and April Fools, Harry Oliver

Ch 2: Working the Land
Home Farm – How to Grow Your Own Food, Paul Heiney
Self Sufficiency, John and Sally Seymour
The Self-Sufficiency Bible, Simon Dawson
On The Farm, Jimmy Doherty
The Illustrated Guide to Chickens, Celia Lewis

Bees & Beekeeping Explained, Gerard Baker
Self-Sufficiency Beekeeping, Joanna Ryde
Self-Sufficiency Hen-Keeping, Mike Hatcher
Several books in the *Shire Books* series, including *Rare Breeds*, Lawrence Alderson; *British Pigs*, Val Porter; *British Cattle*, Val Porter; *Old Poultry Breeds*, Fred Hams. (www.shirebooks.co.uk)
The Smallholder's Manual, Katie Thear
Starting with Bees, Peter Gordon
Starting with Pigs, Andy Case
Starting with Goats, Katie Thear
Starting with Ducks, Katie Thear
Starting with a Smallholding, David Hills

Ch 3: The Country Home and Garden
First Steps in Winemaking, C.J.J. Berry
Grow Your Own Drugs, James Wong
A Year with James Wong, James Wong
Jekka's Complete Herb Book, Jekka McVicar
Good Enough to Eat, Jekka McVicar
Jane Grigson's Fruit Book, Jane Grigson
Jane Grigson's Vegetable Book, Jane Grigson
The Kitchen Gardener, Alan Titchmarsh
How to be a Gardener, Alan Titchmarsh
How to Garden series of handbooks, Alan Titchmarsh
The Gardener's Year, Alan Titchmarsh
Complete Encyclopaedia of Organic Gardening, The Henry Doubleday Research Organisation
Feed Your Face, Dian Dincin Buchman
Herbcraft Naturally, Christine Stapley
Herb Sufficient, Christine Stapley
RHS Encyclopaedia of Herbs, Deni Bown
Wise Words and Country Ways for Cooks, Ruth Binney
Grandma's Ways for Modern Days – Reviving Traditional Skills in Cookery, Gardening and Household Management, Paul and Diana Peacock
Cheesemaking and Dairying, Katie Thear
New Holland Publishing *Self-Sufficiency* Series:
    Self-Sufficiency Preserving, Carol Wilson
    Self-Sufficiency Soap Making, Sarah Ade
    Self-Sufficiency Home Brewing, John Parkes
    Self-Sufficiency Cheese-Making, Rita Ash

Ch 4: The Wild Garden
How To Make a Wildlife Garden, Chris Baines
The English Meadow, Yvette Verner
Native Trees and Shrubs for your Garden, Jill, Duchess of Hamilton and Christopher Humphries
The Natural History of the Garden, Michael Chinery

Ch 5: Country Arts and Crafts

The Forgotten Arts, John Seymour
Fences, Gates and Bridges: A Practical Manual,
    George A. Martin
The Herb and Spice Book, Sarah Garland
Lost Crafts: Rediscovering Traditional Skills,
    Una McGovern
Self-Sufficiency, Spinning, Dyeing and Weaving,
    Penny Walsh
Useful Knots, Geoffrey Budworth

Ch 6: Go Wild in the Country

Sea Fishing Properly Explained, Ian Ball
River Cottage Handbook No 5, Edible Seashore,
    John Wright
Food for Free, Richard Mabey
River Cottage Handbook No 6, Sea Fishing, Nick Fisher
Instant Weather Forecasting, Alan Watts
*The Weather Book, Why it Happens and Where it Comes
    From*, Diana Craig
Weather Forecasting Made Simple, Stan Yorke
The Met Office Book of the British Weather, Met Office,
    authored by John Prior
Wise Words and Country Ways, Weather Lore,
    Ruth Binney
Essential Bushcraft, Ray Mears

SPECIALIST COURSES AND FURTHER INFORMATION

Dry stone walling: the Dry Stone Walling Association
www.dswa.org.uk and the National Stone Centre,
Derbyshire, www.nationalstonecentre.org.uk

Coppicing: the British Trust for Conservation Volunteers,
www.btcv.org.uk

Hedge-laying: The National Hedge-Laying Society,
www.hedgelaying.org.uk

Farming and Wildlife Advisory Group, www.fwag.org.uk

Coracle making: the National Coracle Centre,
www.coracle-centre.co.uk

Bee-keeping: the British Beekeepers Association,
www.britishbee.org.uk

Tracking, hunting, foraging, etc., various bush-craft
schools (search the Internet)

Fishing, foraging, fungi-hunting: River Cottage,
www.rivercottage.net

Kitchen gardening: Garden Organic,
www.gardenorganic.co.uk

Basketry: The Basketmakers Association,
www.basketassoc.org

CENTRES RUNNING COURSES IN A WIDE RANGE OF COUNTRY ARTS AND CRAFTS AND NATURAL SCIENCES

The Weald and Downland Open Air Museum, Singleton,
Chichester, West Sussex PO18 0EU. Tel: 01243 811464,
www.wealddown.co.uk

The Green Wood Centre, Shropshire,
www.greenwoodcentre.org.uk

Denman College (the WI college), www.wi.org.uk

Field Studies Council, www.field-studies-council.org

WALKS AND WALKING

www.countrysideaccess.gov.uk

http://countrywalks.defra.gov.uk

Ramblers, www.ramblers.org.uk

ORGANISATIONS

Butterfly Conservation, www.butterfly-conservation.org

The Wildlife Trusts, www.wildlifetrusts.org

Natural England, www.naturalengland.org.uk

The Herb Society, www.herbsociety.org.uk

The Royal Society for the Protection of Birds (RSPB),
www.rspb.org.uk

The British Trust for Ornithology (BTO), www.bto.org

The National Trust, www.nationaltrust.org.uk

English Heritage, www.engish-heritage.org.uk

The Rare Breeds Survival Trust, www.rare-breeds.com

Botanical Society of the British Isles, www.bsbi.org.uk

The Forestry Commission, www.forestry.gov.uk

The Tree Council, www.treecouncil.org.uk

The Woodland Trust, www.woodland-trust.org.uk

The Department for Environment, Food and Rural
Affairs (DEFRA), www.Defra.gov.uk

The Angling Trust, www.anglingtrust.net

The Royal Horticultural Society, www.rhs.org.uk

INDEX

Alexanders 284
algae 208
All Fool's Day 16
Aloe vera 142
alpacas 92, 93, 255
amber 304
amelanchier 218
Andrew, St 23
angelica 37
ant repellents 146
apple 113, 218
   bobbing for 18
   growing tips 162
   healing properties 31
   jelly 124
   juice 114
   wood 168
apricot 162
ash 37, 38, 168, 171, 199, 225, 232, 278–9
Ash Wednesday 13
asparagus 154

bacon 71
bad breath 143
badgers 281
bank vole 220–1
barley 109–10
basil 157
basket weaving 228–30
bats 212
beach-combing 303
beans 158
Beaufort scale 302
Bed & Breakfasts (B&Bs) 104
bee plants 96, 175, 191, 213
beech 171, 278, 279
beechnuts 284, 285
beer making 109–11
bees 30, 94–8, 213
beeswax 94, 98, 146, 148, 252–3
beetles 156, 176
bell-ringing 12, 32
betony 37
biodiversity 176
birch 168, 171, 178–80, 183, 199
birds 217–18, 263–9, 281
bird's foot trefoil 192–3
Black Death 30
black medick 192
blackberry 165, 284–5
blackbird 266, 267
blacksmiths 33
blackthorn 178–9
bluebell 200, 201
bluetit 264, 267
boats 291, 295
borage 36, 143
Border Collies 89
Boxing Day 20
bramble 184–5, 189
brassicas 158–9
bread ovens 138, 139

Brent goose 268, 269
Brigid, St 30
brimstone 270, 272
brine 131
brooms 226–7
bugle 202–3
burdock 284
burns 142
butter 132–5
butterbur 275, 277
butterflies 213, 270–2
buttermilk 135
buzzard 268, 269

calves 81, 82
canal boat painting 259
candle-making 252–3
Candlemas 38
caraway seeds 143
carragheen 287, 288
carrion crow 268, 269
casting 87, 88
caterpillars 213–14, 270–2
cats 28, 38
centipedes 156
chaffinch 264–6, 267
chamomile 36, 143–4, 149
Chanterelle 286
cheese-making 136–7
cherry 162
chervil 148
chickens 48–55
   battery hens 51
   breeds 52
   broody hens 52, 54, 55
   cockerels 54
   diet 50
   housing 48, 50
   manure 50
   numbers 52
   parasites 54
   predators 50
   wing clipping 55
chicks (chicken) 51, 54, 55
chickweed 283
chimney sweeping 141
Christianity 13, 23, 28, 38
Christmas 19–21, 31, 251
chutney, green tomato 131
cider 113
cinnabar moth 214–15
clouds 300–1
clover 38–9, 193
clustered bellflower 196, 197
coastal habitats 277, 287–92, 303–5
cockles 289
cod 292
colds 143
collared dove 266, 267
coltsfoot 274–5
comfrey fertiliser 161
comma (butterfly) 270, 271

common alder 278, 279
common mallow 275, 277
common vetch 196, 197
commoners' rights 46
community-supported agriculture 105
companion planting 36
compasses 299
compost heaps 152–3
confetti 40, 248
conserve 124, 127
container-gardening 154
cookery 33, 138–40
coppicing 180–1, 225
coracles 295
cordons 162, 166
coriander 157
corn dollies 18
cotoneaster 218
Country Land and Business Assoc. 45
country sayings 31–3
countryside skills 282–305
cow parsley 193
cows 38, 75, 81–3, 100, 132–7
cowslip 192–3
crab apple 218
   jelly 128
crabbing 290
crafts 104–5, 109–71, 223–59
cream 132–5
cricket bats 244
crofts 46
crop rotation 154, 158–9
crossing fingers 28
cuckoo 30
cuckoo pint 273, 274
cucumber, quick pickled 130
curlew 268, 269
cut flowers 160, 249
cyclamen 202–3

dab 292
dagging 84, 87
dahlia 160
dairy work 132–7
daisies 38, 196, 197
damsel flies 210–11
damson gin 115, 121
dandelion 142–3, 283, 284
   coffee 145
David, St 22
deer 36, 281
DEFRA 45, 68
deodorant, natural 148
dill 142, 143
dipping 84, 87
disease 36, 156
ditching 236
dock 100, 102
dog rose 184–5
dog violet 192–3
dogs 89, 305
dog's mercury 274, 275

dogwood 178–9, 230
donkeys 32
dragonflies 210–11
drenching 84, 87
dried flowers 245–8
ducks 56–61
dulse 287, 288
dyes, natural 257–8

earwigs 156
Easter 14
eggs
    chicken 48, 50, 139
    duck 58
    goose 62, 63
    quail 67
egret 268, 269
elder 40, 179, 218
elderflower champagne 115, 116, 179
elderflower cordial 115, 118
energy, green sources 104, 105
English Heritage 304
Environmental Health 45
espaliers 162, 166

fat hen 283
Father Christmas 20
fencing
    electric 99
    post and rail 233–4
fennel tea 144
fertilisers 35, 50, 105, 161
festivals 13–21
fêtes 24, 40
Fiacre, St 23
field maple 184–5
field poppy 196, 197
firecrest 264, 267
fires 141, 299–300
firewood 168–71
fireworks 16
'first footing' 21
fish 140, 204, 209
fishing 291–4
flatulence 143
fleabane 274, 275
florists 26–7
flower symbolism 22
folklore 34–41
foot and mouth disease 68
foot trimming 84
foraging 282–90
fortune telling 18, 24, 40–1
fossils 304
four-leafed clover 38–9
foxes 50, 219–21, 280–1
foxglove 202–3
freshwater whelk 210–11
frogs 210–11
fruit 150, 162–6
    aftercare 166
    hedgerow 166, 285

soft 154, 165, 166
trees 154, 162–5, 166
fungi 286
furniture cream 146

garden societies 26–7
garden tiger moth 214–15
gardening
    kitchen 150–71
    lunar 35
    naked 35
    wild 173–221
garlic mustard 274, 275
gatekeeper 270, 271
geese 62–4, 100, 268–9
George, St 23
germander speedwell 192–3
giant puffball 286
ginger beer 115
goat willow 278, 279
goats 75–9, 100
    milk 75–8
    milk products 132, 136
goldfinch 266, 267
Good Friday 14
good king Henry 283
gooseberry 165
goosegrass 273
gourds 248
grass 99–103
grass snake 220–1
grazing pasture 99–102
great spotted woodpecker 266, 267
great tit 264, 267
great willowherb 275, 277
greater stitchwort 202–3
Greek oregano 146
green woodpecker 266, 268
greenfinch 266, 267
grey mullet 292
grit 50
ground elder 283
guelder rose 179
Guinea fowl 66
Guy Fawkes Night 16–17

habitat degradation 175
hair products 149
hairy bittercress 283
Halloween 18
ham 71
harebell 192–3
hares 280–1
Harvest Festival 16–18
harvesting 36
hawkmoths 214–15
hawthorn 168, 184–5, 218, 235
hay 99–103, 194
haylage 100
haystacks 103
hazel 168, 178–80, 199, 225, 285
    hurdles 232–3

hazelnuts 284, 285
hedge bindweed 185–6, 189
hedge mustard 274, 275
hedge sparrow 264, 267
hedge veg 165
hedge woundwort 202–3
hedgehogs 219, 220–1
hedgerows 182–6, 235–6, 277, 280
helichrysums 247
hemp agrimony 275, 277
herb Robert 202–3
herbs 154–7, 245
    herbal remedies 142–9
heron 268, 269
herring 292
hiccups 143
hiking poles 305
Himalayan balsam 275, 277
hogget 91
hogweed 273, 274
holly 178–9
holly blue 178, 186, 270, 272
home-brewing 109–21
honey 94, 96–8, 118
hops 109, 143, 185–6, 189
horse chestnut 278, 279
horseradish 284
horseshoes 28
horsetail 149
house sparrow 264, 267
houseleeks 40, 142, 143
hoverflies 156
hunts, Boxing Day 20
hurdles 231–3

ice-cream 135
infusions 148
insects
    beneficial 156, 182
    bites/stings 143
    herbal repellents 146
isinglass 139
ivy 185–6, 218

Jack-by-the-hedge 283
jackdaw 266, 267
jam 122–4, 126
jelly 122, 128, 129
jet 304
juniper 143

kelp 287, 288
kestrel 266, 268
knapweed 196, 197
knitting 256
knots 242–3

lacewings 156
ladybirds 156
lady's smock 275, 276–7
lamb 91
'lambswool' (drink) 18

large skipper 271, 272
large white 271, 272
lavender 143, 146, 148, 245
laver 287, 288
lawns, wildflower 190–3
leaf-mould 198–9
leap years 30
lemon curd 129
Lent 13
lesser celandine 202–3
lesser periwinkle 200–1
lesser trefoil 192–3
lightning 40, 300
liquorice 143
litter 303, 305
livestock 43–98
living sculptures 230
llamas 92–3, 255
loggeries 182
logs 168–71, 182
long-tailed tit 264, 267
lovage 148
love 38
luck 28–30, 33, 38

mackerel 292
magpie 28–30, 268–9
mallard 268, 269
mandrake 38–9
manure 50, 105, 161
map-reading 296
marbled white butterfly 271–2
marigold 36, 143, 148, 274–5
marmalade 122, 124–5
marsh marigold 274–5
master of the house 36
May Day 15
mayweed 273, 274
mead 118
meadow brown butterfly 271–2
meadow buttercup 196, 197
meadow cranesbill 196, 197
meadows 190, 194–7, 277
meadowsweet 275, 276
Michaelmas Day 36
milk 75–8, 81–2, 132
milk products 132–7
mince pies 20, 21
miner's lettuce 283
mint 36, 146
   jelly 129
   tea 144
mistletoe 19
mites 54
moles 36, 221
mordants 257
Mothering Sunday 14
moths 212, 213–16, 270
   deterrents 146
   traps 216
mowing 194
mullein moth 214–15
mushrooms 286
mussels 289
mute swan 268, 269

mutton 91
myrtle 40, 218

nail treatments 149
National Farmer's Union 45
National Trust 263, 304
nectarines 162
nest eggs 32
nettle 143–4, 149, 189, 273–4, 283–4
   fertiliser 161
New Forest 46
New Year 21
newts 210–11
Nicholas, St 20
nitrogen-fixation 100, 158, 191
nuts 283

oak 38, 171, 180, 199, 278–9
onion soup 143
orange tip butterfly 271, 272
organic gardening 156
organic matter 50, 105, 151–3, 161
orris root 246
owls 30
ox-eye daisy 196, 197
oxygenating plants 207–9
oystercatcher 268, 269

paganism 13, 15, 19
painted lady butterfly 270, 271
Palm Sunday 14
Pancake Day 13
pantries 139
parent bugs 183
parsley 14, 35–6, 142–3
patchouli 146
patchwork 254
Patrick, St 23, 30
peach 162
peacock butterfly 270, 271
pear 113, 162, 168
peas 158
pectin 122
pelargoniums 157
pennyroyal 143, 146
periwinkle 38–9
perry 113
pests 36, 156
piccalilli 130, 131
pickling 130–1
pied wagtail 264, 267
piglets 72
pigs 21, 33, 68–73, 113
plaice 292
plug plants 187, 189, 190
plum 162, 165
point-of-lay pullets 51
poisonous plants 99, 102, 186
pollack 292
pomanders 251
ponds 62
   for ducks 57–8
   plants for 207–9, 273–5, 277
   wildlife 204–11, 217, 219
ponies 46

pot marigold 143
potatoes 158
potpourri 245–7
poultry 47–67
prawns 290
preserves 122–9
pressed flowers 250
primrose 192–3
pruning 166
pumpkin lanterns 18
purple loosestrife 275, 276
pyracantha 218

quail 67
quilting 254

rabbit 280–1
ragged robin 275, 277
ragwort 99, 102, 275, 276
raised beds 154
Ramblers 263, 305
ramsons 200, 201
ranges 139
rare breeds 46, 51, 71–2, 88
rats 50, 281
rayless chamomile 275, 276
razor shell 289
red admiral 270, 271
red campion 202, 203
Red Poll 82
redcurrant 124, 218
redwing 266, 267
reflections 28
rennet 136
rhubarb 165
ringlet butterfly 271, 272
robin 266, 267
rodents 281
rook 268, 269
rose 35–6, 233, 245, 249
   rose petal jam 127
rosebay willowherb 193
rosehips 284, 285
   syrup 285
   wine 115, 121
rosemary 143
rotavators 103
rowan 37, 179, 199, 218
Royal Horticultural Society 27
RSPB 263–4, 304

sage 36
   tea 143
Saints' Days 22–3
salads 283
salt 30, 142
samphire 287–8
savings 32
scabious 196, 197
scarlet pimpernel 38, 275, 277
Scots pine 279
scythes 194
sea bass 292
sea beet 287
sea fogs 301

sea holly 275, 276
sea lettuce 287, 288
seagulls 38
Second World War 26
seed tray gardens 24
seedheads 247
seeds
    sowing 35, 188, 194
    wildflower/grass mixtures 195
self-heal 192–3
semi-precious stones 304
shaggy inkcap 286
shearing 84, 87, 88
sheep 84–91, 100, 227, 231, 255
sheepdogs 89
shellfish 288–9
shepherd's crooks 227
shield bugs 183, 184
shrew 219, 220–1
shrimping 290
Shrove Tuesday 13
shrubs, native 176–82
silage 100
skin lotions 148
slaters 210–11
slaughter 45, 104
sleep remedies 143
sloe gin 115, 121, 178
slow worm 220–1
small tortoiseshell butterfly 270–1
small white butterfly 271–2
smallholdings 43–105
    definition 46
    legal/administrative side 45
    livestock 43–98
    living off the land 104–5
smoking foods 140
snake's head fritillary 192–3
sneezing 30
snowdrop 199, 200–1
soap making 147
soapwort 149
soil preparation 151
song thrush 266, 267
sore throats 143
sorrel 283, 284
sparrowhawk 266, 268
spear thistle 275, 276
speckled wood butterfly 271, 272
spider crab 290
spiders 156
spinning 255
spirits, warding off 30, 37, 178
squirrels 221, 281
starling 266, 267
stiles 236
stinking hellebore 202–3
stoat 281
storms 300–1, 302
strawberry 36, 165
    conserve 127
stumperies 182
Sundays 12
sunflower 218
superstition 12, 28–30, 34–41

survival skills 296–302
swallows 38
swarms 96–8
sweet chestnut 231–2, 278–9, 284–5
sweet pea 160, 249
sweet violet 200–1
Swithun, St 38
sycamore 199, 278, 279

tadpoles 204, 208
talks, giving 105
tallow 252
tea 109
    fertiliser 35
    herbal 144
    tea leaf reading 40, 41
teal 268, 269
teazel 193, 218
thatching 240–1
thistle 189, 218
thornapple 212
thumb sticks 227
thyme tea 143
toads 210–11
tobacco flower 212
toiletries 147–9
tomato 36
    green, chutney 131
tonics 142–3
tracking animals 280–1
tractors 103
traveller's joy 185–6
trees
    age of 279
    dead 199
    identification 278–80
    planting native 176–82
    seedlings 199
trugs 231
tufted vetch 275, 276
turf, wildflower 191
turkeys 65
turnstone 268, 269
Twelfth Night 20, 31

under-dogs 32

Valentine's Day 22
varroa mite 98
vegetables
    foraging for 283–4, 287–8
    growing 150–1, 154, 158–61
    sea veg 287–8
village fêtes 40
village life 24–7
village shows 24
vinegar 114, 130

walking 263, 296–9, 303–5
walking sticks 225–7, 305
walls, dry stone 237–8
wart removal 143
wasps 98, 156
wassailing 30
water fleas 210–11

water recycling 104
waterlilies 207–8, 273, 274–5
wayfaring tree 178–9
weasel 281
weather 31, 38, 300–2
weaving 256
weddings 40
weeds 99–100, 102, 151
whistles 239
white bryony 185–6, 189
white campion 196, 197
white clover 192–3
white dead-nettle 273, 274
wild boar 72
wild carrot 196, 197
wild cherry 179
wild chicory 196, 197
wild daffodil 200–1
wild hop 185–6, 189
wild privet 184–5
wild strawberry 143, 200–1, 284–5
wildflowers 99, 100, 102, 180, 187–97
    identification 272–7
    lawns and meadows 190–7
    for ponds 207
    pressing 250
    woodland 198–203
wildlife
    deterring unwanted 36
    gardens for 173–221
    tracking 280–1
willow work 228–30
wind strength 302
wine making 18, 115–16, 118, 121
wing clipping 55
winkles 289
witches 37
Women's Institute (WI) 26–7
wood anemone 200–1
wood mouse 220–1
wood pigeon 266, 267
wood sorrel 200–1
wood turning 258
woodbine 185–6
woodland habitats 198–203, 277
woody nightshade 275, 276
wool 84, 91, 255–8
worms (parasites) 54
wort 110
wren 264, 267

yarn 255, 256–8
yarrow 273
yeast 110, 113
yellow flag 275, 276
yellow rattle 195, 196, 197
yoghurt 134
Yule log 19

Special thanks to the following for their invaluable help:

Andy and Tor Sandars; Charles and Lucy Ledgerwood;
Tori Ledgerwood; Fran Ledgerwood; Carl Voysey; Rob and
Sophia Waterstone; Giles and Sarah Kane; Bardsley & Brown
Master Thatchers; Heather Luff; Mark Hayes-Newington;
Dennis Chamberlain; Jimmy and Debby Puxley; The Welford
Estate; the Frank Lane Picture Agency; Jonathan Buckley for
braving the hungry pigs to get the perfect shot; Emma and
Alex Smith for masterful art direction, beautiful design,
expert fishing and fine sloe gin.